INDIAN BLUES

New Directions in Native American Studies
Colin G. Calloway and K. Tsianina Lomawaima, General Editors

INDIAN BLUES

American Indians and the Politics of Music

1879–1934

John W. Troutman

University of Oklahoma Press : Norman

This book is published with the generous assistance of
The McCasland Foundation, Duncan, Oklahoma.

Library of Congress Cataloging-in-Publication Data

Troutman, John William.
Indian blues : American Indians and the politics of music, 1879–1934 /
John W. Troutman.
p.   cm. — (New directions in Native American studies ; v. 3)
Includes bibliographical references and index.
ISBN 978-0-8061-4019-3 (cloth)
ISBN 978-0-8061-4269-2 (paper)
1. Indian dance—North America—History—20th century.   2. Indians of
North America—Music.   3. Indians of North America—Cultural
assimilation.   4. Popular music—United States—History—20th century.
5. Off-reservation boarding schools—North America—History—
20th century.   6. United States—Race relations.   7. United States—
Social life and customs.   I. Title.
E98.D2T76 2009
780.89'97073—dc22

2008038825

Indian Blues: American Indians and the Politics of Music, 1879–1934, is
Volume 3 in the New Directions in Native American Studies series.

The paper in this book meets the guidelines for permanence and
durability of the Committee on Production Guidelines for Book Longevity
of the Council on Library Resources, Inc. ∞

Copyright © 2009 by the University of Oklahoma Press, Norman,
Publishing Division of the University. Manufactured in the U.S.A.
Paperback published 2012.

All rights reserved. No part of this publication may be reproduced, stored
in a retrieval system, or transmitted, in any form or by any means,
electronic, mechanical, photocopying, recording, or otherwise—except as
permitted under Section 107 or 108 of the United States Copyright Act—
without the prior written permission of the University of Oklahoma Press.

CONTENTS

ILLUSTRATIONS

PREFACE AND ACKNOWLEGDMENTS

When I was a non-Indian growing up in southeastern Alabama, my knowledge of American Indian history was maligned by absences. I lived not far from the Lower Creek townsites that the Muscogee people were pressured to relinquish in the early 1800s, yet that historical memory is not entrenched in the minds of the non-Indians who now inhabit the land. My grade school and high school textbooks, tragically similar to those of most of the undergraduates whom I teach today, were virtually silent on any matters related to American Indians, be it pre-Columbian history or contemporary expressions of tribal sovereignty.

These absences in historical memory, however, were marked at the same time by profound proliferations of Indianness—popular ideological representations of indigenous peoples that have often functioned to mask their humanity as well as the history, theft, and violence of colonialism. The names of towns, rivers, and the state itself gave clear indication that the land was once foreign to the Spanish, French, English, and later, Americans who invaded it, but over the years those names became simply woven within the mythologies of colonialism that rendered the land's current tenants blind and deaf to, and distanced from, the nature of their occupation. Likewise, displays of Indianness burst from the seams in local flea markets, where dolls, dream catchers, cheap miniature knockoffs of the *End of the Trail* sculpture, and velvet paintings of "Indian warriors" shared the musty display cases that lay adjacent to Confederate flags and katana swords.

In addition, southern music, to which I also had a great deal of exposure, wafted with the sounds of Indianness.

From Hank Williams's "Kaw-Liga" to Tim McGraw's "Indian Outlaw," country musicians have long woven Indianness into their narratives of loss and desire, and they have often done so with a particular flair for poor taste.[1] Take Loretta Lynn's 1969 album *Your Squaw Is on the Warpath*, for example. If the title track was not offensive enough, on the cover of the album (which reached number two on the country charts), the singer wielded a "tomahawk" and was decked out in a headband, brownface makeup, and a buckskin minidress.[2] In the top-ten 1958 hit, "Squaws along the Yukon," Hank Thompson sang of the sexual desire for a Native woman as the protagonist's efforts to touch her skin were hampered only by her clothing—a "fur-lined parka" and "her underwear [made] from hides of grizzly bear."[3] In McGraw's smash hit, the protagonist was an "Indian outlaw, half Cherokee and Choctaw" who lives in a "wigwam," beating his "tom-tom," offering a guest to "pull out the pipe and smoke you some," while bragging that women get in line to look in his "teepee" while he's wearing nothing but "buffalo briefs."[4] Although these examples represent particularly southern musical articulations of Indianness, such expressions blanket every corner of popular culture in the United States, from animated movies to sports mascots. The power of such images is evident when I ask my students on the first day of class for an inventory of what they "know" about American Indian history. The ignorance reflected in the responses of the non-Indian students, shaped largely by ideas of Indianness in popular culture, remains staggering.

My own reeducation began at the hands of the faculty and students in the University of Arizona's American Indian Studies (AIS) master's program. They taught me that everything I thought I knew about American Indians and about American history in general was in need of not simply an overhaul but an entirely new set of reference points. One of the many lessons that I learned in the AIS program was driven home in my own interest in music. That lesson was, quite simply, that art is not innocuous. One cannot dissociate expressive culture from politics. More specifically, I began to understand that one cannot separate the violence of colonialism—the attempted destruction of tribal communities and the theft of Native lands—from the expressions of American popular culture that unavoidably shape so much of our daily existence, our landscape. Such expressions, like the lyrics of the country songs featured above, are most startling in the seemingly effortless way in which Native peoples and their histories are trivialized and dismissed. I learned that the notion that one could find escape in popular culture is perhaps one of its most deceptive and insidious attributes.

As a musician and an avid music fan, I began to think more deeply about the implications of music while I was in Tucson. What do we make of the sort of songs performed by Lynn, Thompson, and McGraw? How do we know what people thought of them? Some doubtless interpreted them as innocent, well-tread narratives of love-gone-good or love-gone-bad simply set to an "Indian theme." Some certainly interpreted such songs, consciously or not, as a reification of what they thought they knew about American Indians—that "squaws" was an acceptable term and not a derogatory one (if they were even interested in such a distinction), that Native women were eager to please and be sexually available to white men, and that buckskin and peace pipes were ubiquitous throughout Native America. These assumptions of listeners' interpretations are easy enough to make, but how can historians accurately gauge the effects of songs on people's imaginations? The possible interpretations of songs are vast and subjective after all, typically contested between the songwriters, performers, and listeners more often than shared.

Indeed, popular music lends itself particularly well to interpretational ambiguities and contradictions, and even if we focus on song titles and lyrics alone, these songs reveal much less, if anything at all, about Native realities than they do about the cultural work of Indianness. But the ease with which the singers like Lynn and Thompson used this language and iconography seemed extraordinary to me, particularly because they were recorded in a period when Native peoples were receiving more media attention through their efforts to resist the federal policy of termination and to fight an expanded array of attacks on treaty rights. So how exactly did these songs relate to the contemporary concerns facing Native people? Did these representations of Native peoples by Lynn and Thompson, and the thousands of other such images

and songs circulating in popular culture at the time, work to undermine the efforts of Native people to defend their sovereignty and home-
lands? And what could account for the persistence and the recycling of
degrading portrayals, as in "Indian Outlaw," of Native people throughout the history of American popular music and culture?

I continued to think about representations of Native peoples in
popular music as I prepared to leave Tucson; the more recordings I
encountered, however, the more questions they raised. Not all of the
country albums that I came across, for instance, reflected the disdain-
ful language found within the quoted lines above, and not all ignored
contemporary concerns and problems facing Native peoples. In fact,
Peter LaFarge and Johnny Cash wrote an album's worth of songs for
Cash's 1964 release *Bitter Tears* that specifically addressed, for example, the flooding of Seneca reservation lands by the Kinzua Dam and
the death of World War II veteran Ira Hayes.[5] Furthermore, as I came
to discover, American Indian songwriters, singers, and musicians had
engaged the production of popular music in quite interesting ways.
Cree singer Buffy Sainte-Marie rose to international fame in the 1960s
and 1970s, as did Kaw-Creek saxophonist Jim Pepper. This made me
wonder, what was it like for Native artists to perform before a non-
Native public whose only reference to American Indians consisted of
war whoops in western films or the fairy-tale interpretations of the
lives of Pocahontas and Squanto? How did their own use of iconography associated with Indianness and their own songs play into or
contest those dominant ideal types of the noble and ignoble savage?
Did they feel that they could make a difference by creating popular
music, or did they resist the overt politicization of their art? Shortly
after I arrived in Austin to begin my doctoral work at the University
of Texas, I was encouraged by Pauline Turner Strong and my dissertation adviser, Neil Foley, to pursue these inquiries, and I was lucky
enough to meet Rayna Green, who guided my research the next summer at the National Museum of American History.

These questions were not new to Rayna. She had spent thirty years
asking (and answering) them, and on top of that, she knew personally
several of the musicians that I had encountered only on recordings.
The idea behind this book really began to take shape that summer in
Washington, D.C. The Archives Center at the NMAH houses massive

collections of sheet music and ephemera, and as I stretched my inquiries into the nineteenth and early twentieth centuries, I felt as if I had stumbled across a "secret history"—American Indians, it seemed, had engaged the popular music stage in the United States for as long as it had existed. I found sheet music written by Native composers as well as vocal pieces dedicated to Native opera singers and marches performed by brass bands from federal Indian boarding schools. Popular Native singers were featured on postcards donning tribal regalia as well as on glossy photographs autographed for adoring fans. However, the Office of Indian Affairs records at the National Archives revealed a quite different story: at the same time that these individuals toured towns and cities throughout the United States, celebrating their tribal heritage, the federal government, it seemed, was deeply involved in a rigorous campaign, spanning more than fifty years, to destroy tribal dancing traditions and to heavily restrict the type of music that was being produced by Native children at the schools. The political nature of music was never more clear to me than in this juxtaposition, and it led me to another set of questions: Why and how does music become political? What made it appear as dangerous to the federal government? In what ways can popular music serve as a vehicle of liberation, or as a means of containment? How did Native and non-Native people use music and Indianness to challenge or fortify directives of federal Indian policy in the late nineteenth and early-twentieth centuries? The course of my research was then set on a firm path, with many a score to be heard.

I have been fortunate to encounter some remarkable people over the past several years who have offered wonderful direction, assistance, and encouragement for this project, and I would like to thank a few of them by name. Tom Holm, David Wilkins, and Rob Williams provided me with unparalleled guidance in understanding the complexities of federal Indian law and policy. Nancy Parezo and Tsianina Lomawaima are responsible for giving me the confidence to trek onward through graduate school. Their impeccable scholarship, brilliant seminars, and dedication to their students had a tremendous impact on me. They will continue to inspire me both professionally and personally for the rest of my days.

I owe a great deal to the University of Texas at Austin, to its History Department, and to the wonderful faculty who populate it. Neil Foley was a generous and insightful adviser, and he, along with Pauline Turner Strong, Erika Bsumek, and Karl Miller, provided more thoughtful comments and critiques of my dissertation than I could have dreamed of. Howard Miller was a wonderful mentor as well as the perfect officiate for my wedding. I owe him much for his professional and personal guidance over the years. In addition, the university provided exceptional financial and research support, and this book represents one fruit of its commitment to graduate students.

I also owe a great deal to Rayna Green, whose exceptionally smart scholarship paved the way for this sort of examination of the politics of expressive culture, particularly the expressive culture of American Indians. Her support of this project led to my receipt of both a Graduate Student Fellowship and a Pre-Doctoral Fellowship at the National Museum of American History. Along with thanking her, I would like to thank the Smithsonian Institution for the fellowship opportunities and support on which this project is largely dependent.

The Newberry Library's D'Arcy McNickle Center for American Indian History provided a stimulating work environment for me as I assumed the position of assistant director—in one year I met some of the most interesting, cutting-edge scholars and tribal college administrators in the country. On top of that, I worked under the impeccable direction of Brian Hosmer, whose leadership and vision of the McNickle Center and the CIC-AIS program were an inspiration. My thinking for this book was dramatically enhanced through our conversations.

I was honored to receive an Andrew W. Mellon Postdoctoral Fellowship at Wesleyan University's Center for the Americas, where I completed the bulk of my revisions for this book. Patricia Hill, Joel Pfister, and Ann Wightman offered excellent advice and support during my year in Connecticut. The atmosphere at Wesleyan and in the center was always engaging and dynamic—I will never forget playing Dylan songs during the holiday party with Richard Slotkin, participating in a roundtable discussion on music with Mark Slobin, and listening to Neely Bruce perform Arthur Farwell compositions on the grand piano in his home. In addition, while at the center I learned a great deal from Kehaulani Kauanui; her scholarship, professionalism, and constant reach to people and to causes beyond the confines of the campus should serve as a model for all of us in academia. Mahalo!

I have thoroughly enjoyed my first manuscript publication experience with the University of Oklahoma Press. Alessandra Jacobi Tamulevich provided very smart guidance from the beginning and lent more patience than I deserved. The manuscript editorial expertise of Alice Stanton and the work of copy editor Rosemary Wetherold have vastly improved the book as well. I wish to thank Tsianina Lomawaima and Colin Calloway for including this book within their new series. I would also like to thank the readers of the manuscript for so carefully scrutinizing the text and supplying advice and critical commentary where it most counted. Special thanks go to Clyde Ellis, who revealed himself early on as one of the readers. His extensive comments, our numerous conversations that followed, and his willingness to critique subsequent drafts proved to be a true saving grace for significant sections of the book.

Barbara Landis at the Cumberland County Historical Society went out of her way to ensure that my time at Carlisle was well spent and caught more than one of my oversights in the chapter drafts that followed my visit. She has dedicated an incredible amount of her own time poring over and organizing the Carlisle Indian School archives, and I owe her a great deal for her interest, correspondence and help along the way. Likewise, the archivists and librarians at the National Archives, Library of Congress, National Anthropological Archives, University of Iowa, Indiana University, University of California, Berkeley's Bancroft Library, the NMAH Archives Center, New York Public Library, Yale University's Irving S. Gilmore Music Library, Wisconsin Historical Society, and Fray Angélico Chávez History Library provided expertise and guidance during the research phase of the project. I suppose I should thank the creators of eBay as well, since I located many of the images included within this book through its auctions.

I would like to thank my wonderful students and colleagues at the University of Louisiana at Lafayette. After my arrival in Lafayette three weeks before the one-two punch of Katrina and Rita, our first year was a challenge, to say the least, but I appreciate the intense determination and dedication of so many of the students and professors in Acadiana. I would like also to thank the following for their friendship, assistance, and encouragement and/or for reviewing various drafts along the way: Laurie Arnold, Stephen Berrey, Matt Bokovoy, Andrew Brodie Smith, Jessica Cattelino, Brenda Child, Dan Cobb, Brian Collier, Pete Daniel, Philip Deloria, Andrew Falk, Loretta Fowler, Rich Frankel, Rob Galler, Matthew Sakiestewa Gilbert, Adriana Greci Green, Emily Greenwald, Jim Grossman, John Juricek, Marilyn Lehman, Suzanne McLaughlin, Rebecca Montes Donovan, Joanne Palmer, Alyssa Mt. Pleasant, Cathleen O'Connell, Linda Peavy, Gunther Peck, Theda Perdue, Al Quaglieri, Mary Helen Quinn, Elena Razlogova, Luke Ryan, Bill Seidel, David Delgado Shorter, Marie Mullenneix Spearman, Clint Starr, Helen Hornbeck Tanner, Ki Tecumseh, Mark Thiel, Sally Wolff King, and Matt Wray. I would like to recognize the extraordinary talents, tenacity, and courage of the Native people featured in this book who challenged the federal government's policies of assimilation and allotment in such profoundly important and creative ways. As a small tribute to them, and in memory of Hartman Lomawaima, the proceeds from this book will benefit the Hopi Education Endowment Fund.

Sara Ritchey was absolutely integral to the successful completion of this book. She has dedicated much of her love, patience, and time to this project and has tolerated my all-hours-of-the-night writing sessions and my tendency to take whirlwind music gigs from Lafayette to London and anywhere in between. I can only aspire to approach one day the level of creativity, critique, and thoughtful analysis that seems second nature to her. I see the world differently because of her, in so many delightful ways, and I can no longer imagine it any other way. I look forward to our further adventures! I would also like to thank her extended family—and particularly Ron, Mag, Lynne, Clint, Cecelia, and Gertrude—for welcoming me into their lives and for providing such a wonderfully immediate family life for us in Lafayette.

My own family has been incredibly supportive of my dreams and desires, no matter where they brought me. My sister has provided unwavering support and inspiration through the years. My mother has sacrificed more for the fruition of this book, and more for my general happiness over the years, than should be legally permitted for any parent. She has been a wonderful mother to my sister and me, especially when the circumstances turned grim. This book is dedicated to Sara, Malisa, and Rebekah.

JOHN W. TROUTMAN
Cypremort Point, Louisiana

INDIAN BLUES

INTRODUCTION

The 1941 Fourth of July powwow in Flagstaff, Arizona, was in many ways unexceptional: participants and spectators alike traveled from all parts of the country to witness the best Native dancers and singers in the Southwest. The Flagstaff shop and hotel owners welcomed the tourists as the powwow participants reunited with each other, ate fry bread, mended their regalia, and, of course, sang and danced. Many of the tourists arrived there on a quest to experience "authentic" Native traditions and probably expected to find centuries-old American Indian melodies and dances. They were delighted by Paiutes performing a Round Dance and a Sun Dance, while a singer from Jemez Pueblo performed a Hoop Dance song for a young dancer.[1] The powwow performances, however, while incorporating many long-standing traditions, were anything but antiquated. Many of the dances and songs had been introduced to and learned by the participants only recently—at intertribal powwows, by military buddies on base, or by classmates from federal Indian boarding schools. Not only were the dances changing, but the variety of music and the repertoire of dances performed at the powwow were always expanding and in flux, representing a multitude of styles and genres. The Pima Indian Band, a community band with horns and flutes blaring, and marching drums pounding, introduced the spectators to the singers and dancers in the stadium grounds during the Grand Entry. In a classically trained voice, Hopi singer Clarence Taptuka delivered the Indian-themed song "Pale Moon" as if he had penned the words

3

himself. Following some Taos, San Juan, Zuni, and Navajo dances, Margaret Lewis (aka Laughing Eyes) delivered an equally powerful rendition of "From the Land of the Sky-Blue Water."[2]

The powwow participants clearly believed that the latter musical performances were as natural a fit in the powwow as the Hoop Dance. But what of their non-Native pedigree? After all, the members of the Pima Indian Band had received their training from band directors in boarding schools. "Pale Moon" and "From the Land of the Sky-Blue Water" were crafted by Frederick Knight Logan and Charles Wakefield Cadman, respectively, members of a cadre of non-Indian composers who romanticized Native life in harmonized melodies, often borrowed from anthropologists who had lifted them from informants while believing Indian music was a thing of the past.[3] Yet the singers and musicians appeared to have little problem reconciling these histories or the occasion, a Fourth of July celebration, with their performative identities as Native people. This powwow seems particularly extraordinary if we consider that, up until the late 1920s, the Office of Indian Affairs (OIA) had spent decades waging vigorous opposition to dances and on reservations and continually sought new ways to suppress them by practically any means available.

Despite that opposition, musical performative traditions on reservations survived and in fact proliferated during the early twentieth century. New social dances spread quickly through the plains, while ceremonial dances with sacred histories of their own retained their significance, even if they had moved underground. Various forms of giveaway dances served to redistribute resources and wealth in communities, while the singing of Christian hymns, not uncommonly in Native languages, filled the air of reservation churches. But the other musical traditions performed at the 1941 powwow also figured prominently in the lives of many Native people; ever since the late nineteenth century, hundreds of American Indians had traveled the country and the world, performing a musical "Indianness" for their own reasons, often through non-Indian-derived compositions, in venues like powwows, dance halls, opera theaters, and rodeos.[4] Native people constantly innovated and expanded their repertoires of expressive culture in ways that both reflected their experiences and transformed their circumstances.

This book explores how the deployment of musical practice, by American Indians, OIA officials, and the non-Indian public alike, shaped the implementation of federal Indian policy. I argue that musical performance was implicated in the design and execution of the citizenship agenda, which through the 1920s mandated the assimilation of Native peoples into the body politic of the United States along with the allotment and liquidation of tribally controlled lands. In this regard, the Omaha Dance, beyond the multitude of social meanings that Native peoples attributed to it, also served as a battleground over policy issues. The practice of music, in a very real sense, provided a means by which American Indian people could strategically deploy their newfound U.S. citizenship—for example, to reinforce their tribal identities—in the face of OIA officials who sought to dismantle that core of their existence. Likewise, the musical instruction taught in Indian boarding schools could serve as both a means by which the government hoped to shape its own vision of an Indian citizenry, or, as we will see, its own vision of Indianness, and a means for Native peoples to wield Indianness, not simply in order to make a living, but as a weapon of political critique. Musical performances provided access to public forums—through the stage and through wax cylinders, 78 rpm records, and the radio—for questioning and challenging the propriety of the federal government to assume control over Native lands, resources, and education. Music *mattered*, as a means not simply of resistance but of active involvement in the shaping and implementation of federal policy initiatives. Music operated in a decisively political manner, just as it operated in other social and cultural contexts.

Although a new brand of reformers typified by John Collier are generally given the credit for the policy upheavals of the 1930s, these Native individuals deserve their due for waging their own reform work through musical practice. In 1934 the OIA, under Collier, in fact finally caught up in certain fundamental ways with what many American Indians had been shouting and singing for years: that the allotment policy was a disaster for most tribes and that assimilation was not only untenable and undesirable but also impossible to achieve. Music served American Indians and non-Indians alike as a unique way to negotiate, challenge, or fortify the lines of citizenship,

Indianness, and whiteness drawn over the scope of U.S. culture and politics. For this reason the study of music made by American Indians, its practice and politics, can reveal new ways of understanding American Indian history.

CITIZENSHIP AND CIVILIZATION: FEDERAL INDIAN POLICY IN THE ERA OF ALLOTMENT AND ASSIMILATION

How is it that music became so politically charged? To understand exactly why the practice of music was so implicated in federal Indian policy, it is important to understand the context of this particularly trying and often tragic period in American Indian history. By the 1880s, many Americans had convinced themselves that Native peoples faced one of two fates: to disappear from the face of the earth, or to culturally transform into U.S. citizens.[5] Reformers, OIA officials, and congressmen debated the best course of action to take over this "Indian problem," but nearly all of them agreed that tribal traditions, including that of holding reservation lands in common, were antithetical to the individualized, mono-allegiant ideals they invested in U.S. citizenship. They also agreed that whereas high-brow, white American culture epitomized their notion of "civilization," tribal peoples represented the depths of "savagery." If American Indians were to survive into the twentieth century, the reformers reasoned, then they would have to shun the "savage" cultural traits of their tribal identities and transform under very specific instruction and conditions into members of a "proper," Christian, civilized American citizenry. Citizenship was thus conceived for Native Americans as a reward based upon the completion of a set of specific cultural and political requirements. In this way, citizenship became a defining issue in federal Indian policy between the late 1860s and the 1920s, and as the federal government continued to break treaties with and withhold treaty-guaranteed rations to tribes, reformers worked with Congress to develop a plan to bring Native peoples to their own standard of civility.[6]

The reformers and congressmen who crafted the 1887 Dawes Act, the legislation that principally defined the allotment and assimilation era of federal Indian policy (1887–1928), believed that they must destroy every articulation of tribalism in individuals before bestowing them with U.S. citizenship. This detribalization campaign necessitated the destruction of tribally held lands. The Dawes Act enabled the OIA to parcel reservations into individualized plots of 40 to 160 acres.[7] The OIA believed that if individuals or nuclear Native families were forced onto one parcel of land, then American Indians would begin to manage their own property essentially as yeoman farmers, inducing the work ethic and practices of what the government deemed "civilized" life. OIA officials then granted citizenship to the individuals they considered "competent" enough to either sell their land for what it was worth (though in the end, those who sold it were likely defrauded of it) or to hold their plot and farm it. As Vine Deloria, Jr., and Clifford Lytle put it, the Dawes legislators believed that "private property . . . had mystical magical qualities about it that led people directly to a 'civilized' state."[8] As Henry L. Dawes himself said, the problem with tribally controlled communal land ownership was that it discouraged "selfishness, which is at the bottom of civilization."[9] Conveniently, once the OIA parceled the lands in such a manner, millions of additional acres of reservation lands not assigned to Native families were considered "open" and hence available for non-Indian settlement.

In addition to the allotment of lands, the OIA instituted a complex assimilation program with off-reservation boarding schools as its focal point. The government built these schools to remove children from the "uncivilized" surroundings of their families and reservation communities and to educate Native children in what it considered the proper arts, language, literature, and labor of the American citizenry.[10] This instruction included the shunning of tribal affiliations; forbidding the use of tribal languages; dressing and grooming the children to look as "non-Indian" as possible; teaching jingoistic American history; celebrating American holidays such as the Fourth of July, Washington's birthday, and even their own "Indian Citizenship Day"; and subsuming their religious life into strict interpretations of Christianity. As Richard H. Pratt—the founder of the flagship boarding school, the Carlisle Indian Industrial School—put it, the goal of the schools was to "kill the Indian . . . and save the man."[11]

While the remaining Native land base in the United States shrunk through allotment from a scant 138 million acres to a devastating 48 million acres, and while American Indians were left destitute as the result of the denial of treaty-guaranteed rations and supplies and of disastrous economic policies on reservations, the OIA, with support from numerous religious and reform organizations, expanded its efforts to dismantle tribalism and any of its attendant expressive culture.[12] OIA officials, who categorized expressive culture racially, considered "Indian dances" as a breach in the cultural requirements of citizenship and sought to suppress dances on these grounds. At the same time, students in federal Indian boarding schools were instructed in what their teachers considered the arts of civilization. Students were to study the piano, the cornet, the violin—the accoutrements of "white music," as the OIA considered it—at the expense of "savage" musical practices, the "Indian dances" of their parents. During this period in which their lives were so profoundly changed, American Indians had very limited opportunities to engage the formal political arena in which these decisions were being made, yet it was under these same circumstances that the practice of music provided an effective means of resisting and reshaping the implementation of federal Indian policy. But how exactly does music create change? And how can historians assess the power and the politics of something as ephemeral and subjectively interpretive as music?

HISTORY AND THE PRACTICE OF MUSIC

To the best of anyone's guess, it was Elvis Costello who first remarked that "writing about music is like dancing about architecture."[13] Historians seem to agree, given that they have traditionally either ignored the relationship of music to change over time or found difficulty in writing about music, in particular its historical import. Of course, there exist many fascinating and rewarding cultural studies on music in the United States. Since the publication of Amiri Baraka's *Blues People*, for example, a number of scholars have grappled with the relationship between the production of music and the construction of race or ethnicity, and recent works by Ronald Radano and

Karen Sotiropoulos in particular have excelled in that endeavor.[14] To be fair, however, writing about music performed in the past is daunting on a number of levels. Textual analysis of song lyrics, for example, can perhaps reveal something about the songwriter but nothing about the listener—how do we know what significance the audience took from the song if we have no record of its interpretation? Who listened to it? And what was, in fact, the intent of the singer or performer? Such problems of interpretation have clearly precluded a greater inclusion of music—or any form of expressive culture, for that matter—in history texts, and these concerns are quite valid.

What is also clear is that, if you ask anyone on the street whether music is important to them, they will quite often respond with an unequivocal "Yes!" If you ask them why music is important to them, you will receive a variety of responses—"It can make me happy," some might say, and others will tell you, "It can make me sad." Music can transport you to another place and another time; it can remind you of old acquaintances or specific memories. Music can make you want to dance. It can make you cry, and it can make you proud. Music can generate an expectation or a stereotype in your mind (for example, in an undergraduate seminar on music and race that I taught at Wesleyan University, the mere thought of country music made nearly everyone in the room cringe). It can also terrify you. Music did all of these things and more to the people discussed in this book.

Of course, when one looks beyond genres of American popular music to the additional, extraordinary diversity of styles and genres of music that Native peoples have performed, the majority of which lie squarely within tribally specific performative practices, then the task of writing about the meaning of music grows even more daunting. Therefore I must provide some caveats regarding what I do *not* attempt in this study of the practice and politics of music. I do not attempt to craft an ethnological analysis on all of the profound layers of meaning found within, for example, a Lakota Victory Song. I do not dissect dance steps, nor for the most part do I dissect the evolution and spread of powwow dances. Many have written on the musical practice of specific tribal communities, singing groups, or individuals, or on regional focuses that comprise several communities and/or intertribal powwows. Some of the best works on such analysis include the voluminous scholarship by Tara Browner, Clyde Ellis, and Luke Eric Lassiter.[15] Nor do I analyze the extraordinary and complex musical practices involved within church meetings. I also veer away from a decidedly musicological scrutiny of the compositions that were taught in the boarding schools or that traversed the Indian-themed musical landscape of the United States. Philip Deloria eloquently discussed the components of music that formed the "sound of Indian" in American film and popular music in his *Indians in Unexpected Places*, and Michael Pisani's seminal study of Indian-themed music composed in the United States explores the crafting of these compositions.[16] Browner has also written an exceptional study of Indianist composers.[17] An in-depth musicological or ethnological interrogation of social and sacred songs or Indianist compositions lies beyond the scope of this book. I decided instead to focus on only one of many possible layers of meaning—how this music was discussed or performed in relation to the deployment of federal Indian policy.

Within the context of government policy, I am interested in the *practice* of music, the economy of meaning that clusters around organized sound. The remark of Lakota powwow singer Severt Young Bear is instructive: "Song and dance can't really be separated. Even though I'll talk about one or the other, they're always connected."[18] Along these lines, this study weaves together various strains of musical expressive culture—predominantly those of Lakota Omaha Dances, brass band marching music, and art and semiclassical music—through conceiving of music as a practice that encompasses not only singers, dancers, and musicians but audience members (and those who otherwise concerned themselves with the particular musical performances of others) as well. No one can control the meaning that another person attributes to music, but that does not stop people from trying. As with the efforts of the Parents Music Resource Center (PMRC) in the 1980s and the debates over hip-hop that continue to recur every few years, a culture war raged over the practice of music on reservations, in boarding schools, and in other arenas accessible to Native musicians in the early twentieth century, with notions of race and citizenship being continuously manifested and challenged. For historians, it is the *struggle* over the meaning of music that is the most revealing; in archives, newspaper articles, interviews, oral histories, and autobiographies, we can uncover the oppositional interpretations of music that generate perhaps its most valuable historical significance.

To begin to understand the historical relevance of musical performance, we must take into account the individuals who imbue it with meaning. As Susan McClary points out, meaning "is not inherent in music, but neither is it in language: both are activities that are kept afloat only because communities of people invest in them, agree collectively that their signs serve as valid currency."[19] What becomes most significant to us is the mediation of values that people assign to music. On making meaning of text, Michel de Certeau wrote, "It is at least clear . . . that one cannot maintain the division separating the readable text (a book, image, etc.) from the act of reading. Whether it is a question of newspapers or Proust, the text has a meaning only through its readers; it changes along with them; it is ordered in accord with codes of perception that it does not control."[20] Music functions in the same manner and has meaning not only through its listeners but also through those who refuse to listen. If we understand music in this way, as an action over an artifact, then our interpretation of music goes beyond a lyrical, descriptive, or notational analysis and toward the context that produced and contained it.

THE POLITICS OF SAFE AND DANGEROUS MUSIC

The individuals featured in this story—musicians, singers, dancers, OIA officials, boarding school employees, and both Native and non-Native audience members—assigned their own values to musical performances, vividly illuminating the political nature of music. These values are inherently subjective, which is precisely why they serve as a fruitful means of analysis. Steeped in the intellectual tradition of Lewis Henry Morgan and other anthropologists who invested expressive culture in the signification of racial hierarchy, the waltzes, two-step dances, and Euro-American derived musical compositions taught in Indian boarding schools represented to OIA officials the arts of civilized society—in the context of their citizenship agenda, they considered such music "safe"—while on the reservations a Grass Dance, a Sun Dance, or any other kind of "Indian dance," as defined by OIA officials, was interpreted as "dangerous," representing barbarism or savagery.[21] Some performative displays rightly seemed to endanger the assimilationist philosophy that guided the OIA at this time; thus the OIA boarding school curricula included instruction only in "safer," "civilized," typically European-derived forms of music. In their study of Native American education, K. Tsianina Lomawaima and Teresa L. McCarty have argued that in fact the boarding school administrators sought in this manner to contain, control, and otherwise manage all aspects of life for the students by purging any influences the administrators considered dangerous and oppositional to their goals: "Dangerous culture difference was being contained, made safe within the Indian boarding schools, arguably the most minutely surveilled and controlled federal institutions created to transform the lives of any group of Americans. The schools controlled a physical *safety zone* in their classrooms and playgrounds that could symbolically neutralize the Native languages, religions, economies, polities, family structures, emotions, and lives that seemed to threaten American uniformity and national identity."[22] Thus every expression of music was politically charged, because the civilization agenda of the OIA depended upon the close monitoring of every musical utterance both on the reservations and in the boarding schools.

But the notion that music was simply safe or dangerous according to an agreed-upon barometer of "savagism" and "civilization," of Indianness and whiteness, eclipses the complexities of the act. Rather, the political and cultural meanings of the practice of music were contested by and within racial, tribal, community, and generational lines. For example, two-step dances such as the Owl Dance, in which couples danced together, became very popular with returned students on many reservations in the early twentieth century, including those of the Lakotas. Though such two-step dances had been influenced in some ways by the dances taught in boarding schools, OIA officials nevertheless usually considered them "Indian dances" when they were unregulated on reservations. More significantly, however, such dances caused some older Lakota people great consternation: prior to the introduction of the two-step dances, Lakota dances had typically precluded the dancing of men and women as couples, and particularly the quick changing of partners. Some Lakotas believed that two-step dances led to sexual promiscuity and immorality. In their eyes, therefore, the new dances were as dangerous to these Lakotas as they were to the OIA.

Moreover, particular practices of music never held static meaning; the meanings changed over time and were continually contested, especially as new groups of Native people began to participate in them. The practice of music often came to signify a manifestation of power and control. For many OIA officials, dance came to represent every aspect of federal Indian policy that failed during this period. For many Native people, it served as a vehicle of freedom through which they expressed an increased sense of autonomy over segments of their own lives or a rejection of OIA control and surveillance; for others, dancing was considered an inalienable right and could even serve as a declaration of the rights bestowed on them through U.S. citizenship and participation in World War I. To borrow from the work of James Scott, the practice of music could serve as a blatant, yet hidden, transcript of resistance— blatant in the public nature of performance, yet hidden in the sense that music could be considered an innocent social entertainment as much as it could represent an assault on the assimilation policy.[23] That is what made the practice of music such a viable, cunning, and complex political form—its transformative power often lay in the eyes and ears of the beholder as much as in those of the performer. And as we shall see, through such performances even the OIA tenets of allotment and citizenship became dangerous in the minds of the officials who most vociferously supported them.

MUSIC AND INDIANNESS

The struggle for self-determination over Native performative practices was not limited to reservations and boarding schools. Students who ventured into nearby towns and urban centers discovered a non-Indian public who did not treat them, as Richard Pratt had hoped, as assimilated Americans. Although some faced discrimination, much of the public by the early twentieth century had largely bought into the idea that a nonthreatening, "safe" Indianness, could actually benefit rather than stifle modern American society. As Philip Deloria and others have argued, in the early twentieth century Indianness became much valued in the movement of antimodern primitivism.[24] Many middle-class white Americans who had become disillusioned with the pace of urban modern America began to turn toward Indianness as a form of rejuvenation, a touchstone of authenticity found in Otherness. Indian people seemed natural to them, an idealistic reflection on a simpler time in which proper ideals of manhood and womanhood were not obscured by the emasculation of a desk job for men or the straying of women from the maintenance of domestic duties.[25] The Boy Scouts of America, the Camp Fire Girls, and other organizations created a template of order and "proper" modern social values through their decidedly antimodern interpretation of Indianness.[26] Likewise, as Deloria has elsewhere demonstrated, the non-Indian public maintained expectations of Indian people that confined these individuals to roles suited more to perpetuating colonial dominance than to transcending it.[27]

Indeed, these publicly mediated understandings of Indianness had little to do with the daily realities of Native people's lives. Indianness, as I will refer to it, along with the rhetorical categories deployed so often by the OIA of "Indian dances," "Indian music," or "Indian songs," consisted of racial expectations of the era, full of history, certainly, but otherwise empty of substance. The "sound of Indian," as Deloria argues—the stereotypical melodies and drone of the drum that signified Indianness in Hank Williams's "Kaw-Liga," for example—resulted mostly from non-Indian sources, for even music collected on reservations was mediated through the recording device, transcriptions, and harmonizations as non-Indian ethnologists, musicians, and composers sought to evoke their interpretation of Indianness in song.[28] The non-Indian public held visual perceptions of Indians firmly in place as well: they expected beautiful princesses in buckskin dresses and hypermasculine chiefs wearing nothing short of a very large headdress and a very small breechclout.[29]

Although non-Indian constructions of Indianness did not reflect the ways in which Native people defined themselves in terms of tribal or pan-tribal affiliations, they become substantive when we consider the ways in which American Indians themselves began to deploy Indianness. Beyond developing additional individual, tribal, and pan-tribal identities through intertribal relationships and shared experiences in the schools, many American Indians also played into dominant popular conceptions of Indianness by the non-Indian public for reasons that served their own interests and, in some ways, contributed to a much larger, more complex matrix of identity formation.[30] American Indians had acknowledged the desire of non-Indians to experience Indianness for some time and immediately took advantage of it, selling arts and crafts at Fred Harvey railway stations and trading posts or dramatizing famous battles for Buffalo Bill's show.[31] As long as expressions of Indianness were safe and properly contained within the fairgrounds or a piece of Pueblo pottery, it seemed, non-Indian Americans could attempt to identify with Indian people. While, on one hand, such actions could reify stifling representations of American Indians, on the other hand many Native peoples learned to use these opportunities to their own ends. Between the 1880s and the 1930s, hundreds of students musically trained in the schools performed Indianness on the road in musical troupes, jazz and marching bands, string quartets, and other outfits. In doing so, road-weary bands and Native celebrities gained the opportunity as well to present individual, tribal, and pan-tribal musical identities that complicated and often contradicted the public's assumptions of Indianness and the assimilative goals of the OIA.

The non-Indian public's interest in Indianness in the early 1900s had a growing impact on federal policy as more Native musicians traveled the country. Tourists, theatergoers, and lecture circuit attendees began to discover how former boarding school students had turned the assimilative vision of their instructors into new avenues to celebrate their difference as Indian people. By the 1920s the assimilation policies that had for decades guided the OIA began to seem antiquated and out of step with the non-Indian desire, even demand, to experience authentic Indianness, just as the anthropological theory of cultural relativism began to significantly infiltrate universities and the press. As the press debated reservation dance bans, as the Harvey Company and other purveyors funded such performances, and as non-Indians flocked to performances by Native musicians in the cities, the political nature of American Indian music became exceedingly public.

This book consists of five chapters that explore the politics of American Indian musical performance principally between the opening of the Carlisle Indian School in 1879 and the passage of the Indian Reorganization Act in 1934. The chapters are organized, not chronologically, but along particular arenas in which the practice of music was engaged or debated. Chapter 1 examines the rejuvenation of dances on Lakota reservations primarily from 1900 through 1922, the year that Commissioner of Indian Affairs Charles Burke called a meeting of all the North and South Dakota superintendents and missionaries over what he termed the "dance evil." The chapter explores why and how dancing became an important and useful political device for Lakota dancers with regard to federal policy, and the ways in which Lakota people manipulated tropes of citizenship and patriotism through dance in order to reassert some control over the arena of the reservation environment in the midst of aggressive assimilation and allotment policies. Chapter 2 investigates the impact of the press and popular cultural trends on federal Indian policy as many American Indians protested loudly over the OIA's renewed efforts to suppress dancing nationwide in the mid-1920s. Chapter 3 turns to the boarding schools, where the increased surveillance and control that the enclosed school grounds afforded the OIA facilitated its attempts to manage student bodies, knowledge, and performative practices. I examine the implications of the forms of music that school officials deemed appropriate, and how the students responded to the instruction. Chapter 4 maintains a focus on the schools. While the marching bands, string quartets, and vocal lessons ostensibly served the OIA in its quest to inculcate its vision of "safe" musical whiteness into the students, teachers, particularly after 1904, also engaged in a movement to use musical education as a means of instructing the students on how to perform "safe," "proper" Indianness. I investigate the relationship between these agendas, the impetus behind the movement, and the ways in which the students approached the performance of Indianness. The final chapter turns to the public arenas of popular music performance in the United States. Comprising a series of biographical vignettes, the chapter examines how five Native professional singers and musicians, trained in Euro-American-derived musical instruction, applied their training beyond the boarding schools, at times drawing from their school experiences of using Indianness to lure audiences, and at times using that audience access to advocate for change in federal Indian policy. Together, the five chapters provide a window into the musical production of Native people on reservations, in boarding schools, and on public stages in the late nineteenth and early twentieth centuries, and each chapter demonstrates how various parties sought to use music as means of enforcing or transgressing federal Indian policy.

These stories—of the dancers, the musicians, the musical productions in the schools—are deserving of their own microhistories, and indeed this overview of the politics of music in the allotment and assimilation era will no doubt gloss over important, locally oriented distinctions in both expressive culture and the implementation of federal policy. The newest wave of scholars working on boarding school histories will undoubtedly provide great clarification and reveal nuance, if not further contradictions, in the specific musical histories found within each school.[32] As well, much more work needs to be done to examine the proliferation of Indian clubs that began to develop in the schools after the passage of the Indian Reorganization Act in 1934, the moment at which this study concludes. Studies of Native musicians from the mid-twentieth century to the present will reveal the creation of entirely new musical practices. David Samuel's ethnography of a San Carlos Apache rock band will certainly herald more such studies of how music works within processes of modern identity formation.[33] My hope is that this book will introduce the overarching conflicts and contradictions that lay at the heart of Native musical practice in this era, at least as far as federal Indian policy initiatives were concerned.

The practice of music worked in various capacities in this period; while American Indians could use it as a vehicle for expressing political dissent or for reconfiguring the meaning of U.S. citizenship, the OIA hoped it would serve to support that office's program of assimilation in the schools. Yet this goal of the OIA was turned on its head as alumni began working in all-Indian bands and touring the country, developing their own repertoire and displaying their boarding school skills through a decidedly "Indianized" performance. Indeed, this study in part seeks to return Indianness to Native agency and to emphasize the role of music in shaping federal policy. Native musical performances of all sorts provided political voices that often effectively critiqued federal policy and its underlying philosophy of assimilation, both in cities and on reservations. This book seeks to feature Native performers on the center stage of struggles over federal Indian policy in the early twentieth century.

CHAPTER 1

The Citizenship of Dance

Politics of Music in the Reservation Environment

Music is at the center of Lakota life in the old days and since the reservation days started. No matter what you do, whether it's a man singing to himself because he's a brave warrior, or because he is feeling bad, or is singing to himself because he wants to identify more closely with God, anything you do in your band or community requires singing. Music helped Lakota people survive a great deal of hardship and endure lots of pain because there was a song there.

—Severt Young Bear, 1994

When the tom tom sounds the cloak of civilization drops off the shoulders of the Sioux Indian. The tom tom is the same kind of an instrument that is used by the lowest savages of today and they use it in their religious rights. Pure savagery. The singing that accompanies this dance is the same as the sound you hear from the religious ceremony of the lowest savages. . . . When the Sioux Indian goes into the dance ring he is a savage. A savage garbed in a suit of underwear dyed red.

—Superintendent E. D. Mossman,
Standing Rock Sioux Reservation, 1922

In the first three decades of the twentieth century, a resurgence of Native musical practices among the Lakota peoples began to resonate through and alter the implementation, and eventually the course, of federal Indian policy.[1] Disillusioned with or disgusted by the directives of OIA allotment and assimilation policies, many Lakotas challenged them through a series of inventive political acts of revitalization and resistance. Their efforts were exceptional, given the circumstances: since 1878, but particularly following the massacre of Ghost Dancers at Wounded Knee in 1890, missionaries and local Indian agents, concerned about their dances and economic practices, placed the Lakotas under extraordinary surveillance. For those reservation-based Lakotas who opposed the allotment and assimilation policies, challenging those policies on a public or national level was nearly impossible; the OIA controlled the resources necessary for subsistence on reservations, and many OIA agents were not averse to withholding rations for any "trouble." The traditional avenues to express dissent in the American political system—through speeches before the American public, congressional hearings, the media, and the courts, for example—were quite limited, if virtually nonexistent, for most Native people at this time, particularly for those living on reservations.[2]

Yet many did effectively challenge the economic and cultural mandates of the allotment and assimilation policies, as well as the very meaning of American citizenship. Too often overlooked by historians of federal Indian policy, these local-level struggles reveal the adaptability of alternative methods of resistance. American Indians manifested such political engagement in myriad ways: through delegations, petitions, and religious movements, for example, or more subtly through their participation in fairs, rodeos, or other events that, in borrowing from James Scott, nurtured "hidden transcripts" of everyday resistance—resistance disguised and located "behind the scenes . . . [when the oppressed] create and defend a social space in which offstage dissent to the official transcript of power relations may be voiced."[3] Like many other American Indian peoples, the Lakotas combined the subterfuge of "hidden" acts of resistance with blatant and effective challenges to federal Indian policy through a most unexpected yet highly political medium: musical performance. From the turn of the century through 1922, the Lakotas succeeded in vastly expanding their dance traditions, despite increased efforts by the OIA agents and missionaries to curtail them. They fought their battles on a very local level, against specific adversaries found within the ranks of OIA agents and missionaries; their success was due in part to their establishing a "citizenship of dance"—that is, their framing of a right to dance as a right of their newfound U.S. citizenship. In the first three decades of the twentieth century, many Lakotas used dance in this vein as a means of engaging the politics of American citizenship and, in so doing, disarmed the more culturally insidious, local manifestations of federal Indian policy.

In this chapter and those that follow, I discuss numerous musical forms, which each have histories of their own, as well as relationships with one another. This chapter focuses on the Omaha Dance complex and some related forms. These forms of expressive culture derive from Lakota or other indigenous contexts, whereas other forms discussed in the following chapters might derive from Europeans or from non-Indian Americans. It is tempting to refer to the Lakota dances and songs in this chapter as "traditional" in order to create shorthand for referring to tribally derived musical practice. The term is fraught with problems, however, as it cannot help but denote stasis rather than change, reversion rather than innovation, and it can also refer to certain dance styles in contemporary powwows that may or may not relate to the dances discussed here. Such use of "traditional" would be of little use here, for the history of the Omaha Dance complex, which includes many varieties of social dances and giveaways, was and remains exceedingly dynamic in Indian Country. Therefore use of "traditional" is avoided here, and songs and dances are described as specifically as possible, given the nature of the archival sources, which often referred to any dances on reservations of the time simply as "Indian dances."

Of course, many forms of Lakota dancing and singing are extremely powerful, important, and complex, and as Lakota singer Severt Young Bear was quoted as saying in the introduction, they are also interrelated acts. They may articulate individual, band, social, and communal identities as well as serve ceremonial and social purposes; they can foster intense competition at intertribal powwows as well as mediate tensions or heal and reconstitute individuals and communities.[4] The practice of sacred and social music within Native communities can take on many layers of meaning that derive from multiple indigenous systems of knowledge. In addition, the ceremonial or sacred dances in particular often contain knowledge and meaning that is not intended for most individuals, and certainly not for outsiders. Even the "sacred" and "social" distinctions are problematic. According to Shoshone elder Esther Horne, "Dance could be sacred or social, private or public, but always is hallowed with spirituality."[5] The practice of music elicits multiple meanings, but the present discussion focuses specifically on the possibilities of one level of meaning—the early twentieth-century Lakota practice of music as a means to engage and shape the local implementation of federal Indian policy. For our purposes, the reactions of government officials and missionaries are as important to consider as the intentions of the dancers and singers, for it is through these reactions that we can see exactly how dance affected federal policy. Surveying the landscape of Lakota social dances of the period in this way demonstrates not only one manner in which music was negotiated as a significant political force but also the resolve and brilliant success of the Lakota dance practitioners who wielded it to such effect.

SETTING THE STAGE: LAKOTA RESERVATION CONDITIONS AND POLITICS OF SOCIAL DANCE IN THE LATE NINETEENTH CENTURY

In order to understand why music came to play such an important role in engaging federal Indian policy initiatives, it is useful to command an overview of late nineteenth-century Lakota history. From the mid-nineteenth century through the early twentieth, federal policy had detrimental social and economic consequences for the Lakotas. Instead of creating productive, individualistic, independent American citizens, the polices of the assimilation and allotment era succeeded in crippling many Native populations, forcing them into positions of dependency by not providing the equipment with which to become successful, self-sufficient farmers, by taking away more of their lands through allotment, and by attempting to stamp out their communal means of providing for one another in times of need. The OIA sought to mandate its own requirements for U.S. citizenship and established an assimilation agenda accordingly. However, the Lakotas used the practice of music as a means to redefine U.S. citizenship and the rhetoric of patriotism to serve their own needs.

The 1860s were a period of great conflict between the United States and the Lakotas. In 1865, at the conclusion of the Civil War, the U.S. government began building a string of forts through Wyoming and Montana along the Bozeman Trail. This was prime hunting territory for the Lakotas, Arapahos, and Cheyennes, who considered the new construction to be an offensive maneuver. By 1865, mounting violence between encroaching whites and the Lakotas had begun to render diplomatic efforts such as the 1851 Fort Laramie Treaty ineffective, so that as the U.S. government built its forts, the famed Oglala warrior Red Cloud voiced stiff opposition to this latest breach of trust.[6] By the end of 1866, Red Cloud had carried out a number of successful attacks on the forts to protect his people's hunting territory, resulting in the U.S. government's inability to maintain the forts. In 1868 the United States and the Lakotas returned to the negotiating table and signed the second Fort Laramie Treaty, which established the Great Sioux Reservation; the reservation included the entirety of present-day South Dakota west of the Missouri River. The treaty also guaranteed the right of the Lakotas to hunt in the territories of Wyoming and Montana and in significant parts of Kansas and Nebraska.[7] Red Cloud, writes William Powers, "emerged from battle as the only Indian ever to win a war against the United States Government."[8]

Despite this victory, conflict continued between the Lakotas and the U.S. Seventh Cavalry. When the federal government stole the Black Hills and warned the Lakotas to leave the hunting lands that had been guaranteed them in 1868, tensions reached a frenzy. In June 1876, Custer and his men were routed at the Battle of the Greasy Grass. In response to this defeat, the federal government stepped up its efforts to systematically force the bands dwelling outside the reservation to return to the government agencies on the reservation. In addition to these extraordinary pressures on the Lakotas, in 1889 the Great Sioux Reservation was broken up into a much smaller set of five reservations: Standing Rock, Cheyenne River, Lower Brule, Rosebud, and Pine Ridge. The federal treaty negotiators deemed the remaining eleven million acres of land, once guaranteed to the Sioux by the 1868 treaty, to be "surplus" to the Lakotas' needs and turned it over to the public domain.[9] The non-Indians who moved onto the former Sioux lands, however, also eyed with envy the remaining lands of the smaller five reservations. The 1889 Great Sioux Agreement stipulated that, in time, the entirety of all Sioux reservations should be liquidated into the hands of private landholders.[10] The loss of massive amounts of land—in conjunction with an economic depression that swept the country after the 1898 Spanish-American War, followed by a drought that devastated the plains—amounted to a critical economic situation on the Lakota reservations, exacerbated by the OIA's extraordinary mismanagement of resources and economic policies.

The situation quickly deteriorated. Beginning in 1878, when the Lakotas had been forced onto ever-diminishing reservation lands at gunpoint, the U.S. government, fearful of and concerned about their cultural and communal activities, mounted a massive surveillance apparatus over practically every aspect of Lakota life.[11] Where OIA agents and missionaries did not dwell, the government assigned non-Indian farmers to conduct reconnaissance on their Lakota neighbors. Additionally, the Indian police force served at the beck and call of the agency superintendents and conducted raids on Lakota homes when the OIA deemed it necessary. Many of these agency superintendents even withheld treaty-guaranteed rations to bend Lakota families to their will. Indeed, the distribution and withholding of rations by the OIA became a mechanism that, as Tom Biolsi has argued, further restricted the movements, activities, and social organization of the Lakotas.[12] OIA agents often withheld rations from individuals that they considered troublemakers: specifically, those who moved about on or between the reservations, and also dancers.[13] Because of the loss of land and limited mobility, the Lakotas became increasingly destitute throughout the final decades of the nineteenth century. Starvation due to lack of rations, through either their being withheld or the inability of the local agents to secure proper amounts, was partially responsible for encouraging the cultural revitalization that culminated in the so-called Ghost Dance movement and the massacre at Wounded Knee in 1890. The Lakotas by necessity became dangerously dependent on an exceedingly undependable distribution of rations.

On top of these adverse circumstances, the OIA promulgated allotment and assimilation policies that irrevocably transformed all aspects of American Indian people's lives, cultures, and economies. The results of the General Allotment Act, combined with the citizenship agenda of the OIA, were nothing less than catastrophic for Native peoples, and the Lakotas were no exception.[14] Designed to train Indians to become proper American citizens, assimilation efforts provided little aid for the Lakotas, who by this point simply struggled to survive. Many of the Lakotas were too young, too old, or too sick and disabled to cultivate the allotted farms as designated and parceled out by the OIA, and the OIA did not provide enough tools or supplies to farm.[15] To make things worse, what land remained in the hands of Native people, particularly the Lakotas, was practically untenable for farming. As Biolsi observed, "Western South Dakota, as everyone knew, could not sustain commercial dry farming for long: rainfall was unpredictable and often insufficient (even subsistence gardening was unreliable in this climate), soils were poor, and local markets or nearby shipping points were not always available. What is more, the Lakota could not compete with the better-capitalized white commercial farmers."[16] The OIA officials felt that ranching and seasonal wage labor could supplement income derived from individually owned farms and further induce what they considered a suitable work ethic, but again, the OIA's plan to deliver "civilization" through such labor failed before it could even begin: ranching required more capital than the Lakotas could raise, and the amount of land allotted to individuals was vastly insufficient for the enterprise. Even when some Lakotas gained success in stock raising in the first decade of the twentieth century, this too came to an abrupt end in 1916, when cattle prices soared due to the war in Europe and OIA agents convinced the ranchers to sell the entirety of their herds. According to Edward Lazarus, "White cattlemen (who also had incited Sioux enthusiasm for cashing in) moved onto the empty Indian lands, leasing huge tracts to support their continuing war boom business." As the profits were spent, the Lakotas found themselves in as destitute a position as they had yet faced.[17] Beyond farming and stock raising, jobs were in very short supply around the reservations.[18] Lakota relief measures such as giveaway dances, which had pooled resources such as tools, seeds, and food for those in need, were typically forbidden because of their communal nature. The assimilation policy's emphasis on independence, self-reliance, and private property was utterly incompatible with the communal way of life cultivated by the Lakotas.

Lakota dependence—a dependence created by the federal government's theft of Lakota lands as well as by its allotment and assimilation policies—grew throughout the first three decades of the twentieth century. During these years the OIA continued to foist an economic and cultural agenda on all of the reservations while intensifying its coercion and efforts to monitor and otherwise control every aspect of Native people's lives, leaving them with no effective means in the legal system to defend themselves or articulate their opposition.[19] The OIA consistently responded to the dire economic circumstances by insisting that only by fulfilling its conception of the cultural requirements for American citizenship could the crises of the reservations be resolved, the crises that the very policies of allotment and assimilation had exacerbated if not in some cases entirely created. Within this context of economic crisis, pervasive surveillance, and implementation of the assimilation campaign, the Lakotas and the U.S. government engaged in several battles over the practice of music—battles over power, executed through dance.

"INDIAN OFFENSES": DANCE IN THE RESERVATION ENVIRONMENT, 1868–1900

The allotment of Lakota lands and the assimilation impetus of the Indian reformers' citizenship agenda led in precise ways to the development of an OIA policy on the practice of music on reservations. The policy was heavily influenced by missionaries, Native and non-Native alike, as well as by agency superintendents. For these individuals, the power of unregulated musical practice by the Lakotas was not only profound but also incredibly dangerous. Yet for the dance practitioners, the danger lay in *not* singing their songs. On the northern plains, this debate revolved around the Sun Dance and the Omaha Dance complex.

"Back in the days before the reservations were set up," noted Severt Young Bear, "our dances were mostly part of the warrior societies that men belonged to, or the different ceremonial dances we used to do."[20] One of the most prominent Lakota ceremonial complexes was the Sun Dance. Throughout the 1880s the Sun Dance held great importance for Native peoples across the plains; its annual performance, according to Tom Holm, "reaffirmed each tribe's place in the world, provided for a restrengthening of intertribal relationships, and like most other Native American ceremonies, fulfilled tribal obligations to the Creator's universal scheme."[21] The ceremony, which lasted eight days, included fasting and dancing and, among the Cheyennes, Lakotas, Arapahos, and Blackfeet, might also involve the piercing of skin by skewers, demonstrating the supreme sacrifice of flesh before the "Great Mysteries of the world."[22]

Local Indian agents and missionaries misunderstood the purpose of the ceremony and fixated on the skin-piercing rituals, which to them signified primitive barbarism. Beginning with the Sun Dance, the OIA sought to regulate every aspect of life for the Lakota people. Because missionaries, reformers, and many OIA officials considered Lakota dance as a practice most offensive to their tastes and exceedingly dangerous to their assimilation project, the OIA worked quickly to restrict or forbid dancing. The OIA began its assault on the Sun Dance in 1882, and by the next year the federal government had deemed "all similar dances and so-called religious ceremonies . . . 'Indian Offenses,'" punishable by "incarceration in the agency prison for a period not exceeding thirty days."[23] Adriana Greci Green, however, notes that punishments for dancing also included the withholding of treaty-guaranteed rations, and imprisonment for up to six months; furthermore, local agents resorted to tearing down the dance houses and halls that facilitated dancing in the winter months.[24] OIA officials and missionaries, who considered the dances as "heathenish" and antithetical to their goals, struggled to eradicate them, often with the help of the Indian police, a group of sympathetic Lakota men hired by local agents ostensibly to enforce their agendas.[25]

In addition to the Sun Dance ceremonial, the Omaha Dance complex figured prominently in the lives of the Lakotas and their neighbors.

The ceremony was adopted from the Yanktons by various Teton bands, according to winter counts, between the years 1860 and 1865; the Yanktons, in turn, had received the dance from either the Omahas or Poncas.[26] Originating among the Hethuska and Inloshka societies of the Kaws, Omahas, and Poncas, and in the Iruska society of the Pawnees, the dance spread in the mid-nineteenth century to reservations across the northern and southern plains.[27] Dances were owned by various societies—the Omaha Dance belonged to the Omaha society, and originally only members of the male society and their families could participate. The Omaha tradition entailed a complex of social activities, including oratory, dancing, ritual drama, giveaways, and feasting, as well as Honoring Songs, songs about deeds, Charging Songs, Society Songs, Victory Songs, and social songs.[28] The complex, according to Mark Thiel, was nationalistic in nature and celebrated victories and achievements in warfare; it grew to serve many additional functions in society such as the distribution of goods through giveaways and, increasingly, as a means of negotiating the restrictions on dancing and traveling that constricted Lakota social and ritual life.[29] With the advent of World War I, the Omaha complex took center stage in the conflict between dancers and the OIA.

As is true of most dances, the meanings of the Omaha Dance for the various groups who practice it have changed and are continually redefined. It appears that the Omaha Dance was originally very closely related to the Grass Dance, though this relationship is understood in different ways, depending on the authority. According to Young Bear, these dances were originally separate but became one: "[The Grass Dancers] would go out and pick some tall grass, tie it together, and put it on their backs at the waist. Some even braided the grass and wore it like a sash across the chest. They have their own set of songs and their dancers do a lot of fancy footwork. They dance backwards, cross their legs, and go in circles." Describing the Omaha Dancers, Young Bear noted: "The Omaha and *tokala* [Kit Fox society] dancers were straight dancers. They might go down low, but not like these grass dance guys, who were a little bit fancier and somehow identified with grass. Some say it represents scalps and others say it symbolizes generosity. Originally, Omaha dance and grass dance were two different dance customs. Later on, I think in the 1880s and 1890s, they came together in their songs and their costuming."[30] According to Oglala Lakota Norma Rendon, "Grass Dance originated a ways back. The Lakota, a long time ago they had these men, and they would wear a row of grass around their head, around their arms, around their ankles and right under their knees. . . . As they [the dancers, after returning from a successful raid or war party] went into the dance arena before the People, they would stomp down the grass with their feet."[31] The origins and meanings of the dances are attributed differently by different authorities, but the popularity of the dance, and the speed with which it spread through the plains, is staggering.

As the Omaha Dance complex rose in prominence as a central component of Lakota social and ritual life, the meaning of the dance and its accompanying songs began to change after the Lakotas were forced onto reservations in 1878. Although the use of the dance to seek protection from enemies in battle began to fade after the virtual incarceration of reservation life, the songs became much more oriented toward themes of "good health [and] sermons on righteous conduct," and "new inspirational songs became popular."[32] Over time the social aspects of the dance were increasingly accented. For some of the younger dancers, the Grass Dance eventually even served as a means of courtship, as women began to dance outside the men, in the opposite direction.[33] As the dance's warrior element waned along with opportunities for young men to demonstrate their skills on the battlefield, giveaways gained importance, celebrating Lakota virtues such as generosity, and individuals were also increasingly recognized by their dance abilities.[34]

Despite the virtues the Omaha complex celebrated, the OIA called it the War Dance. Describing it as a dance that included "all ceremonies formerly associated with armed hostilities including the popular Omaha dance," the OIA banned the Omaha Dance, just as it had banned the Sun Dance.[35] The inability of the OIA to recognize the myriad ways the Lakotas found meaning in dance is embedded in its decision to condemn the dance as a War Dance, thus flattening into a single trope of "savagery" a very complex act of expressive culture. But why was the OIA so concerned about these dances? What about the practice of music caused the OIA to mount such a vigorous campaign against it? And how successful was that campaign? Given that the government was set on suppressing these dances and had by 1882 exerted tremendous control over the movements of the Lakota people, indeed over practically every aspect of their lives, then how did the Lakotas succeed in perpetuating these dances and even innovating them? It is in this context that dance took on a powerful political resonance with regard to the implementation of federal Indian policy.

In broad strokes, OIA officials and missionaries from the 1880s through the 1920s typically considered "Indian dances" as "heathenish" and antithetical to their assimilation and citizenship campaign; throughout that period, but particularly between 1890 and 1922, many local OIA agents and nearly all local missionaries struggled feverishly to eradicate the dances. In seeking to suppress dances on the reservations, federal OIA officials rarely exhibited any sensitivity to or concern for the larger historical significance of the dances and the meanings they held for dancers. Tara Browner argues that distinctions between the Omaha Dance and the Grass Dance, or between the entire array of individually distinctive Lakota dances in this period, were misunderstood or overlooked by non-Indians who did not have the eyes, the ears, or the proclivity to differentiate the songs, movements, and regalia associated with each dance.[36] Indeed, correspondence between OIA agents and officials regarding Lakota dances in the early twentieth century refers nearly exclusively and interchangeably to "Grass Dances" and "Omaha Dances," if they are even that specific in their descriptions, and these dances, whatever they signified to the Lakotas, caused great consternation among the non-Indians who sought to curtail them.

Despite the collective horror expressed by these reformers, religious figures, and government employees toward "Indian dancing," they never provided a list of characteristics that differentiated an "Indian" dance from a "white" dance—primarily because they assumed that anyone who witnessed them could tell them apart. Furthermore, their understandings of the differences between specific songs and dances, or even between Omaha and Sun Dance expressive culture, were limited at best. The meanings and uses of the dances to the Lakotas were beyond their purview. Based on correspondence between OIA reservation superintendents and the commissioner's office, however, we can establish some of the basic organizational principles by which their racialized performative designations were ostensibly assigned.

The OIA maintained a polarized view of Native performance in this period: "Indian" dances were typically organized by Native people, usually those considered the "traditionals" or "conservatives" by the OIA—those least prone to accept the tenets of a citizenship agenda geared toward the eradication of their language, of non-Christian religious customs, of their socioeconomic and cultural organizations, and so on. These dances were deemed heathen or otherwise incorporated what were considered non-Christian elements. What the agents saw and heard was people dancing in regalia to singers belting out unrecognizable phrases in unrecognizable melodies, certainly not the acceptable melodies or modes of European or white American composers. The dances would typically feature drums and voices as the primary instruments, and dance gatherings could last for days or sometimes weeks. All of these characteristics directed the OIA to conclude, time and time again, that any tolerance for such dancing would hinder the "uplift" of Native people.

Many of the Lakotas, however, did not agree. As soon as the government banned the Sun Dance and the Omaha Dance, the Lakotas began to develop a variety of tactics to evade the orders from Washington. The 1880s were thus marked, not by an empty dance calendar on Lakota reservations, but rather by a full schedule that mirrored the calendar of American festivities in remarkable and strategic ways. Indeed, the first tactic the Lakotas developed to perpetuate many of their traditions after they came under fire from OIA officials and missionaries was to perform them on American holidays. The Lakotas began petitioning their local OIA agents for permission to hold dances on the Fourth of July, for example, ostensibly to celebrate American patriotism. This innovation was not unique to the Lakotas; during this period Native communities throughout the plains and beyond had begun to adapt their dancing calendars to coincide with American holidays.[37] Remarkably, OIA officials increasingly found themselves forced to concede to the clever request of the Lakotas and others to hold dances the week of the Fourth; after all, did not such celebrations demonstrate in some ways the success of the assimilation agenda?

Of course, the agents understood little about the dances, nor did they recognize the relationship of these celebrations to the Omaha Dance complex or even the Sun Dance complex—for example, some aspects of the Sun Dance complex were maintained at these celebrations, such as the Hunka Ceremony, or Hunkapi, for "the Making of Relatives," and the Buffalo Ceremony, commemorating girls' first menstruation.[38] Additionally, Lakota ceremonial calendars often fit well with American ceremonial calendars; the Sun Dance celebration, for example, was initially held on the same days, approximately, as Fourth of July celebrations.[39] The celebrations, according to Mark Thiel and Adriana Greci Green, typically lasted between three and eight days and often consisted of most of the components found in the Omaha Dance tradition: various song traditions and styles, mock battles, oratories, and giveaways.[40] Although it is not known precisely when the first Lakota so-called Fourth of July celebration occurred, it is clear that the groundwork for such practices, though not universal on the reservations, was firmly in place by the late 1880s.[41] By the early 1900s the Lakotas had become particularly masterful at using American holidays as an excuse to dance.

Clearly, while the government maintained an official policy that restricted if not forbade Lakota dancing, local officials would occasionally relent to Lakota pressure to permit dances. One important arena in which some dancing, particularly Omaha dancing, was permitted in this period was tribal fairs. Tribal fairs came into existence by the late 1880s and were organized to encourage agricultural and ranch labor as advanced by the OIA. As with the Fourth of July celebrations, however, the Lakotas were quick to transform the fairs, and even preparation for them, into celebrations of Lakota peoplehood. Young Bear described it this way:

> Here in Porcupine they went to the [OIA] superintendent or boss farmer and said, "You outlawed traditional dancing and singing, but we want to honor the New Year and have masquerades for good health and so that our cattle and horses and produce will grow well for the next district fair or tribal fair." And the agent said, "All right, that's a good idea." . . . We also were allowed to dance at fairs in late summer or early fall because there would be displays of vegetables, rodeos, and other signs that we

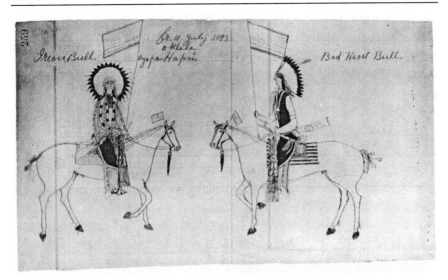

Amos Bad Heart Bull depicts his and Iron Bull's roles as "chiefs" of a Lakota dance held on the Fourth of July in 1903. Participants danced under U.S. flags and incorporated them into their dance regalia, particularly in beadwork, in part to convince OIA officials that their Omaha dances should be permitted at Fourth of July celebrations. Reproduced from *A Pictographic History of the Oglala Sioux*, by Amos Bad Heart Bull, text by Helen H. Blish, by permission of the University of Nebraska Press. Copyright © 1967 renewed 1995 by the University of Nebraska Press.

were becoming good modern citizens instead of sticking to all that old ceremonial and warrior stuff. But we still got to dance.[42]

The Lakotas used these fairs as grand occasions for visiting friends and relatives on other reservations, particularly after the government so heavily restricted movement between the reservations. The fairs became so popular that in 1913 the OIA commissioner mandated that all reservation districts hold them on the same days, to avoid such visiting, and that the districts include band concerts and athletic contests, to erode the popularity of the Omaha Dance. Rather, the popularity of the fairs themselves diminished as a result, and by 1927 both the Pine Ridge and Rosebud reservation fairs had closed.[43] As the Lakotas discovered, however, in the late nineteenth century, fairs and American holiday celebrations were not the only available outlets for maintaining various dance complexes. The non-Indian public's fascination with Indianness provided additional venues.

It is not coincidental that the ability of the Lakotas to hold celebrations in the Omaha Dance traditions, amid the OIA's policy of dance suppression and assimilation, increased after the launch of Buffalo Bill Cody's Wild West Show in 1883. In fact, what served as Cody's trial run for a Wild West show occurred at a Fourth of July celebration in North Platte, Nebraska, in 1882.[44] Cody and organizers of other Wild West shows, medicine shows, and local fairs and rodeos all hired Lakota men to perform dances in the Omaha tradition in the 1880s and 1890s, typically billing the performances as "war dances" to titillate audiences eager to experience "authentic" Indian dances. It is unclear whether Bill or OIA officials first began to refer to Omaha Dance as War Dance, but what is clear is that popular perceptions of dances and the federal government's dance policy were interacting with one another from the beginning of the reservation period. Whereas to the OIA these "War Dances" connoted danger and placed its assimilation policy in jeopardy, the "War Dances" in Wild West shows connoted to the audiences a danger safely contained in Cody's arenas, but a titillating danger nonetheless. The Lakotas' success in manipulating and resisting the federal policy of dance suppression was in part strengthened by the burgeoning interest of the non-Indian public in Indianness—popular ideological perceptions of Native Americans, typically at odds with the realities of Native life but also, in terms of Indian relations with non-Indians, a prominent influence in proscribing Native economic or social roles and opportunities.[45]

The OIA was not of one mind regarding the Wild West shows but seemed to begrudgingly tolerate them as they increased in popularity. Reform organizations such as the Indian Rights Association (IRA) immediately condemned the shows for seemingly glorifying the displays of "savagery" that needed strict suppression. An 1899 IRA report, for example, stated, "It is worse than folly for the government to say to the Indian child, through the school: Think, dress, act like a civilized white man; and then to say, through the show business: Think, dress, act like a savage Indian."[46] OIA officials seemed to typically share such concerns, but Cody never seemed to have too much of a problem in securing permission from the OIA to hire dancers. As

Moses and Murphy have argued, the OIA seemed more concerned that Cody ensure a morally sound environment for the dancers while on the road, and apparently none of the OIA commissioners felt that their refusal to permit the performances stood on solid legal ground.[47] Murphy argues that in fact the OIA tolerated the type of performances in the shows because "they saw it as much less threatening than a continuation of the Indian religious ceremonies and ways of life off the stage." She notes, "Cody's Wild West started presenting Indian 'war dances' as theater in the mid-1880s, at precisely the moment their practice off the stage was prohibited. This staging served to assuage fears of the force of Indian dance, and to convince the powers that be that the force of the dance, once converted to spectacle, had thus been contained."[48] Of course, the hired dancers understood their work in very different terms.

L. G. Moses' account of Wild West shows argues that "show Indians," most of whom were Oglala, were not dupes for "playing Indian" before whites but rather used these newfound opportunities to make a living in difficult times, to publicly assert their tribal identity, and to demonstrate their virtue and skill both in dances that they selected and controlled and as warriors in sham battles in which they interpreted previous heroic acts against the U.S. Army.[49] Indeed, among the Lakotas the "show Indian" tradition, or *oskate*, was about much more than money, although the money was welcomed: it fostered honor and, along with it, tremendous innovation in dancing, particularly within the Omaha Dance complex. In the 1880s and 1890s, it was not uncommon for two hundred Lakota men to be on tour, in full regalia, performing Honor Songs and Victory Songs and creating new innovations along the way.[50] The show Indians were at times themselves honored with songs, as Young Bear recounted:

Here's [a special *oskate* song] from the early 1890s: "Pte San Wicasa bli-hic'iyayo. Oskate wayinkta waciniyanpelo. Mni wanca watakihotun hi najin ki catne iyani pa kte lo" (White Buffalo Man—his name was San Stabber—be brave! There's a big Wild West show coming for you. When you hear the sound of the boat, your heart will beat faster). This next one is one that my cousin Irving Tail often sings: "Oskate wan iyayinkte ca iyapi wapaha iwekcuna winyeya he wa u." Then they name that person, like Pte San Wicasa, and then it goes on, "heina oskate ekta iya." This says, "There will be a Wild West show that will start soon, so I got my war bonnet ready and I'm ready to go. This is what White Buffalo Man said, and then he went to the Wild West show."[51]

The Wild West shows and fairs provided new contexts for Lakotas to innovate their dances—dances simultaneously threatening to the OIA yet enthralling to the Wild West show audiences.

Eventually Wild West shows became one of the only outlets for public dancing, and because of a number of influences, by the turn of the century public dancing on the Lakota reservations seemed to be well on its way out. One of those influences was the massacre at Wounded Knee on December 29, 1890, when nearly three hundred practitioners of a new movement that had swept the plains—the Ghost Dance movement—were slaughtered by the U.S. Army. Following the Seventh Cavalry's rampage against Big Foot's band, the Ghost Dance massacre caused such trauma among the Lakotas that dancing of any sort was greatly diminished in the 1890s. Following the massacre, the OIA stepped up its efforts to "rigidly" control all ceremonials.[52] On the Standing Rock Sioux Reservation, Father Bernard Strassmaier reported that dancing was "universal" until "the Messiah craze came on and Sitting Bull and some of his followers had been killed on December 15, 1890," at which point the dances were "entirely annihilated."[53] Indeed, the massacre of Ghost Dancers and their families at Wounded Knee crippled the ability and desire of the Lakotas to hold dances or large gatherings of any sort.

At the same time, Christian organizations stepped up their efforts to eliminate the options for their followers to practice Omaha Dance, Ghost Dance, or Sun Dance traditions. Like the Lakotas, many Yanktons were heavily influenced by the missionaries by the 1880s, and this influence affected Sioux dance traditions in various ways. For example, in 1887 the Yanktons began to split over the Fourth of July dances; while the older men participated in Omaha dances, a group of younger men looked on in disappointment. According to one observer, "After one or two dances another appeal was made to the young men. 'This is the Fourth of July. It is all right to dance on the Fourth of July. . . .' But as powerful as the argument was, the young men would not come in."[54] This reluctance was attributed to the influence of a Native pastor who discouraged dancing.[55] By 1904 the Yanktons had formed three separate camps during the week of the Fourth, with two attending the "dancing, horse racing, and [giveaways]," while the other attended a YMCA convention held on the reservation as an alternative avenue of entertainment based in scripture readings, patriotic speeches, and the performance of "national songs."[56] With perhaps one exception, missionaries among the Sioux sought to suppress all forms of tribally derived dances; the missionaries were consistent in the frustration they expressed over the fairs and Fourth of July celebrations that facilitated what they considered to be heathen and immoral dances.[57]

The missionaries witnessed significant victories in their struggle over Lakota dances in the 1890s. By organizing mutual aid societies and timing gatherings to coincide with fairs and holidays, they seemed to influence more and more Lakotas to refrain from dancing. The Catholic convocation, or Indian Congress, as it was known, was scheduled during the first week of July from 1891 through 1905. Protestant missionaries developed their own calendar of celebrations that were void of any use of or reference to Lakota dances, although implicit in their design was an admonishment of dancing. The most ardent Catholic and Protestant Lakotas saw no honor in the "show Indian" tradition and rather viewed it as antithetical to meeting their own ideals of religious devotion and cultivated, Christian living. By 1900, according to Thiel, the popularity of the Omaha Dance had decreased dramatically, and most missionaries were satisfied that as soon as the older Indians who continued the Omaha tradition died, no one would remain to perpetuate its customs.[58]

RETURNED STUDENTS, THE FAILURES OF OIA
ECONOMIC POLICY, AND THE LAKOTA DANCE REVIVAL,
1900–1922

The missionaries and OIA agents, of course, were most concerned with the younger Lakotas. By 1900, agents and missionaries felt that Indian dancing was certainly on the way out, as they encountered unprecedented success in suppressing most Lakota dances and driving the remainder underground or out to the hills and into contained Wild West show arenas, far away from the agencies. Most felt that the older Lakotas were beyond redemption, both spiritually and culturally, and they believed that if they set age limits on dancing, granting only those over the age of forty to fifty permission to dance, then dancing would not seriously intervene in their assimilation and allotment project. This prediction was proven incorrect, however; within twenty years, dancing permeated all of the Lakota reservations and served as perhaps the most significant antiassimilation weapon that the Lakotas could wield. The strategic use of dance by the Lakotas resulted in the defeat of a powerful anti-dance element in the OIA in the 1920s. It also contributed to the passage of the Indian Reorganization Act in 1934, which halted any further allotments of Indian land and effectively dismantled the philosophical underpinnings of the assimilation policy that supported dance bans. Moreover, this impressive reversal of policy was undertaken by the youth—the returned students from federal Indian boarding schools. By looking closely at the local power struggles between the Lakotas and the OIA officials over dance in this period, we can get a sense of how the practice of music was effectively wielded as a catalyst for political change.

The younger generations of Native people were seen by the OIA as the last hope for "civilizing" American Indian communities. Children were placed in federal Indian boarding schools with the idea that they should shed all cultural attributes of their tribal identities and affiliations in order to assume the cultural ideals the OIA envisioned for "proper" U.S. citizens—a goal that most fin de siècle Indian Office critics and OIA officials seemed to share. Those ideals of U.S. citizenship included their taking new "American" names, learning and speaking only English, dressing in conservative attire, if not in discarded military uniforms, and gaining a passion for Christianity, Euro-American expressive culture, wage labor, and private property. But the separation of the children from their relatives, often from the time they were five or six until they were eighteen or even older (with occasional visits home in between), bore many unexpected results. Although the students had gained certain tools such as literacy and a command of the English language, students returning from the schools often had a lesser education in their people's history or in their personal community, societal, and familial obligations, and many missed the ceremonies necessary to bring them into adulthood. This was expected by the OIA and was the point, particularly for the off-reservation schools. Yet OIA officials had not considered the possibility that the students, after receiving an education to become proper American citizens, would desire to remain Lakota citizens. For this reason more and more "returned students," as they were called, began to use dancing as a means to reincorporate themselves within their families and communities. Dancing in part became a method for the students—fresh from the halls of schools designed to American- ize them—to Indianize themselves and gain the respect and accept- ance of their reservation community. Thus the off-reservation boarding schools in effect spurred the on-reservation dancing renais- sance of the early twentieth century.

New battles over dance played out in local politics in the early twentieth century. Particularly troubling to OIA officials and mis- sionaries was that the renaissance was attracting, and in many cases was led by, younger American Indians. Harmon Marble, superin- tendent of the Crow Creek Indian Agency of South Dakota, wrote, "These dances have not proven a serious problem in the past. How- ever, I note a growing tendency of the younger people . . . to partici- pate in the dances. . . . I have endeavored to place upon the older people, sponsors of the dance, the responsibility for excluding these young persons. However, it does not appear this plan will work out satisfactorily as the old people are timid about enforcing such rules."[59] Marble's concern resonated with agents throughout South and North Dakota. From 1902 to 1922, James McLaughlin observed a steady increase in dance participation at the Standing Rock Agency until it had begun to include "nearly every male adult of the reservation."[60] Arthur Pratt, the stockman in charge of the Porcupine district at Standing Rock, noted that Lakota parents began to bring their chil- dren, home on vacation from the boarding schools, to dances. At the dances they learned "the ways of this old custom and all that goes along with it," Pratt wrote. "I notice on this reservation at one time during a big celebration a bunch of boys from 10 to 12 years old sit- ting around an old can and singing Indian songs to a perfection, this happen just outside of one of the feast tents while the adults were singing inside the tent." He continued: "The young children of the reservation are receiving training in this savage doings which are directly opposite to what the government is doing for them and proposes to do along the civilized ways."[61] The OIA officials believed that the younger generation's participation in these dances would undermine the inculcation of an acceptable Indian citizenry within the schools. The participation of returned students more than anything else caused the OIA to begin a series of new strategies of their own to eliminate tribally derived dances from the repertoire of the youth.

American Indian youth began publicly dancing en masse on several reservations. A non-Indian stockman who was conducting surveillance on dances in the Porcupine District of Standing Rock, a reservation on which not only Lakotas but also the closely related Dakotas and Nakotas lived, stated in 1922 that "the young Indians or the citizens now practically dominate the dances and the old people are taking [it] somewhat easy and [seem] to be on the background."[62] Bishop Hugh L. Burleson additionally noted that among the Lakotas the revival of the dances in the early twentieth century was not a continuation of old customs or traditions but rather a new creation fostered by Native youth: "It is not survival of an old ceremony or custom. My own observation is that the majority of the dancers are not over thirty and in some cases are under sixteen. The old people are on the outside and the young people are in there dancing."[63]

Some of the youth, including boarding school students, accepted payment by local white fair organizers to dance, essentially getting paid by whites to resist the government's assimilation policy. Such students often baffled OIA officials and the spectators at their expense, dressing, as one superintendent observed, "in gundy sacks and instead of dancing the old dance they would stand on their head and some would lay down, and they would do all kinds of stunts."[64] As did McLaughlin, Superintendent C. M. Ziebach here felt that as long as "dancing could be restricted to the old people," then no real danger could come from allowing the dances to continue.[65] Clearly, however, Ziebach was unable to control the returned students. Noting that "dancing is on the increase," the Sisseton Reservation superintendent witnessed "one small boy some three or four years of age

Sioux dance house, 1911. The Lakotas held many of their Omaha dances and giveaways within structures such as this one. Here a number of people are attempting to look inside what is presumably a packed house. Local OIA agents and farmers also wanted to look inside, as part of intensive surveillance measures geared toward controlling the dances. J. A. Anderson Collection, Prints and Photographs Division, Library of Congress, LC-USZ62-101270.

keeping step just as nicely as the elder Indians."[66] Although the Grass Dances that occurred before the turn of the century on the Standing Rock Sioux Reservation had been held mostly by the older people, since that time the youth had taken up the dance and gave Superintendent E. D. Mossman the most "trouble."[67]

It seems that a cultural renaissance taking place on the Lakota reservations was intended in large part to directly oppose the imposition of the assimilation policy, and that the renaissance was led not by the older generation but by Lakota youth and young adults who had left the reservations for boarding schools and returned with a desire to rejuvenate pride in Lakota expressive culture. This revival of older dances and the creation of new ones by larger and larger groups of young people threatened the sense of control that federal officials had tried to maintain over their local Native populations. Dance weakened this control in several ways. One was that American Indians could use the dances to further their own economic interests and thus weaken their dependence and thus the control of the local agents and the federal government, while compromising nothing. For example, Superintendent Whillihan complained that at an off-reservation fair at Forman, North Dakota, some of the Lakotas had created a ring and charged twenty-five cents admission for whites to witness the dance, and sent "a tax to the state for operating the show."[68] Native people essentially got paid to "play Indian" before non-Indian audiences who, as Philip Deloria has argued, at this time often sought to experience their perceived "authenticity" of American Indians in response to increasing anxieties over the modern world.[69] With the popularity of the Wild West shows and fairs, Indianness became more lucrative for Native musicians and dancers willing to perform for non-Indians than virtually any OIA policy or program of assimilation they could adopt. This proposition challenged the underlying assumption of the assimilation policies, which asserted that the performance of tribally derived cultural traditions was antithetical to full participation in the market economy of American society. Rather than recognize or admit the irony that some Lakotas found a semblance of economic security in the celebration of their peoplehood through music and dance as opposed to simply taking up individual homesteads and breaking tribal ties, the agents in North and South Dakota saw this cultural activity as a danger that threatened their efforts at controlling the mental, physical, and social economies of the Lakotas.

The participation of the students also demonstrated to the OIA officials and the missionaries who lived on or near the reservations the very failure of the "civilization" program in assimilating Indians. The program of coercive education implemented in the schools—to break tribal and communal ties, eradicate Native religious beliefs and languages, and foster Christianity, individualism, and economic independence through instruction in the arts of industry and thrift—was having unexpected results. Lakota missionary Dallas Shaw spoke of the students and their participation in the dances:

> A good many of my brothers and friends have been to school. I teach them that they must not go back to the blanket but on the Rosebud Reservation all the returned Carlyle students have returned to blankets. They are the cause of a great deal of this trouble. . . . [I went to a dance at Black Pike]

and saw a number of men who had on war bon[n]ets and there was one young man there dressed just like the old men and this man came near and I seen that this young man had a mustache on—it looked so funny. And I was ashamed of myself. I felt so ashamed of myself. He talked better English than I do and I was ashamed. The outward look of him was more like a white man. He spoke the English language and yet he was all painted up. And so there is a great problem.[70]

Shaw's comments at once reveal the complex meaning and seemingly contradictory signals sent by the young dancers. These returned students brought an array of cultural influences from the schools—they learned to read and write English, for example, as well as they learned to dance. Because the schools were often filled with Native students from reservations all across the country, they inadvertently served as hotbeds of new and foreign customs, songs, dances, and traditions that the students could adapt and bring back to their reservations.[71] For these reasons, and also because dance served as a way for the returned students to gain acceptance by their older peers and elders after being away for so long, the off-reservation boarding schools fostered the on-reservation dancing renaissance of the early twentieth century. Furthermore, as the students developed increasingly sophisticated understandings of the English language and American culture, so too did Lakota dance take on political meanings in entirely new and expanded contexts.

Although clear indications of success continued to elude OIA officials in their quest to Americanize and detribalize the youth in boarding schools, the vision of the utter economic and agricultural fiasco of allotment surrounded them in the fields and prairies of the Lakota reservations. As Janet McDonnell has argued, American Indians generally "lacked the capital and credit that they needed to purchase seeds, equipment, and stock," and "most of the reservations were located in arid regions with marginal agricultural potential."[72] However, by the 1910s most OIA officials blamed the economic disaster in Indian Country on the Indians' lack of abilities or interest rather than on the real obstacles that doomed the agrarian policy from the start. Even efforts by Native people to overcome the obstacles were thwarted if those efforts were not attempted in a manner acceptable

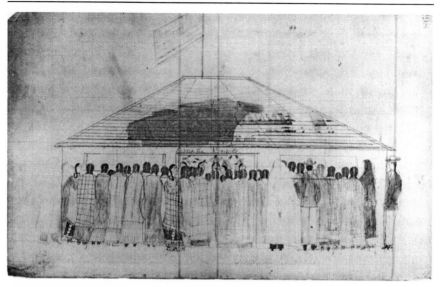

Ledger drawing by Amos Bad Heart Bull, featuring his take of the modern Omaha dance house used during the Fourth of July celebrations in 1903. The U.S. flag flies high above the regalia-clad dancers inside. Reproduced from *A Pictographic History of the Oglala Sioux*, by Amos Bad Heart Bull, text by Helen H. Blish, by permission of the University of Nebraska Press. Copyright © 1967 renewed 1995 by the University of Nebraska Press.

to the officials' cultural standards. In 1908, for example, a group of men from the Oak Creek District of Standing Rock formed a singing association for the ostensible purpose of raising money to buy a threshing machine or a separator "for the use of this association and for others." It seems that the local agency did not have these crucial technologies available. Because the local agent forbade the association from holding the song meetings, Ignatius White Cloud, a member of the association, directly petitioned the commissioner of Indian Affairs to gain permission to sing. The acting commissioner contacted the Standing Rock agent, who informed the commissioner that he believed the association was really raising funds, not for these machines, but for more and more song meetings and feasts that would subsequently interfere with their tending of crops.[73] In what was certainly a devastating rebuke, consequently the agent confiscated the singing association's drum.[74]

Regardless of the intentions of the association, this correspondence provides an early example of the way musical performance had become enmeshed within the directives of federal Indian policy as well as within Native strategies to perpetuate cultural practices in the wake of an orchestrated attempt to dismantle them. Even by the 1920s the OIA appeared unable or unwilling to recognize the heart of the problems, to increase the availability of seeds, tools, arable lands or other means of improving reservation conditions, or to consider an alternative trajectory for federal Indian economic policy. In 1922 Bishop Burleson reiterated the view of blaming American Indians for the failures of allotment:

> The welfare of the Indians, just as the welfare of the white man, depends upon their effort and their application, and we must always keep before them the things that they have in life, and it is bound up with agriculture. There isn't anything else you can put before them. They have to learn to live on the land and by the land. . . . What should we be training him to do? It must be agriculture. In the general life they are handicapped.[75]

Burleson went on to express additional fear that Native women in "commercial life" were "in great danger," considered by white men as "fair game." He reiterated his view that agriculture was the only option and that rural life was perhaps their only "safe" mode of existence.[76] Burleson and the other missionaries, and government officials, felt that the Native boys and girls were unfit for anything other than a life of agriculture, because of their supposedly limited abilities as well as the perceived threats of rape or prostitution for Native women and of miscegenation for white men.

In the 1910s and 1920s, missionaries, OIA agents, and farmers blamed the nemesis of dance for the dire reservation conditions created by the government's ineffective agricultural policy. This tactic of blaming American Indians for the failures of government policies conveniently provided yet another reason to restrict dancing, as complaints that dances would keep the Indians from tending their fields increased in OIA correspondence. Like the other officials, Superintendent Ziebach of the Crow Creek Agency saw a causal relationship between the dances and the unsuccessful reservation crops of the

Nakota and Dakota residents: "The main trouble is that the dances come more often during the summer months and the Indians neglect their crops to attend them. We must get the Indians to put in a good crop, and raise a good garden and to have some horses and pigs and chickens."[77] Superintendent Mossman of the Standing Rock Agency agreed: "All the trouble I found [during a four-day trip in the Porcupine District], lack of hay, idleness, dissatisfaction, poverty, lack of interest in our Farm Bureau and Community Work, were apparently directly the result of the heathen dance and its influence."[78]

Local agents thus stepped up efforts to curtail dances, while the Lakotas began to expand them through covert tactics. The Sun Dance, particularly the aspects of the dance that included the ritualistic piercing of the skin, moved underground soon after it was first attacked in the 1880s. The OIA continued to press for the cessation of key elements of the Sun Dance and maintained its pressure against the Omaha tradition, even though it occasionally granted permission for fairs, holidays, and Wild West tours. In the 1900s this pressure to curtail public dances resulted in an expansion of social dances in private homes. Severt Young Bear described the situation:

> The Indian police that the government had put in place to break the power of the chiefs and their *akicita*, or warrior societies, would come around to any ceremonial or warrior gatherings to break them up. If they found a sweat lodge set up, they would throw ropes and pull it down. Also if any of the dances were held with people in costume, they would show up and break them up and harass the participants. As a result, our people started to have dances at night at someone's home, with the curtains drawn. If any car lights showed up in the distance, the young guys who were on lookout knew this had to be the [OIA] police or the boss farmer, since they were the only ones with cars at the time. People would put their hand drums away, and since no one was in costume for these social dances— you didn't wear headdresses, feathers and bells—the police had nothing to go by. What was happening was the start of the social dance tradition.[79]

Arthur Pratt reported similarly evasive tactics regarding one dance near Shields, North Dakota, on May 5, 1923, when "two ring leaders . . . invited all the people outside to come[,] urging them to dance, telling them there was no one there to watch them." The leaders, Peter Black Hawk and Albert Walker, had pointed out that "the policeman was in Mandan and the Farmer was in bed, so after 12 o'clock every body danced."[80] Despite the ramped-up attempts of the OIA to restrict dancing in the early twentieth century, the Lakotas continually found creative ways to prevail.

Although the war over dance was typically carried out in local battles, the commissioner of Indian Affairs was very well apprised of the situation, often by correspondence or visits from Native people. Hollow Horn Bear, a renowned Lakota warrior who fought the U.S. Calvary in the 1870s, became a well-traveled "Native representative," or diplomat, on the East Coast in his later years and had many contacts among Washington officials.[81] Living at Rosebud, he was well aware that the OIA not only blamed Indians for the economic disaster of allotment but also justified dance restrictions for this reason. Though frail, he traveled to Washington, D.C., one last time in 1913 and met with Assistant Commissioner F. H. Abbott. Hollow Horn Bear wished to dispel this connection, and the exchange between the two merits close attention:

HHB: Some are educated people; they have finished their schooling; they are married and have farms and are living on farms. Like in my tribe they have the social dances at certain places but they keep these young people away from them, they won't allow them to look in there or go near. Back there they have a dance for social gathering and talk it over like spring plowing, how to get together to help each other, plowing, and putting in seeds and such as that. We also take up a collection at such socials. That collection is to support a round up fee—it is called the round up fund— we collect it to buy goods and such as that. We collect it at social dances. We have such a ruling there that if those educated people go into those socials to take them out and make them suffer their punishment—either stop the dancing altogether when they go into a dance [or] they take them out and punish them.

Abbott: The Commissioner [Cato Sells] does tell all the superintendents not to permit dancing so frequently that it interferes with their industry or causes them to waste their time and their money but urges them to raise crops and to hold fairs and then have their socials in connection with that. He urges them not to have these people get together in dances and go away from their work and neglect their live stock and their farming.

HHB: What I want is this; I want those young people there. They want the enjoyment. I do not think it is right to keep them away from such pleasures. We know when we were young. Those young people like this pleasure the same as we did. What we are accused is wasting time in working time. We are men; we know when anything is against us, when anything is wrong for us we know it. Those people think they know more than we do. We never try to dance but when it is out of working time, as in the winter time. That is the time we have pleasure, the same as you white people do. We don't spend time as they thought we did. We have got to put in our time the same as white men do. Last fall we shipped our cattle to the market and got money for them and that was encouragement to us. Now we don't like to gather all the old people up. We can't do anything with the old people. The young people have got to do the work and we have got to be with them, just the same as white people. I want you to fix this up for our children.

Abbott: They want the young people at the dances?

Estes (the interpreter, explaining): Yes. The old people have the dances and the young people cannot even look in there.[82]

Hollow Horn Bear was very diplomatic to Abbott and couched his terms in apologies and soft tones. Yet he was very direct in his requests to Abbott, and Abbott promised that he would consider his concerns and write him with a response. Hollow Horn Bear developed pneumonia in Washington soon after this meeting and died before receiving the following response from Abbott, which he no doubt would have found disheartening at best:

As to allowing the young people and returned students to attend the dances, you are advised that, owing to the fact that oftentimes the older Indians indulge in the old-time customs, and also fail to carefully guard the young people from falling into evil and immoral practices as a result of their associations at the dances, it has been considered wisest to keep them away, in order that the good that has been done at school and by the teachings of those who have the interests of the young people at heart, may not be overcome. The Government is very anxious to bring the Indians up to a high state of civilization, and the greatest opportunity for accomplishing this lies in the young people. They must be encouraged to drop the old customs.[83]

Despite facing a direct, well-intentioned, well-reasoned argument that illuminated the misguided principles of the dance restrictions and its illogical connection to farmwork, OIA officials continued to refuse to acknowledge their own policy failures.

CULTURAL CITIZENSHIP AND THE POLITICS OF PATRIOTISM, WORLD WAR I, AND DANCE

When Abbott invoked the "high state of civilization" in his letter to Hollow Horn Bear, he spoke in the language of cultural citizenship, a citizenship he desired for American Indians that would come only through their abandonment of "evil and immoral practices" in favor of a set of decidedly Anglo-American cultural sensibilities. These sensibilities included a singular political allegiance, not to tribes or Lakota bands and customs, but to the United States. But the language of cultural citizenship, much to the consternation of many an OIA agent, was not univocal and could not be contained or controlled. Dancers young and old appropriated aspects of what the OIA would consider "proper" Americanism—such as the celebration of national holidays and service in the armed forces—to deflect OIA criticisms and efforts to suppress their dances. In fact, they used such tenets of the OIA citizenship agenda to enhance and encourage their own cultural agenda, whether or not it coincided with that of the OIA. Indeed, on the Lakota reservations, by the end of World War I, the battle to control the language of cultural citizenship remained firmly entrenched.

As the OIA began to reinvigorate its attempts to suppress dance, dance became increasingly important for the well-being of many Lakotas, partly because of the Great War. World War I served as the pivotal catalyst, along with the participation of returned students, for a rejuvenated and emboldened dance culture on the northern plains. Dancing reached a new apex just as ardent dance opponent Charles Burke entered office in 1921 as the commissioner of Indian Affairs, and just as the miserable failures of allotment were becoming increasingly clear on most reservations. At this same juncture, dance took on a new resonance, both as the OIA's excuse for its economic and assimilation failures and as a means for Lakotas to shift the power dynamics on the reservation in new, exciting ways, through strategic deployments of U.S. citizenship. The Lakota people increasingly used dance to contest the meaning of U.S. citizenship, once lauded by reformers as the primary goal and marker of success of the assimilation and allotment policies. Participation in the armed forces, and the U.S. citizenship that veterans gained as a result, became a way for the Lakotas to perpetuate and expand their dances.

In great contrast to this use of citizenship, the assimilationist philosophy of Indian policy, originating in the nineteenth century, reflected the belief of OIA officials that American Indians must meet a set of specific cultural requirements—and shed the cultural traits of tribalism—before assuming the legal status of U.S. citizens. This belief, which rested upon the idea that tribal culture was learned and not immutable, was the cornerstone of the assimilation philosophy and was made explicit in the General Allotment Act (Dawes Act) of 1887, section 6 of which stipulated that Indians must demonstrate that they were living "separate and apart from any tribe of Indians" and had "adopted the habits of civilized life" before receiving the bestowal of U.S. citizenship.[84] A significant amendment to the Dawes Act, the Burke Act of 1906, empowered the secretary of the interior to render allotments to individual Indians in fee simple title, provided that the secretary deemed the Indians "competent and capable."[85] The amendment essentially equipped the secretary with the authority both to perpetuate the OIA's all-encompassing legal power over Indians who were considered "incompetent" and thus could not demonstrate the cultural requirements of citizenship, and to make the land of any Indians deemed "competent" available for sale without restrictions to non-Indians. Citizenship was thus granted to American Indians in a rather haphazard, case-by-case manner from the 1870s through 1924, when the remaining one-third or so of American Indians who did not already have U.S. citizenship automatically received it.[86] An exception to the general case-by-case rule prior to 1924 was the Citizenship for World War I Veterans Act of 1919, which permitted American Indian veterans to receive citizenship in appreciation of their patriotic service overseas.

Lakotas and other Native peoples challenged the meaning of U.S. citizenship in different ways. Because returned students and their parents were quite cognizant of the desire of OIA officials to inculcate a spirit of Americanism and patriotism within reservation communities, they effectively used these tropes for the express purpose of establishing and maintaining practices of tribally derived song and dance. When agents in North and South Dakota continued their substantial pressure to cease the dances, the Lakotas built upon the nineteenth-century tradition of holding dances on American holidays. Although the OIA typically maintained sufficient coercion on reservations to limit dancing through the 1910s, the one moderately tolerated dance, the Fourth of July celebration, was revived and quickly recognized as a significant cultural victory for the Lakotas. Soon after, Native people throughout the northern and southern plains found more and more dance holidays to request of their agents. By the early 1920s at the Tongue River Agency in Montana, for example, the Cheyenne held small dances on National Indian Day in addition to their largest dance, usually lasting three or four days, held on the Fourth of July. During that week, half of the Cheyenne would celebrate at Busby, and the other half would travel to Miles City to dance at a fair organized by whites.[87] A group of ambitious Lakotas met in 1922 with Rosebud superintendent James McGregor and the local missionaries to request permission to hold dances not only on the last Friday of each month but also on several national holidays, including Washington's Birthday, Indian Day, and Armistice Day.[88] Similarly, in 1923 a delegation from the Simnasho District of the Warm Springs Reservation in Oregon petitioned their superintendent to hold dances on Christmas, the Fourth of July, and New Year's. They planned to hold another dance on April 15 called the Root Feast, which they told the superintendent was "of the same nature as the Thanksgiving Day among the white people."[89] Soon dances were held on reservations all over the country on the Fourth of July, before or after Lent, on Christmas, and on New Year's.[90] It seemed clear that American holidays were not few and far between, at least if you looked hard enough for them.

Like those who began the Fourth of July dance tradition in the nineteenth century, American Indians used the patriotic underpinnings of holidays like the Fourth of July and Thanksgiving to convince the agents that their cause for dancing was justified. A dance understood by the agents as a celebration of the founding of the Republic could be interpreted as much less of a threat to the "civilizing process" of the assimilation campaign; such celebrations would even appear to laud the U.S. government's concept of civilization. Severt Young Bear noted that the Lakotas in the Porcupine District petitioned for dances on "New Year's, and Washington's and Lincoln's birthdays, Memorial Day, Flag Day, July Fourth and Veterans Day," adding, "I guess the [OIA] agents thought those weren't dangerous occasions, so we got to dance."[91] The success of these tactics, which loosened the reigns of reservation surveillance and the control of OIA agents, called into question the very ownership of concepts like patriotism and Americanness. Furthermore, they suggested that the cultural agenda of the dancers was gaining more headway than that of the OIA.

Of course, many agents reckoned that the Fourth of July was more of an excuse than a reason to dance. Dean Ashley, a missionary of the Cheyenne River Reservation, reported to a group of OIA officials in 1922 that since 1916 the Fourth of July dances had grown rapidly and were led by the Lakotas for reasons other than the celebration of the United States:

> The 4th of July celebration in the Indian Country and the 4th of July celebration by the whites are two totally different things. It is proper and eminently fitting that our Indians should be called together and impressed with the ideals of our government, but I am going to ask how many of you present here have ever heard the ideals of our government set forth at a 4th of July celebration? Have heard the principles for which our government was founded? The Indians celebrate the 4th of July with a regular Indian Pow wow with all its frills and fixings that go with it.[92]

Ashley's abhorrence of the dances, even when held on a national holiday, was shared by many of his peers. When Superintendent Mossman came to Standing Rock in 1921, he arrived at the beginning of July, when, according to him, "Hell and damnation were let loose. . . . The celebration amounted to just this much: seven great big Indian blowouts."[93]

Although many local superintendents did not originally feel threatened by the Fourth of July dances, Native peoples used the celebration of the Fourth to serve their own cultural agenda. One white visitor to a dance at Little Eagle on the Grand River in 1920 was horrified at the sight of a dancer "dressed in imitation of the American flag!"[94] In fact, American flags proliferated at the Fourth of July dances and at Lakota dance halls, where the Lakotas could dance under the "protection," as it were, of the flag. A celebration conducted under the rubric of nationalism became threatening in the minds of the superintendents only when they realized that they could not contain the symbolism of the holiday that they wished the Lakotas to observe. This symbolic appropriation by the Lakotas alerted the agents to a further loss of control over Native people's lives, served as another indication of the failures of assimilationist policies, and demonstrated the singers' and dancers' ability to wield the politics of dance in very creative ways, succeeding even when the agents questioned the sincerity of their patriotism.

However unpatriotic these dances may have seemed, the missionaries and federal officials could not deny that an estimated seventeen thousand American Indians had served in World War I, where "Indians volunteered and . . . [were] inducted at a rate nearly twice as high as the rest of the American population."[95] The war provided the chance for many American Indians to fight for the United States, perhaps to demonstrate their value and patriotism to the country. But more significantly, they fought to gain status within their own communities. Tom Holm argues that the military "Indianized" more than Americanized these veterans. Indian veterans have "given military service meaning within the context of their own tribal social structures, beliefs, and customs," he writes. "What more than anything American Indians have done in regard to military service is syncretize it with their own systems."[96] William K. Powers suggests that the tremendous rate of volunteerism by the Lakotas in military service was due to their desire to "defend their own tribal land as well as the territory of the United States from potential foreign invasion."[97] Accordingly, some tribes declared war on Germany independently of the United States.[98] Commissioner of Indian Affairs Cato Sells (1913– 21), who originally thought that military service by American Indians would demonstrate their preparedness for eventual U.S. citizenship, was discouraged when he heard that recently returned veterans "had counted coup, taken part in victory dances, watched as their sisters, mothers, and wives performed Scalp Dances, and had been ritually cleansed of the taint of combat by medicine people."[99] Holm argues that Native participation in World War I prompted a rejuvenation of warrior societies and that these veterans received the honor and status granted warriors "one hundred years before. . . . In short, he was a warrior and, whether clad in traditional dress or in olive drab, he had reaffirmed his tribal identity."[100]

The rejuvenation of Lakota warrior societies transformed Lakota ceremonial life. As Lakota soldiers went off to war, new songs were created to honor them, and their warrior deeds were memorialized in songs upon their return. The songs were often built on old warrior song texts and on Omaha Dance and Iwakicipi, or Victory Dance, melodies.[101] Powers recorded a number of World War I songs on the Pine Ridge Reservation in the late 1940s through the 1960s, including this one:

Eya ica wan maucanze ca
Tamakoce na tawapaha ko
Mak'uwakiye *lo he ye he ye yo*

The Germans made me mad
So not only their land but flag
Are what I made them give me *lo he ye he ye yo*[102]

R. D. Theisz compiled a number of Lakota songs dating from World War I, including the following—the former a Veterans Song, and the latter a Waktegli, or Victory Song:

Tehatan natanpe lo (4 times).
Iya ica kin ceya napape lo.

Lakota hok ila tehantan natanpe lo.
Iyašica kin ceya napape lo.

They are charging from afar (4 times).
The Germans retreat crying.
The Lakota boys they are charging from afar.
The Germans retreat crying.[103]

Iya ica kin owe wanciyanka he.
Wahte ni t'a.
Toke le k'eya niciciye ka.

German, I have been watching your tracks.
Worthless one!
I would have followed you wherever you
Would have gone![104]

Returning Lakota servicemen were honored by their people with many new songs, demonstrating the vibrancy of these musical traditions that honored warriors and the extent to which the war affected all of Lakota life at the time. The tradition of Tawapaha Olowan, or Flag Songs, began after the Great War. The following is an example:

Kowakantan okicize yelo *he ye he ye ye*
Lakota Hok ila ekta ain kte lo *he ye he ye ye*
Mila Hanska kin heyakeyape lo *he ye he ye yo*

There is fighting over there *he ye he ye ye*
That's where the Lakota boys will go *he ye he ye ye*
They say the Americans were saying that *he ye he ye yo*[105]

Around the Pine Ridge Agency, Lakotas held the Crow Dance "on the order of a victory dance, the words of the song being exultation over victory, real and supposed, over [their] late enemies in the World War." This was one of the most popular dances at Pine Ridge by 1923.[106] Although government officials and missionaries had strenuously suppressed the Sun Dance on the reservations, the Lakotas held at least three Sun Dances at Kyle between 1917 and 1919, the first two in dedication of the war, and the last in commemoration of the Allied victory.[107] The veterans who danced at the Standing Rock Agency were "among the more enthusiastic participants of the dance, which ex-soldier element gives it increased prestige."[108] Young people around the Crow Creek Agency in South Dakota, "led by the returned soldiers," were likewise involved in more and more dances.

In addition to the creation of Honor, Victory, and Flag songs, during the war entire Lakota communities gathered together and held giveaways to honor the local men who had enlisted and to raise money for the war effort. Superintendent Mossman of the Standing Rock Agency stated that the Indians "gave a large amount of money to the Red Cross and other kindred causes but as a rule this money was raised at Indian Dances." He continued:

> Had it been given outright or raised in any other way the volume of patri-
> otism would have been wonderfully diminished. The method of raising
> this money is as follows: The Indians are congregated in the dance hall, the
> women and children on one side, the men on the other. The master of cer-
> emonies makes a speech in Indian in which he depicts the German army
> being destroyed by the valiant Indian soldiers. An old man rises and says,
> "I give ten cents in honor of my grandson." The grand son rises and goes
> to the old man and shakes his hand and probably puts the ten cent piece
> on the drum. The six or more men sitting around the drum then sing in a
> loud voice the merits of the donor, or as they express it "honor him."
> When the song is done every one dances chanting and making motions of
> killing Germans. By the time the entire crowd has worked itself into a
> frenzy of excitement, horses, cattle, machinery and all kinds of property
> are given away. . . . That is the way the war funds were raised.[109]

The Lakotas were raising money for the war effort, but because they did so through the medium of giveaway dances, Mossman recommended to Commissioner Burke that he forbid the Lakotas from raising funds for "fairs, [the] Red Cross, and any other proper purpose at heathen dances."[110]

The irony of the government's precluding the raising of relief funds through dances was not lost on Native people, who took full advantage of arguing the politics of such "patriotic" dance before the OIA higher-ups. In 1919 a group of Standing Rock Sioux urged Commissioner of Indian Affairs Sells to reprimand school superintendent James Kitch and the local missionaries for banning the giveaways: "The only time that we do give anything at dances is when there are donations to be made to the Red Cross, War Work Fund and Liberty Loans and we feel that it is our duty to do so."[111] They believed that the missionaries who complained about the giveaways would not have done so if the dance participants had given the dance proceeds to the churches and not the war effort, and thus they considered the missionaries to be German sympathizers.[112]

The Standing Rock Sioux, composed of Lakota as well as Dakota and Nakota people, were particularly proud of their participation in World War I on both the home front and abroad. However, in their efforts to carry out service to the war and to honor the local servicemen and veterans, they felt impeded by Superintendent Kitch, a man who truly despised all forms of Native dance. Kitch imposed a laundry list of bans, rules, and prohibitions regarding dances, and though he claimed to have reduced Indian dance on "his" reservation to a bare minimum, his correspondence indicates that he was constantly thwarted, if not outmaneuvered, by people determined to have their dance. Thomas Frosted and John Brown of Standing Rock, feeling that Kitch was misrepresenting the significance of their dances in his anti-dance stance and in his correspondence with Washington, wrote a letter directly to the commissioner of Indian Affairs to detail the relationship between the dances and the war.[113] The Standing Rock Sioux held Red Cross giveaway dances, they argued, because they wanted to "do [their] part and be true Americans in every way."[114] The side-step giveaway dances, which were only occasionally approved by Kitch, were absolutely necessary, according to Frosted and Brown, in order to "do [their] part as true Americans in helping get the kaiser." They reminded the commissioner that 150 Standing Rock Sioux were soldiers at the time, "doing their part in patriotism." To maintain optimism and hope throughout the war, they argued, the Standing Rock Sioux needed these dances, which they emphatically labeled as Christian, and not heathen, dances. And finally, they stressed to the commissioner that "the persons opposing these simple danc[e]rs are unconsciously opposing a good work and without intending it, are pro-German to the extent that they are hindering the full efficiency with which we must all work together to win the war."[115] Whether or not we take the seemingly pro-American pleas of Frosted and Brown at face value, their arguments demonstrated a sophisticated understanding and use of the contested language of cultural citizenship.

But what can we make of federal employees and strong advocates for the assimilation of American Indians into (white) American society arguing that Indians should *not* be allowed to raise money for the Red Cross or to organize patriotic gatherings? How did such dances become threatening to these officials, not simply when they were held on a national holiday as an excuse but even when they were held for the explicit purpose of honoring American veterans of the war and to raise money for the Allies?

"It's funny," Severt Young Bear noted, "when you think of the Christian principle of charity, that once we were put on reservations, both the missionaries and the BIA opposed the sharing of material goods because it kept us from becoming modern, self-supporting American citizens."[116] Indeed, Mossman and Kitch abhorred giveaways because their patriotic purpose was undermined by the way in which the funds were raised: through giving away the very commodities that Mossman and the OIA had been trying to teach the Indians to individually accumulate and cherish. During the war years and into the 1920s, the dances that most threatened the officials and clergy were those that challenged their own conceptions of civilization and their belief that American Indians should value private property and commit to a life of noncommunal agrarianism. But these giveaway dances, as noted by their wartime functions, represented so much more than what the officials could understand. The giveaways served as a modern Lakota adaptation by which communities could honor their warrior soldiers as well as their commitment to maintaining an expressive and vibrant sense of pride in their tribal identities while simultaneously engaging the patriotic and American traditions of raising funds for the war effort through local support. Despite the complex nature of the giveaways and their role on the home front, however, the comprehension of these dances by federal officials remained somewhat one-dimensional, and after the war most Lakota communities felt an increased pressure to cease performing them.

The giveaway dances especially threatened the OIA even beyond the war years because the philosophy of the event shattered one of the most fundamental elements in the OIA's cultural citizenship agenda, that of instilling the sacred value of private property. The giveaway dance was held by Native communities, in some form or fashion, on reservations throughout the country. The dances were, and still are, held in part to celebrate communal values and redistribute resources, not hoard them individually—honor is derived by giving, and by being asked to host a giveaway. The dances could bring together the people particularly in times of need, so that they could contribute what resources and goods they had available to be redistributed throughout the community, or for more direct causes, in the case of the Red Cross during World War I. In 1923 Smith Pain on Hip remarked to Commissioner Burke that superintendents and missionaries "don't know what dance is. . . . And they don't know why they 'give away.' . . . [T]his is done so to help the poor and needy Indians."[117] The philosophy of the giveaway fundamentally contradicted the messages sent by OIA agents that emphasized the importance of individual accumulation. According to Severt Young Bear, "the traditional way of thinking tells us that when you have material possessions, the best thing you can do with them is to give them away, especially to those who are without or are having a hard time. A leader is not the guy who can store up and keep lots of things, but instead someone who will share them with the people."[118] He continued, "We are taught as young boys and girls that in order to honor ourselves and our relatives, we should always be ready to share. One of our Lakota songs tells us: 'There isn't anything I won't give away because my parents are still alive.'"[119] The logic of the giveaways confounded OIA officials who associated the redistribution of wealth with anarchy, communism, and self-destruction rather than with an affirmation of community and self-preservation.

Giveaways were held for a variety of purposes, and they continually perturbed OIA agents. People living on the Lower Brule Reservation, for example, sometimes held a giveaway or a "singing" to raise funds for Fourth of July celebrations and fairs. They would also hold them in order to eulogize a member of the community, either dead or alive. On one such occasion in 1923 the superintendent, C. H. Gensler, fired an Indian policeman who had given away a horse when he had been sent to "see that that very thing was not indulged in."[120] Superintendent Gensler usually jailed anyone who participated in such dances, a punishment he felt was easy for the "wards" (noncitizens), but he complained to Burke that some of the citizen Indians could not be imprisoned as easily because they were familiar with habeas corpus proceedings and knew that such imprisonment was illegal.[121] To exert control over the dances, Gensler tried to attend each one, but his attempts were not quite successful, as "they would talk Sioux and [he wouldn't] know what they [were] doing."[122] Many superintendents and missionaries, including Native missionaries, reported to Burke numerous stories of people who would give away valuable goods and property.[123]

The giveaways near the Standing Rock Indian School, perhaps due to their flagrantly political nature, particularly aggravated Superintendent Kitch. The giveaways were usually, according to Kitch, held to defray the costs of sending a Lakota delegation to Washington, D.C., to petition for the return of the Black Hills.[124] These giveaway dances, sharply politicized and narrowly focused, prompted Sioux participants to amass hundreds and even thousands of dollars toward these diplomatic meetings, even in the midst of Kitch's order that "no collections be taken while Indians are under the influence of dancing or drum music."[125] Having fought in the U.S. armed forces and received U.S. citizenship, many Lakotas then exhibited their vision of U.S. citizenship, which included the right to hold giveaways for their people and to petition, in this case, for the return of the sacred Black Hills, a fight that continues to this day.

By 1920 Kitch had established a set of rules that, if followed, would have prevented all fee-patent Indians, employees, returned students, or "any persons under the age of forty years" from participating in the only dances he felt he could begrudgingly tolerate, which according to these rules could consist only of the side step with "no paint, feathers, or costumes."[126] The side-step dance that became very popular among some tribes in the early twentieth century was understood by some agents as similar to a "white" round dance and therefore more tolerable (both require males and females to dance together and with multiple partners). Although Arthur Pratt, a stockman assigned to the Porcupine District of the Standing Rock Agency, acknowledged the similarities between the "Indian" side-step dance and the "white" round dance, he could not look beyond the lens of savagery and civilization that obscured his view; he wrote to Mossman in 1922, "I have heard arguments in favor of the side-step dance that it is most similar to the white round dances and very likely this is true in the outward form, but the former represents pure savagery and the latter supposed to represent civilization."[127] The side-step dance was often popular with returned students, though the contact between males and females during the dance upset many older reservation residents who believed that men and women should not make contact while dancing. A few agents with certain strong religious convictions were averse to any form of dancing by American Indians, whites, or anyone for that matter. Typically, however, agents applied racial and hierarchical distinctions to all dances, and the cultural bedrock of American citizenship was at stake.

THE DUTY TO REFRAIN OR THE RIGHT TO DANCE?
THE POLITICS OF CITIZENSHIP

Citizenship lay at the crux of the early twentieth-century debates on dealing with the "dance evil" on Lakota reservations. Despite the emphatic conception of U.S. political citizenship as a responsibility fit with *duties* of cultural citizenship, many American Indians, often aware of the ramifications of citizenship through their boarding school education, increasingly emphasized the *rights* of citizenship when defending the cultural prerogatives of their dance.

Citizen Indians, typically World War I veterans or recipients of allotments in fee-simple title, were not restricted in their activities on the land, as they were when their legal status was that of a ward. The scattering effect of the allotted lands on the reservations, along with the rights of citizenship granted particular American Indians, prevented the superintendents from exerting the control they wished. Some Lakotas, understanding the new limitations of this control, exercised their prerogative of holding more public dances under the newfound status that their allotted lands and their citizenship granted. Others even hired attorneys to defend their right to hold these dances when the local superintendents forbade them.[128] By 1922 Commissioner Burke had recognized the difficulties of maintaining a dance policy of coercion when Native Americans resisted it:

> We didn't want to make an order that wouldn't be enforceable. . . . On a closed reservation we could handle the matter without the slightest trouble. But it is a different question where you have Indians residing in different localities, a portion of them citizens to the fullest extent. Now tell me how we are going to say just what shall happen in a community like that in the Porcupine district where practically all of the Indians own their own land. I don't like to issue an order that does not mean anything, and so in whatever we do I want to go only so far as I am confident that we can enforce whatever act we do.[129]

Burke in this statement seemed to actually lament the institution of the allotment program and the U.S. citizenship that many Native people had already received. He recognized that if an American Indian was a citizen and a holder of a patent in fee of property, there was no way he could prevent that citizen from giving away his or her property. Because "conditions are different than when these Indians were on closed reservations," he searched all possible means for restricting citizen Indians from dancing.[130]

Indeed, Standing Rock Indian School superintendent Kitch had reported in 1920 that the dance "trouble" was "caused mainly by fee patent or citizen Indians, who claim that they are not under the jurisdiction of the United States and that they have the right to dance or costume themselves as they deem advisable."[131] For OIA officials, "Indian" dancing was completely incompatible with the responsibilities of citizenship. Assistant Commissioner E. B. Meritt wrote in 1921 that "by such excesses [as dancing] they cannot become worthy, self-supporting citizens and a credit to their race."[132] Burke and the federal officials knew they had lost a considerable amount of the legal power they had wielded over Indians when they were strictly "wards of the government," and these officials seemed to regret deeply this loss and this shift in federal Indian policy. As Meritt lamented,

When an Indian receives a patent in fee to his land, under the law he becomes an independent citizen in control of his property and subject to state and federal laws as any other white citizen. With so large a percentage of citizen Indians [about half of the adult Standing Rock Sioux were citizens by 1921], it becomes quite difficult for this office through the Reservation Superintendent to control social tendencies, such as dancing which is frequently conducted on patented land.[133]

Again, citizenship, once deemed the goal of the assimilationist policies had become a double-edged sword for agents who were uncomfortable with the ways in which the dancers and singers were expressing their rights of citizenship. The citizenship that Burke desired for American Indians was a very limited and controlled citizenship that contradicted fundamentally the rights bestowed them.

Inspector McLaughlin agreed with Burke that the increased popularity of the dance among the younger men could not be suppressed as easily as it had in the past, "the Indians being then wards of the Government" and receiving "subsistence bi-weekly [and] also a fair allowance of clothing annually."[134] Unable anymore to threaten the Lakotas by withholding such goods, he felt that all the government could hope to do would be to regulate the dances more fully. Because more and more Lakotas, especially younger people, were taking up the tribally derived dances, the dances grew more and more dangerous in threatening the federal goals of assimilation. Simultaneously, the danger felt by the agents was fed by the increasing lack of coercion and control that the agents could muster over the Lakotas. For McLaughlin at this time the danger of the practice of music was located not so much in the "savagery" or "pagan" aspects that the missionaries so abhorred, but rather in his growing inability to confine and control the activities of the Lakotas—in the diminishment of his power. At this point the OIA officials set out to develop a dance policy that would control the performative traditions of American Indians while recognizing the limitations that citizenship posed in their attempt to enforce it.

The early twentieth century was one of the bleakest periods the Lakotas had yet faced: people were starving, their reservation lands undergoing rapid liquidation, they weren't provided with treaty-guaranteed rations, and neither was agricultural work a tenable solution to their problems. Even wage labor was difficult to attain, and by the 1920s, when they found themselves under the zealous scope of Commissioner Burke, the U.S. government had reached a new apex of implementing an Indian policy designed to destroy virtually every element of their decidedly Lakota identity.[135] However, most of the Lakota people never seemed to waiver from a shared goal of regaining control over their own lives, and the practice of music served them as an effective weapon in their fight.

The Lakotas' struggle over the right to dance and the meaning of U.S. citizenship continued to shape in many ways their modern political vision. Even after the passage of the General Citizenship Act of 1924—the act that bestowed U.S. citizenship on the remaining one-third of Indian people who had not yet assumed it—the implications of citizenship on their dances was foremost on the minds of many American Indians. Superintendent Mossman of Standing Rock reported that at a meeting of the Standing Rock Business Council following the act, "the new citizenship proposition was discussed vigorously." With distress, he noted that "the only thing about it which seemed to interest the larger portion of the council was its effect upon the regulations against the dance and the giving away."[136] The daily struggles of the Lakotas, and their daily acts of resistance, were often played out in expressive culture: dance served the Lakotas as the primary political weapon against the local OIA agents and their policies of cultural destruction. Likewise, the meanings that the OIA officials assigned the concepts of allotment and citizenship were turned on their heads by the Lakota practice of music.

A consideration of music on reservations as political practice reveals complex local manifestations of an expansive array of tactics that Native people used to actively engage and often combat the prerogatives of allotment, assimilation, and ultimately cultural and geographic dispossession that characterized governmental visions of (Indian) American citizenship and, more broadly, this era of federal Indian policy. Of course, the politicization of Lakota music vis-à-vis federal policy implementation represents only one of many possible layers of meanings the Lakotas would have attributed to each performance, and they were not the only people to use performance in such a manner; Native peoples across North America experienced similar challenges in this period, and dance represented one avenue of resistance among many. However, dance succeeded particularly well as a catalyst for change on the reservations of the northern plains. Faced with policies of assimilation on all fronts, Native Americans used dance to communally redistribute food and other resources to those in need, to reincorporate boarding school students into their reservation communities, and to properly honor and recognize their soldiers and veterans—warriors—of World War I. Dancing became more prevalent on reservations in the early 1900s as a direct result of the efforts to detribalize them through the increased deployment of boarding school education and the recruitment of young men into the armed forces. As a result, the meanings of the dance transformed as well, to reflect an expanded incorporation of shifting cultural, social, and economic influences. Dance fostered the community understanding, meaning, and healing needed a to counter the dire social and economic toll of the citizenship agenda. A medium of resistance, adaptation, and incorporation, dance was imbued with political resonance and meaning that sparked a series of culture wars on reservations throughout the country. Dance transformed the tools of assimilation—boarding schools, the legal status of citizenship, service in the armed forces—into tools of Indianization, of Lakota revitalization and celebration.

CHAPTER 2

THE "DANCE EVIL"

CULTURAL PERFORMANCE, THE PRESS, AND FEDERAL INDIAN POLICY

On February 23, 1923, Commissioner of Indian Affairs Charles Burke issued a message addressed "to All Indians," warning them not to perform several dances. The students working in the print shop of the Chilocco Indian boarding school in Oklahoma printed fifteen thousand copies of the message for distribution to every reservation agency in the country. Beyond certain "decent amusements or occasional feast dances," all Native peoples were instructed not to hold dances unless the dances had been approved by their local OIA superintendent. Burke stated that instead of issuing a direct order to stamp out the dances, he would much prefer that the people give up the dances of their "own free will." If the superintendents reported in a year's time that any unapproved dances continued, then "some other course [would] have to be taken."[1]

Why did the practice of music motivate the commissioner to have these circulars printed and distributed directly into the hands of thousands of American Indians? How did Native and non-Native people respond to the circular? Turning from the local politics of music among the Lakotas, in this chapter I explore the reaction of the implementation of Burke's anti-dance policy among a national audience of media outlets and among Native communities and individuals throughout the country. The cacophony of voices resulting from the anti-dance order demonstrates that both Native peoples and the non-Native press played powerful roles in shaping federal Indian policy, which resulted in the gutting of what remained of Burke's power to wield control over the performative practices of American Indians on reservations. The debate over the politics of music brought media coverage to Indian affairs that was at least as great as, and perhaps more widespread than, the coverage spawned by any other OIA policy issue of the decade. The sympathy of the press, although based in reasons often contrary to those of the ban's Native opponents, nonetheless signaled a sea change in public support over the federal government's assimilation policy.

STRATEGIZING TO DEFEAT THE "DANCE EVIL"

In the first quarter of the twentieth century, and particularly in the years following World War I, Native peoples began dancing with renewed vigor and assertiveness that directly challenged the attempts of local agents and missionaries to restrict their dancing, and directly attacked the overarching policy of assimilation that had defined OIA efforts for the previous several decades. Although dance bans had remained in effect since 1882, tribal and intertribal dances had only increased in frequency, particularly due to the efforts of returned boarding school students and veterans, groups whom the OIA considered to be most primed to shun their tribal identities and assimilate into American society.

Charles H. Burke was appointed the commissioner of Indian Affairs in March 1921 by President Warren G. Harding. Burke had spent many of the previous years representing South Dakota in Congress. By the time of his appointment he fancied himself an expert on Indians, having served on the House Committee on Indian Affairs. Almost immediately, Burke demonstrated his disdain for reservation dances, even though he really knew nothing about them and based his opinion solely on hearsay from various conservative reform organizations and from missionaries and OIA agents in South Dakota.[2] Within a month of entering office, Burke launched a renewed effort to control the dances by issuing circular 1665 to all the superintendents, outlining exactly which dances he found problematic. In the circular Burke did not condemn "the dance *per se*"; he understood it rather as "something inherent in human nature," stating that "as a medium through which elevated minds may happily unite art, refinement, and healthful exercise it is not inconsistent with civilization." Dance became dangerous for Burke, however, when it was performed "under most primitive and pagan conditions." He specifically listed the qualities of dances that he thought were dangerous to the livelihood of Native peoples and the promotion of "civilization."[3] Beyond the Sun Dance and other "so-called religious ceremonies," he stated that the ban would also include

> any dance which involves acts of self-torture, immoral relations between the sexes, the sacrificial d[e]struction of clothing or other useful articles, the reckless giving away of property, the use of injurious drugs or intoxicants, and frequent or prolonged periods of celebration which bring the Indians together from remote points to the neglect of their crops, livestock, and home interests; in fact any disorderly or plainly excessive performance that promotes superstitious cruelty, licentiousness, idleness, danger to health, and shiftless indifference to family welfare.[4]

Burke thought the superintendents should exercise their own judgment in regulating and, in effect, sanitizing the dances on the reservations. He believed that with such regulation the officials could continue the "social and moral elevation" of the American Indian, "not by offending his communal longings or robbing his nature of its rhythm, but by encouraging these instincts to serve his higher powers and by directing his desires and purposes towards the things he needs to make him strong and capable and fit to survive in the midst of all races."[5] Burke wrote that certain forms of dances and other practices of music were permissible, but only if their negative elements, such as those mentioned above, were removed and the dances were held under the regulation and watchful eye of the government. Dancing was safe for those with "elevated minds," but because federal Indian policy was organized around the assumption that the Native "mind" was certainly not "elevated," dancing by American Indians in nearly every form was seen as a threat.[6]

Burke's circular 1665 proved an inadequate solution, for dancing continued to increase. Determined dance participants were responsible for limiting the success of this measure, and many did so without realizing it, for Burke did not have copies printed and distributed throughout the reservation populations. The concern expressed by many OIA agents and missionaries over dancing, particularly among the Lakotas, grew into frenzy and fear. Burke responded accordingly, scheduling a meeting on October 24, 1922, in Pierre, South Dakota, to hear direct reports from the field and reconsider his strategy for combating what he considered to be nothing less than the "dance evil."[7] South Dakota seemed a reasonable site for the meeting; because of the success of the Lakotas in proliferating their dances, exercising their rights as citizens to dance, and loosening the control of their superintendents, Burke considered the region to be the national epicenter of his dance crisis.

The attendants consisted of OIA agents, school superintendents, missionaries, and government farmers who lived on or near Lakota reservations; they unanimously voiced their disgust at Lakota dances and provided several reasons as to why the dances were objectionable. Along with the use of patriotism and citizenship as a defense of dance, the giveaways became the heart of the issue addressed at the conference. The dances seemed dangerous to government employees and missionaries because of their anti-individualistic nature and their valorization of distributing private property to community members. As was demonstrated in chapter 1, the idea of giving away rather than hoarding one's property repulsed them and seemed completely at odds with the individualistic values they held dear. They also blamed the dances for the failures of OIA agricultural policy, and as the reservation economies worsened, leaving more and more people destitute, they clung with increasing desperation to that notion. In addition to these concerns, the officials and missionaries were disturbed that they had lost much of their legal control over the Lakota people as the Lakotas gained U.S. citizenship or received allotments in fee-simple title. Finally, these anti-dance factions couched their descriptions of all dances in the rhetoric of "civilization" and "savagery," rhetoric that had for so long framed virtually all matters of federal Indian policy.

The federal officials and missionaries at the Pierre meeting were unanimous in their fear of the dances and perceived the practices around them as dangerous, anti-American, and a hindrance to their "civilization" policy. The Pierre meeting also demonstrated, however, a tactical shift within the overriding directives of federal Indian policy. For the previous forty years Indian policy had been based on the promise of "civilization" that allotments, formal schooling, Christianity, and citizenship would bring to American Indians, at the expense of perpetuating tribal identities and cultural persistence (not to mention a massive loss of Native landholdings). In effect, these measures, the OIA policy makers believed, could mute tribal identities within a potent blend of specific white, middle-class Victorian values and institutions. As Frederick Hoxie has argued, however, by the early twentieth century the OIA grew pessimistic that such a radical transformation was possible.[8] This pessimism grew out of Native resistance to underfunded agrarian and misguided assimilation and allotment polices more than anything else. But the methods of resistance caused a shift in policy as well—American Indians used the harbingers of "civilization" in a variety of ways, often in fact, but not always in the same manner, to reaffirm their bonds of tribal affiliation. By the time of the Pierre meeting, OIA officials and missionaries were focused on a new policy concern: that of reclaiming and maintaining management and control over the daily lives of American Indians—bringing things back, in a sense, to the way they had been before so many had become U.S. citizens. More specifically, the meeting's attendees sought new methods to control Native cultural and political allegiances and the symbols of "civilization" that Native people continuously refigured. By the early 1920s OIA officials and missionaries believed that the threat to this control was most egregiously manifested in the musical practices of tribal and intertribal expressive culture.

Some of the Pierre meeting participants thought that, to reassert their control on the reservations, an order to prohibit dance, imposed by force, was the best course of action. The participants realized, however, that any strong course of action taken against the dances would meet with swift resistance from large constituencies of Native people. According to the recent memory of the meeting participants, many young Lakotas, often citizens and veterans, were already resisting the suppression of the dances with increasing vigor. Around many of the Sioux agencies the superintendents had recruited government farmers to monitor such activities.[9] At the Pierre meeting the Episcopalian Rev-

erend Dallas Shaw told of a story in which, after a farmer had refused
the request of three or four men to allow a dance, the men took him
outside and beat him.[10] Superintendent E. D. Mossman of the Standing Rock Sioux Reservation tried to enforce a restriction against dancing, only to have it rejected by several residents. He attempted to set
up farm bureau meetings in order to replace the dances, but as he put
it, "the Indians got together and they wouldn't attend a farm bureau
meeting because they thought that was made, as it was, to take the
place of their dances, and this is what I have been up against. . . . The
last man I saw before I left and the first man I will see when I get back
home will be a man who wants to dance." He continued:

> In the Porcupine district the young citizen Indians got together there and
> said that they would boycott the farm bureau. This outfit formed what
> they called the star club. They stuck a stick in the ground on the top of
> which they fastened a tin star. When they got around each one would go
> up and make obeisance to this fetish. They would all dance around this
> star. It is a religious rite with those people. And those very young men,
> tho[ugh] they are educated and citizens of the United States, are wor-
> shiping at the shrine of that star. I don't know where we are going.[11]

Mossman's desperation was echoed by many at the meeting.

Burke had to be cautious, because it was also clear to the meeting
participants that their traditional authority over Indian affairs, as recognized for several decades by the public, was under increased
attack, and not only by American Indians. By the advent of tourism in
the Southwest, larger numbers of non-Indians had begun to consider
their perceived primitivism of Native cultures as an antidote to the ills
of the modern world. They became transfixed by Indianness, and
some, like John Collier, became prominent critics of the OIA's allotment and assimilation policies. For his part, Collier was overcome by
an experience at Taos, New Mexico, that led him to direct his reform
efforts to advocating for the religious and ceremonial freedom of
Native Americans.[12] Their campaign against OIA policies in the years
preceding the Pierre meeting revealed an array of scandalous practices, most recently the efforts of the OIA to secure passage of the Bur-
som Bill.[13] The bill, which was eventually defeated, was designed to

further alienate the Pueblo Indians of New Mexico from their lands by legitimating the title claims of white squatters. It was clear at that point that as scandals continued to plague the OIA, the mission of assimilation was only gaining critics.[14] Burke was already inundated by correspondence condemning the suppression of dances—correspondence that was often generated through the efforts of Collier and his like-minded anti-assimilationist reformers—and he was not eager to open himself to further attack.[15]

In addition, superintendents and missionaries were keenly aware of the popularity of hiring dancers from the reservations to put on exhibitions in local towns for fairs and rodeos. And Native people were aware of it as well; many had made good money performing in local fairs and in national touring troupes that featured Native music and dances. Numerous off-reservation towns had built successful tourist enterprises by 1922 that depended heavily upon the performance of "authentic" Indian dances. The dominant images of "authentic" Native people in popular culture were images, not of men in short hair and trousers and women in bloomers, but of men and women in plains regalia, the last vestiges of a "dying race." Although the government since the 1893 Columbian Exposition had used "live" exhibits at world fairs to demonstrate their assimilative efforts in boarding schools, such exhibits were typically overshadowed by sideshows and midways that exhibited a Wild West of feather-donned warriors and buckskin-clad princesses in all their glory.[16] The OIA faced an uphill battle over its rights to control the music and cultural displays of Native people; it met with resistance not only from Native people and other OIA critics but also from this burgeoning popular culture that appropriated the same images, music, and cultural displays.

Faced with these difficulties, the men in Pierre struggled over how to further suppress the dances without facing more antagonism from opposing forces on the reservations and among the press and the public. They realized, in the end, that such antagonism would be unavoidable if they passed a direct order banning the dances. The idea to control the dances by instead shifting the tide of public support to the OIA was recommended by several participants at the Pierre conference. Dr. Riggs, a missionary among the Lakotas, put it bluntly: "It seems to me that in the years past we have failed so often [to build public support]. We must build up public opinion that will control these dances. We can't build character for them. We can't make them civilized human beings by putting trousers on them and cutting off their hair. We must build up public opinion that will control them."[17] Riggs understood that the possibility of rapid assimilation, for many years the working assumption of Indian reform organizations and OIA officials, was simply impossible to achieve. But rather than examine the flaws of such a philosophy, or the unwillingness of American Indians to cooperate, Riggs believed that a new strategy of propaganda in the press would ameliorate the loss of control that he and the other meeting participants felt. Superintendent Munroe of the Cheyenne River reservation agreed: "We are bothered year after year by these little fairs, roundups and frontier days all over the country."[18] Munroe pointed out that many of these events offered, among other things, water, meat, and admission to Indians who were willing to participate. He continued, "We must get the cooperation of the decent white people and promote the right kind of public sentiment and then we will be in a position to stamp this out. We haven't authority over these white people and the only way we can reach them is thru propaganda."[19] Commissioner Burke concurred with the suggestions to attempt to control public opinion in the matter:

> I don't hesitate at all to say that anything that can be done to bring this matter to the attention of the public and creat[e] public sentiment will be productive of more results than anything else that we can do.... [In regard to another decision that faced public opposition] I did deliberately cause to be spread what might be called propaganda.... Acting in cooperation and collectively we will be able to correct a good many of these things by simply making sentiment.[20]

The power of public opinion in shaping the implementation of federal Indian policy had never been clearer to Burke, and he was determined to devise a plan so that no one would derail his efforts to finally eradicate the dances, once and for all.

The power of Indianness in popular culture weighed heavily on the minds of Burke and the others in Pierre and factored into the result of the meeting, a dance circular issued by Burke in 1923 that included an attached list of recommendations derived from the participants of the meeting. The circular supplemented OIA anti-dance circular 1665, introduced in 1921, which had failed to effectively reduce or control the dances.[21] The participants believed that a direct order would be unenforceable because of the resistance of Native peoples and the public, so they decided to print and distribute copies of the message "To All Indians," requesting that certain practices be discontinued. If the Indians did not comply, the circular threatened that "some other course" would then be taken.[22] Although the meeting focused on Lakota dances, clearly Burke decided to implement a uniform policy throughout the country. Therefore the response to the circular supplement and "message" was not limited to the Lakotas but, rather, encompassed Native people throughout the country.

In the message, a causal relationship was established between the dances, powwows, and other celebrations on the one hand and the "neglect of stock, crops, gardens, and home interests" on the other.[23] Burke instructed Indians, first of all, to "try to make your own living, which you cannot do unless you work faithfully and take care of what comes from your labor." He obviously did not consider performance at fairs and rodeos for money or food a legitimate means of making a living. Burke wrote that he did not want to "deprive [Indians] of decent amusements or occasional feast days," but he also did not want them to spend several days at a dance, to participate in "evil or foolish things" like the giveaway dances, or to "torture [their] bodies or to handle poisonous snakes" in ceremonies, referring implicitly to the Sun Dance and the Hopi Chu'tiva, or, as it was known by tourists, the Snake Dance.[24] Printed by students of the Chilocco Indian School in Oklahoma, the circulars were mailed and handed out to residents of every reservation in the country.

An attached list of recommendations, derived from the Pierre meeting, was meant for only the superintendents to read. It prohibited altogether the giveaway because it was said to be a form of gambling, limited dances to one per month in the daylight hours of "one day in the midweek," prohibited anyone under the age of fifty from participating, and specified that "a careful propaganda be under taken to educate public opinion against the dance and to provide a healthy substitute," that federal employees and missionaries work to convince the operators of local fairs and rodeos "not to commercialize the Indian," and that federal employees and missionaries continue to work together in matters dealing with the "moral welfare of the Indians."[25] Anticipating resistance to the circular, Burke reiterated his intention to the superintendents that the document was "only an appeal," focused largely upon the Lakotas. At the same time, however, he privately confided that he would in fact ban the Hopis from handling snakes, demonstrating the reservation-wide scope of his circular. He also condemned the performance of any Native dance by children in the schools and stated that, in terms of a "healthy substitute," they should learn "safer," more morally sound dances such as the "Maypole Dance."[26]

PUBLIC REACTION TO THE DANCE CIRCULAR OF 1923

Burke recognized that to control any oppositional sentiment generated by the public, he would need to reach out to sympathetic reform organizations such as the Indian Rights Association (IRA), the YWCA, the Philadelphia Indian Aid Association, the Home Mission Council, the Council of Women for Home Missions, and the Bureau of Catholic Indian Missions.[27] The IRA had lobbied Burke for years to strictly forbid all tribally derived dances and took its case to the public through letters to the editors of newspapers and through interviews and speeches. Since the founding of the IRA in 1882 the reform organization was emphatic in the notion that American Indians must assimilate into white American society if they were to survive. This vision of the IRA reformers was annually reinvigorated at their Lake Mohonk conferences and reinforced if not guided the late nineteenth-century implementation of the allotment and assimilation policies. In the 1920s the IRA had found a true friend in Charles Burke, who shared many of its views on the proper course of handling the "Indian problem." Burke's dance circular 1665 and supplement could have come directly from an IRA playbook, and when Burke came under attack in the press, the IRA stood by its friend.

Herbert Welsh, founder and president of the IRA at the time of the dance ban circular, was one of the first to defend Burke in public. In a

May 1923 letter to the editor of the *Philadelphia Record*, Welsh not only supported Burke but also chastised those who challenged the policy or Burke's moral vision. Welsh was in fact responding to an editorial in the *Record* that opposed Burke's ban. Welsh wrote: "[There is] no midway resting place between the policy of civilization, on the one hand, which involves, sooner or later, the practical abandonment of old heathen customs, and that of retrogression, which would leave the Indian undeveloped, uncivilized, insuring his disintegration and final extermination."[28]

In line with Burke's recommendation of gathering public support to combat the dances, the IRA in fact served as the OIA's main arbiter of propaganda. Based on an interview by *Washington Times* reporter George Franklin with IRA representative S. M. Brosius, Franklin wrote that one of the aims of the IRA was to "eliminate as far as possible the 'give away' dances, pow-wows and other celebrations which are held by the Indians," because, as he put it, "during these affairs many of the red men remain away from their homes and farms, and as a result stock, crops, gardens and home interests are neglected."[29] Claiming that the IRA was unbiased, nonpartisan, and nonsectarian, its members continued to advocate, purely "for promoting the civilization of the Indian and for securing his natural and political rights," the stance that Burke had taken against Native dances.[30] When Burke was chastised by the press, the IRA grew more ardent in its support. In one communication the IRA stated, "It is to be regretted that, presumably through the ignorance of the real facts, this suggestion of Commissioner Burke to the Indians has brought forth vigorous protests. There is no intention on the part of Commissioner Burke to deprive the Indians of decent and proper amusements."[31] The real problem with the dances lay in the "secret dances of a bestial and revolting character," according to the IRA, which also stated: "Christian people of the country must warmly welcome this policy of Commissioner Burke. To become worthy American citizens every encouragement should be given to Indians to abandon pagan practices and to travel patiently the road of thrift, care of crops, and continuous labor."[32]

The IRA supported Burke's assessment that one could draw a direct correlation between the dances and the impoverished conditions on the reservations. Similarly, according to the OIA, the lack of successful harvests was in no way related to its failure to deliver successful agricultural initiatives or to provide proper funding for the tribes. But the IRA was much more concerned not with the impoverished economic conditions but rather with what they considered the impoverished moral conditions of the tribes brought on by the dances. Since 1920 the association had circulated among its members and some government officials various accounts of Pueblo dances in a "Secret Dance File." The file, nearly two hundred pages long, was composed of sworn testimony from around a dozen Hopis and seven white observers, recorded by U.S. government inspector E. M. Sweet.[33] As interpreted by Sweet, the witnesses told in graphic detail of a number of secret Pueblo dances laden with, in the view of the IRA, uncivilized, immoral, and intensely sexual acts of debauchery. The accounts were so indecent, according to members of the IRA, that they could not even send them through the mails or publish them.[34]

The IRA defended Burke and the dance ban in the press principally upon its interpretation of the contents of the infamous "Secret Dance File," which apparently was never released to any newspaper. The IRA titillated the public not with direct evidence from the file but with nuances and rumors. IRA secretary M. K. Sniffen wrote to the editor of the *New York Times*,

> I have in my possession statements from six men who were eyewitnesses to a secret dance, describing what they saw. I also have an affidavit (reluctantly given) of three ladies describing immoralities they witnessed at a public dance during 1924. In addition we have the sworn testimony of Indians who, in the past, participated in these ceremonies, and they ought to know whereof they speak. . . . [T]hey are too indecent to be printed or sent through the mails, but they are available to any seeker of the truth.[35]

Sniffen was responding to a letter published in the October 26, 1924, edition of the *New York Times* in opposition to the dance ban. Regarding its author, Sniffen wrote, "I judge that he sympathizes with the view of a Harvard ethnologist that 'morals are merely a matter of custom.'"[36] Sniffen argued that pro-dance pagan caciques of the Pueblos prevented the "moral Indian" from having "the right to think and act for himself." Therefore, according to Sniffen, it was Native leadership, and not the OIA, that was withholding religious freedom from American Indians.[37]

Some reformers and organizations published letters in newspapers that condemned the dances on the belief that women were given away and that depraved acts of sexuality were either committed or simulated in the dances. The front page of the April 27, 1923, *Chicago Evening American* featured an article and interview with Elmer Higley, the superintendent of Indian missions for the Methodist Episcopal Church. The Hopi Snake Dances, wildly popular with tourists, were "unspeakably immoral," according to Higley.[38] According to the newspaper Higley carried with him "a sheaf of sworn affidavits of men who at the risk of their lives spied upon the Indians' esoteric festival . . . and there witnessed the excesses." In one of the Hopi dances, "gradually the contortions of the dancers become more and more vulgar," Higley lamented. "Towards the end they are unspeakably so." After much vulgarity, he asserted, the dance climaxed in the bartering of prostitution, resulting in "an orgy—an orgy comparable only to the practices of ancient Druidism."[39]

Edith Dabb, director of YWCA Work Amongst Indian Girls, was one of the most outspoken reformers who supported Burke and the dance ban. Responding to an editorial in the *New York Tribune* in opposition to the dance ban, she wrote that the *Tribune* overlooked the fact that "many customs connected with these dances, whatever they may have meant to the primitive, are degrading to the Indian living in the world of today. . . . Burke is a warm friend of the Indians . . . and understands . . . the struggle being made by the younger Indians for a cleaner and more self-respecting life on the reservations."[40] Dabb, who believed that "young girls are often the greatest sufferers" as a result of the dance, stated that girls were much better off when their time was consumed by the "healthier recreational activities" that the YWCA, for example, offered.[41] In an interview published by the *New Orleans Times Picayune* entitled "Thirty-two Dances of Indians Beat Jazz," Dabb argued that the giveaways were the real problem: "The idea is born of that stupid conception of generosity which inspires a person to pauperize himself, to beggar himself and his family. There are, in the Indian 'give away' code, some serious complications, especially when, in a fit of acute generosity, he gives away his wife or his daughter."[42] Margaret Jacobs has argued that such reactions to the dances by female reformers were conservative responses to changing sexual mores in American society rather than from any sound understanding of Pueblo sexuality or of the dances as a whole, and that Dabb's concerns were rooted solely in hearsay generated by like-minded reformers, not by observation.[43]

Nevertheless, Dabb and others in favor of the circular attempted to circumvent the arguments of its detractors in every way possible. To combat the claims that the dance ban violated the religious freedom of American Indians, reformers who supported the circular argued that the dances viewed by whites were "inauthentic," done only for commercial purposes and thus purely secular in nature. The remaining religious dances, according to Dabb, were "almost invariably done in secret" and resulted in "orgies" and "all night camps" that, along with the commercialized dances, led Native men away from the care of their families.[44] The Board of Indian Commissioners, an influential group of missionaries and reformers who in 1923 voted unanimously that Indians "should not dance," argued that "with only a few exceptions, the Indian dances are no longer connected with religion, but have become entirely commercialized."[45] According to board member Samuel Eliot, "the so-called religious festivals of the Indians have become mere money-making debauches."[46] Although none of the circular supporters provided examples of any tribally derived dances that they or Burke approved of, many of them continued to reiterate that Burke was not forbidding all dances, just those that were immoral or prevented Native Americans from working in the fields or providing approved forms of labor for employers. Their concerns reflected those of many white middle-class reformers who were troubled not just with the expressive culture of American Indians but with that of European immigrants and African Americans as well. Nonetheless, never before had such a coordinated effort been directed against the cultural expressions of one racialized group, from organizations that had invested decades of work in encouraging its forced assimilation.

Burke's assertion that the press would play a vital role in the dance debate proved to be quite accurate. His "careful propaganda," however, supported by the IRA and other reformers such as Dabb, was buried beneath a massive volume of articles and editorials written in opposition to the dance ban. The control that the OIA sought on reservation life was as dramatically challenged by the non-Indian public as it was by Native people themselves, and the opposition of both undermined this federal policy initiative. But the public and press attacked the OIA and the dance ban for a variety of reasons not often in concert with those of American Indian people resisting the ban.

Newspaper editors and reporters recognized their role in the debate and quickly took sides. The Associated Press issued a bulletin from Santa Fe on March 8, 1923, indicating that "ceremonial dances by the New Mexico Pueblo Indians which annually bring thousands of visitors from the entire country have been forbidden except in the wintertime by Charles H. Burke."[47] This initial press report attracted reformers both in favor and against the ban, who quickly began to write editorials in the eastern newspapers. Collier, by that time the executive secretary of the American Indian Defense Association (AIDA), and anthropologist Frederick W. Hodge quickly defended the dances in the *New York Times* after missionaries in another reform group, the Council of One Hundred, had propagated a resolution in support of Burke's circular.[48] The *Times* and the *New York Tribune* sided with Collier and Hodge and published several articles and editorials in support of the dancers.

Journalists around the country pointed out the influence of the media in shaping the debate. The *Danville (Va.) Bee* noted that although the Hopi Snake Dance had "aroused [the] curiosity of non-Indians for years," it had never before attracted such "widespread attention" as when Burke issued his latest circular.[49] In an article titled, "Taking the Indianism Out of the Indian," the *Literary Digest* noted that the dance order seemed "to strike at everything but the Indian's material interests," adding, "At least so it is understood by the newspapers that have commented on the matter, nearly all in favor of the Indian and against the Commissioner."[50] Many articles also speculated that, in the words of the *Utica Observer Dispatch*, "there is no probability that the country will stand for an attempt to enforce it."[51] The title of a letter to the editor of the *New York Herald* read, "The Indian's Dances: Every True American Will Want to See Them Preserved."[52] The *Helena Record Herald* was more blunt when its editorial staff noted that "lovers of liberty" considered Burke a "provincial ass" for his previous oppressive policies and that with this dance ban such a moniker would remain unscathed.[53] Papers in smaller cities and communities sometimes reprinted editorials from larger eastern newspapers that were almost universally opposed to the ban. An editorial from the *Times*, incredulous at the prospect that the government would pass such "a dangerous and wicked order" against Pueblo dances, was reprinted in the *Santa Fe New Mexican*.[54] Indeed, the newspapers of small or rural towns close to reservations were often as adamantly opposed to the dance ban as were those of eastern urban centers, and a day after the *Times* editorial was printed in the *New Mexican*, the latter reported that the Santa Fe Chamber of Commerce was looking into the possibility of having the order rescinded.[55]

Much of the language in the local and national newspaper coverage of Burke's circular was framed in valuations of Indianness. This language in fact linked the concerns of the major eastern newspapers with those of reservation border towns or non-Indian communities that might otherwise profit from Indian dances. Because of the growing fascination with Indianness in American society, the correlating sense of disillusionment with modern, urban life that a growing number of non-Indian individuals felt, and the expansion of tourist opportunities in the early twentieth century, thousands of middle- and upper-class white American families took pilgrimages to the "Wild West" tourist locales of towns like Santa Fe, Phoenix, and Flagstaff. In the process they invaded the surrounding reservations and bought up as much Indianness in the form of pottery, baskets, and admission to dances as they could afford. Border towns and train stops profited all the while. The increased interest in commodified Indianness and southwestern tourism is reflected in the 1922 launching of what became known as Santa Fe's annual Indian Market, just one year before the message "to All Indians" was circulated.[56] By the 1920s it was increasingly clear that Indianness was serving important ideological and economic purposes for a significant segment of the non-Indian public.[57] Along the same lines, folklorists valorized Indians as a part of the true American folk as they sought to establish authentic "American" traditions not necessarily derivative of European music and art. An article in the *Chicago News* in support of the Ojibwas' desire to continue their dances despite opposition from the OIA summed up the idea:

> American palefaces have permitted their own folk dances to fall into disuse, and have forgotten their folk songs. . . . [U]pon the picturesque aborigines rests the burden of maintaining a worthy American folk tradition. It is the Indians, too, who starkly maintain the primitive, rugged virtues that once were shared by white Americans, for they have not been led astray by money, lust, ragtime, colored supplements and summer furs. They are the guardians of the temple, the tenders of the flame. We should not interfere with them. Then when we have spent our substance in riotous living, have wearied of truffles and pate de foie gras, have gone stale through walking the dog and foxtrotting to jass bands and have turned, soul sickened, away from the tinsel and tinkle and garish glare of more or less great and somewhat smudged white ways, we can gird up our loins and go back to the lodge of our red brother and learn again the delights of the simple life. At the same time Brother Lo, the good Indian, will have conserved his financial as well as his artistic and moral resources and may stake us to a new start in the quest of fortune, beauty, and salvation.[58]

The sentiments of antimodern primitivism laced many editorials and articles in opposition to the dance ban, and although they idealized and thereby dehumanized American Indians, they could also add a layer of support to the Native people struggling to continue, create, and expand various dancing traditions. It is through the language of Indianness that we find continuity among the multitude of journalists who opposed the ban.

Cities and towns that supported local tourism around reservations, particularly in the Southwest, recognized that they would face devastating losses if all Indian dances, or even if only some of the more infamous such as the Hopi Snake and Antelope Ceremony, ceased to exist. Chu'tiva, or what became known as the Hopi Snake Dance, had by the 1920s become one of the largest tourist draws in the Southwest. Led by members of the Snake (Tsuutsut) clan, and coupled with members of the Antelope (Tsöötsöpt) clan, the Snake Dance originated at Walpi on the First Mesa of the Hopi Reservation in Arizona. During the last day of the nine-day ceremony, members of the Snake clan danced with snakes in their mouths. The dance still typically takes place in August and is responsible for ensuring plentiful rain for the corn crops.[59]

The dance became known to non-Indians after anthropologists and even Theodore Roosevelt observed and published in titillating detail descriptions of the ceremony in the late nineteenth and early twentieth centuries; before long, the dance was promoted by hotels, railroads, and nearby chambers of commerce as an essential southwestern tourist experience.[60] For that reason, newspaper coverage of Burke's dance circular in Arizona and New Mexico was overwhelmingly negative. The *Bisbee (Ariz.) Review* noted that Burke did not pass an executive order banning the dances outright, because he had foreseen the opposition he would receive not just from American Indians but also from nearby towns that reaped financial rewards from the dances. According to the *Review*, "thousands of people annually tour the northern part of the state for no other reason than to view [the Hopi Snake Dance], and no doubt the chambers of commerce of Flagstaff and other surrounding cities will put up such a wail that Commissioner Burke will think twice before he issues his final order."[61]

Members of the press learned early on of Burke's intention to spread propaganda among the public and were often quick to criticize what they considered his misuse of power. The *Los Angeles Illustrated Daily News* reported charges that a "paid lobby" of the OIA had attended the convention of the General Federation of Women's Clubs "to put through . . . Burke's reported suggestion to Indian Bureau subordinates that a careful propaganda be undertaken to educate public opinion against Indian religious dances."[62] The "paid lobbyists" in fact included Clara D. True, associate secretary for the IRA, and a group of seven like-minded Christian Pueblo Indians who opposed some of the Pueblo dances.[63] After quoting Burke's "Message to All Indians," in which he intimated that if any Native persons did not give up the banned dances of their own free will, then "some other course will have to be taken," an *Oakland Post-Enquirer* editorial quipped, "Surely a strange conception of 'free will'! 'You are free to give up these ceremonies, or I will make you,' announces the commissioner. As if a hold-up man should say, 'You are free to hand me your watch, but if you don't I will take it.'"[64] The *Louisville (Ky.) Post* agreed: the message from Commissioner Burke "carried with it an implied threat so that it amounted really to an order." The *Post* added: "The only objection to the dances seems to have been they were not consonant with civilization. Such an attitude is singularly intolerant and narrow-minded. . . . They do not express themselves in this or in other matters the way Anglo-Saxons do. But simply because their method of expression is different does not prove that it is wrong."[65] Despite overt racism experienced by American Indians at the time, a degree of cultural pluralism and tolerance—at least toward Indianness—had begun to infiltrate some editorials by the early 1920s, as exemplified by the *Post*. Taking a jab at reformers seeking moral "improvement," the *Chicago Evening Post* sarcastically suggested that the response to the American greeting, "How's everything going?" would soon become "moraller and moraller," followed later by "duller and duller."[66] Concurrently comparisons were drawn between the policy of the OIA and that of other countries around the world:

> There is something savoring of crass stupidity in the order by Charles H. Burke. . . . It is almost grotesque vandalism coming at a time when the whole world is awakening to new interest in the records, civilizations, religions and customs of the past. . . . The order of the commissioner of Indian Affairs is altogether an act of tyranny almost worthy of a Bolshevist dictator. Having been persecuted, murdered and systematically robbed for several hundred years by the white race, the red man ought at least to be spared this last indignity from a people whose own popular dances placed alongside the symbolical dances of the aborigines make the latter seem in contrast like patterns of purity.[67]

Many editors and reporters indeed drew comparisons between Indian dances and popular "white" dances at a time when jazz dances and dance contests also caused irate responses from detractors. The "dance craze" that swept the middle-class youth of the 1920s, rooted of course in African American music, was controversial among conservatives and religious organizations; reformers sought to sanitize jazz dance as quickly as white boys and girls appropriated it.[68] The media heavily covered jazz dance marathons, for example, and both allies and enemies of Burke forwarded many such articles to him for comparison with aspects of his policy. As opponents of Native American dance focused on the giveaways as a justification for the ban, national columnist H. I. Phillips argued that if an Indian "got away" with giving a $350 cow at a dance, he was getting off easy: "When a white man goes to the modern dance he knows his girl will eat up twice that much in dinner checks, not to say a word about the taxi bills" and that a man who spent only that much at a "fashionable dance" would be considered "a mere piker."[69] The sexist, fallacious comparison ignored the nature of giveaways—the redistribution of resources within the community—and showed the public's lack of understanding of them, but Phillips's goal of ridiculing the OIA was clear. The *Meridian (Miss.) Star* suggested that if American Indians were to give up their dances for the jazz dances popular among white youths, then "it may be just as corrupting to Indian morals as tribal dancing . . . but it would presumably satisfy bureaucratic ideals of regulation."[70] The *El Paso Times* reprinted a *New York Times* article that was similarly critical of Indian boarding school curricula that taught "white man's games" at the expense of Indian games.[71] Remarking on Burke's suggestion that the dances drew crowds and "made confusion," the *Fresno (Calif.) Bee* reported that "one might fairly say as much about the revival service of Billy Sunday."[72] The *Utica (N.Y.) Observer Dispatch* noted: "Instead of holding football games, races, conducting excursions, getting drunk and participating in sport generally upon a day of thanksgiving or a day of prayer, the Indians assemble and engage in a ceremonial dance. The chant is a form of supplication or thanksgiving, as the case may be—a prayer for bountiful crops, for rain, for the safety of their homes, for increase of their stock, or for the welfare of their children."[73] Some papers also argued that many symbols that were involved in the celebration of Christian holidays, such as Christmas trees and Easter eggs, had origins as pagan as any symbol found in Pueblo dances—an ironic statement, given that many Pueblos incorporate Catholic traditions into their dances.[74]

As soon as Burke renewed his attempt to curtail reservation dancing, non-Indians leapt into the fray. While Burke gathered support from the reform organizations most heavily invested in the assimilation policy or in the maintenance of Victorian sexual mores, most

It's the Bunk, by J. N. Darling. Editorial cartoons such as this one from 1926 criticized the government's attempts to ban reservation dancing by casting the laments of barbarism within the context of popular jazz dances at the time, such as the Charleston. Reproduced with the permission of the "Ding" Darling Wildlife Society.

newspaper reporters were extraordinarily critical of Burke's efforts. Newspapers from large eastern cities and reservation border towns were not the only media outlets that opposed the government's efforts to restrict dances. Rather, newspapers from large and small towns across the country, some nowhere near any reservations, reacted negatively to the circular. Their critiques were often rooted in non-Indians' fascination with Indianness, but they also stemmed from a distrust of the OIA or of the provincial reform organizations that supported Burke. Despite his concern with managing the public reaction to the circular, Burke could not have anticipated the depth of animosity that he encountered over his attempt to restrict reservation dancing.

NATIVE AMERICAN RESPONSES
TO THE DANCE CIRCULAR OF 1923

Although a survey of newspaper coverage reveals an extensive national reaction by non-Indians to Burke's circular supplement and "Message to All Indians," Native peoples reacted strongly as well, not only in the press, but especially through correspondence with Burke. Some agreed to give interviews to newspaper reporters, others contacted Burke directly or discussed the matter with their local OIA agent, and still others mobilized their communities in reaction to the dance circular or publicly and blatantly defied the order. An examination of each of these methods reveals a cross section of reactions to the dance restrictions in Indian Country.

A number of Native people used the local and national press to convey their views on the dance circular. A local paper in Washington State queried a group of Yakama and Umatilla people on their way to a Fourth of July dance at White Swan. One respondent said, "They tell us to do as the white man does. Well, everywhere we went on the Fourth the white people were dancing. Surely we dance, and our maidens dance with more modesty than daughters of the white man."[75] Ponca dancer Horse Eagle presented his case to a *Kansas City (Mo.) Times* reporter: "Oklahoma Indians spend less time dancing in a year than white folks do in one month."[76] Horse Eagle continued:

"What if the Poncas do give away to visiting tribes? We get it all back when we go visiting. We Indians dance so much because we need the money. Our dances are considered among the most artistic in America. Professional dancers of America and from foreign countries come to us to learn our dances to copy them."[77] The *Daily Oklahoman* interviewed several Ponca and Otoe dancers and reported that although they sometimes dance "for the white folks entertainment," they do so to generate much-needed income. The Poncas and Otoes also were said to "hold up their hands in horror at the idea of holding snake dances."[78]

Some Native people who used the press to further their views defended dance in religious terms. One reporter interviewed a Navajo medicine man named Ya-otza Begay, who was in the process of conducting a sing to heal a woman who made a living weaving blankets for tourists at the Harvey House in Albuquerque.[79] Begay adamantly defended the sing:

> What do we thin[k] of the commissioner's wish to stop our ceremonies and dances? What would the white men say if they were told to give up their religion and their medicine? We do no dance at a medicine sing for fun. It is to cure sickness that we dance at a sing. . . . You ask what will we do about it if the commissioner does as he threatens to do. The answer is that we do not want to die, and without our medicine and our ceremonies we have no protection against the witches who cause much of the sickness. We cannot give up our ceremonies. We must have the right to worship our gods and to protect ourselves as we have always done. It must be that the great commissioner does not consider what the Navajos feel, and what is best for us.[80]

When the reporter asked another Navajo man, Tsen-ah-chene-chu, whether or not he believed medicine men were paid too much for their work, given that the OIA provided white doctors for the Navajos, he responded, "We do not pay the medicine men much; maybe five or six sheep. It is true that we have to pay nothing for the treatment of the white doctors that Washington sends out. But what do your white doctors know about the witches that may be causing the sickness that is to be cured?"[81] The Navajos interviewed for the article all defended their ceremonials on the grounds that they were absolute necessities in Navajo life—that the Navajo people would die without them—and that the order from Burke was without merit. Members of the Pueblo tribes in New Mexico felt personally offended by Burke's circular and called an emergency council meeting with representatives of the Acoma, Santo Domingo, San Felipe, Santa Ana, Jemez, Sandia, San Juan, Santa Clara, San Ildefonso, Nambe, Isleta, and Cochiti pueblos.[82] The Pueblo Council, working closely with John Collier, faced one of the first attempts by Burke to enforce the circular: he had demanded the return of two boys to school who had been temporarily withdrawn to undergo religious training at Taos Pueblo.[83] Within an hour and a half a committee composed of Tony Abeita from Isleta, Sotero Ortiz of San Juan, and Alcario Montoya of Cochiti had drafted a memorial to Burke that condemned the circular and reminded him of a letter from Secretary of the Interior A. B. Fall, dated June 17, 1921, that guaranteed no interference from the government in regard to their customs.[84] Asking Burke to rescind the "Message to All Indians," they wrote, "You know better than we do that the Constitution of these United States gives the right and liberty to all people to worship according to the dictates of their own conscience."[85] Newspapers across the country reprinted their memorial to support their condemnation of the dance circular.

It is clear that Burke had sparked a chaotic national reaction to his order. Although the content of his circular and "Message to All Indians" was based directly on recommendations specifically regarding the Lakota dance situation in North and South Dakota, Burke's determination to distribute fifteen thousand copies of the letter throughout Indian Country turned the local battle over Lakota dance into a national war, and even Burke's knowledge of the Lakota dances was limited to what the missionaries, agents, and government farmers told him.[86] He based his prejudice against Pueblo dances and the Hopi Snake Dance solely upon hearsay and the affidavits from the "Secret Dance File" that he had extracted from OIA files and handed to sympathizer S. M. Brosius of the IRA.[87] Since the vast majority of Native people had never even heard of a "Snake Dance," its reference in the "Message to All Indians" led to even more confusion on reservations. Native dancers and proponents of dances were aroused to challenge federal Indian policy in the local and national press. Burke began to quickly crumble under the combined pressure of their efforts with those of interested non-Indian parties. In fact, no less than five months after the supplement to circular 1665 and "Message to All Indians" was delivered, Burke bowed to the wishes of the Arizona governor to petition the Hopis for permission to photograph the Snake Dance in late August.[88]

Not all American Indians were supportive of the dances, however, and some used the press to articulate their oppositional views. Otto Lomavitu, a Hopi from Oraibi whom the OIA considered to be a "progressive" sympathetic to the assimilationist philosophy, was a contributor to the "Secret Dance File"; in the summer of 1923 he wrote a lengthy letter to the editor of Flagstaff, Arizona's *Coconino Sun* in response to the paper's protest against the dance ban.[89] The town of Oraibi, on the Third Mesa of the Hopi Reservation, split in 1906 after mounting disputes and machinations among the politico-religious leaders. Two factions, referred to by the government as the "friendlies" and the "hostiles," vied for political control up until the split. While the dispute had a long history and the split was prophe-sized and very complex in nature, part of it had to do with the accept-ance or rejection of acculturative pressures from the OIA.[90] The factionalism continued to dominate the lives of the people of Oraibi and the villages and social structures of Hotevilla and Bacavi that formed afterward. Lomavitu, one of the earliest Oraibi Mennonite converts, shunned the Snake Dances and struck out against the *Sun* for promoting them.[91] But he went further in his attack, illuminating the hypocrisies he witnessed from the tourists who came to the mesas every year while simultaneously staking out his own cultural dispo-sition:

> In the judgment of a Hopi a white man is a superior being, and naturally he desires to imitate him. But when he comes year after year, spending thousands of dollars in small hotels and cafes tingling the greedy ears of the portly inn-keepers and then stretches out his covetous hands to a poor, dust-covered Hopi of the desert with assumed friendly smile only to sneer when meeting him on his own town streets, the ever alert "superstitiously-reverent" Hopi begins to suspect rottenness in the game.[92]

Lomavitu attacked the tourists and white people in general, wondering why a white person would spend hundreds of dollars "just to see an ignorant Indian wriggle with his wriggling god the snake."[93] He stated that he was proud of the Hopi people, despite what he considered their lack of education, because they would "mark out a woman clothed in nudity, ever admiring herself in a glass, twisting her head like a reptile, ever powdering her nose and painting her lips and eyelids, as absolute shamelessness." Then he asked: "Is this civilization?"[94]

The *Sun* reporter had argued that the Hopis would suffer financially and would be deprived of thousands of dollars each year because of the ban. The tourists, Lomavitu responded, showed their "blackest side" to the Hopis and paid exorbitant sums to see the dance—money that did not reach the pockets of the Hopis nearly as much as it did the hotel and café keepers in the villages nearby or on the way to the dances. Questioning the validity of the reporter's statements, he wrote, "Is this another case of peace treaty with the Indian so plausibly and ambiguously worded as was done with our forefathers?"[95] Lomavitu pointed out that the dance so heralded by the tourists was a fake, that the dancers extracted all of the venom prior to the dances, and that because of that deception "the Indian 'laughs in his sleeves' at the poor, deluded, pompous pale face."[96] Finally, Lomavitu praised Burke and asked those who disagreed with him to step aside: "We owe all our education and civilization to the man in Washington besides our greatest benefactor, the Almighty God. We must pay our debt by becoming better citizens."[97]

Lomavitu's letter and convictions not only represent the complexity of the dance debate but also reveal the ways in which Native communities were created and broken over the impact of assimilation policies. Born in a village that almost destroyed itself largely because of OIA pressures to assimilate, the people of Oraibi developed perhaps an even more acute attunement to the politics of expressive culture. Even while Lomavitu criticized the Snake Dance, he took many more pains in his acerbic letter to the *Sun* to chastise the white tourists who both promoted it and exploited the Hopi. A year and a half later, Lomavitu provided the welcoming address at the Oraibi Day School Christmas party. He looked on as students participated in a ceremonial of their own: the singing of Christmas songs and the participation in perhaps their most recently adopted pagan ritual, that of watching Santa Claus crawl out of a specially constructed fireplace and chimney. No snakes were present.[98]

The "Message to All Indians" produced a tremendous and varied response from Native people, directly to local government agents and to Commissioner Burke. As was noted at the onset by the presence of Native missionaries at the Pierre meeting, along with some anti-dance tracts in the press, several Native people approved of at least parts of Burke's measures. Peo-peo-tah-likt, a sixty-six-year-old Nez Perce, wrote Burke in praise of the circular but added that he still partook in "celebrations lasting only a few days" when they did not interfere with work on his farm.[99] Bird Above, of the Crow Reservation in Montana, concurred with Burke's condemnation of the giveaways, which he said occurred frequently in his community. But he also blamed the Catholic and Baptist missionaries for their lack of attention toward individual family homes. He argued that they forced the members of the community to meet together often: "They made the Indians camp together and made or allow them to have all these wrong[] things instead of helping or try to tell them what to do towards making homes." Bird Above argued that, rather, his own "innocent religion" kept him and the followers in small groups and at their homes: "We believe in stay home and look after of farms or home and have our little prayer meeting right in our own home."[100] According to C. H. Asbury, superintendent of the Crow Agency, Bird Above was "one of the leading peyote devotees."[101] Bird Above in essence agreed with Burke as to the detrimental nature of the giveaways, but his alignment with Burke and his policies stopped there. Using the language of the circular, which stressed the importance of remaining and working in the home, he advocated the peyote religion, a practice that Burke also sought to suppress.

Like Bird Above, other American Indians who opposed the dances voiced their support of the "Message to All Indians" in conjunction with requests for the OIA to validate their own unique agendas. One month before Bird Above wrote his letter, two Crow women named Nina Big Day and Annie Pryor congratulated superintendent Asbury on his plan to limit the Medicine Dance. Big Day and Pryor criticized the Crow men for pulling their boys into the dances when "these boys got education to go ahead in other games such as Basket ball and wrestling match and other games which will help to develop their health and be ready to do any kind of work even to go to the army."[102] The women supported boarding school education and believed that it was not reconcilable with Medicine Dances. But in their critique of the dance, Big Day and Pryor set their sights on appropriating a building presently occupied by an agency official. Because of the detrimental impact of the dances, "it will be a good idea if you let us have the old commissary for a gymnasium," they argued. "Some of the boys looked at the building and makes them feel good to see the great big room where Mr. Campbell is now. I think he ought to move to the white building where Dr. Oberlander lives [because] it's a better building."[103] Throwing themselves into the debate, the Crow women had inventively used their opposition to the dance as leverage to argue for the commandeering of a government building.

The varied responses from Native people indicate their diversity of opinions, including those within communities, over the nature of their dances. Some, like the Lakota missionaries, believed that the dances were ultimately a threat to the "advancement" of Christianity and "civilization" among their people. Most, however, were upset and offended by Burke's circular. The negative responses to it were based on several grounds. Some defended the dances because of their cultural and/or religious significance, some criticized the government for blaming crop failures on the dances, some argued that white dances were more morally threatening than their own, and others found the circular genuinely amusing.

Another group of Crows, this time twenty-three of them, wrote Burke in response to the circular. They noted that only a few members of their community practiced the giveaways. Their real complaint, however, was that he had blamed dances for unsuccessful harvests, so they told him what they believed were the real reasons they were having difficulties with their crops. Horses Mane and the other Crows argued that they had been farming for many years and used to have "great crops of wheat and hay," but they had "lost interest" for several reasons:

1st: The grasshoppers destroyed our crops.

2nd: When we needed the irrigation ditch, we could not obtain it, because the ditches were not in good condition.

3rd: Although we obtained no water, yet we had to pay for the maintenance fee. *More money* than the whole crop was worth.

4th: There was no money in wheat and oats.

5th: Those who had to help us, from the office, did not give us intelligent help.

6th: The construction work of the ditch is a scandal here. Why must people pay *Service* for construction work? Would be better to have no land at all.[104]

"Yet," they wrote, "with all those obstructions which were brought to us, yet, we are willing to farm."[105] The Crows recognized that the difficulties of farming on the reservation had much less to do with dances than with the outmoded and underfunded agrarian economic policies of the Office of Indian Affairs; they understood that the OIA was using dance as both a rationale for its own failure and a way to blame the victims.

Several Native people defended their dances on religious grounds. Many Pueblo leaders who had invited Collier to work with them on the matter were appalled at Burke's lack of respect for their religious beliefs and, after meeting in council, wrote, "One way of worshipping our God is by dancing and singing, praying and fasting. . . . [W]e do not hold or have any dance, race, or other tribal custom merely for the fun there is in it. It all [has] a solemn meaning to us." They claimed a constitutional right to religious freedom and asked Burke to rescind the circular.[106] Frank Anwash of Oneida County, Wisconsin, also argued that Burke should not have the right to suppress the dances: "This our religious dance. That's the only religion we got in this world and we can not get without it[;], Jessus gave us his power to have this Religion dance."[107] They held dances four times a year, in the spring ("to have our bodies clean and souls"), on the Fourth of July, in the autumn, and on Christmas Day, each dance lasting about four days. Anwash stated that the dances were essential for their religion and that they still worked hard to plant and harvest their gardens, even though they did not receive any money or land "of any kind" from the government.[108]

Many Native people felt that the dances of white people were much more morally threatening than the dances that Burke attacked. Equating high moral standards with those who attend church more regularly, Oliver Jumping Eagle of Pine Ridge, South Dakota, told his superintendent that the level of decency and morality was very high at the Omaha dances, arguing that "many more of the mixed bloods and others who attend the Omaha dances may be found the following Sunday in church than among those who attend the white dances."[109] Such scrutiny of white dances (the particular dances were not mentioned) was not uncommon and indeed challenged the moral hierarchy of "white" over "Indian" dances that Burke maintained. Smith Pain on Hip from Pine Ridge wrote Burke and argued that the dances were conducted with "strict order" and behavior, not like white dances, in which he said "several fellows get drunk or some one may get kill or steal, such thing as that."[110] He did not understand why the missionaries were complaining about the Lakotas, as they "are baptized and attend church." Pain on Hip also wrote that many of the missionaries were corrupt: "They might as well [have] retired from church work if they cannot live up to it. It will be better for them to quit and farm for themselves."[111] In addition to criticizing the missionaries, Pain on Hip considered the morality, practice, and rules of the Lakota dances as superior to the dangerous, immoral behavior that he equated with the non-Indian dances, and he defended giveaways as a means to help "poor and needy Indians."[112]

Native peoples from throughout the country criticized the ban through comparisons with "white" dances. A group of Washington State Indians, appointed by the Colville General Council, responded to Burke's circular by arguing that their dances were "given for pleasure only, like white people's dances." They primarily danced to "celebrate old times," and they argued that the dances did not interfere with their work.[113] Four years prior to the circular supplement, in a 1919 letter to Commissioner of Indian Affairs Cato Sells a group of Standing Rock Sioux argued, "What is the difference in Indians dancing and white men dancing? There is no more temptation in the Indians' dance than there is in the white mans." They also wrote that "we are getting old and cannot enjoy ourselves in dancing the white mans' dances."[114] Two years later Joseph No Hearts of the Standing Rock

Agency pleaded with the commissioner: "We would like to dance now and then. We are old and that is the only enjoyment we get. . . . [If the law prevents us from dancing, then] you should put a stop to White dances. It is not fair."[115]

The letters to Burke from Native individuals who opposed the circular were often read by their superintendents before being mailed (if at all) to him. O. L. Babcock received several negative letters from people living around the Spokane Indian Agency to mail to Burke, but he forwarded only one, from Jonas (John) Joseph, an older member of the community, who wrote,

> I wish you would stop write me letter like that [circular.] I could say that foolish for you to do that isn't your business Indian dance and feast you don't know what your talking bout . . . you white p[eo]ple have dance all summer and all winter know body stop you folk because we know it your way and Indian way to I am tired all ready that why you should not send me letter like that I am work hard every day fence my wife place I am hungry I don't like to get letter like that that foolish letter and other thing you can stop Indian they got right to going somewhere to work make little money for they children if you had give Indian money they wouldn't going know where . . . you know well I am old poor I am not able to work just now come I tell what I think oh yes I am send your letter back I don't like keep it to your self give to someone that like dance give him this letter to him John Andrew is one that going all over World for fun if you want give to him He see that letter I think he stay at his own place But me we all stay home we don't going nowhere good by.[116]

Joseph was offended that the circular was sent to him when he didn't believe he was responsible for any of the activities described in the circular. He considered himself a hard worker who stayed at home and lived in poverty because he had little access to the means to buy the seed from the government that his people were directed to use for their crops. Joseph wrote Burke to criticize the government for wasting time sending circulars about trivial matters to cover up its own failures, when it could instead devote more resources to improving the dire conditions that he and his neighbors were facing.[117] Because governmental inadequacy kept Native peoples impoverished and often hungry, because it failed to implement an agrarian policy that gave them access to the resources they needed to work an already unsuitable land, Joseph felt that those who danced at fairs and Wild West shows for profit had every right to do so, as the dances provided more of a means for supporting their families than the allotment and assimilation legislation could provide. Native people were of course extremely aware of the failures of the allotment policy due to the lack of suitable land and resources. Yet the agents and the commissioner continued to cast their own failures onto the shoulders and the expressive culture of American Indians, to the point of condemning the practices even when they brought a semblance of economic relief.

The circular also occasioned collective responses from a council of Wichitas, Delawares, Wacos, Keechis, Tawakonis, and others in Oklahoma.[118] They "were in a good humor all the way through the reading of the letter" and dictated a lengthy response that outlined their customs and religious practices, such as the redistribution of seeds in the spring so that all families were provided with enough for their planting.[119] They considered themselves very religious and highly moral in nature; their nonreligious gatherings included big feasts when the children were about to leave or were returning from boarding schools: "It is a ser[i]ous matter for [the mothers] to know that their little ones are to be gone away from them for so long a time. Others try to comfort them, and use this occasion to make as merry as possible." They felt that they had not breached any of the moral directives that Burke laid out in his circular.[120] The council was "curious" and "smiled a little" over Burke's allegations. They felt that he made an unsubstantiated "blanket charge" that did not apply to them. They asked the Office of Indian Affairs to be more specific and laid out several questions that they hoped Burke would address:

1. Please explain the meaning of "Pow-wow."
2. What is a "Snake Dance?"
3. When have the Wichitas or Delawares neglected their crops, gardens, and homes?
4. When and where did these tribes give public shows of their customs?
5. Tell us more about handling poisonous snakes.

6. We are desiring to have respectable gatherings. We do not know all;
   we want to learn what is right.[121]

Burke's assumption that people on every reservation would know what a "Snake Dance" was reflects his facile comprehension of the diversity of expressive culture in Indian Country; the Wichitas and others took the opportunity to point out the ludicrous nature of his "Message to All Indians." On a more serious note, they challenged the OIA to question its own hierarchical assumptions of religious and cultural practices.

Their challenge did not end without a comparison with the dances popular among white youth. They wrote: "The jazz-dance is offensive to us . . . . [W]e would be very glad to have the Board of Health of Reviews or Censors to contrast our manner of dancing with those of the white-folks and from the stand-point of saneness and morality and healthfulness show which of the Dances are more in keeping with standards as set out."[122] They turned Burke's equating of Indian dances with immorality on its head, opining that the "white" dances were much more threatening than the "Indian" dances in the very terms that Burke used to define them. They pressed this point even further: "We would not allow our children to degrade themselves to go to one of such dances as the white folk put on if we could help ourselves. . . . We are willing to go on trial . . . to prove to the world that we our manners and customs are much superior in many points of virtue over our boasted white brethren."[123] The letter to the OIA was drawn up and signed in the presence of John Thomas, a Wichita preacher who led his own exclusively Native congregation. While non-Christian Indians, or those who had more successfully syncretized Christianity within their own cultural traditions, could have much at stake in rejecting Burke's letter, so too did American Indians heavily involved in more doctrinal Christian organizations. The members of this congregation took pride in their sense of morality and tribal heritages and would not allow Burke's charges to stand without a challenge, especially given that the dances and gatherings of their peoples had been designated as more morally dangerous than "white" dances. They expressed their own notions of what constituted safe and dangerous cultural performances, in direct opposition to Burke's allegations. But

The Hopi snake dance, as it was known by non-Indian tourists and government officials, created immense concern within the Burke administration and the Indian Rights Association. Yet non-Indian tourists, fascinated with the dance, pressured the government to lift the ban. This performance took place on May 15, 1926, in front of the U.S. Capitol, only three years after Burke banned the dance in his "Message to All Indians." National Photo Company Collection, Prints and Photographs Division, Library of Congress, LC-DIG-npcc-15822.

these notions were not a response to Burke as much as an affirmation of their own morality, and a rejection of the immorality they felt surrounded the "white" dances that they had witnessed. Dances, no matter what style or origin, served as barometers that registered the desires and values of Native peoples, agents, and missionaries alike.

Burke asked all agency superintendents to provide a report one year after the dance circular supplement was issued. The reports varied in length from one or two sentences to several pages, but many agents took the opportunity to express their own views on Indian dance and the circular. While some indicated that dancing either had never been a "problem" or was curtailed under their own watch during the year, many responded that dancing was on the increase; some provided Burke with their own opinions as to what was causing the frequency of dances on their reservations.

The most outspoken dance opponents previous to the issuance of the circular were typically those most disappointed with its lack of success in the years following. Arthur Pratt, the farmer in charge of the Standing Rock Sioux Reservation's Porcupine District was particularly aghast: "The letter had a wide publicity among the Indians here, but it appears that they soon forgot it and continued to go on with the dances as though the letter was never written to them by the Commissioner. No effort on the part of the Indians has been made to uphold and carry out the instructions that were given them."[124] The people in Pratt's district had threatened to take the matter up with U.S. senators if he did not grant them permission to dance. They formed a committee ostensibly to self-regulate the dances, but Pratt, in an illustration of his lack of control and authority over the dancing, felt that instead their job was to ensure that "every savage custom is performed that are a perman[]ent part of all these Indian dances."[125] Upset that many dancers argued they had a right as citizens to dance without governmental regulation, he wrote that he did not think "that the Constitution means that any class of people in the United States are to follow their old savage, heathen customs. . . . These Indians have a government of their own and it is the Indian dance."[126] H. W. Sipe, a farmer in the Yankton Agency, disliked the "white" dances that some of Lakota participated in as much as "Indian" dances and had forbidden "all dancing on the agency ground."[127] His stance seemed to do little good, however, as he reported that dancing had continued in full force, and in no case had the dancers even bothered to request his permission.[128]

A number of superintendents reported to Burke that local non-Indians caused as much resistance to the enforcement of dance restrictions as did American Indians. According to Superintendent Jacob Breid, the "most harmful gathering" of the Sac and Fox occurred as an annual powwow sponsored by the state historical society.[129] He added, "Those participating in the pow wow say that they must make some money with which to pay their obligations, but this would not be necessary if each had a larger acreage to cultivate. This is only an excuse but there are good grounds for the assumption of such an attitude."[130] The Blackfeet Agency superintendent complained that a number of Blackfeet "professional dancers . . . made Glacier Park Hotel their head-quarters" and received constant solicitation from moving picture companies, rodeos, and artists.[131] The frustrations of agency superintendents continued to mount. A year after the dance circular supplement was issued, one farmer among the Yankton Sioux complained, "The dance craze took on new life last year as a result of the dancing at the Yankton Sioux fair. There were more visiting dancers and a great many more participants in the different dances than I had seen before in five years I have been at this place."[132] He was particularly concerned at the "surprising number of the younger generation who frequent them."[133] While banning any dances considered "Indian" among his pupils, the superintendent of the Phoenix Indian School observed an increase in dances across the Southwest, particularly those "staged for the white population at railroad points and elsewhere" such as the annual Gallup fair.[134] Between forty and fifty Sisseton Sioux danced each year at the annual fair near their reservation, each earning one or two well-needed beeves as payment. However, once the dance circular supplement was issued, the local superintendent felt it his duty to forbid them from participating and thus caused tremendous agitation.[135]

In Wisconsin the Grand Rapids Agency superintendent noted two powwows held the previous year where "admissions were charged and considerable money made on the gate receipts charged the white people."[136] That year dancers also made "considerable sums" when hired out on a daily wage in Kilbourn, Marshfield, Wausau, Tomahawk, Rhinelander, and Chicago, among other areas.[137] The superintendent expressed some frustration over both his inability to control the dancers and the lack of economic incentives available to them as an alternative:

> Being citizen Indians and not under reservation restraint and very widely scattered, I find it very difficult to prevent my Indians from leaving home when they have little or no money or provisions and are promised good wages to dance. . . . Farming and stock raising has been paying very poor returns and it is doubtful if much progress can be reported until the price of farm commodities is higher, but I will not allow this argument to influence my course.[138]

Indeed, only a handful of OIA employees seemed willing to challenge Burke's correlation between dancing and poor agricultural returns.

Of these few, some superintendents argued that even if dancing were to continue, it was not a problem that the OIA should focus its energies on. H. P. Marble was more direct than the Grand Rapids Agency superintendent in refusing to acknowledge a causal relationship between dancing and the lack of agricultural success on reservations. "As indicated in previous reports," he wrote, "the dances amongst the Pueblo Indians are not thought to interfere with farming or productive labor. On the contrary most of their dances are in celebration of the completion of some particular task in connection with their agricultural activities."[139] The Coeur d'Alene superintendent wrote Burke that the "war dance element" on the reservation held two or three potlatches (a form of giveaways) during a dance, but that such practices were typically harmless: "The value of the presents given is, as a rule, not great. Generally the gift is a repayment of an obligation, also the recipient is expected to reciprocate. I do not know of a case where any hardship has ever resulted from the Potlatch dance."[140] Superintendent Bauman of the Zuni Agency reported that the Zuni danced with great frequency, but that he respected the ceremonial nature of the dances and did not believe they interfered with any industrial or agricultural activities. Like most tribes, the Zunis held dances more frequently in the winter months than in the summer, because, according to Bauman, after the harvest they had "little else to attend to" until the next season.[141] Despite these few calls for Burke to reassess the placement of blame for failed OIA economic policy on the reservations, Burke and the majority of agency officials continued to place it on the backs of the dancers.

The controversy over the Burke circular and the attempted regulation and suppression of reservation dances by the government continued for several years. By the time the circular was issued, however, many Native people, having spent decades battling OIA superintendents over dance, had grown adept at using dance as a voice in national politics, a voice that could simultaneously critique assimilation, allotment, and the very definitions of Americanness, civilization, and citizenship held by the OIA. Others such as Otto Lomavitu used the dance debate to affirm contrary views or to critique the non-Indians who had become engrossed in the dances. The OIA was never successful in turning the tide of popular culture and public opinion against the dances, nor could the office persuade many Native people to agree with its particular vision of citizenship and "civilization." The lack of OIA success in this regard is perhaps most fully evidenced by the 1933 appointment of John Collier, the outspoken reformer and leading non-Indian proponent of the dances, as the commissioner of Indian Affairs.

Collier became a fixture in D.C. and in the press when he sided with the Pueblo peoples against the dance ban. By doing so, he effectively launched his career in Indian Office reform. His appointment became a possibility only after a sympathetic president took office and the 1928 Meriam Report, prepared by an independent investigative team for Congress, revealed what Native people had known all along: that the allotment and assimilation policies had created catastrophic economic, health, and social conditions.[142] Collier's Indian Reorganization Act of 1934 ended the sale of any further allotments, and as his siding with Native peoples who opposed Burke's dance circular in the 1920s demonstrated, he supported the celebration of tribalism through dance, arts, and crafts. This vision and its implementation were not born solely out of the minds of reformers, however—rather, they depended as much on public interest in Indianness, reflected in critiques of the dance ban found in newspapers from across the country, as they did upon the creative strategies of Native people to find ways to publicly denounce federal assimilation policies during the most oppressive of times. Far from lacking a voice in issues of federal Indian policy, Native people found that, in this case, dance spoke louder than words.

Dancers used Americanness to advance the protection of their difference as Native people, and they used their performance of Indianness as a platform to advance their case before the American public. Dance participants used the tropes of morality and citizenship to combat the supplement to circular 1665, while newspapers, organizations, and non-Native individuals used Indianness to articulate a vision of America that was often, but not always, counterintuitive to Burke's. The press also used the dance debate to criticize reform movements affecting their own communities. As the *Great Falls*

(Mont.) Daily Tribune remarked, "super-denominational uplifters . . . furnished blue laws for red skins, and poor Lo is cribbed, likewise much cabined and confined."[143] Certainly this was a reaction by the newspaper's editors to all of the reformers and prohibitionists of the day. The debate waged in this and other newspapers reveals a divide not only concerning the approval of tribally derived dance but also over competing views of society, race, and culture. Cultural relativism had begun to influence the beliefs of some reformers like Collier as much as older theories of social evolution persisted in the minds of Burke and others. Where Burke's policies were based in hierarchical views of race and culture straight out of the nineteenth century, however, the ideas proposed by the new generation of reformers were often steeped in romantic desires of primitivism that placed value on cultural difference and were based upon problematic or incorrect assumptions of their own.

Despite his prejudices, even Burke was willing to compromise his stance on dancing to serve a higher goal of the OIA, that of liquidating the tribal estates. In 1923 and 1924 he approved the hiring of dancers from the Rosebud Reservation to participate in the annual Frontier Days fair, established specifically to attract non-Indians into the area to purchase allotted parcels of the scant remaining Lakota lands. The organizer of the event, C. E. Kell, wrote to the Rosebud superintendent James McGregor:

> I believe you understand the nature of the celebration and its purpose. . . . We have the show each year purely for advertising purposes. While some men in town make money out of it, by selling foodstuffs, drinks etc., the Association is not organized for profit, but for the purpose of advertising the country; to get people to come here and see the country. If we derive no benefit from that source, then the show is of no benefit. We do not exploit the Indians and use them to attract the crowds for money making purposes, but merely to add to the entertainment, and if the show is beneficial to any person, it is beneficial to them because they are the heavy land owners in this country.[144]

Upon a renewed appeal for the dancers' services at the next fair, in 1924, McGregor requested from Burke that "such Indians as had their crops properly cultivated and their farm work up to date" be given permission to dance at the fair, but that any Lakota caught dancing who had "not properly cultivated their grain and crops, would be placed on the black list and their funds held up." Burke agreed, writing, "I think you have probably taken a view of the situation most practical and in the real interest of the Indians, that is to make their participation contingent upon having their farm work well in hand and up to date. Even then their absence would probably cover a week and would be followed by considerable neglect of home conditions."[145] Burke seemed compelled to associate the dancing of Lakotas, even those who were succeeding in their harvests, with detrimental "home conditions." Yet this concern did not compel him to call off the dancers when he was convinced that their work could help liquidate remaining Lakota lands.

Indeed, it seems that the real concern of Commissioner Burke was to retain OIA authority over Native lands and Native lives. The dance debate that raged in the press was as much about white desires to access Indianness as it was a debate over who should control Native performative practices, and the OIA found itself on the losing end of that fight. For many Native peoples the conflict was less a debate than a full-fledged attack on the expressive culture that defined their relationships and their communities. However, they had experienced the tragedies of allotment and assimilation for several decades, and their expressive culture was much more resilient than any policy initiatives that Burke could create. In this regard, the dance debate is instructive in that it reveals the profound sense of disempowerment felt within the OIA as Native people found new ways to celebrate the tribal, community, and pan-tribal sense of difference that the government had for so long struggled to dismantle.

The dialectics of what constituted "dangerous" and "safe," or more and less threatening, cultural practices fueled much of the debate between Native peoples, OIA officials, missionaries, and public representatives. Never stable, the values and meanings assigned to the practice of music changed according to the circumstances of the American Indians, missionaries, or agents defining them. Native people were divided over the issue, ranging from the responses of the Lakota missionaries such as Dallas Shaw who condemned their practices as "heathenish" to the angry polemics of many individual Indians and leaders who were offended by the ignorance and hypocrisy of the officials' interpretation and attack of their expressive culture.[146] Some such as Otto Lomavitu considered Hopi dances and ceremonials as antithetical to "progress" among the Hopis, while others, like the concerned group of Wichitas, believed that these dances were morally superior to the "white" dances taught in federal Indian boarding schools.

Sometimes the instability of these concepts grew even more profound. In 1927 a group of Standing Rock Sioux who represented themselves as members of the American Progressive Association petitioned Commissioner Burke to prohibit three specific dances on the Standing Rock Sioux Reservation: the Kahomni, or Owl Dance; the Rabbit Dance; and the Slide Naslohan Dance.[147] They argued that the dances were barbarous and heathen as well as injurious to the Sioux who practiced them. They also pointed out that these dances violated Burke's directives in the circular #1665 supplement and his "Message to All Indians," which had their origins in the "dance evil" meeting in Pierre. Many returned students took up these dances, Joseph Otter Robe and the other petitioners complained, and thus "instead of trying to do what they have learned in school they go back to the old barbarism ways and disobey the orders from the Indian Office."[148] They reported that in the five years since the circular and the supplement were delivered, they had noticed no perceptible reduction in the number of "barbarism dances" or in their threat to hindering the goals of making Indians "good citizens."[149]

Burke asked Mossman, still the superintendent of the Standing Rock Agency, to report back to him regarding these dances and complaints. Mossman, previously perhaps the most outspoken critic of Lakota dances, responded: "I agree partly [with] what is said in this petition. However, these dances as enumerated are not really Indian dances. They are a hybrid between the old Indian dances and the modern white dances."[150] He explained that the dances "do not call for Indian costumes" and that the Owl Dance was "something like a waltz" in that male and female partners faced each other and swung around holding hands. Mossman's only objection to the Owl Dance was that "they insist upon dancing it with a tom-tom and singers[;]

otherwise it would be a white dance."[151] Mossman believed that if the OIA officials and government farmers encouraged the dances but separated them from the "old Indian dances," then the "old" dances would eventually die out.[152]

Nevertheless, the Lakota American Progressive Association understood these three new dances as barbaric and a hindrance to the government's program of assimilation and civilization. Otter Robe said that the dances would "demoralize their character and their homes and family," foster the drinking of alcohol, keep them from working the fields, and lead them astray from their lessons of proper citizenship taught in the boarding school classrooms.[153] While demonstrating the polarizing and political nature of music in this period (and the subjective nature of its interpretation), Otter Robe and the others further exacerbated this complex story in item five of their letter: "This here petition does not interfere with the Omaha dance or Grass dance and other dances that is allowed by Treaty law, as a memorial dance."[154]

The various Native people, OIA officials, journalists, reformers, and missionaries involved in the dance debate framed the danger involved in either the proliferation or the suppression of dances in different ways, for different reasons. However, all recognized the importance, magnitude, vitality, and deep political resonance of the practice of music throughout this period of American Indian history. The struggles of Native people over the control and meaning of their expressive culture exposed the limits and transformed the directives of federal Indian policy, challenged the notions of citizenship, Indianness, civilization and savagery that shaped that policy, and demonstrated the malleability of those concepts in the early twentieth century.

CHAPTER 3

THE SOUNDS OF "CIVILIZATION"

MUSIC AND THE ASSIMILATION CAMPAIGN IN FEDERAL INDIAN BOARDING SCHOOLS

They called us the *skin* band, but . . . our band can play better than those white boys in the town.

—*Morning Star*, March 1886

Richard H. Pratt, founder and head of the Carlisle Indian Industrial School, concurred with the anti-dance sentiment of most OIA employees, and he was always anxious to learn of any reports of reservation dancing. Yet in January 1891 news of the massacre of Ghost Dancers at Wounded Knee electrified his entire Pennsylvania campus. Although the Carlisle newspaper had kept the students abreast of the rising tensions since early December 1890, nevertheless students were stunned when reports of the killings arrived. Reports of the violence at Wounded Knee were mediated by Marianna Burgess, superintendent of printing and the editor of the school paper, the *Indian Helper*.[1] Burgess seemed perfectly attuned to Superintendent Pratt's assimilationist zeal and his expectations for his students, and firsthand reports were heavily edited to reflect her, and presumably his, perception of the events.[2] Burgess clearly articulated her impression of the Ghost Dance as wholly antithetical to their civilization project in the articles and letters she edited for the *Indian Helper*. On December 5 she wrote,

"The Messiah craze among the Indians may have been sprung upon those poor ignorant people by white men who are after their lands, or their money, or who want a war with the Indians so that they can rush into battle, kill them and thus win renown. What a shame and an outrage it is! What is the real reason for it all? Ignorance on the part of the Indians, nothing else. Our boys and girls who have learned to read and reason, know better than to be led into trouble in that fashion. Thousands, perhaps of your people will suffer and many [will] be killed before they get their eyes open. Dear boys and girls, if you were there you could not help them. Be content that you are where you can get the education that will save you from such a fearful mistake in the future.[3]

Burgess encouraged the returned students living around the Pine Ridge Agency to submit their interpretation of the events, but she appears, however, to have been rather selective in the reports she chose to publish, perhaps even fabricating some to support her and Pratt's philosophical views. As Amelia Katanski has demonstrated, Burgess regularly manipulated the voices of Native students in the school publications, and certainly this situation would serve as no exception.[4] She published a letter from former student Edgar Fire Thunder, who wrote in December, "We haven't any trouble except some of the Indians had Ghost Dance, but I think they will stop now[. A] good many soldiers came here a few days ago, eight companies in all. The newspapers told that the Indians wanted to fight white men. That is all a mistake. They are going to have council with the soldiers."[5] Although she typically included the names of returned students who sent her accounts of the situation, Burgess perhaps took some editorial liberties when she recounted the following letter, whose author she referred to only as "W," that supported her views: "Oh, it makes me laugh when I saw in the paper, that they said someone told them that they must kill all the whites and they are the ones [that are] going to have the world for themselves. Poor Indians! They don't know what is best for them. Dear! The idea they left their farms and houses [and] are going to be turned into savage ways."[6] On December 26 Burgess reminded the students that "when each Indian gets his eyes open sufficiently to see that the sooner he learns to lead *himself* instead of following the advice of ignorant chiefs the better it will be for him."[7]

The Ghost Dance movement polarized the returned students living around the Pine Ridge Agency. Early and erroneous reports from the

Helper indicated that students Mack Kutepi, Paul Eagle Star, and others had been killed by the soldiers.[8] Pratt solicited George Means and other returned students to assess which former Carlisle students were among the Ghost Dancers. Two months after the massacre, they reported back that fifty-seven of a total of sixty-three former students residing near Pine Ridge during the events were still alive and accounted for, and that six of those accounted for had been involved at Wounded Knee.[9] Pratt, fearful that his students' participation in the movement would tarnish his reputation along with that of his school, suggested that those ex-students "remained long enough [at Carlisle] to gain a smattering of English only."[10] Those who opposed Pratt's project at Carlisle charged that his students were among the Ghost Dance leaders; indeed, it seems that Pratt's greatest concern over Wounded Knee lay in dismissing that charge.[11] However, he and Burgess were also worried about how their students would interpret both the dance and the news of the massacre by federal troops.

Pratt and Burgess were concerned about not only the Ghost Dance but all forms of tribally derived dances performed on reservations or fairgrounds, and the year the students learned of the massacre, Burgess published a small instructional guide for students entitled *Stiya: A Carlisle Indian Girl at Home. Stiya* was a fictional account of the journey home for a Carlisle student and was designed to serve as a moral compass for the returning students.[12] Like all of the teachers and administrators in off-reservation boarding schools, Burgess was keenly aware of the difficulties that returned students often faced in applying their vocational and domestic training on the reservations. Furthermore, she, like the rest, had heard many stories of students "going back to the blanket"—that is, shedding their "citizen" clothes and their "civilized" skills in favor of the "old Indian ways." Burgess was determined to demonstrate through the story of Stiya that the inability of the students to apply their Carlisle instruction was the fault of their families and communities, not that of the school.

Stiya, who represented for Burgess the model of civilized behavior for an alumna of Carlisle, found life in her Pueblo village particularly horrific: she thought her parents and her people were culturally grotesque, the very models of "savagery" that Carlisle had taught her to abhor. She found herself sleeping on the floor of their home, washing clothes without the aid of a washtub, and warding off her parents' urges to give up her school clothes for her cousins' dress and leggings. But the climax of Burgess's story revolved around Stiya's refusal to participate in a Pueblo dance. Against the Pueblo governor's orders, she convinced her parents that none of them should take part in the "disgraceful dances" that represented the very antithesis of all that she had learned in Carlisle as right, proper, "civilized," and morally sound.[13] Indeed, the lines between "civilized" and "savage" expressive culture were stark for Burgess and Pratt, and both did what they could to burn those lines into the minds of their students.

Whereas the failure of Charles Burke's dance circular and "Message to All Indians" (discussed in chapter 2) reflected to a great extent the power of Native peoples' creativity to control the practice of music on their reservations, OIA officials asserted much more control over the music produced in off-reservation Indian boarding schools. The 1890 massacre at Wounded Knee and the perception of the degrading effects of dances such as that depicted in *Stiya* invigorated OIA officials' desire to suppress Indian performative practices and supplant them with those of "civilized" white society. As the Carlisle publications demonstrate, federal Indian boarding schools provided an apt arena in which officials tried to shape the meaning of the practice of music for both the students and even for non-Indian audiences. Inculcating the male students with the regimented disciplinary movements associated with military brass bands, and then displaying those disciplined Native bodies before a predominantly white public, bolstered the prestige, Congressional support, and perceived reformative successes of OIA officials and school administrators. While the bands served the public relations campaign of the boarding schools, however, the assimilationist philosophy of the schools had potentially devastating consequences: beyond the long distances that often separated the children from their families, school officials sought to sever the children's ties to their home community's people, knowledge, expressive culture, and values.

But how exactly was music to function as an instrument of "civilization," and what did students make of their instruction? What forms of musical practice were permitted on school grounds, and what forms were criticized or forbidden? Musical practice served as a moral and cultural battlefield in the schools, just as it did on reservations. In this chapter I parse that battleground, elucidating how OIA officials used music as a "civilizing" tool, how non-Indian audiences reacted both positively and negatively to the singers and musicians, and how the students themselves received and used the music they were taught, in ways that reflected the variety of their musical experiences both at home and at school in the late nineteenth and early twentieth centuries. Although students had little control over musical practices they were permitted to engage in on school grounds, they did what they could to make their school experiences tolerable, and music played an important role in doing just that. Many came to excel on their instruments and began to contemplate a life beyond school that incorporated their newfound talents. While the musical experience varied between schools and among the students, this chapter provides an overview of boarding school musical instruction in the allotment and assimilation era.

THE ROLE OF MUSIC AND DANCE IN A "CIVILIZATION" CURRICULUM

Federal Indian boarding schools such as Carlisle were founded in the late nineteenth century under the premise that, through school education and vocational training, Native children could become "civilized," Christianized, and assimilated, eventually prepared to assume the rights and duties of American citizenship. While primarily the girls were trained in domestic labor and the boys were trained in industrial labor, the students' "transformation" also required, according to the OIA, training in the "proper arts of civilization." For example, the returned students, as represented by the character Stiya in Burgess's fictional account, were trained in Euro-American forms of music and dance that were intended to replace the "heathen" dances that would tempt them upon their return to the reservation. Richard Pratt epitomized the philosophy of Americanization in the first decades of the boarding schools with his infamous slogan that the Carlisle school, in accord with the mission of all boarding schools, should "kill the Indian . . . and save the man."[14] Musical education was absolutely fundamental to Pratt's purpose, and the role of Euro-American music in the schools continued to grow even after his departure.

After 1879, when Pratt opened his school in Carlisle, Pennsylvania, the government established several additional large off-reservation boarding schools such as Chilocco Indian School in Chilocco, Oklahoma; Haskell Institute in Lawrence, Kansas; Flandreau Indian School in South Dakota; Chemawa Indian School in Salem, Oregon; and the Sherman Institute in Riverside, California, along with a number of boarding and day schools on reservations. Many of the largest schools were situated far from the homes of most of the students, for the explicit purpose of diminishing what Indian service officials considered the "demoralizing" cultural influences of parents and other reservation community members. By 1900 nearly 18,000 children attended 153 government-operated boarding schools (25 of which were off reservations), and nearly 4,000 attended the 154 day schools.[15] These figures did not include the Hampton Institute, which was privately run, nor the 50 or so missionary schools in operation at the time.[16] Carlisle was the most widely recognized nationally among these schools; its famous football team and marching band brought young Indian athletes and musicians before thousands of people who had never seen a single American Indian, let alone an entire team or orchestral band of them.

Boarding school educators sought to use musical instruction in the schools as a means to cultivate the students' tastes for "proper"—Euro-American—arts. The administrators who oversaw the schools viewed the practice of music in much the same way that most reservation superintendents did—in very stark, culturally and politically loaded terms. They believed that music lessons in the schools would combat the insidious influences of performative practices that predominated on reservations. Richard Pratt correlated "Indian dances" with savagism when he instructed Lakota chiefs visiting the Carlisle school to go back to the reservations and "make the Indians stop their dances, change their Indian habits and dress for civilized ones and make different and better surroundings for our returned pupils."[17] By instilling in the students a sense of "proper" and "civilized" music, federal Indian boarding schools sought to churn out students like Stiya, who

shunned the tribally derived songs and dances that corrupted reservation life. Even when OIA officials on rare occasion voiced concern that
musical instruction in the schools would not prepare students for the
job market or was too costly an expenditure, nonetheless Euro-
American musical instruction remained a steadfast component of the
students' lives.[18] While Native people and OIA superintendents waged
battles throughout the country over the right to dance on reservations,
OIA teachers hoped that their unrelenting surveillance in the boarding
schools would permit few challenges to the replacement of those
dances and songs with "safer" Euro-American-derived arts.[19]

As Santee Sioux and Carlisle class of 1915 graduate James Garvie
saw it, "The whole object of the school was to turn out loyal Americans. That was the object of the whole thing."[20] The concept of "loyal
Americans" included the idea that the students should develop the
responsibilities of becoming proper citizens. Their musical training
served, not only to create disciplined Americans or to demonstrate to
the public the benefits of that education, but also to provide the students the necessary cultural background for assimilation into the
mainstream of American popular culture.

According to the educators, the appreciation of Euro-American-
derived music could perhaps more easily acclimate the students to
the cultural requirements of American citizenship. "Uncle Sam's officials at the Indian Department," according to a *Pittsburg Gazette-Times*
article in 1914, "were quick to realize the civilizing influence [that an
education in Euro-American music] could exercise upon the Indian
himself, if developed."[21] Carlisle school bandmaster Claude Stauffer
even suggested to a reporter in 1914 that his success in "softening"
Native students through music could be applied to uplifting the character of recent European immigrants and poor whites: "Here lies a
splendid social uplift idea for the masses of the supposedly more cul-
tured and civilized white race. Would little slum dwellers, if thoroughly versed in music in the settlement houses and other uplift
agencies around or among them, develop into strong-arm men and
thugs?"[22] The appreciation of and ability to perform "civilized"
music, according to the article on Stauffer, would enable the students
"to enter certain classes of society which might otherwise remain
closed to them."[23] The musical education in the schools was therefore

aimed at structuring the tastes of students along the cultural palate of a very specific whiteness—a whiteness defined by Victorian moorings and entertainments. In other words, the curriculum was designed to teach the students how to exhibit what administrators considered the proper expressive culture of whiteness.

To acquire the cultural habits, followed by the values, of this white citizenry, the students participated in a wide variety of musical exercises and performances deemed appropriate to the project at hand. Certainly the marching bands were the most obvious musical extensions; the Carlisle Band formed in 1880 and soon afterward developed pieces by Grieg, Mozart, Rossini, Schubert, and Wagner.[24] The students' repertoire was further shaped by hymnals, orchestral compositions, and songbooks, some of which were even written by students or their teachers.

Claude Stauffer himself wrote a number of songs for the Carlisle student body. The words to "Hail to Thee, Carlisle" followed the formula of the typical spirited school anthems of the day:

Carlisle we love you, yes we do! do! do!
Our hearts to thee will e'er be true! true! true!
Thou can'st depend upon us without fail;
To thee our Alma Mater, dear, we hail.
Then wave our colors true of Red and Gold,
Onward to vict'ry send her braves so bold.
No son shall ever thy good name beguile—
All Hail to thee, our Dear Carlisle.[25]

The Chilocco School song performed in the 1930s was similar in tone:

Oh Chilocco! Oh Chilocco!
Where the prairies never end,
Oh Chilocco! Oh Chilocco!
You are still our famous friend.
School of schools you are the best,
You're the school that stands the test,
You're the school that brings us fame,
Ever we'll revere thy name.

Oh Chilocco! Oh Chilocco!
We love your campus grand,
We love your lawns and shady walks
Where graceful maples stand.
We love the sunsets and the stars at night,
Reflected by the lake so bright.
We love the cardinal's cheery call,
And the bright red maples in the fall.

Oh Chilocco! Oh Chilocco!
Where you old stone buildings stand.
Oh Chilocco! Oh Chilocco!
Ivy covered they are grand.
They are monuments of hope
As we on learning's ladder grope,
School that makes our dreams come true,
We are ever loyal to you.

Oh Chilocco! Oh Chilocco!
When the morning bugle calls,
Oh Chilocco! Oh Chilocco!
We are glad to fill your halls.
We come here that we may learn,
Life's great secret to discern,
Teach us how to work and play,
Bring us something new each day.[26]

Beyond the curious reference to "braves" in "Hail to Thee, Carlisle"(discussed further in chapter 4), nothing would distinguish these songs from any other performed in schools across the country. As the OIA opened schools in the late nineteenth century, the selection of songbooks was somewhat haphazard, although the musical styles were not. By 1923, however, the OIA had established a standard set of songbooks for use in the schools. H. B. Peairs, OIA chief supervisor of education, wrote, "It is believed that as the Indian young people are preparing for citizenship among young people of all other nationalities who are citizens of the United States it is better to have them use the same songs, sacred and secular."[27] These books included "*Gloria* by Shephard (sacred), *Song of the Nation, Revised*, by Johnson (Patriotic, secular and sacred) and *Golden Book of Favorite Songs, Revised and Enlarged* (Miscellaneous well known secular, sacred and patriotic)."[28] Peairs added that "these books are giving very good satisfaction and the Indian children sing the songs as enthusiastically and as well as do the children of the public schools."[29]

The schools boasted a variety of musical organizations, including string quartets, harmonica and mandolin clubs, and choirs. The Sherman school's Mandolin Club, for example, consisted of around twenty girls in 1909, with an additional fourteen beginners who were waiting in the wings. Supervisor of Indian Schools Harwood Hall reported, "Prof. Charles Wayland is a high class musician and most excellent instructor, as well as a gentleman in the full sense. He has no bad habits and his actions and influence stimulate the boys and girls to good conduct."[30] The popular Carlisle Literary Society performed music at several school-related and public events. Boarding school literary societies performed recitations as well as music and were often featured entertainment in the communities surrounding the schools. Beyond the literary societies, the schools offered up a wide milieu of musical activities within the framework deemed acceptable by administrators. Flandreau Indian School, for example, maintained a harmonica band, an orchestra heavily laden in mandolins, an operetta, and boys' and girls' glee clubs, while a select group of Chemawa Indian School students formed the Indian String Quartet, which toured the country on numerous occasions.[31] Students typically accessed art music but in some ensembles also performed the latest in popular songs from Tin Pan Alley.

Music filled the grounds and the halls of Indian boarding schools from morning until night, but perhaps the most central music organizations in the schools (and certainly the loudest) were the brass and marching bands. Beginning at 7:30 A.M. every Monday through Saturday, the grounds of Carlisle reverberated with the first band practice of the day. The bands performed for practically every formal school function as well as for extracurricular activities such as football games, parades, and dances. For the school administrators, the performance of marching and brass bands served a variety of essential functions within the curriculum. Particularly in off-reservation schools from the 1880s through the early 1920s, discipline and regimentation were among the highest educational priorities, as American Indian people at this time were often seen by the OIA as lazy and undisciplined.[32] Richard Pratt was in fact a commissioned army officer before and during his tenure at the school. An ardent believer in the idea that the "Indian problem" was not genetic but cultural, he felt that through rigid discipline and education, and by living near communities of white citizens as far away from their families' homes as possible, students could acquire the discipline, refinement, and cultural attributes necessary for them to eventually become proper American citizens.

Marching bands were regarded as a perfect vehicle for instilling such discipline, not only in the musicians themselves, but in the entire student population: while their minds were to be cultivated within the classroom, their bodies were to respond to the cadence and calls of the band.[33] For some boys and girls, the OIA goal of using the band to shape their movements worked all too well, as this former Phoenix Indian School student explains:

> At first the marching seemed so hard to learn, but once we had mastered the knack, we couldn't break the habit. Sometimes on our once-a-month visit to town, a talking machine would be blasting band music outside a store to attract customers. Then we girls would go into our act; try as hard as we could, we just couldn't get out of step. It was impossible! We'd try to take long strides to break the rhythm, but soon we would fall back into step again. How embarrassing it was![34]

In just this manner school administrators sought to use music to posture Native bodies on and off campus.

The students were regulated and regimented not only through the music of the band but also through bugle calls and whistles that commanded them, twenty-nine times per day at Carlisle, to wake, eat, work, attend class, study, and go to sleep at night.[35] The boys in the schools typically donned old military uniforms and drilled with rifles to the sounds of the band. Luther Standing Bear attended Carlisle

INDIA SCHOOL BAND AND GIRLS QUARTERS, CARLISLE, PA

In the late nineteenth and early twentieth centuries, students in federal Indian boarding schools drilled on their campus in parade fashion to the sounds of school marching bands. OIA officials believed that the students lacked regimentation and discipline in their lives and that marching bands provided the perfect antidote. Note the bandstand in the background of the image. Postcard from the author's collection.

from 1879 to 1885 and, once he learned to play, served as the school's bugler during his tenure. Standing Bear wrote,

> After I had learned to play a little, I was chosen to give all the bugle calls. I had to get up in the morning before the others and arouse everybody by blowing the morning call. Evenings at ten minutes before nine o'clock I blew again. Then all the boys would run for their rooms. At nine o'clock the second call was given, when all lights were turned out and we were supposed to be in bed. Later on I learned the mess call, and eventually I could blow all the calls of the regular army.[36]

James Garvie (Santee Sioux) was likewise perhaps the most audible and visible musician during his years on campus between 1912 and

1915—he was the assistant bandmaster and the school bugler. Sixty-five years later he recalled his experience in terms remarkably similar to those of Standing Bear: "One hour before breakfast we would go out and drill. I would stand over there and blow 'Reveille' in the morning to wake them up and blow 'Taps' at night for the lights to go out. Strictly military! Oh god, we might as well be at West Point!"[37]

Indeed, the regimentation of the schools was often etched into the former students' memories. William Collins, Jr. (Ponca), who attended boarding school in the 1930s, recalled: "The most profound aspect of my sojourn at the Pawnee Indian School is the specter of discipline. Discipline in its most rigid, non-yielding, almost brutal, shocking and galling state. Non-Indian was the order of the day."[38] A Riverside Indian school student later stated, "[Riverside] was really a military regime. . . . Every year an official from Fort Sill would come down and review our companies and our drilling maneuvers. We marched everywhere, to the dining hall, to classes; everything we did was in military fashion. We were taught to make our beds in military fashion, you know, with square corners and sheets and blankets tucked in a special way. . . . On Sundays we had an inspection . . . just like the military."[39] As David Wallace Adams notes, no element of daily life in the schools left a more pronounced impression on the students than its militaristic nature.[40] And the bands served as the principal disciplinary engine.

PUBLIC PERFORMANCE AND DEMONSTRATION

In addition to structuring the regimentation of daily life in the boarding schools, bands served an essential public relations role, influencing the non-Indian public's perception of the schools and of OIA education policy on the local and national level.[41] According to Richard Pratt, the Carlisle Band and other music groups "gave the school and all government Indian school work great publicity" when they performed beyond the school grounds.[42] Such publicity was necessary, for Pratt recognized that he must maintain the support of the public in order to keep the school running with government funds. In fact, after federal appropriations to Carlisle decreased in the 1890s,

In music class, such as this one photographed at Carlisle Indian School in 1901, students learned to sing compositions deemed appropriate by the government's "civilization" campaign. Frances Benjamin Johnston Collection, Prints and Photographs Division, Library of Congress, LC-USZ62-71318.

despite an increase in student attendance, Pratt at times relied on student labor—musical, athletic, or otherwise—to supplement school coffers.[43] Bands were the perfect vehicle through which school superintendents such as Pratt could heighten awareness and enthusiasm for their own programs and even generate a modest economic return through musical performances.

Boarding schools generated a national profile and entered the public consciousness in large part through the musical performances of the students; the highest-profile performances were those at world fairs and presidential inaugurations. The Carlisle Band, in particular, performed at many national events, including inaugural parades for William McKinley, Theodore Roosevelt, and Woodrow Wilson.[44] At the 1893 Columbian Exposition in Chicago, the Carlisle Band played all of the bandstands, and the band and choir gave a concert in Festival Hall, attracting tremendous crowds of curious onlookers. Dennison Wheelock (Oneida)—a Carlisle graduate, a friend of Pratt's, and later the bandmaster at Carlisle—organized a band of sixty-five boys from the school to make the journey, with the band and choral performances at the fair covering their expenses.[45] One year prior to the Columbian Exposition the Carlisle Band traveled to Chicago and New York to perform at Columbian quadricentennial parades. Two students marching in time with the band carried a banner through the streets that read, "Into Civilization and Citizenship."[46] Not uncommonly, just as Pratt hoped, reporters latched on to these messages, as did a New York reporter covering a national tour by the Carlisle Band in 1900. "An interesting roof of the plane of development to which the American Indian is capable of being elevated," he surmised, "is afforded by the Carlisle Indian Band. Little of the primitive influence of the monotonous beat of the tom-tom or the clash of the rattle, which are the main stays of the instrumental recitals that accompany Indian religious rites or merry-making, can be detected in the performance of the musicians."[47] For the reporter, who assumed that his readers would concur, music effortlessly cued distinctions between "primitive" and "civilized" people, which made it such an incredibly powerful instrument for Pratt as he sought to tap into and shatter the public's racial expectations.

For the 1904 Louisiana Purchase Exposition in St. Louis, the OIA assembled a band that included the most highly regarded Native student musicians in the country.[48] Chilocco school superintendent Samuel M. McCowan petitioned the superintendents of all of the other Indian schools to submit the names of their most exceptional student musicians, from which Chilocco bandmaster N. S. Nelson selected thirty-five; many of them relocated from other schools to Chilocco in order to prepare for the fair.[49] The band performed twice daily for the duration of the fair and drew large crowds at each show. According to a promotional brochure, the band members represented "in every way the educated, civilized and enlightened American Indian."[50] In criticizing Native cultural traditions, the brochure also lauded the Chilocco Indian Girls' Quartette, noting that "their singing is the more remarkable when we consider that but a few decades lie between them and savagery, with its monotone, while our civilization, musical and literary, dates back thousands of years."[51] As far as the OIA was concerned, the musical lines between civilization and savagery were as clear as the girls' harmonies that wafted through the fairgrounds.

These national events provided the OIA with a unique opportunity to advertise the product of its assimilation policy: the finely tuned, dressed, and postured Indian student. Marching with such discipline, playing "civilized" compositions through brass instruments, the bands offered a glimpse of assimilation at its most mechanical and perfect. Keeping a military stride, celebrating a national, American event, wearing military uniforms, the band spoke volumes for Pratt and other OIA educational leaders in the late nineteenth and early twentieth centuries. At times, however, it became unclear whether these public performances more greatly served the students, the audience, or the government employees. If the overriding policy of assimilation logically mandated the eventual downsizing and dismantling of the OIA, employees in its ballooning bureaucracy during the early twentieth century were not lining up to suggest that their posts be the first to become obsolete. For school officials, parading school bands before the public demonstrated the nobility of their purpose and the reason for the continuing support of politicians and taxpayers alike.

Bands performed public relations work for the boarding schools and the OIA in both national and local events. While national events drew the largest onlookers and the most publicity, equally important to the OIA was the need to edify local communities that the Native students who lived nearby were safely contained, free of any of the dangerous activities that the non-Indian public associated with American Indians, and that the schools were worthy of their support and appreciation. The bands again served the school officials as the primary instrument in this endeavor, performing at a variety of local functions. In 1908 and 1909, for example, the Sherman Institute band performed twice during the presidential campaign, for the Riverside Driving Park Association, for a variety of charitable associations, and to "serenade" Senator Frank P. Flint.[52] In 1914 the Sherman band led the parade in Riverside before an exhibition baseball game between Chicago and Los Angeles.[53] Ralph Stanion, superintendent of the

Theodore Roosevelt Indian School in Fort Apache, Arizona, reported
to the OIA commissioner that the performance of the school band in
several local cities "attracted much in the way of sympathy and
understanding to the cause of Indian education."[54] Similar to the
presentation of the Chilocco girls' quartette at the 1904 fair, female
students were introduced to nearby communities through music as
well. According to the 1931 annual report of the Bismarck Indian
School, "During the last few years the Bismarck girls have acquired
considerable reputation by their proficiency and artistic ability in
vocal music. They are popular and in considerable demand among
the communities nearby for entertainment purposes."[55]

Some boarding school bands held regular public performances on
Sundays in parks and other venues. The bands were widely heralded
in newspaper articles for their performances as well as their drawing
power for townspeople who were curious to see the effects of the
schools and the novelty of Native musicianship. In 1930 the Phoenix
Indian School newspaper, for example, reported that one such performance featured "a cornet solo by Stanley Chiago who played
Rollinson's 'Columbia Polka,'" and the trombonists who played the
ragtime hit "Lassus Trombone," by James Henry Fillmore.[56] In January 1913 the Sherman Institute band played a Sunday concert that
drew fifteen hundred attendees.[57] At times the drawing power of
Indian school bands persuaded local communities to expose the
bands nationally in order to advertise their towns to distant tourists;
for example, the Phoenix Board of Trade in 1914 asked the Phoenix
Indian School band to tour the East during the summer to promote
tourism for Arizona and the Southwest.[58]

Local reporters often fixated on the elements of the performances
that affirmed both the "accomplishments" of the schools and their
assumption of cultural superiority. "Bishop was captured by the Indians," reported the *Owens Valley Herald*, with regard to a performance by
the Bishop Indian School students at the Bishop Opera House in 1914.[59]
"The battle was not accompanied by the war songs of the past," the
Herald advised, "but was won by the arts of peace, as exemplified by
Principal George Simeral."[60] The *Herald* writer considered the military
marches and drills by thirty-two boys and girls as the most interesting
feature of the evening and reported that the students' performance

Indian school bands, like the Fort Lewis Indian School Band in this 1896 photo-graph, often performed within local functions such as parades. Such public events enabled school administrators to use student musical performance to demonstrate the success of the "civilization" campaign, while students often simply appreciated the opportunity to leave the school grounds. The students pictured above formed part of the Sunflower Carnival parade in Colorado Springs. A fraternal organization, perhaps the local Improved Order of Redmen, is lined up behind them. Denver Public Library, Western History Collection, Horace Swartley Poley, photographer, P-2174.

along those lines was the "result of careful training and discipline."[61] "The Indian School band," according to the *Herald*, "played a number of pieces and played them well, in time and harmony. There was [also] a duet by two dusky maidens Kate and Lena Turner."[62] Regarding the same performance, the *Inyo County Register* noted, "We don't appreci-ate the Indians as we should; they are entitled to our best sympathy and cooperation in efforts for their upbuilding."[63] Although the *Regis-ter* criticized the "vocal ability" of the Paiute children, the paper reas-sured its readership that "doubtless it will come in time, as it has with the Hawaiians and other peoples who have had longer contact with white influences."[64] The reporter was impressed that "each year sees a higher standard more generally recognized; more of agreement with white codes of right and wrong and of mortality [*sic*]."⁶⁵ Reporters often concurred with the OIA's valuations of whiteness and Indianness, and of civilization and primitivism, which music generated in their minds.

Similarly, school superintendents sought to shape the meaning of these musical performances through the solicitation and advertisement of public performances by the band. The Sherman Institute band, for example, entertained and competed at the 1917 California State Fair. The band members were originally sent, according to the Sherman superintendent, to introduce the public to the success of the school by demonstrating "that our Indian boys and girls are worthy, in every way, [of] a more appreciative consideration tha[n] has been accorded them by the white citizenship of this state."⁶⁶ The fair organizers then reiterated in fair literature the superintendent's hopes that the exhibition of the band would

> tangibly demonstrate what the Government is accomplishing with the Indian—through the various Indian Agencies and Schools in California as to the end, that, ultimately all prejudice against him be dissipated and he be allowed to take his place as a law-abiding, self-respecting and self-supporting citizen of the State. . . . As the Indians will, sooner or later, be absorbed into the citizenship of the State their progress as tillers of the soil and industrial workers, and their fitness in trades and domestic arts, should be matters of interest and importance to the people of California. It is expected these exhibits will prove that the Indians contribute a commendable share toward the prosperity of our State, and that owing to the work of the Government in their behalf they are fast assuming a standing as workers whose results are not to be belittled through competition with similar results of the whites.⁶⁷

Superintendent Miller of the Greenville, California, Indian school believed that the inclusion of the Sherman band was essential to forwarding the mission of the Indian schools before the public. The band, he wrote, would "aid very materially to attract attention to the work of the Riverside Indian school as a Government institution for Indians and will liven up the exhibit in a way that can not be accomplished in any other manner." He added, "There is no question about the exhibit's success if we have a desirable musical organization attached to it."⁶⁸ The

Promotional photos such as this one taken at Carlisle Indian School, portrayed Indian students poised to play Euro-American-derived instruments as evidence of the perceived success of the government's assimilation campaign and, more specifically, of the schools. Cumberland County Historical Society, Carlisle, Pennsylvania.

band members probably felt "livened up" by the experience as well: they had their expenses paid and earned a daily wage of one dollar for spending money, performed twice daily, at 1 P.M. and 7 P.M., slept in tents on the fairgrounds, formed a "conspicuous" part of the downtown parade, and won first place in the class B band contest.[69]

RACISM AND UNION RESISTANCE

Although school officials tried to establish control over the meaning of public musical performance for both the students (in terms of the perceived civilizing effects of Euro-American music) and the audience (in terms of its demonstration of the success of OIA policies), their control was challenged in myriad ways. Despite the OIA objective that the public performances generate for American Indians "a more appreciative consideration tha[n] has been accorded them by the white citizenship," nevertheless white citizens at times demonstrated a reluctance to embrace or even accept the musicians. Some of the Indian bands were actually too good: the success of the school bands in securing local community performances often created jealousy and contempt among non-Indian bands rather than bolstering their support of federal policies. In a letter to his father, a Carlisle student voiced frustration at the attitude of some of the local bands:

> There was an entertainment held at the opera house last night and they wanted our band to play for them, so we went to town and played for them. There were two bands besides our band. One band was going to play one piece but we played the piece before they got ready so after they heard us play, they got vexed at our band and didn't play any. The other band played two times, then after they got through we played so that band got mad at our band and they called us the *skin* band, but we played until the band went home, then we came home too. Our band can play better than those white boys in the town.[70]

Bands were highly competitive in this era, as they provided some of the most popular public entertainment of the time. The stakes were high, and non-Indian musicians often reacted in negative ways to the popularity and prowess of the Indian school bands.

The boarding school students faced resistance from not only individual non-Indian musicians but also from musician associations. The Sherman, Haskell, Phoenix, and Salem Indian school bands were so successful in their communities that the OIA received a number of complaints from American Federation of Musicians (AFM) local chapters that believed their union members were unfairly losing jobs to these "inmates" and "wards" of the government.[71] In 1908, AFM president Owen Miller, distressed by the success of the Salem Indian School band, wrote to the OIA: "The American Federation of Musicians has not the slightest objection to these Indians being educated in all the arts. If any understand, we certainly do, the great humanizing and civilizing influence of music, therefore the Indians should be given an opportunity of the benefits of this method of civilization."[72] Nevertheless, the AFM staunchly protested practically any paid community event in which the Indian school bands performed. Joseph Weber, president of the AFM in 1926, wrote Secretary of the Interior Hubert Work, condemning the Haskell band: "On behalf of the musicians of the United States, I beg to protest against the activities of H. B. [Peairs], Superintendent of the Haskell Institute of Lawrence, Kansas. Mr. [Peairs] places a band composed of Indian boys in direct competition with musicians. . . . Such activities by the inmates of an Institute are absolutely contrary to the principles why the Institution is maintained [and] are injurious to civilian musicians, therefore [we] turn to you for redress."[73] In 1913 the AFM protested the performance of the Sherman Institute band at a rodeo in Los Angeles.[74] In most cases the OIA investigated the complaints but allowed the schools to use their own judgment for band performances, typically believing that public performance was beneficial to both the musicians and the schools.[75]

Sometimes band leaders, working with both Native and non-Native musicians, exhibited intense concern in their territorial squabbles. For example, a dispute in Phoenix between several bands and individuals reveals the competitive nature of local bands in the early 1900s, and the complicated politics that arose from a situation wherein non-Indian bands tended to distinguish the Indian school bands by what they considered unfair government subsidies rather than their talent. In May of 1913 the Musician's Mutual Protective Association, AFM Local 586 of Phoenix, petitioned the government to investigate and put a halt to the attempts by the Phoenix Indian School band to "defeat organized labor." J. M. Shott, manager of the Pioneer Band of Phoenix and representative of the local union, argued that the school band was stealing jobs from non-Indian musicians:

They are able to play practically for nothing or a small compensation for the reason that the Government is supporting them in their undertaking for the purpose of defeating Organized Labor and our Local Musicians Union #586. . . . The latest system that they have ina[u]gurated to defeat Organized Labor is to have Mr. Peter Vanne the leader of the Indian School

Band get in behind some Scab Band as leader and He draws pay for this
as well as leader, Then he will have as many of the Indian School Band as
is needed to fill in and make up the Band. This is for the express purpose
of defeating . . . Organized Labor and the best interest of our Local band
and the purpose that it was organized for thereby defeating us out of our
daily earnings which belong to us.[76]

Peter Vanne was, in fact, leading another band at the time, the
Industrial Liberty Band. Composed of "young Mexican boys and
returned students of the Indian School," the band seemed to Indian
Affairs commissioner Cato Sells a "splendid opportunity of helping
these returned students to whom the school owes an obligation." Yet,
in response to Shott's complaint, school superintendent Goodman
forbade Vanne from participating further.[77] Vanne and his students,
however, were not satisfied with this agreement and one month later
proposed that he, along with several other students of the school, both
current and former, enroll in the Arizona National Guard for the
express purpose of serving in the First Arizona Infantry Band.
Because the request could be justified as "post-graduate" music education for the students, the OIA agreed to it, after several months of
correspondence and the encouragement of a member of the House of
Representatives.[78]

Less than a year later, however, the leader of the First Arizona
Infantry Band made a formal complaint to the adjutant general of Arizona about the Phoenix Indian School band, even though the infantry
band had recruited several members from it. Adjutant General Harris of the State National Guard of Arizona filed a complaint to Secretary of the Interior Lane, who, familiar with the complaints from the
previous year, addressed the issue with the OIA and Phoenix Indian
School. Harris argued that the school band was robbing the infantry
band of jobs and income: "This protest has nothing whatever to do
with the fact that the Band is an Indian Band, but the same protest
would be made should the students of any institution, who are educated at the expense of the Government, be allowed, as an organization, to compete with men who derive their living from their
occupation."[79] Harris accused the band of playing ballpark engagements and other public events with only expenses covered in remu-

neration, thus undercutting the infantry band by stealing its potential opportunities to perform.

After an investigation and the submission of reports by the disciplinarian and superintendent of the school, the OIA determined that the First Arizona Infantry Band had no cause for complaint. The twenty-six members of the school band played six free engagements that year: during fair week; for "Dr. Hughes anti-saloon celebration"; for a church benefit; for a Salvation Army benefit (that did not involve a giveaway dance); and at two baseball games (Tucson versus Phoenix and Albuquerque versus Phoenix). The band also played three paid engagements (payment was a nominal fee for expenses that totaled sixty-eight dollars): the Illinois picnic, the Mesa Mayday celebration, and the opening for a Mesa skating rink. At the time there were three organized bands in the Phoenix area: the First Regiment Band (i.e., the First Arizona Infantry Band), the Pioneer Band, and the Phoenix Indian School band.[80] The scale for band musicians in the Phoenix area was three dollars per day, but despite Harris's statement to the contrary, neither the Pioneer Band nor the First Infantry Band was composed of musicians who depended on the bands for their livelihood—both bands typically played concerts only on Sunday, a day on which the Phoenix Indian School band in those years never played.

Oddly, the disciplinarian of the school, Edgar Grinstead, reported that the Pioneer Band had "always been on friendly terms" with the Phoenix school band and that "manager Mr. J. M. Shott says they have never regarded the Indian School Band as competing with them."[81] Recall that Shott had only recently petitioned the OIA to prohibit the school band from competing with his. On the other hand, reported Grinstead, the First Regiment Band had no room for complaint, because the U.S. government supplied its instruments. Three members of the thirty-piece band were current Phoenix school students, and eight others were former Indian school students, seven at Phoenix and one elsewhere. The leading representative of the band, who apparently made the most trouble for the Indian school and Pioneer bands, was Francis Redewill, the leader of the First Regiment Band and the same man who had petitioned the school the previous year to allow some of the student musicians to enroll in the state National Guard in order to play in his band.[82]

After the investigation determined that none of the bands mentioned consisted of musicians making their living at music, and with the conviction that public performances did nothing but aid the goals of the school, Assistant Commissioner of Indian Affairs E. B. Merritt defended the school band and encouraged the superintendent to continue the public performances. Throughout the complaints from local bands and unions, the OIA consistently defended the school bands because they tangibly demonstrated for the non-Indian public the supposed success of the assimilation policy. The complaints also reveal that former boarding school students were filling the ranks of all of the local bands alongside whites and Mexican Americans and that, it seemed, they were certainly doing so by choice.

STUDENT DANCES

In addition to the bands' high profile off the school grounds, the musical experiences of students on campus were vast and included social dances on Saturday nights. The type of dancing permitted at most boarding schools was restricted, with teachers carefully surveying the bodies on the dance floor. Nevertheless, many former students had fond memories of the dances, and in many schools the Saturday night dances were one of the boys' and girls' favorite activities. According to a description from the Sherman Institute in 1909, "Every second Saturday evening a general dance party is given in the student dining hall. The school orchestra furnishes the music. These parties are much enjoyed by the pupils. Indeed they conduct them as young people of the white race do and dance all the popular round dances. The employe[e]s join with the pupils and a general good, healthy time is had."[83] Speaking of her father's experience at Carlisle, Luana Mangold said,

> Dad had a lot of girl friends. And we often wondered how in the world, you know, he had time to have all his girl friends when he was doing all those other things he said he was doing. But they would have socials, and they would have dances. As a matter of fact, Mr. [James] Garvie, who used to always play in the band, he says, "it was really hard, we didn't have as

many socials as the others did because I always had to play in the band."
Every once in a while they would have one for the band to socialize. And
they did, they got to, you know, socialize a little bit that way.[84]

While the OIA sought to suppress tribally derived dances on reservations, most schools actively instructed students in dances such as the
waltz and the fox-trot, and dancing became a regular, eagerly anticipated part of many students' lives. Some schools instructed students
in an entire Victorian culture of dancing. With boys dressed in uniforms and girls in white dresses, a teacher at the Fort Mojave school
recalled that "a boy bowed before a girl when requesting a dance, conducted her to her seat afterward and thanked her."[85] In this way the
students were expected to learn every element of the dances taught in
school, including the specific comportments that accompanied them.

These dances could serve as pivotal social moments for boys and
girls. Jim Whitewolf (Kiowa Apache) recalled his hopes at one dance
for a Comanche girl to select him for the first "promenade":

We had hair oil on our hair, and we had flowers in our buttonholes, hand-
kerchiefs in our pockets, and our neckties all tied. All of us boys marched
in twos. We stood real straight and had our coats buttoned up. There were
about ten of us, and we were all seated on a bench in a row. We were facing a big crowd of all the students there. I noticed that there was a chalk
line drawn around the floor along the edges where we were all seated.
Pretty soon, as we were sitting, all the girls came in dressed in white, with
red flowers on. They were sure pretty. My heart was just shaking. I didn't
know which was the girl who had invited me. The girls knew who they
invited, and they each sat down by the boy they invited. A girl came over
and sat down by me. I just sat there real straight. It was the Comanche girl
who had written me that note before.[86]

According to David Wallace Adams, Whitewolf and the girl later won
the competition, "which consisted of judging which couple was best
able to promenade around the room keeping time to the music." As
Whitewolf recalled, "I was about fifteen years old at this time. It was
the first time I ever had a date with a girl and talked with her like
that."[87]

Although the dances proved quite popular with the students and allowed the boys and girls to interact on a much more personal level than their rigid, disciplined activities typically permitted, the school dances often came under protest from Native and non-Indian people alike. The OIA did not have a strict policy on sponsoring such dances; rather, it allowed each school superintendent to determine the extent to which his students could participate in them. Proponents of the waltzes and round dances, in which boys and girls danced hand in hand, believed that the dances socialized the students to the American norms of acceptable adolescent male and female interaction. Some students, however, complained that the dance policy in the schools was confusing and awkward, if not altogether unpleasant. Riverside boarding school student Juanita Yeahquo preferred the dances of her own people and complained that she did not enjoy being forced to "dance all those white man's dances—like the boogie woogie."[88]

A number of school officials shared Yeahquo's antipathy regarding the boogie-woogie, although they were not agreeable to Native-derived dances either. Some school superintendents, such as Jesse House of the Rapid City Indian School in South Dakota, banned dancing altogether.[89] Charles Davis, the superintendent of the San Juan School in Shiprock, New Mexico, concurred and in 1910 listed for the commissioner of Indian Affairs four reasons why he thought dancing of any sort should be prohibited. First, he argued that because some of the church organizations sponsoring mission work on the reservations forbade dancing among their communicants, when pupils belonging to those churches danced in the schools, they disobeyed the rules of the church and the wills of their parents. Second, he wrote, "The principal form of amusement of white communities near Indian reservations is dancing, and in many localities much drinking and other forms of vice are practiced at these dances. . . . In short the social tendencies of the dances on or near the Indian reservations is for evil instead of good."[90] In addition, Davis associated dancing with promiscuity or the threat of rape and suggested that "several girls returning from boarding schools . . . have met with ruin through going to these dances near their homes."[91] Third, he pointed out that the round dances that were practiced and sometimes required in the schools involved contact between boys and girls. Such contact, he argued, "requires the Indian youths to violate social rules obtaining among their people from time immemorial. . . . This form of dance is usually quite obnoxious to the parents, and they dislike to see thier [sic] children thus violating their home rules and teachings."[92] Finally, Davis argued that permitting the "white man's dance" in the schools would hinder the ability of the department to curtail "Indian dance" on the reservations: "The *real* Indian contrasts the Indian dance and the white man's dance, and in his own mind comes to the conclusion the white man's dance is quite as prone to evil as that of the Indians. . . . This being the case, the Superintendent of a reservation who permits or requires dancing in his school is greatly handicapped in attempts to control the evils of the Indian dance."[93] He was also deeply troubled that returning students seemed to organize these "white man's dances" on reservations: "It would be far better for the Indian youths returning to their homes if they were trained in other forms of social amusements that they may entertain their friends without the necessity of calling a dance. It is now frequently found that dances are about the only forms of social amusements engaged in by young people on the reservations."[94]

Dance of any form was charged with racial and cultural meaning. Some school superintendents clearly regulated "white man's dances" as much as "Indian dances." The lines became blurred, however, as students returning to reservations introduced into their communities the dances they had learned in the schools. They did so neither with the approval of the more conservative superintendents, nor necessarily because they identified more strongly with Euro-American derived music traditions than those that were tribally derived. Most important was that the dances became what the students made of them. Assimilative directives and in-fighting among OIA officials could not contain the significance that the students attributed to them. It was clear that these dances were enjoyed by many of the students; they perhaps represented one of the few aspects of boarding school life that students appreciated. Margaret Jacobs notes that among the former students who took menial jobs in the San Francisco Bay area between 1920 and 1940, socializing in the city's dance halls proved one of their favorite pastimes.[95] Superintendent Davis's concerns reveal not only the degree of seriousness with which OIA officials regarded the practice of music (he deemed the Virginia reel or listening to the phonograph as more acceptable practices) but also the degree to which Native peoples took these dances seriously as well.

STUDENT INTEREST

Although the school officials orchestrated the bands, dances, and music clubs in order to contribute to the citizenship training of their students and to the public relations campaign of the OIA, the students sought their own benefits from the musical instruction. Gathering student perspectives on their boarding school experiences from this period is a daunting challenge; at the same time, their perspectives are the most critical component to assessing the outcome of the boarding school experience. As Lomawaima and McCarty write. "[This] most important perspective for the story . . . can be heartbreakingly ephemeral. Gaps and fissures fragment our knowledge of Native experiences over the last century."[96] In searching for student perspectives on musical education, I have located passages in autobiographies, letters, interviews, and oral histories, and federal records can also offer some clues, even if mediated by non-Indian authors. Yet as Lomawaima and McCarty assert, these offer only small, fleeting inroads into understanding those experiences, and thus analysis of the documentary materials requires care. And in examining this evidence, it is important to remain aware of the silences as well—although we know that Juanita Yeahquo did not approve of the "white dances" taught in the schools, voices of blatant disapproval rarely float so easily to the surface of the archives.

What is clear is that many students thoroughly enjoyed their musical experience at the schools. James Garvie was given his first bugle at the Haskell Indian school when he was seven years old, and he demonstrated a passion for American band and popular music for the rest of his life.[97] However, his musical experiences in Carlisle from 1912 to 1915 also reflect a sense of pragmatism in avoiding other aspects of life at Carlisle altogether. "By being a Sergeant Bugler, I got out of a lot of things I didn't like," he said with a chuckle years later.

"That's right," he continued, "I refused the promotion when I was a senior. I was getting out of things I didn't like so I might as well stay as Sergeant."[98] He was most eager to get out of the "strenuous training" required in the gym: "By being a bugler, I got out of that. I didn't tell them why I refused it—the promotion—but that's why I did it. I wanted to get out of things I didn't like."[99] According to Robert Trennert's study of the Phoenix Indian School, band members occupied prestigious positions on campus and enjoyed many "fringe benefits."[100] One of the benefits for students with exceptional musical ability was to be relieved of typically required chores by the bandmaster in order to practice.[101] In addition, students found the communal experience of playing and socializing with bandmates an antidote to the monotony and isolation often found within the regimentation of the schools.[102]

Garvie, like other exceptional musicians at the schools, tailored his coursework to suit his own interests, and training in the shops to prepare for farming or for the low-wage, minimum-skill jobs that the OIA envisioned for future Indian citizens was not among those interests. His aspirations took him beyond the limited confines of the OIA's imagination:

> I didn't bother with any shops because I wanted to devote my time to music. . . . So I specialized in music, and it paid off. In the fall of the year, that is for the coming year, the band votes on one member, whoever it is, they vote on him. He becomes the student director. In case of emergencies, supposing Mr. Stauffer gets sick, well, then I take his place temporarily. Now the good that that does is that it keeps you under supervision how to direct the band. Now when you get out in a civilian band you have a better idea what you are doing. That's what it did for me. That's how I got into it professionally from there.[103]

Garvie's recollections of band life in a 1980 interview were mostly positive. Although he missed most of the Saturday outings in the town of Carlisle due to band obligations and had to perform rather than dance at most Saturday evening socials, he fondly recalled taking the train for band trips such as those for football games.[104] The band members, he said, "got a lot of shoe boxes from the shoe factory.

Shoe boxes to put lunch in for us to eat because we didn't have time
to eat over there, so each one of us got a box of lunch when we got on
[the train]. It was up to you to eat it whenever you wanted it."[105] There
was strong camaraderie between the band members, he recalled, and
they even cared for a dog as their mascot, a rat terrier that looked "like
that dog's picture on the Victor records."[106] The boys adopted it from
a man who brought the dog along with him when he delivered food
to the school from a local bakery.[107]

Other students clearly enjoyed their musical training in the schools
as well. Luther Standing Bear reveled in his musical instruction at the
school and fondly recalled the day he picked up his first horn, a B-flat
cornet.[108] He was also proud to lead the band when the bandmaster
was unavailable. Recalling his trip with the band to New York City in
1883, he wrote,

> Captain Pratt came to me and asked me if I thought I could lead the band.
> Then we discovered that we were to play at the opening of the Brooklyn
> Bridge, and were to march across it. . . . We were instructed to keep play-
> ing all the way across the bridge. When the parade started I gave the sig-
> nal, and we struck up and kept playing all the way across the great
> structure. So the Carlisle Indian band of brass instruments was the first
> *real American band* to cross the Brooklyn Bridge, and I am proud to say that
> I was their leader.[109]

Some students took pleasure in the extensive travel that the bands
were often permitted. The Phoenix Indian School band in 1904 took
an eleven-week tour of California and reservations in the western
states.[110] Band members often traveled during the school year as well
as the summer, providing them with a bit of a vacation from the
school routines and a chance to experience life in other parts of the
country. These opportunities fed the passion that many of the boys
expressed for the school bands. A 1910 Sherman graduate, Victor Sakiestewa (Hopi), petitioned the school's superintendent in 1913 to allow
him to return to the school so that he could join the band for its scheduled 1915 performance at the world's fair in San Francisco.[111] Brenda
Child recounts a letter written in 1913 by George White Bull, a fifth-
grader from Porcupine, South Dakota. Because he felt that his educa-

Luther Standing Bear was a prominently featured cornet player and bugler at Carlisle who led the band across the Brooklyn Bridge during its opening ceremonies in 1883. Cumberland County Historical Society, Carlisle, Pennsylvania.

tion at the Oglala boarding school was wanting, he asked to be enrolled in the Flandreau school. He added that "the very first thing I want to do when I get over there is to join the band."[112] Haskell student and later schoolteacher Esther Horne (Shoshone) reflected fondly on her music teacher: "Another teacher who broadened my horizons for a lifetime was Miss Stella Robbins. She . . . gave me an appreciation not only of great music but of the background of the great composers."[113]

Music performances could be enjoyable for the students, particularly when not forced to march around the parade grounds and especially when they found creative ways to make the performances their own. In the early days of the Carlisle band, for example, Amos High Wolf was asked to deliver a solo on the bass horn during a performance for the student body. As recounted in the Carlisle paper of what *not* to do,

At the appointed time, Amos walked up to the stage with the dignity and grace of an artist, and adjusting his mouth-piece without dropping his horn, he began playing "Sweet bye and bye." He began rather firmer than sweet, but continued to the end of the strain without any serious catastrophe, except that toward the finish, while he was taking his usual breath, it suddenly dawned on him he was making a distinguished success, and he became unable to go on [to] the second strain, and to get out of it he gave a grand "War Whoop." This was taken up by the other pupils and the noise they produced with their Indian yells and whoops will find few duplications in American history.[114]

High Wolf and his comrades placed their own stamp on the performance, breaking the boundaries of comportment that they were expected to maintain. Whereas Pratt's newspaper editor considered the "War Whoop" a blemish on an otherwise noble performance, High Wolf certainly counted on getting a rise from the student body, which delivered with glee.

Indeed, student musicians did not always behave complacently, and because the bands had such high visibility, any resistance to the demands of their superintendents spilled out quickly into the local newspapers. On one occasion such resistance spawned an investigation by the Office of Indian Affairs into allegations circulating in the local newspapers that Carlisle housed a "dungeon" for rebellious children. James Riley Wheelock (Oneida), a Carlisle graduate and the brother of the former Carlisle bandmaster Dennison Wheelock, desired to procure temporarily the service of Carlisle students for his professional band during the summer of 1909. He believed this training would fit into the parameters of Carlisle's outing program, which typically placed Carlisle boys and girls in the homes or work environments of non-Indians to provide them with life experience among successful white people. For unknown reasons, but perhaps because he planned to use the band to serve his own public relations campaign that summer, Superintendent Friedman refused to allow any of the band members to participate in the outing program. Of the more than nine hundred students enrolled in the 1908–1909 school year, only two hundred remained on campus during the summer.[115] Seeking life experience and perhaps a bit of adventure outside the confines of the campus, two of the boys from the band attempted, against Friedman's wishes, to join Wheelock's band and had their trunks taken to the train depot. Friedman discovered the plan and had the trunks returned to the Carlisle barracks. The boys were locked in the guardhouse as punishment for their actions. The rest of the band was so resentful of what Friedman had done that they expressed their grievance by refusing to perform during that evening's "salute of the flag," a daily ritual at Carlisle.[116] Wheelock was infuriated by Friedman's actions and charged in the newspapers that the superintendent was jealous of his band's success, was the cause of disciplinary problems in the school, and held students illegally in a "dungeon" (the guardhouse). Friedman responded that he had "refused permission to students to enter his organization to play, simply for the reason that invariably in the past they have indulged in the kind of dissipation and debauchery during the summer which taints and brings about an unhealthy condition in the fall when they return to the school."[117] Wheelock dismissed these allegations by stating that the only Carlisle students he had ever before included in his four-year-old band were graduates, and not enrolled students.[118] The story made local headlines and thoroughly embarrassed both Carlisle and the OIA. After several weeks and an OIA investigation, the government supported Friedman and the matter was dropped. The students who forged resistance through the flag controversy, however, did not do so because they did not wish to play. On the contrary, they rebelled because of their intense desire to perform beyond the campus and the city of Carlisle, and certainly beyond the gaze of Friedman himself.

Music education figured prominently in the lives of many of the students after they left, and though it is impossible to ascertain a broad impact of this education among the students from this period, some letters, autobiographies, and interviews, including a series conducted in the homes of former Chilocco students in 1934, provide an interesting cross section of responses. Some students not only excelled in the musical curriculum but also, as we have seen, returned to Indian schools to carry on the instruction. Chilocco ex-student Francis Chapman (Cherokee) is such an example. Chapman would have graduated in 1904 from Chilocco, but after his band and his classmates were exhibited in the 1904 St. Louis Exposition, he was unable to return to

James Riley Wheelock (Oneida), brother of famed Carlisle bandmaster Dennison Wheelock, took his own band on tours throughout the country. James Wheelock created a controversy in Carlisle, Pennsylvania, when he was denied the opportunity to take some students on the road with him during their summer break. Two students who attempted to join him anyway were caught by school employees and locked up in the Carlisle Indian School guardhouse. Postcard from the author's collection.

Chilocco to finish his requirements.[119] However, by 1934 he was the director of the Chilocco band.[120] Other students surveyed also seemed to retain an interest in the music they were introduced to in the schools. A discussion with Claude Hogg, who made the home visits to Chilocco ex-students, revealed that Oscar Pratt (Arapaho) had an affinity for "good, semi-classical music."[121] It is not clear, of course, whether Pratt turned the radio of his Geary, Oklahoma, home to a semiclassical station every morning or whether he did so only when an Indian bureau official was snooping around. James Ussrey (Cherokee), of the class of 1929, found in his musical education a much more viable and interesting career path than that of his vocational training; after leaving Chilocco, he pursued a profession in band music through the Northeastern Teachers College in Tahlequah, Oklahoma. However, when asked if he ever used his vocational instruction, he said jokingly, "I certainly do. I couldn't have a car at all, if I didn't know how to repair it myself. It is an old rattle trap, but it goes."[122]

Instruction of any sort in the boarding schools at this time was heavily defined by gender. By the early twentieth century, boys were instructed almost exclusively in rurally oriented, small-scale crafts-manship such as harness making, blacksmithing, printing, masonry, carpentry, and other such trades. In contrast, girls were instructed in the "domestic arts" of housekeeping, laundry, and cooking.[123] While not necessarily unique to Indian schools, this type of training also con-tributed to a larger purpose: to teach Native boys and girls to become docile, subordinate citizens who knew their "place" in the social order and recognized that, through allotment, their relationship with the land and their role in the modern world were severely curtailed.[124] The music instruction in the schools was likewise constrained by con-siderations of what was deemed culturally appropriate for male and female students. Only young men participated in the brass bands, which were associated with the more dangerous, public world out-side the home, while girls took piano, guitar, and mandolin lessons—proper instruments for the parlor. Important exceptions existed in some schools: some instruction permitted both boys and girls to par-ticipate—women occasionally participated in orchestras, and both boys and girls took vocal lessons and sung in the choirs and glee clubs. In 1907 the Sherman Institute's all-female, thirty-seven-member mandolin club performed for the National Education Asso-ciation convention in Los Angeles.[125] For the most part, however, the girls had far fewer opportunities to leave the school grounds than the boys in the band, and the OIA strove to segregate musical instruction between the sexes.

Many of the girls had other plans. Young women were trained in parlor instruments, but that did not mean that the instruments would keep them in the home or, for that matter, on the school grounds. Many young women thoroughly enjoyed their piano lessons, which certainly would have been preferable to toiling away in the school laundries, yet it is also clear that by seeking additional musical train-ing beyond the capacity of the school's instruction, they intended to continue to play after they left. In 1908, Carlisle student Elizabeth Penny sought such additional training, and the commissioner of

Indian Affairs agreed to keep her on the Carlisle rolls if arrangements were made with Wilson College to further her training. Penny told the superintendent that she desired to "thoroughly equip herself to go back to her people and assist them by furnishing music for their devotional work."[126] In this way, it is perhaps possible that she saw herself as using music to provide what she considered an important role for her people, a role that would also place her in fact out of the home and presumably in a publicly recognized position within her church. Nearly thirty students at Flandreau in 1923 sought additional, private lessons from teachers outside the school because the school's teacher was already completely booked. It is unclear whether the lessons were provided on school grounds or off, but certainly they enabled the students to gain greater control over their weekly routines. More than thirty girls who were enrolled in the Bismarck Indian school in 1933 paid two local piano teachers for additional lessons with their own money. Ten Bismarck girls paid for orchestra lessons as well, and around twenty-five paid for dancing lessons.[127] Parents supported their children's musical ambitions too; a number of Flandreau parents wrote Superintendent House, expressing their willingness to pay for additional musical instruction of their daughters.[128]

Looking beyond the limited employment opportunities that domestic training was to provide them, some young women successfully turned their musical instruction into a trade. Chilocco ex-student Alice Frazier Braves (Santee Sioux) learned to play piano and eventually became a piano teacher in Shawnee, Oklahoma.[129] Ruby Falleaf Jeunesse (Delaware) graduated from Chilocco in 1928 and by 1934 had worked for eight years as a music teacher.[130] Mary Ellison (Choctaw-Chilocco class of 1930) became the clerk of the Southern Navajo Agency but supplemented her work by playing in the orchestra and for student dances.[131] After separating from her husband, 1920 Chilocco graduate Ethleen Pappan (Pawnee-Winnebago) sang over the radio to help support herself and her son.[132] Although fewer Native women pursued and succeeded in professional musical careers than men, Dora Armstrong (Eagle Harbor–Alaska) brought her training beyond Chilocco to the halls of New York City, where she had an opportunity to sing in light opera and continue her study.[133] Such opportunities for women were opened through their music instruction in the schools, often beyond the expectations of their teachers.

Church singing allowed many Chilocco graduates, both male and female, to cultivate their vocal instruction, and they were often very proud of their musical abilities. According to Clyde Ellis, "a rich and vibrant hymn tradition was inaugurated at the Rainy Mountain Mission in the 1890s, and Kiowa men and women—many of them boarding school graduates—took active roles as lay readers, deacons, and ordained ministers."[134] Kenneth Mills (Shawnee), a Chilocco graduate of 1917, sang in the same Arkansas City, Kansas, Presbyterian church choir as Minnie McKenzie (Cherokee), who had graduated just two years later. "In spite of her housekeeping duties, her sewing, etc.," wrote interviewer Hogg, McKenzie also found time to "engage in Choir work at the Presbyterian Church, the 'C' Club activities" and was "a very proficient golfer."[135] Palmer Byrd (Chickasaw) of St. Louis told Hogg that he and his wife were "both members at the Lafayette Park Baptist Church" and added: "This choir recently won in a contest over fourteen other church choirs. We sang on Christmas over KMOX, St. Louis. I am bass soloist in the choir and have for the past four years been the president of it."[136] Singing in church choirs was practically the only constant in the life of one Kaw Chilocco graduate:

Francis has a wonderful baritone voice, and everyone expected great things of him when he should leave school. He went to Southwestern College of Fine Arts, at Winfield. He sang in the Methodist Choir in Winfield, and was doing really well. However, he met a girl, a white girl, and married hastily. He gave up school, and they moved to Arkansas City where he sang in the Presbyterian Choir, and did such work on spare time as he could get to do. Apparently they were not as congenial as they thought, for they have separated. He is now working on the E.C.W. at Chilocco, still singing in the Presbyterian Choir on Sundays.[137]

Many former Chilocco students took deep pride in their church singing, and those who interviewed with Hogg made sure to indicate that they were fully using the training they learned at the school.

Former students also performed in local community bands. Van Horn Flying Man (Cheyenne) of Colony, Oklahoma, graduated from

Chilocco in 1908: "He really used the musical training more than any that he received here, for he had developed bands and orchestras that had won much praise, of which he was very proud. This statement was born[e] out by some more men who were sitting about on the porch where we were talking."[138] Kenneth Mills, who performed with Minnie McKenzie in the Arkansas City, Kansas, Presbyterian church, also played the bass horn in the municipal band.[139] Louis Brueninger (Cherokee) simply told Hogg that "the musical training he received here has been of the greatest advantage to him since leaving school."[140] And class of 1922 graduate John Johnson (Seneca) reported that although he had not pursued the trade he learned at Chilocco, "the training in discipline, music, etc., has benefited me greatly."[141] Bert Brown and three other Otoe men—Francis Pipestem, Amos Black, and Joe Young—formed the Otoe Quartet after leaving Chilocco. Pipestem had, according to Hogg, "a very promising baritone voice" while at Chilocco. A patron funded his additional vocal training at the Baptist College in Bolivar, Missouri. However, the patron failed to advance the student's second semester's tuition and did not tell him. Pipestem did not learn of this until after he had secured his board, room, and clothes and returned to the campus after the holidays. He was "let down" and bitter, according to Hogg, but he later married and began farming.[142] The Otoe Quartet, however, allowed him to continue his interest in singing. The group even left Oklahoma on occasion and made good money while traveling on the road with an evangelist.[143]

Finally, as has been discussed in previous chapters, boarding school students did not typically abandon the songs and dances taught them by their families, elders, and other community members and were often eager to catch up on the latest such dances and songs. In the early twentieth century, returned students were some of the most active singers and dancers of tribally derived songs to be found on reservations and allotments. That the knowledge of those songs persisted within the schools is evidenced by the recollections of students such as Francis La Flesche (Omaha), a resident of a mission school in the 1860s. La Flesche recounted a day in which three government inspectors visited the campus. After observing reading and arithmetic demonstrations (along with a prank by the ever-devious

La Flesche), one of them asked the children, "Have your people music, and do they sing?." One of the older boys answered in the affirmative. The man responded, "I wish you would sing an Indian song for me. . . . I never heard one." La Flesche continued:

> There was some hesitancy, but suddenly a loud clear voice close to me broke into a Victory song; before a bar was sung another voice took up the song from the beginning, as is the custom among the Indians, then the whole school fell in, and we made the room ring. We understood the song, and knew the emotion of which it was the expression. We felt, as we sang, the patriotic thrill of a victorious people who had vanquished their enemies; but the men shook their heads, and one of them said, "That's savage, that's savage! They must be taught music."[144]

Indeed, the knowledge of tribally derived songs did not dissolve in the schools, nor, as indicated by the inspectors' response, did the resolve of government employees to control the practice of music in the schools.

Each school engendered different sorts of musical experiences, however, and further studies of expressive culture in the individual schools will certainly reveal that for all of the efforts by OIA commissioners to manage a coherent government educational policy, much of the musical instruction in the schools resulted from decisions made on the local level. These decisions were based upon the desires of students, and occasionally even tribal leaders, as much as they were based on the needs of superintendents to advertise the perceived success of their bid at assimilating the students. In one remarkable example, Matthew Sakiestewa Gilbert recounts the story of Tawaquaptewa, a Hopi chief who played a pivotal role in the Oraibi split and who was sent to the Sherman Institute as an adult by the OIA in a further attempt to assimilate the Hopis.[145] Tawaquaptewa and the five hundred Hopi children, as well as additional Hopi adults, who were enrolled at Sherman in 1906 were not exactly isolated from their people in the Riverside, California, off-reservation boarding school, and Tawaquaptewa saw his residency at Sherman as an opportunity to remain with the children who had been forced to enroll there.[146] Perhaps due to the overwhelming number of Hopi students at the school, the teachers were compelled to acknowledge Hopi cultural expressions, if for no other reason than to ascertain how to harness those expressions in a way that would advance their pedagogical goals.[147] For the instruction of Tawaquaptewa and the other Hopi adults at the school, Gilbert writes that "by using objects and materials familiar to the Hopi adult students, teachers related lessons in math with real life situations on the Hopi reservation.[148]

Tawaquaptewa excelled in his language and other classes, serving as a role model for the students, and as a model student for the school superintendent.[149] As his influence continued to grow in the school, so too did the opportunities for the Hopi students to maintain their expressive culture within the school grounds. By March 1907, Tawaquaptewa and eight other Hopis, according to Gilbert, "performed a traditional Hopi song in the school's auditorium." Gilbert observes, "As an impressed audience looked on, the program began as a Hopi boy kept a steady beat of a drum. With a school banner in hand, Tawaquaptewa led the small procession of Hopi singers into the auditorium, singing and dancing with 'signal ease and excellent time.'"[150] Two months later, he and other Hopis performed the Eagle Dance, popular among the Pueblo Indians. Gilbert notes that, "at the request of Tawaquaptewa, each costume used in the Eagle Dance came from the village of Oraibi, and consisted of complete and fully authentic pieces."[151] Such performances continued during Tawaquaptewa's residency at Sherman and indeed inaugurated a tradition of Hopi singing and dancing that persists at Sherman Indian High School to this day.[152] Whereas the superintendent may have seen these performances as a way to advertise the school, Tawaquaptewa and the other Hopis clearly had their own goals in mind. Gilbert adds that "the government had established the boarding schools to assimilate Indian students, but those very students used the boarding school as a place to preserve and protect their own cultural ways."[153] As the Sherman example illustrates, each school provided a different sort of musical experience for the students, and that experience changed over time. Whereas most school officials were persistently strict in managing the type of musical expressions permitted on school grounds, a handful, on occasion, allowed extraordinary latitude regarding the ambitions of the students.

As for the legacy of *Stiya*, the work of fiction that Marianna Burgess hoped would inspire returned students, Leslie Marmon Silko recounted a story in which her Grandma A'mooh (Maria Anaya Marmon) and Aunt Susie (Susie Marmon), both Carlisle students during Burgess's tenure, got into "the only big quarrel" they ever had—and it was over that book.[154] Shortly after they had returned from the school, shipments from Carlisle arrived at the Laguna Pueblo, containing copies of the book for all of the students.[155] The responses of Silko's relatives, however, were anything but what Burgess would have wanted. According to Silko, "Grandma A'mooh began reading the book, but, as she read, she became increasingly incensed at the libelous portrayal of Pueblo life and people." Her Aunt Susie wanted to discuss the book, but Grandma A'mooh would have none of it. "Aunt Susie," writes Silko, "was a scholar and a storyteller; she believed the Stiya book was important evidence of the lies and the racism and bad faith of the U.S. government with the Pueblo people." Grandma A'mooh "told Aunt Susie the only place for this book was in the fire, and she lifted the lid on her cookstove to drop in the book." For Grandma A'mooh believed that "a book's lies should be burned just as witchcraft paraphernalia is destroyed."[156] The argument was resolved only when her Aunt Susie asked Grandma A'mooh to give her the book instead, which according to Pueblo etiquette, the latter could not refuse.

Where do we place the experiences of these students within a historical inquiry of the boarding schools? The music education curriculum, the publication of *Stiya*, and Pratt's and Burgess's admonitions and shared concerns during the Ghost Dance fervor and ensuing massacre reveal that boarding school officials most often desired to eliminate from among their students the expressive culture that the officials considered hostile, dangerous, and antithetical to their civilizing program. However, the central role of returned students in the renaissance of the Omaha Dance complex among the Lakotas demonstrates clearly the range of the students' response to the assimilation program. The Hopi experience at Sherman in 1906 and 1907 indicates that in some cases tribal prerogatives regarding some forms of expressive culture were maintained even within the schools. Pratt and the other officials sought to supplant the performative practices they considered dangerous with those that were acceptable to the tastes of a Victorian, middle-class, white American citizenry, but many students seemed more eager than ever to participate in tribally derived dance traditions at home, if not in the schools themselves.

At the same time, many of the students seemed to love the popular swing, waltz, and jazz dances of their school days and took them back to the reservations, sometimes to face criticism from community members who exhibited a variety of responses of their own. Many of them held that men and women should not dance together at all and that the dances learned in the schools were dangerous and challenged the proper mores of their society. Music and dance thus served as a stark moral and cultural battleground that invoked the desires and beliefs of the OIA officials, the students, and the members of their home communities.

Between these extreme reactions, however, lay perhaps a more representative array of actions exhibited by the students, who often felt that while many aspects of boarding school life were extraordinarily harsh and oppressive, they had benefited from and even enjoyed certain aspects of their formal musical education. Although a few of their favorite entertainments were shunned by some of their community members, and although Claude Hogg found an occasional ex-student whose "present occupation," she snippily wrote of James Thomas (Delaware and Shawnee), was "probably attending all the Indian pow-wows," most used their musical talents in a way that reflected the sheer multiplicity of their experiences, both at home and in the schools.[157] They culled what they desired from their boarding school education and implemented their learning in ways that suited them, transforming the possibilities of Native expressive culture into an even wider array of articulations that represented their often difficult yet astounding life experiences.

CHAPTER 4

LEARNING THE MUSIC
OF INDIANNESS

As the sixty Paiute students from the Bishop Indian Day School fil-tered into the local Bishop, California, opera house on March 28, 1913, their nerves could not have been more on edge. Not only were they about to perform for a sold-out audience of strangers at a benefit for their own band, but their parents and friends also awaited them in the galleries with eager anticipation after traveling through horrendous weather to witness their stage debut.[1] Their parents had worked hard to provide them with the proper attire for the performance: new blue overalls and white shirts for the boys and blue-sashed white dresses and red hair ribbons for the girls.[2] School superintendent Spalsbury was nervous too; prior to the performance, the townspeople seemed to have lost their former interest in his pupils, and no white people had visited the Indian church in months.[3]

All of their fears abated, however, when from the moment the stu-dents walked onto the stage in drill formation, waving small Ameri-can flags above their heads, the audience burst into applause.[4] Band member Harrison Diaz played a baritone solo "in absolute key," then later joined in a duet with cornetist Edward Lewis. Six-year-old Hiram Meroney performed a recitation entitled "Our Flag."[5]

These recognizable public displays of citizenship and discipline by Native students, however, were followed by an altogether different type of performance. Twenty-four of the children launched into a rendition of "Old Indian Love Song," a popular composition with which, according to one newspaper, the students were "all familiar."[6]

Concluding the evening in an eagerly anticipated climax, eight of the older Paiutes, who were parents and relatives of some of the students, performed an "Indian dance" replete with Indian "costume" that catered to the specific tastes of whites or, as one newspaper report would have it, "due concessions to white conventionalities in the way of attire."[7] The performance was a rousing success, and the students earned over two hundred dollars for the school band.[8]

In the midst of an extraordinarily oppressive assimilation agenda in the schools, why did the Bishop Indian School administrators allow the children to sing an Indian-themed song and their relatives to dance in regalia? How did it come to be that such expressions were presented as part of an official OIA school function? How did the OIA reconcile such musical displays with its overarching citizenship agenda? This chapter examines how such performances of Indianness reflected a shifting set of policy initiatives with which American Indians grappled in the first quarter of the twentieth century. Though the curricula and public displays of expressive culture had varied between the schools and among the school superintendents since Carlisle opened its doors in 1879, a new order of OIA administrators in the early twentieth century effected a dismissal of Superintendent Richard Pratt's beliefs that American Indian children should or could shed all expressive culture attributed (erroneously or not) to Native peoples.[9] Instead, administrators soon began to propose the seemingly contradictory premise—that students must learn to perform Indianness as well. This recent appreciation of Indianness, however, had little to do with a desire to acknowledge cultural pluralism; the OIA educational policy inaugurated by Commissioner Francis Leupp served rather to modernize and enhance previous notions of the cultural and racial superiority of whiteness through ancillary student musical performances of Indianness. The performed practices of Indianness permitted in the schools were specifically tailored to fit the OIA's overarching concern to produce "proper," safely contained, docile citizens, and the performances remained contrasted, and subordinated, to performances of expressive culture deemed "civilized" and white. Performances of Indianness and whiteness could thus work in tandem to further OIA objectives of detribalization and assimilation. The politics of music in the schools was multifaceted, however, and moved beyond struggling to negotiate the contours of "dangerous" tribal expressive culture and "safe" white expressive culture toward accommodating an increasing demand for Indianness by the non-Indian public. Furthermore, the concerns of the policy makers were not those of the students, who, like the Bishop school students, often took pleasure in the opportunities to make their own the school performances of Indianness afforded by the new OIA directives.

MUSICAL INDIANNESS IN POPULAR CULTURE

The instruction of Indianness in Indian schools budded in part from the growing investment of non-Indians in the idea that they could personally benefit from experiencing "authentic" Native culture in tourism, arts, and entertainment. The American Indians who performed in Buffalo Bill's Wild West Show in the late nineteenth century served as a vanguard in the emergent consumer culture of popular entertainment that would profoundly shape the character of twentieth-century American society. Prior to the formation of all-Indian bands and other entrepreneurial ventures that sold entertainment through Indianness, Native American performers—or "show Indians," as they were sometimes called—had already discovered a way to gain entry to the market economy, sometimes earning ninety dollars a month, then about two-thirds the salary of an Indian agent, and vastly more than most American Indians working allotments were able to procure.[10] As demonstrated in L. G. Moses' study of Wild West shows, hundreds of American Indians performed Indianness—typically as "war-bonneted equestrian raider[s] of the plains"—in shows that recounted battles with the U.S. Cavalry and "primitive" Indian life within a contemporary representation of the past.[11] These individuals profited from performance as the audience cast its own ideals of Indianness upon them; because most of Bill's Native performers were Oglala, their Plains regalia of eagle feathers, ornate beadwork, bone breastplates, and buckskin clothing solidified popular conceptions of what Indians "should" look like.[12] Some reform organizations such as the Indian Rights Association loudly denounced the shows for their perceived degradation and exploitation of the participants, as well as the occasional deaths of some traveling performers.[13] Many of the paying spectators, however, were less concerned with the welfare of the performers than with the displacement and uncertainties that modernity wrought; for them, Indianness gathered appeal because of its apparent cultural authenticity in an unseemly, inauthentic, vapid modern world—a world in which popular fantasies of Indianness served as an antidote to the fabrication and immediacy of modernity. Philip Deloria argues that the romanticization of Indianness thus played a crucial role in the movement of antimodern primitivism and helped lay the foundation for a modern American identity.[14] Indianness became a commodity in the emerging consumer culture, with "show Indians" offering a live, authentic experience for the non-Indian audience.

American Indian–authored literature also played into the public appetite for Indianness. *Old Indian Legends*, by Gertrude Bonnin (Zitkala a), published in 1901, and *Indian Boyhood*, by Charles Eastman (Ohiyesa), published the following year, established a vanguard of twentieth-century Native writing that was celebrated as firsthand, "authentic" accounts of Native American life. Some Native writers also became prominent anthropologists: Omaha author and anthropologist Francis La Flesche, for example, not only collaborated with Alice Fletcher to collect Omaha music but also hired Indianist composer Charles Wakefield Cadman as his assistant for transcribing music while he completed a four-volume work on the Osages.[15] Often these Native authors brought public attention to their concerns with federal Indian policy, but they also often gratified non-Indian desires for authenticity, primitivism, and nostalgia. Deploying the Indianness expected by American consumers was, as Lucy Maddox argues, often a "political necessity" aimed at forwarding specific agendas.[16] The deployment of Indianness in this sense was quite strategic, and these writers shared much more in common with "show Indians" than they might have comfortably acknowledged at the time.

At the same time, non-Indian composers, supported by the public's fascination with Indianness, increasingly attempted to capture the "sounds" of Indianness. American Indians had appeared in European and later in American compositions since the 1600s, either, as Tara Browner has categorized, in symbolic ("native-inspired"), indexical ("attempting to approximate native sounds,") or iconic ("using materials from native music") themes.[17] Michael Pisani engages the various musical incarnations of Indianness found within European courts, opera houses, and salons, up through the vaudeville stage and film scores of the twentieth century. He demonstrates that musical representations and indexical tropes of Indianness were not fixed ideas from the days of the European courts but, rather, developed over time, and very rapidly during the late nineteenth and early twentieth centuries.[18]

Since 1880, when Theodore Baker first began an attempt to systematically document Native music, non-Indian composers began to take notice of the potential for incorporating Native melodies into their works.[19] Early "Indianist" composers, as they became known, such as Edward MacDowell and Amy Beach, along with later composers such as Arthur Farwell, Charles Wakefield Cadman, and Thurlow Lieurance, established a large body of work dedicated to the production of Indian themes palatable to non-Indian ears.[20] Influenced in part by Dvoák, MacDowell used Indianist compositions to establish an "authentic" American, nationalist musical tradition. The nationalist emphasis on the compositions remained strong after the turn of the century, and at this point the works of the composers began to resonate in primitivist circles as well. No other race or ethnic group represented a closer relationship to the American landscape. By the early twentieth century, many such aural ethnic signifiers pervaded American music; fabricated sounds of Chinese, African American, and American Indian peoples—peoples who had the least amount of power in the country but who nevertheless seemed to pose the greatest threat to the maintenance of the social order—were increasingly encoded and contained in the art, minstrel, vaudeville, and Tin Pan Alley compositions that founded the modern epoch of American music.[21]

Philip Deloria interrogates the "sound of Indian" in this period and demonstrates that it now permeates popular culture, not only in musical genres but even in cartoons and the chants at sports coliseums. He argues further that musical incarnations of Indianness evoke more than sounds or images but "complete worlds of expectation concerning Indian people, rich with narratives and symbolic meanings."[22] One of the most resonant components of the "sound of

Indian," including the "war drum" (DUM dum dum dum DUM dum dum dum), came in the first half of the twentieth century to cue pioneers on the silver screen to shriek with horror or muster their manliness. By the mid-twentieth century, Deloria argues, the sound of Indian was "so familiar it was like sonic wallpaper, only dimly heard as anything other than completely natural."[23]

Unlike Indianist composers, Tin Pan Alley songwriters maintained absolutely no pretense, beyond stoking the burgeoning indexical tropes of musical Indianness, of producing any sense of "authenticity" in their work. For them, Indians simply provided a way of injecting a racial—and, in so doing, often quite racist—dynamic into their narrative formulas. The lyrics typically had nothing to do with the realities of life in Indian Country. The chorus of one such song, "Indian Blues," demonstrates the geographic and cultural malleability composers imparted to themes, names, and tribal designations, in their work:

> Won't you come back to me, my own Iona
> I am so sad for I am all alona
> Won't you please leave your tribe in Arizona
> Leave that tribe of Sioux, my little papoose.
> You went away, now I am always crying,
> My love is true, why there's no use denying,
> My heart is broken, I am always sighing
> I've the Indian Blues.[24]

Examples abound of lyrics that demonstrate the incongruity between lived Native experience and the representation of Indianness in Tin Pan Alley songs. In another example, despite the incredible rate of volunteerism by American Indians in World War I, and their generosity in raising war funds, Native soldiers were ridiculed in compositions such as "Big Chief Killahun":

> Big Chief put his war-paint on and kissed his squaw good-bye
> Threw away his pipe of peace and went to do or die.
> He said, "Uncle Sammy feeds me, gives me all I get,
> Now that Uncle Sammy needs me, Big Chief no forget."

(Chorus)

Big Chief's on his way to Berlin, just to do his share;

Big Chief's goin' to make 'em squawk,

When he hits 'em with his tom-a-hawk.

Big Chief's goin' to scalp the Kaiser, take a-way his gun;

Oh! Oh! He have heap much fun;

Good-bye Herman, no more Ger-man; Big Chief Kill-a-Hun.[25]

To take to task but one of the erroneous and degrading assumptions offered by these words, the lyricists of "Big Chief Killahun" are gleefully oblivious to the trust relationship that underlay the treaty responsibilities promised by the federal government (however much abandoned by the government at the time) in return for the massive, if not total, conveyances of tribal lands by Native nations. Instead, they chose to characterize the Native warriors in the armed forces as paying an obligation to the federal government for giving them everything they could claim as their own. Such songs permeated not just dance halls but, through the main Tin Pan Alley medium of sheet music, the parlors of American families across the country as well.

As such songs grew in popularity, the Indianist composers, the so-called serious students of American Indian music, took pains to establish their authority over what they deemed "true" Indian music. To legitimate the authenticity of their works, the second generation (1900–1920) of Indianist composers, led by Farwell and Cadman, often collaborated with or based their compositions on melodies collected by contemporary ethnologists such as Alice Fletcher, Frances Densmore, and Natalie Curtis. Although their interpretations were extremely distilled versions of transcribed and decontextualized melodies, nevertheless Indianist composers gained much authority in the eyes and ears of the non-Indian American public; at the same time, as their compositions were transcribed, idealized, and harmonized, they seemed in the end to share much more in common with the imagery found in Tin Pan Alley numbers than with the performances as originally observed and recorded by the ethnologists. Combined with the songwriters who labored to plug common perceptions of American Indian names, words, and sounds into their pop themes on Tin Pan Alley, these ethnologists and composers contributed to a widespread movement in American music that continued to generate interest in American Indian cultural traditions, no matter how manipulated and contrived.[26]

FRANCES DENSMORE AND THE INFLUENCE OF ETHNOLOGISTS WITHIN THE OIA

As the "sound of Indian" infiltrated more and more American musical genres, ethnologists interested in music increasingly penetrated the OIA; their efforts to "preserve" Indian music neatly coincided with mounting public pressure on OIA officials to produce American Indians who could perform musical Indianness on cue.[27] The work of ethnographers to produce "authentic" Indian music, however, represented a significant challenge to OIA policy: their investigative process—gathering data by interviewing living "informants"—required the OIA to grant them permission to record songs for the same dances that the office was trying to suppress. However, by the twentieth century, the growing public interest in American Indian music, no matter how distantly removed from its original context, provided additional pressure and support into allowing the work to take place. Popular culture, anthropology, and federal policy were thus wed in highly unusual circumstances, but these circumstances, as we will see, contributed to the shift within OIA educational policy toward the instruction of musical Indianness in the schools.

Frances Densmore's long career reveals in many ways the tangled intersection of anthropology, popular culture, and federal Indian policy in the early twentieth century and provides an introduction to the ways in which the OIA constructed a "proper," safe Indianness for didactic purposes within the schools. Densmore, born in 1867 in Red Wing, Minnesota, spent most of her life visiting reservations to record and transcribe the songs she collected from Native communities. By the time of her death in 1957 she had recorded an extraordinary 3,500 songs and transcribed 2,500 of them for her numerous publications and lectures. Today her recorded legacy is seen by many Native and non-Native people alike as a remarkably rich and vitally important archive, particularly given that she recorded many of the songs in the midst of the OIA's dance suppression.[28] Nevertheless, it is important to consider her own intentions and motivations in order to best understand how she and other ethnologists of the time influenced the boarding school music curricula and federal Indian policy generally.

Although Densmore believed deeply in the historical value and beauty of American Indian music, she recorded the songs because she believed that American Indians could not afford to perform them much longer in an increasingly modern world. She dedicated most of her fieldwork to the "preservation" of Native songs, believing that their value as racial artifacts was more significant than their value within Native communities to foster community ties or communal, tribal identity. Viewing the songs as historically rather than actively relevant, Densmore and other ethnologists worked toward preserving performances of them as relics of the past, relics of a race that would either disappear or sacrifice the practices in order to assimilate into an assumed detribalized American social fabric.[29]

The immediate problem for Densmore and others, however, lay in the OIA's policy of suppressing the performances that the ethnologists wished to observe and transcribe. At the same time, her ability to find singers reveals that many of the performative traditions banned by the OIA had persisted in at least the memories if not also the practices of the Native people she encountered. For example, the Sun Dance had been officially blacklisted since the 1880s, yet Densmore on multiple occasions—such as her trip to Fort Yates on the Standing Rock Sioux Reservation in 1911—successfully tracked down singers and persuaded them to perform the songs.[30] Often singers questioned Densmore as to why she, as a government worker, was asking them to perform songs that the OIA had forbidden. Densmore recalled,

I was asking the Indians to tell me about customs that [the reservation superintendent] was forbidding them to practice. I was asking them to sing songs that were con[n]ected with those customs. It was hard for the Indians to understand this anomaly but I was always loyal to the Government of the United States. My explanation to the Indians was, "I want to keep these things for you, just as you keep valuable things for a child until he grows up. You have much to learn about the new way of life, and

you are too busy to use these things now. The young men are too busy
with the new life to learn the old songs but I will keep the songs and the
information for them."[31]

Densmore's paternalistic explanation positioned her, rather than these
singers, as the keeper of knowledge for the Lakota/Dakota people,
and her complicated and conflicted valuation of Native songs soon
reflected that attitude: while she told the people at Fort Yates that the
younger generation of American Indians did not have the time or incli-
nation to learn the songs she was recording, she was already directly
involved in a plan to introduce her own version of their songs to both
Indian school students and the non-Indian public.

Densmore's efforts to present Indian songs to Indian students
began as early as 1904, the year in which she delivered a talk on the
subject to the students at the Morris Indian School in Morris, Minnesota (the same year that Pratt was forced to concede his authority
at Carlisle).[32] In 1906 she recorded two songs by a Dakota woman
named Wapatanka. Densmore "wrote down the songs as they were
sung"; then she played the melody on a nearby piano, "adding simple chords like those used by Miss [Alice] Fletcher."[33] After she transcribed and harmonized the melodies of the songs to fit within
Euro-American scales and notations, she transformed one into a
"choral march," and both were printed in the April 1907 edition of
Chilocco's *Indian School Journal*.[34] She made several more trips to
schools, including those at Sisseton and Phoenix through 1921, transcribing the songs that students would sing for her as often as she was
teaching these new musical forms to them—forms far removed from
the musical systems that originally structured the content and performance of the songs and far removed from the indigenous systems
of knowledge that originally structured their meaning.

Although she did not believe that the songs she collected on reservations should play a role in the lives of modern Indians other than to
testify to their ancestral past, Densmore recognized a need for modern non-Indians to experience the "authenticity" of Native songs. In
fact her correspondence indicates that she seemed most proud when
composers applied her transcribed songs within operas and other
forms of Euro-American orchestration. She considered such applica-

Using developing technologies, Frances Densmore recorded thousands of songs during her career in an effort to preserve the music of "disappearing" Native peoples. The reasons that some of her subjects participated were to receive financial compensation, to provide a record of current songs for their future generations, and, in some cases, to gain an outlet for criticizing local OIA agents or policies. This photograph was captioned: "Piegan Indian, Mountain Chief, having his voice recorded by ethnologist Frances Densmore." National Photo Company Collection, Prints and Photographs Division, Library of Congress, LC-USZ62-107289.

tion to be the "practical use" of her studies and used their success as justification for the renewal of her contracts with the Bureau of American Ethnology (BAE). Among those who incorporated Densmore's transcribed melodies into their orchestration were Alberto Bimboni, in his operas *Winona* and *The Maiden's Leap*; Alfred Manger, in his *Fantasie on Sioux Themes*; and Carl Busch, in two compositions for string orchestra entitled *Second Indian Rhapsody* and *Sun Dance Rhapsody*.[35]

At a time when federal policy was directed toward the allotment and eventual liquidation of all remaining tribal lands, ostensibly to prepare American Indians to live in a modern world, the non-Native public sought refuge from that very same modern world in the music of Indianness. Of course the adaptations of Indian melodies were culturally and temporally removed from the context in which they were originally intended to be performed; nevertheless, the music purported to represent a distant yet preserved racial heritage, an apparently authentic experience of the American natural landscape. Densmore and her preservation work were explicitly involved in providing this refuge—a refuge, apparently, to be void of Native peoples as well as the modern ills of society. In June 1913 Densmore walked into the office of the commissioner of Indian Affairs and asked if the allotment of John Red Fox, a Lakota from the Standing Rock Sioux Reservation who had befriended her, could be transferred to the Smithsonian, whereby the institution would sell his property in order to pay her expenses for "making an investigation of music in the Sioux country."[36]

In fact, Densmore was not the first ethnologist interested in Native music to become intimately involved in the liquidation of tribal lands. The most well-known ethnographer of American Indian music in the late nineteenth century, Alice Fletcher, worked as a special agent in the Indian service for ten years for the express purpose of facilitating allotments. According to her biographer, Joan Mark, she earnestly "believed that treaties needed to be broken, for she believed Indians were occupying more land than they could make good use for."[37] Fletcher not only was involved in the assignment of allotments but also was responsible for some of the most important allotment legislation; her efforts led to the successful passage of the bill providing for the allotment of the Omaha Reservation, where she allotted 75,931 acres of land while lying on her sickbed for five months. She referred to the infamous Dawes Allotment Act as "the Magna Carta of the Indians of our Country" and, according to Joan Mark, was more responsible for the final shape of the bill than any other individual. Henry Dawes agreed with this assessment, stating in regard to Fletcher's contributions, "I stand in reference to that very much as Americus Vespuscious [*sic*] stands to Columbus." By the end of Fletcher's work as a special agent for the OIA, she was personally responsible for assigning allotments to 4,400 individuals, while her legislative efforts led to allotments on virtually every reservation in the country.[38]

Densmore considered Fletcher a role model, and perhaps this contributed to her own interest in allotments. But she, like Fletcher, was more known for her research in Native music, and this interest could cause complications in her fieldwork. Although in certain ways Densmore's efforts seemed perfectly aligned with OIA policy, the principal of the Sisseton Indian school was in fact fearful of the response Densmore's visit would provoke among the students. When she visited the school in 1911, she wrote,

> I find here the greatest possible prejudice against the teaching of Indian songs to pupils in the school. As the principal here said, "when the boys take to singing Indian songs in the evening I know it's time to look out for a lot of runaways." The first question asked me by the school principal was whether I "had any notion of putting the children up [to] singing Indian songs" and I had to prove very conclusively that my work was purely scientific before I could get any attention from him.[39]

In the early twentieth century, despite all of the efforts of the OIA to manage and contain the musical expressions of Native people, returned students were often those most responsible for combating government directives aimed at the suppression of dances on reservations.[40] The principal recognized the difficulties of controlling the musical expression of the students and the potentially oppositional meanings generated from the performance of songs; he was therefore suspicious of Densmore's attempt to inculcate a "proper," sanitized appreciation of Native music even though she defended her work as clinical and scientific.

Though Densmore may have felt that her experience with the principal was difficult, she faced a multitude of challenges from Native singers as well. In some cases, she avoided those challenges by not even letting them know she was there. For example, Densmore was particularly pleased by her transcription and publication of "Geronimo's Song," based on her encounter with Geronimo at the Louisiana Purchase Exposition of 1904 in St. Louis. Although a prisoner of war since 1886, by 1904 Geronimo was a celebrity, albeit an unfree one, and the War Department often relented to requests by promoters to feature him in their fairs and parades. Geronimo made the most of it, selling his autographs, photographs, coat buttons, whatever people wished to buy—and they wished to buy everything he offered. Densmore, however, was simply interested in securing a song from him. In a 1906 edition of Chilocco's *Indian School Journal*, Densmore recounted that one day, after observing Geronimo for some time, she finally said to a boy who was traveling with his group, "Tell Geronimo that I like Indian music and wish I could hear him sing." She continued: "There was a flash in the old eyes behind the steel-rimmed spectacles, a slight drawing up of the aged figure and I confess to a feeling of relief when the crowd swallowed me up." Fearful of Geronimo, apparently afraid even to speak to him while he whittled arrows to sell to his legions of onlookers, Densmore nevertheless resolved that "Mr. Geronimo shall be conquered by my craft," and she bided her time "with the patience of my red brethren." She exercised this patience for some while, and finally her glorious conquest paid off: one day, while spectators gawked at Geronimo and then purchased some arrows he was making, she heard him hum to himself. This was her moment, and she realized that she had to act quickly: "I slipped into ambush behind him where I would not attract his attention, and noted down his song. He sang it softly but with a peculiar swing, beating the time with his foot. The curious throng did not stop to listen to his singing. They saw only an old Indian sitting on a box, whittling an arrow—but before his eyes there stretched the plains and the mountains, with never a white man to bar their beauty."[41] Despite her consideration of this story as a success, Densmore quickly learned that lying in wait to ambush singers would not get her very far.

Densmore grew very successful at securing performances, as the numbers of her wax cylinders demonstrate, but the singers she solicited challenged her on many occasions.[42] For example, in 1914 she visited the Uintah and Whiteriver bands of Northern Utes in an effort to record their songs on cylinders. By this point in her career she had spent more than ten years traveling to Native communities in order to capture voices and melodies, but it was not always easy for her to convince Native people that her efforts were sincere or worthwhile. She recalled,

From the day of my arrival the Utes did not like the idea of my work. . . . I set up the phonograph in the front room, secured a good interpreter and hoped for singers. Many Indians came out of curiosity, looked in the windows, sat around the room and *laughed*. In vain I explained, through the interpreter, that I had been with many tribes who were glad to record their songs. I told of the building in Washington that would not burn down, where their voices would be preserved forever, but still they only looked at each other and laughed. . . . It was absurd to think that a white woman would pay money to record their songs, for the government to keep forever in that building that would not burn down![43]

Densmore tried to persuade them to sing by placing a quarter on the phonograph and leaving the room, telling her visitors that whoever was willing to sing would earn the quarter. After hearing only snickers for several minutes while she waited in another room, someone eventually sang into the machine. But when she returned, she discovered that the singer was her interpreter, who kept the quarter as well as his regular pay.[44]

Densmore's intentions to record Native songs were multiply foiled by the Utes. After failing to persuade them to sing, she asked them to find Red Cap, the Ute leader adamantly opposed to allotment who had gained notoriety in 1906 by attempting to join the Utes and the Sioux together in war against the United States. She believed that if she could convince him that her mission was worthy, then he would tell people in his community to sing for her. After meeting with him, he seemed convinced and told her he would bring the best singers to her. When she finished recording them, Red Cap said, "I have done as you wished. Now I want to ask a favor. I do not sing, as I said, but I would like to talk into your phonograph. Will it record talking?"[45] Densmore replied that it would. He continued,

Well . . . Then I will talk and I want you to play the record for the Indian Commissioner in Washington. I want to tell him that we do not like this Agent. WE want him sent somewhere else. We don't like the things he does. What we tell him does not get to the commissioner but I want the commissioner to hear my voice. I want you to play this so he will hear my words, and I want you to give him a good translation of my speech. We want to get rid of this Agent.[46]

Red Cap immediately seized on the technology that Densmore could only discuss with Native individuals in patronizing terms. When describing "preserved voices" and big buildings in Washington that "would not burn down," Red Cap parsed the supercilious rhetoric and discovered political opportunity, just as many Native peoples had discovered how to deploy Indianness, for example, as a political weapon. Densmore, conceding to Red Cap's upper hand, agreed to play the recording for the commissioner. However, Densmore declined Red Cap's request to provide a good, or any, translation. She played the recording for Commissioner Cato Sells without providing any information as to the content of the speech, nor a translation.[47] She later wrote, "Numerous employees of the Indian Office were asked to hear the recordings, but no one understood the Ute language and the contents of the speech remained a mystery. The record has not been played since that day."[48]

THE IMPLEMENTATION OF INDIANNESS
IN THE SCHOOLS

Despite Red Cap's innovative use of the recording and transcribing technologies that began to permeate reservations, Densmore and OIA officials continued to believe that their vision of Indianness, one that wed public desire with federal Indian policy directives of allotment and assimilation, was the only one that would matter in the end. Although Densmore agreed with many in the OIA who believed that tribal identity was antithetical to their agreed-upon cultural requirements of American citizenship, she nevertheless sought to infuse Americanness with Indianness for the benefit of the white American citizenry. Such an infusion began to complicate federal Indian education policy, as OIA officials of the post-Pratt era such as Commissioner Francis Leupp and Carlisle superintendent Moses Friedman built upon the work of Densmore, Fletcher, Curtis, and Indianist composers to create a sanitized, decontextualized form of Indianness within the schools that responded to public pressure, modern social science, and the overriding citizenship agenda. They launched an effort to introduce a form of "Indian" instruction in the schools that would not undermine, but instead enhance, their goals of establishing a racialized citizenry of vocational and domestic laborers.

Leupp, who was the commissioner of Indian Affairs from 1905 through 1909, brought a disposition to the OIA that was much different from Pratt's. Leupp did not hold much faith that Native students were capable of fully assimilating within white society, and he did not necessarily believe that they even should.[49] Frederick Hoxie has argued that at this time the OIA had grown pessimistic about the idea that Native peoples could meet the high expectations demanded of first-class citizens and that educational initiatives were then geared away from common-school training and toward rudimentary vocational and domestic training more suited for the second-class citizenship of a nonwhite minority.[50]

It is not difficult to find exceptions to this rule, as teachers, superintendents, students, and parents cultivated unique circumstances in each school. Estelle Reel, for example, supervisor of Indian Affairs from 1898 to 1910, had advanced a pessimistic assessment of Native abilities before the turn of the century. She even voiced concern that piano instruction was not practical for students who should only learn to labor.[51] However, due to strong student interest along with challenges by school superintendents, piano instruction remained a mainstay in the schools.[52] Hoxie's argument is well founded, however, in the sense that Leupp's appointment and Pratt's resignation in the first decade of the twentieth century largely quelled the voices of those in the OIA who advanced the belief in a common intellectual capacity between whites and Indians. OIA policy as shepherded by Leupp was also steeped in a decidedly modern understanding of race, one that embraced the notion of immutable racial difference at the same time that the commodification of Indianness grew to be highly valued by many whites.

Influenced by friends in the social sciences and new trends in anthropology, Leupp subscribed to some seemingly relativist ideas— that there was some value in Native cultural traditions.[53] Along these lines, Leupp prefigured John Collier (commissioner of Indian Affairs from 1933 to 1945) in asserting that Native arts and crafts retained value for Indians and non-Indians alike and that an Indian "will never be judged aright till we learn to measure him by his own standards, as we whites would wish to be measured if some powerful race were to usurp dominion over us."[54] Because he supported the instruction of Indian arts and crafts in the schools, in 1905 a new building at Carlisle was named the Leupp Indian Art Studio, much to the mortification of Pratt.[55] However, Leupp also believed that the standards of Native Americans were lower, arguing that they retained "primitive instinct[s] common to all mankind in the lower stages of social development."[56] He wrote that most American Indians were "fundamentally incapable of certain of our moral, social, and intellectual standards."[57] Leupp's positive valuation of Native arts and crafts, steeped in his staunch belief that American Indians held inferior cultural practices and values, not only justified the OIA's paternalistic approach and oversight of tribes but also reflected his attention to the emerging market of Indian crafts and the creation of primitivism as a modern style. Leupp's expectations were significantly lower than Pratt's and were shared with the most prominent of Pratt's successors at Carlisle, Moses Friedman, who believed that American Indians (whom he often referred to as "savages") should instead resign themselves to becoming a class of laborers that could serve the country ably as citizens, though second-class at that.[58] This labor included the production of Indian arts and crafts for white consumers; by the 1920s, the OIA conspired to place Indian artisans in the employ of corporations involved in the tourist trade. In 1921 Charles Burke, the commissioner of Indian Affairs who had vociferously sought to quell Native dancing, actually praised this "safer" production of Indianness: "The railway system found it profitable to continue to provide attractive work rooms for families of Indian artisans at stations along the line, where their handiwork sells readily."[59] Goals of racial assimilation were thus transformed to and perhaps more aptly described by goals of "proletarianization," as one scholar put it.[60]

As performances of Indianness grew increasingly popular through Wild West shows, the cottage industry of Native arts and crafts in the Southwest and in the schools, and the published works of ethnologists and composers, so too grew the OIA's realization that the citizenship agenda as envisioned through allotment and assimilation was not succeeding as policy makers intended. Despite harsh and consistent efforts to detribalize them, Native Americans had largely refused to shed their tribal identities. Allotment had resulted not in Jeffersonian farmers but often rather in tragedy and disaster, as unarable lands and broken tools at times left people starving. Giveaways began to proliferate, partially in response to these woes. Still seeking to suppress such cultural flourishes, OIA officials not only blamed American Indians for OIA failures but began to argue that Native peoples simply did not possess the faculties to transcend their perceived cultural deficiencies. These arguments merely bolstered Leupp's views on race; despite the emergence of cultural relativism in anthropological circles, racial inferiority rather than learned cultural practices seemed to distinguish American Indians from whites in the economic and educational policies of Leupp and his contemporaries.

Faced with what would appear to be the failure of allotment and assimilation, the OIA did not abandon such policies but instead accelerated their execution. For example, the Burke Act of 1906, passed to restrict alcohol consumption on reservations, amended the Dawes Act such that citizenship would be deferred for twenty-five years after allotments were assigned (thus perpetuating the wardship status of the allottees) and, more important, allowed the secretary of the interior to grant patents of fee-simple title at his discretion to any Native allottee he considered "competent and capable of managing his or her affairs."[61] This facet of the Burke Act in practice greatly increased the number of allottees who received title to their lands, and between 1906 and 1908 more than 60 percent of those receiving fee-simple titles under the amendment had quickly lost their lands and the proceeds through sales to non-Indians. This trend continued, and between the years 1916 and 1921, Commissioner Cato Sells issued more than twenty thousand patents in fee, twice as many as had been issued in the ten years prior.[62] Likewise, the assimilative educational curriculum remained largely intact from the creation of Carlisle through the 1920s.

Vocational training for American Indians was a mainstay at Carlisle from the very beginning, even though Pratt believed that higher education was within their grasp. In 1906 Leupp sent troops to arrest Hopis who refused to send their children to boarding school, and in 1908 he proposed legislation to force fee-simple title allotments on those who refused to send their children away, knowing full well that they could easily lose their allotments through swindle.[63] And, finally, the bestowal of citizenship remained the goal of the OIA, even though it became clear that Indians would continue to fail, from the OIA's perspective, to meet the responsibilities and cultural requirements of citizenship.

Yet Leupp also ushered in a new era in federal Indian policy, one that actively advanced displays of musical Indianness within the schools. In 1907 he wrote education circular number 175, which contrasted dramatically with previous policies in the OIA regarding Native songs in the schools:

I have, in a few speeches and other public utterances, made special mention of the successful practice of one of our teachers in the Southwest, of inducing her pupils to bring to the class-room the little nursery songs of their homes, and sing them there in concert, in their own tongue and with their own inflections and gestures. As everyone who reads this letter probably knows, I have none of the prejudice which exists in many minds against the perpetuation of Indian music and other arts, customs and traditions, *provided they are innocent in themselves and do not clash needlessly with the new social order into which we are inducting our aboriginal race.* Indeed, I am glad to have the simple songs which the Indians have learned at home in their childhood preserved by their young people, just as among the children of the Caucasian race the nursery songs and lullabies are among the sweetest memories they carry into later life. Although I would use every means to encourage the children to learn English, that being one of the objects for which they are brought to school, I do not consider that their singing their little songs in their native tongue does anybody any harm, and it helps to make easier the perilous and difficult bridge which they are crossing at this stage of their race development.[64]

Leupp's seeming acceptance of Native music, even if only "innocent . . . nursery songs," reflects one of his innovations in the OIA: influ-

enced by anthropologists who forwarded theories of cultural disparity, he believed that American Indians could not, as Pratt believed,
shed their "Indian" traits through education.[65] Rather, he argued, the
OIA must accept that Indians and whites were in some ways fundamentally different. These differences, he believed, did not necessitate
outright elimination unless they clashed with the "new social order."
Although the instruction in Euro-American music was designed to
teach the students to become proper Americanized citizens, it appears
that in 1907 the OIA undertook a new experiment: that of using music
to teach the students how to become "proper" Indians as well.

Leupp's particular decision to embrace the inclusion of curricular
material that celebrated Indianness was largely in response to the
growing canon of literature by ethnologists on Indian music. Natalie
Curtis's collection of Native songs, called *The Indians' Book* (1907),
seems the most likely publication that urged Leupp to reconsider the
music curriculum in the schools. Curtis's book, which drew positive
reviews and has remained in print ever since its publication, initially
attracted attention because of President Theodore Roosevelt's
endorsement. He wrote a note that introduced the book: "These songs
call a wholly new light on the depth and dignity of Indian thought,
the simple beauty and strange charm—the charm of a vanished elder
world—of Indian poetry."[66] Roosevelt's support of Curtis's work, in
the midst of a federal policy that rendered Native traditions antithetical to citizenship, caused quite a bit of controversy within the OIA.[67]
Yet Leupp was a friend of Roosevelt's and a member of his "cowboy
cabinet."[68] While the anti-dance sentiment remained intact within the
OIA, the popularity of *The Indians' Book*, coupled with Roosevelt's
support, prompted some within the bureaucracy to rethink educational policies.[69] Leupp's challenge lay in how to integrate his directive to support the inclusion of tribal and Indian-themed songs with
the federal government's overriding citizenship agenda.

Leupp's valuation of Indianness remained entrenched within a cultural hierarchy crowned by the perceived superior attributes of whiteness. Musical performances of Indianness were not to support calls
for self-determination or self-governance by tribes. It seems that their
primary purpose was to underscore the "civilized" nature of Euro-
American music while catering to the desire of a white public to experience "authentic" displays of "Indian" culture—to inhabit a critique

of "white" culture that at the same time reaffirmed its inevitable dominance. Safely contained, seemingly impotent, yet marketable displays of Indianness were contrasted by Leupp to the dangerous tribally derived dances that the OIA continued to attack.[70] To justify the racial order that seemed relatively fixed in the minds of Leupp and others who were pessimistic about the abilities of Indians to transcend their cultural "binds," particular exhibitions of Indianness were deemed in line with, and not in opposition to, the continued assault on Indian lands and communal values. In other words, racial displays of Indianness, sanitized and removed from all elements harmful to white society, not only supported the notion of white superiority but also justified the economic conditions of American Indians.

Not everyone agreed with Leupp's assessments. Accordingly, Leupp, who faced criticism from both Native and non-Native people alike for allowing performances of Indianness in the schools, emphasized his reconciliation of the policy of celebrating racial difference in the schools by sanitizing the meaning of tribal song and dance— removing the context and value of the songs from the indigenous systems of knowledge that operated within the reservation environment. If the songs did not challenge the "new social order," they could serve instead as signifiers of an ancestral racial pride, safely relegated to the past and removed from the contemporary conditions that fueled the dance resurgence. Therefore Leupp sought to manage how students understood their Native identity in relation to the government civilization and citizenship agenda, in this case through a carefully designed music curriculum. The OIA immediately began to implement this curriculum in the schools.

TEACHING THE MUSIC OF INDIANNESS

In 1907, the same year that Leupp composed the circular, the same year that Curtis's *Indians' Book* was first published, the Carlisle school band performed Stauffer's arrangement of "Song of the Ghost Dance" for the school's commencement exercises.[71] Even the Ghost Dance, considered one of the most dangerous of recent developments in Indian Country, was seen by the OIA as safely contained in the students' repertoire less than twenty years after the massacre. By 1909 the OIA had even created an appointment to collect Native music and transcribe it.[72] By this time Indianist composers had already requested a lead role in the effort of teaching Indianness to Native schoolchildren. Eagerly seeking government endorsements, as well as a share in the Indian school market, these composers flooded the OIA with offers of their services. In 1914 Charles Wakefield Cadman recorded "tribal songs" by the "full blooded" Pima children at the Phoenix Indian School in order to develop compositions for further use.[73] There exist volumes of correspondence between composer Thurlow Lieurance and the OIA from the 1910s and the 1940s. Lieurance frequented the schools during this period and often reported to the OIA when he heard "a piece of Indian music" in the schools, as he did by the Haskell school band in 1913. Though not a government official in any capacity, Lieurance composed several "Indian-English songs, adapted for use in the Indian schools," and gave them to the superintendent of the Crows. "I taught them, the children, a complete list, gratis," he wrote.[74] The next year, Lieurance took the Santa Fe Railway to visit several schools, collecting music along the way.[75] Through such cooperative efforts with American composers, the OIA discovered a way to further the policy of assimilation while recognizing the public pressure to produce a body of alumni who could, when prompted, produce safe, controlled, docile displays of Indianness.

At the same time that such Indianness flourished as performance in the schools, students were constantly admonished, in the tradition of the tale of *Stiya*, not to cross the line into a dangerous performance of tribally derived expressive culture. In a 1911 article from Carlisle's *Red Man*, students were warned of the grave consequences of participating in the Shoshone Sun Dance: "Its practice is wholly inconsistent with the teachings of Christian civilization and progress. It effectively counteracts the best efforts of teachers and missionaries, and not only is an impediment to the advancement of the tribe, but it yearly takes the Indians from their farm work at a time when crops need the most careful attention."[76] The article continued, "It is a wild, weird and fascinating performance; a fanatical fantasy; an orgie [of] nearly naked and frenzied Indians. . . . Certainly a religious rite devoid of morality and virtue, an idolatrous and pagan worship from which women and dogs are excluded!"[77] This voyeuristic description not only revealed the barometer of savagery that OIA officials applied to Native expressive culture but also informed the students that the dance remained intensely popular among the Shoshones, despite the ban.

Although the description of the Shoshone dance may have appalled some of the students, it is equally plausible that it fascinated others and gave them something else to look forward to when they returned home. Indeed, school publications such as that advertising the Shoshone dance served as a means both for school officials to critique certain forms of expressive culture and for students to inform each other of upcoming events at home. The same edition of *The Red Man* dedicated a section to the "legends, stories, customs of Indians" written by Carlisle students.[78] Editions of other Carlisle periodicals maintained a long-held tradition of including published letters from alumni, though carefully screened, updating their friends about life back home.[79] From as early as the mention by Henry North of a Kiowa medicine dance planned for the summer of 1887, these periodicals had referenced specific dances and even provided a dance calendar of sorts to the students.[80] While Marianna Burgess in editorial capacity wrote about the evils of dance ("Of course, the lazy, worthless Indian will try to do all they can to hinder the progress of those who have taken the right road"), the alumni, it could be argued, found ways to use the Carlisle publications to advertise dances to their friends, to learn about the dances taking place at home, and to recall dancing traditions.[81] Such dances, of course, were forbidden on school grounds.[82]

Perhaps believing that a sanitized evocation of Indianness would somehow satiate student interest in these dances, the OIA in 1913 proceeded formally to implement a form of musical Indianness education within the boarding schools. The office hired composer Geoffrey O'Hara to record Native songs on reservations, arrange them in the medium of Euro-American orchestration, and then teach them to the Indian school students.[83] In this way OIA officials believed they had cleansed Native music of any elements of "heathenism" that were associated with songs and dances in the reservation environment. One OIA official stated, "It is not considered desirable to smother everything distinctly aboriginal in the young Indians, nor is it deemed necessary that they should entirely lose their identity as a race in the process of civilization."[84] Commissioner F. H. Abbott added in the same year,

> There is much of good in the music and life of these people which should not be lost to the world as it will be if they become mere imitators of another race. . . . [T]o preserve the best in their music, arts, and economics is not a backward step in the course of their material progress. . . . The purpose of this conservation of native music is not a fad but an earnest sympathetic effort to help both races in giving to life one thing that is worth preserving of a vanishing race. Nor is it intended nor will it have the effect of perpetuating any of the baser or ignoble parts of Indian life.[85]

O'Hara began his work by immediately descending upon the Carlisle Indian School. At the request of Commissioner Abbott, O'Hara traveled to the school from New York City to hear a sacred concert by the pupils. Only one week prior, a group of Blackfeet had arrived at the school to witness the commencement ceremonies; O'Hara quickly recruited them to sing into his phonograph machine in New York. After the records were made, as reported by a Carlisle paper, they would be "sent to Washington to be put among the Government archives, therefore preserving for all time the music of the Original Americans who are rapidly passing to the Happy Hunting Ground."[86] Not all of O'Hara's work ended up in the "Government archives," however; the next year, Victor commercially released a recording of O'Hara singing three Navajo songs, backed with a recording of "Gambler's Song" by a group of Blackfeet Indians, most likely the group from Carlisle.[87]

Despite the apparent zeal with which the OIA eventually established the teaching of decidedly Indian music in the schools, uniform instruction, regulated by the OIA, never occurred. It is unclear exactly how much of the music O'Hara collected was actually included in individual school curricula. When, in 1914, Senator William S. Kenyon asked Commissioner Sells to forward to him "a set of Indian music taught in the schools of the different Indian reservations," Sells indicated that Indian music had not been uniformly included in the school curricula and instead directed him to a set of recordings that the OIA had licensed to the music merchants M. Witmark and Sons in

New York and Chicago.[88] Nevertheless, it is clear that by that same year Indian-themed music had infiltrated many schools in nearly every component of musical instruction. Attempts within the schools to foster music that consisted of Indian-themed content, whether in the form of ideological representations or otherwise, were much more localized and school-specific than based on the centralized policy proposed by Leupp or undertaken by O'Hara. Although the school superintendents and teachers developed their own curricula, similarities in content between the schools are remarkable. The resemblance in music curricula reflects not only an unwillingness to include songs and dances performed currently on reservations but also an acceptance of the images and sounds of Indianness that already circulated in popular culture, as well as a working knowledge of many of the popular Indian-themed songs of the day.

Native schoolchildren's performances of such songs at this time provide insight into how Indianness was envisioned and disseminated within the schools. Superintendents struggled to reconcile the celebration of performed difference with the principles of assimilation, which demanded homogeneity. School administrators and OIA officials, to differing degrees, believed that their inclusion of Indian-themed material in the curricula met the demands of the non-Indian public via an innocuous calculus of Indianness, safe from causing the students irreparable cultural damage even though it often reaffirmed the stereotypes the OIA ostensibly sought to dismantle.

The Carlisle school, for example, incorporated references to Indianness into the fight songs of its heralded football team. Claude Stauffer, head of the school's music program, wrote a number of these songs that the band and students performed at games, often to huge crowds of curious spectators. Rather than accentuating the similarities between Native and non-Native people as demonstrated in the games, the songs emphasized Native American "warriors" who would "scalp" their foes by trouncing them on the field. Stauffer's "Tammany" is one such example:

Harvard, Yale and Willie Penn
   With half a score or more
Of the other Colleges

Are looking for a war.
Won't they be surprised to see
Among the Red and Gold
All Big Chiefs like Tammany,
Who was a Warrior Bold.
Now that's what we've been told.

(Chorus)
Wau-se-ka! Wau-se-ka!
Heap Big Chief, he make a rush
Their whole line go down, "oh slush"
Wau-se-ka! Wau-se-ka!
Keep them humping by your bumping
Wau-se-ka![89]

Stauffer's song "Cheyenne" included the line, "You're up against a real proposition,/The 'Big Chiefs' from Old Carlisle," and a verse from his adaptation of "My Wife's Gone to the Country" proclaimed, "We aim to take Penn's scalp today,/There's no other way."[90] Stauffer's words penetrated the psyche of the public (and Carlisle's football foes) by satisfying their expectations of Indianness and simultaneously prompted the students to invest their repertoire with lyrics reifying the stereotypes that a Carlisle education would supposedly eradicate.[91]

Indeed, the role of the general public, and its expectations of Indianness, should not be underestimated in contemplating the implementation of federal Indian policy in this period. The fight songs in part reflected the burgeoning popularity of Indian-themed songs and compositions found on cylinder recordings, 78s, and sheet music. Soon after they and the publications of Curtis, Fletcher, Densmore, and others began to grow in circulation, the non-Indian public began to petition the OIA for information on how to access more of such music. In 1909, when Henry Finck of New York's *Evening Post* was preparing for a vacation to the Southwest, he asked the commissioner of Indian Affairs where he could hear some "real Indian singing right 'on tap.'" The office told him to visit the Colorado River, Sherman, Klamath, Mohave City, and Havasupai Indian schools and in fact sent him letters of introduction for each superintendent that read, "No doubt you have among the Indians around the agency those who should be willing to sing for him. I would like very much to have him hear something really characteristic. Please furnish him such facilities as your place affords to get genuine Indian singing."[92] It is important to note that the OIA invited him to the schools so that he could find the "genuine" article. In addition to providing the letters, the OIA made a special recommendation that he visit the Sherman Institute, where he could hear "a class of Hopi pupils, some of rather mature age, who were sent there over a year ago." The recommendation continued: "They are 'of Indians most Indian,' and you could probably hear something interesting from them."[93] Other letters commended the new musical program in the schools, especially in the wake of O'Hara's 1913 appointment.[94] Mazzini Slusser and his wife wrote Interior secretary Franklin Lane: "As long time friends of the American Indian we were made very happy by finding in the *Chicago Tribune* of today the announcement that you had appointed a musical composer to study and prepare native Indian music for use in the Indian schools. The far reaching and beneficial effect of such an act can not be measured."[95]

The OIA even turned the eager public toward the work of the ethnologists who were partly responsible for the rising popularity of Indian-themed music. After Lucy Barlow from New Albany, Indiana, witnessed a Mohave song and its accompanying dance, she later "reproduced it" on paper and submitted it to the department. She noted that she did not know the meaning of the words and that the song was "sung with a jerky movement."[96] Chief clerk J. M. Conser forwarded her transcription to the *Southern Workman* at the Hampton Institute, but he noted that if the school did not publish her "reproduction," he would send it to Alice Fletcher, a "pioneer in the work of preserving Indian music."[97] When J. H. Bratley, a former teacher and superintendent of various Indian schools for nine years, decided that he "would like some Indian music," the acting chief clerk recommended he look at *Indian Story and Song*, by Alice C. Fletcher; *The Indians' Book*, by Natalie Curtis; the *Indian School Journal* published at Chilocco Indian School; and Hampton Institute's *Southern Workman*. He also recommended the work of composer Arthur Farwell of

Boston, who had published "Four American Indian Songs" through the White-Smith Music Publishing Company, as well as "Navajo War Dance No. 2 for Piano" in 1904.[98] Amid the continued suppression of reservation dances, the highest-ranking OIA officials seemed perfectly secure in their acknowledgment of the influence of ethnologists within the schools. Additionally, in the midst of a federal policy certainly defined more by the goal of assimilation than by a goal of self-determination or even cultural tolerance, they saw no contradiction in teaching the students Indian-themed songs, which they perhaps considered a practical means of producing a labor force that could even, when called upon by non-Indians, provide safe and entertaining "real Indian singing right 'on tap.'"

NATIVE RIPOSTES AND OIA REBUTTALS

As the study of Indianness in the schools suggests, it became less and less clear who among the ethnologists, the non-Indian public, and the OIA officials was steering federal Indian educational policy, and American Indians immediately jumped into the fray as well. In fact, Native teachers had been working from inside the schools to celebrate, and thereby resist the imposed suppression of, Native arts.[99] Shortly after Pratt left Carlisle, noted artist Angel DeCora (Ho-Chunk) began teaching at Carlisle and remained on its art faculty for nine years. She dedicated her work there to encouraging the students to express pride through Native art traditions.[100] After Pratt's departure, she established in 1906 a Native arts and crafts program at the school. She wrote that "[white] educators made every effort to convince the Indian that any custom or habit that was not familiar to the white man showed savagery and degradation." She continued, "In looking over my pupil's native design work, I cannot help calling to mind the Indian woman, untaught and unhampered by the white man's ideas of art, making beautiful and intricate designs on her pottery, baskets, and beaded articles, which show inborn talent."[101] DeCora lashed out against the assumptions of cultural superiority that colored her own student experience at the Hampton Institute.

Others wrote the commissioner about the Indian-themed music initiative. A self-described "full blood," J. W. Gibson (Delaware) offered to furnish songs to the office:

> I can muster about 100 or more ancient and modern songs of the various tribes. . . . I am the only living Indian today who can sing that many songs. Among the songs one the War dance from 5 different tribes the Ghost Dance. Medicine. Sun dance. Buffalo. Wolf. Turkey. (not Turkey Trot) doll. Stomp dance and many others. I am the Indian who presented the late Senator M. S. Quay to the Delaware Indians and was made a chief of the Delawares. 1904. I am here representing the M K & T Ry. [Missouri, Kansas, & Texas Railway Company] with headquarters in Rosedale [Kansas].[102]

Acting commissioner Abbott forwarded the letter to O'Hara and assured Gibson that "there is no doubt but that [O'Hara] will appreciate every opportunity to get into touch with Indian musicians."[103]

While some American Indians were excited about the OIA's interest in Indian music, others were outraged and clearly considered as dangerous the themed music that seemed so safe to Leupp. Some of the most vociferous Native supporters *and* opponents of the policy in the press came from within the ranks of the vanguard of Native writers, poets, lawyers, and musical performers, who became actively involved in the reform and progressive movements of the period. Carlos Montezuma (Yavapai) was one of the most vocal Native opponents of the teaching of Indianness in the schools, and he lashed out in print against it.[104] Montezuma, who was born in 1871 and alternatively went by the name his parents gave him, Wassaja, was captured by the Pimas, or Akimel O'odham, when he was four and sold to a man who adopted him for fifty dollars. He attended public schools and eventually worked his way through the Chicago Medical College. He served as a reservation and Indian school physician at various locations for a number of years and ended up at Carlisle, where he felt a deep kinship with Pratt. Montezuma, like Pratt, believed in immediate assimilation as the only course for American Indians. He later established a private practice in Chicago and cofounded the Society of American Indians (SAI). He was an outspoken critic of the OIA, and later of the SAI when it challenged his views.[105] He was proud of his heritage, but he nonetheless condemned the instruction of tribal music in the schools in a letter to the *Chicago Herald* in 1913:

> Indian music, Indian art and like fads are shame and the real Indian abhors such foolishness. . . . Indians do not want to be kept as Indians, but seek education and light and more ability to cope with their pale face brother. . . . The people of this country are taxed to civilize and elevate the Indian children into modern usefulness and Americanism, and to eradicate their Indianism with its primitive life, which has cursed them with the title of "uncivilized." The development of the Indian to civilized usefulness is far more important than filling his mind with Indian legends and Indian songs. These have a place in the Smithsonian Institute, but certainly not in Indian schools. A thousand times better is it for the Indian to fight out his own salvation than to have sentimentalists and special interests add their impractical and deteriorating efforts to his so-called uplifting. . . . For nearly eight years the Indian bureau has been experimenting on the Indians and cultivating Indian fads to the neglect and serious injury of his advancement. If the present administration is going to continue exploiting Indian fads, then our race will continue to suffer.[106]

Montezuma's convictions ran deep, and he dedicated his life to reforming federal Indian policy in a way that fully supported elevated formal educational guidelines for Native students, particularly in regard to opening up more opportunities for higher education. He was discouraged by Leupp's 1907 education circular and altogether outraged by the hiring of Geoffrey O'Hara. A Cherokee named John Oskison wrote to the secretary of the interior in support of Montezuma's arguments, adding, "Too much experimenting on the Indians has been done, and . . . too much publicity has been given to the more spectacular features of Indian life. The big job to be done is to prepare them for industrial competition with the Whites."[107]

The OIA in fact received a number of newspaper clippings from individuals that reported Montezuma's opposition to the policy. Assistant Commissioner Abbott responded to one such individual by acknowledging that white citizens could benefit from an assimilation of their own:

There is much in the aboriginal life of the Indian of which he may be proud and we should not be ashamed to adopt and assimilate all that is good in him, nor can I see harm to the Indian or to the white race in so doing. . . . The American people of today is an assimilation of the best of many nations, it is a composite of the great races of the world, and to draw the best and noblest of the original American will not detract from our own civilization or affect the Indians adversely.[108]

Abbott continued by taking Montezuma to task:

The purpose of this conservation of native music is not a fad but an earnest sympathetic effort to help both races in giving to life one thing that is worth preserving of a vanishing race. Nor is it intended nor will it have the effect of perpetuating any of the baser or ignoble parts of Indian life. *It is to the shame of some educated Indians, that in their veneer of white civilization, they overlook the real Indian, who is quite as much, if not more, entitled to our friendly sympathy than he is.*[109]

Abbott's critique of school-educated Indians, "in their veneer of white civilization," seems astonishing given that the OIA had spent decades attempting to assimilate individuals in just the manner that Montezuma advanced. On the other hand, Abbott's statement accurately reflected the beliefs of most OIA officials of the time: that Native people were doomed to a life in which they would cloak themselves either in a pretense of whiteness, ever transparent, of course, or in the dress of the OIA's "real Indian," a simulacra fabricated through the negotiation of Indianness and deserving of sympathy rather than dignity. As Indianness continued to infiltrate the directives of federal Indian policy, such performances of both Indianness and whiteness grew to support the assimilation and allotment agenda. At the same time, federal officials could not maintain control over the meaning of those performances by the students.

To begin with, not everyone agreed with the codependent nature of those performative roles of whiteness and Indianness, and the public desire for Native students to perform Indianness often confounded the attempt of school superintendents to manage, or in some cases to thwart, such expressions. The resulting tension often caused confusion and consternation among the students. Sometimes even when students were instructed against performing Indianness, the public nevertheless pressured them to do so. In 1880, Booker T. Washington, then in charge of the Native students at the Hampton Institute, wrote an article in the school newspaper describing the resultant student frustrations in even this early period of boarding school education: "There have been a great many excursions here this summer and of course all of them had to see the Indians. At first the girls did not mind them very much; but they came in such bodies, crowded around them in such numbers and asked so many absurd questions that they soon got tired and would hide when they heard them coming."[110] The desire of non-Indians to experience Indianness pervaded and colored Native student experiences with the non-Indian public and continued to do so throughout the ensuing decades.

In 1911 Carlisle superintendent Friedman sent five students, four males and one female, to sing at an exposition in Boston. He, along with OIA commissioner Robert G. Valentine, believed the students would demonstrate the "Indians' progress" and would "be of assistance in a demonstration of Indian Missions and Indian education."[111] Their repertoire, however, consisted of Indian-themed songs by Charles Wakefield Cadman, who based his compositions on transcriptions of Chippewa songs collected by Frances Densmore.[112] The quartet gathered large audiences with their renditions of songs such as "Ho, Ye Warriors on the Warpath." Like clockwork, they performed nine times a day for a month to crowds that averaged two hundred people. Apart from other special appearances, they also performed the songs for about five thousand schoolchildren every Saturday morning during the duration of the fair.[113] Although several people who heard them sing wrote the OIA praising the work at Carlisle, the office also received word that the students did not exactly follow the letter of Friedman's instructions. Friedman wrote to one of the students, James Mumblehead (Cherokee), halfway into their Boston visit:

I understand that you attended the Lacrosse game between Harvard and the Indians in your Indian costume, which was, of course, a serious mistake. I understand also that you emphasize the primitiveness of the

Indian, rather than the Indian's progress in civilization. I am grieved to hear this and I am sure that you will agree with me in my desires that you four young men shall represent in "The World in Boston" what Carlisle stands for, namely, progress, industry and Christian civilization. . . . I desire that you boys at all times . . . dress yourselves as other men are dressed, and that you shall act in conformity with the training that you have received. . . . Show my letter to the other boys and use your influence in getting them to make the most of this opportunity, not in emphasizing "Indianism," but rather in showing to those about you the progress of the Indian in Christian civilization.[114]

Despite Friedman's allowance of Indian-themed songs in the students' repertoire, Mumblehead and the boys had crossed the line as to what Friedman deemed appropriate. After an investigation and response from Mumblehead, however, it became clear that the boys were in fact told to dress in "Indian costume" by the leaders of some Indian missions who were charged with "taking care" of them in Boston.[115] Like Pratt years earlier, missionaries recognized the essential need to "sell" the value of their missions to the non-Indian public, who often supported them. They, like many boarding school officials, time and time again titillated the public with displays of Indianness alongside their stated goals to destroy tribalism—in order, if for no other good reason, to justify the necessity of their transformative project. Indeed, for many missionaries and OIA officials in this period, it seemed that merely justifying their projects, if not their employment, occupied a much higher priority than the needs they deemed appropriate to their Native subjects. Pratt bitterly shared this view of the OIA bureaucracy and discussed it in a chapter of his autobiography, aptly entitled "Propaganda": "The government-salaried denizens in the Indian and Ethnological bureaus saw their occupations vanish with every development of the Indian into the ability of citizens. Their headquarters in Washington and administrative opportunities gave them daily access to legislators and administrators, and 'self-preservation is the first law of nature.'"[116] As Tom Holm points out, despite the claim made by Secretary of the Interior Franklin K. Lane in 1913 that the OIA was a "vanishing bureau," the number of OIA employees had more than doubled since 1900.[117]

As we have seen, justifying their projects deftly coincided with providing non-Indian audiences with the commodified displays of Indianness that they so desired. School officials who disagreed with the mandate faced admonitions by the press, similar to those Burke encountered during the dance controversy. In 1915 the *Oklahoma Oil and Gas News* reported that OIA commissioner Cato Sells had forbidden the Chilocco band students from donning tribal dress. Referring to him as an "official nincompoop," they wrote that he expressly forbade the Chilocco band from playing one of its "especially attractive" pieces, an "Indian folk composition requiring the use of tribal attire." The paper reported: "If the members of the band appeared in typical Indian costume the band would not be permitted to exist longer but would be disbanded permanently. That's going some, if you leave it to us. They'll have to use chloroform to keep us quiet after that."[118] Sells, however, had not issued such an order. The YMCA had invited the Chilocco band to play in Tulsa, and although, according to Chilocco superintendent Edgar A. Allen, the band never dressed "Indian," the organization requested and advertised that one boy would dress in "costume" during the performance of one of Harold Loring's Indian suites.[119] The superintendent said that under no circumstances would such a performance occur, which led the newspaper to lash out against the OIA. Clearly, the performative deployment of Indianness varied between schools, even as top OIA officials attempted to assert bureauwide policies on the matter. Students who transferred between schools, as they often did, could find themselves encountering wildly different rules regarding displays of expressive culture.

School officials struggled much more than the far-removed OIA commissioners in configuring public presentations of their students that at once demonstrated their abilities to assimilate while also captivating the public's interest through displays of Indianness. The majority of the public who supported the right of American Indians to dance on reservations in the early twentieth century also preferred and demanded presentations of Indianness over the musical displays aspiring to the perceived discipline and regimentation of whiteness traditionally featured in the school programs. The overwhelming representations of "authentic" Indian people in popular culture, after all, were not of students in band uniforms or "citizen"

clothes but rather of "warriors" and "maidens" donning war bonnets and buckskin. What resulted was a performance by the students
of both Indianness and whiteness, a performance school administrators hoped would emphasize the assimilative qualities of education
by students who were simultaneously bound by the racial bonds of
immutable difference.

Eventually school officials and bandmasters created various "educational" evolutionary paradigms in which they could incorporate
performances of Indianness within the logic of their "civilizing"
assimilation campaign. Even this strategy was old hat for some, as
several bandmasters had, by the late 1800s, dabbled in evolutionary
narrative within their compositions. In 1896, Oneida bandmaster
Dennison Wheelock composed such a piece for the Carlisle band.
According to a review of one performance, "Dennison Wheelock with
his cornet band . . . brought out a new and entirely original composition—"From Savagery into Civilization" in which the sounds produced led up from the wild tom tom, through curious and intricate
twists and turns to the sweet and classic strains of civilized horns. It
was very appropriate for the occasion and was highly appreciated by
the audience."[120] Pratt considered Wheelock, according to Laurence
Hauptman, "a surrogate son, one of his special Carlisle boys . . . a near
perfect model of what the superintendent had envisioned when he
founded the school."[121] Indeed, if any of the student musicians took
the assimilation campaign to heart, it would have been Wheelock, yet
even he could have reveled in the passages of Indianness for reasons
that Pratt would not have approved or understood.[122]

Superintendent Samuel McCowan was eager to incorporate
Indian-themed songs in the repertoire of the Chilocco School band
and choir as well, particularly for their performances at the 1904
Louisiana Purchase Exposition. After Alice Fletcher had pulled him
aside earlier that year in order to convince him of the merits of teaching the students "Indian" songs for the fair, McCowan wrote her back
in agreement: "I believe with you that Indian music touches chords in
the human soul beyond reach of most of the stuff used today. I am
really anxious to get something in the musical line for the Band that
portrays something at least of what Indian music really means to the
Indian and his interpretation of nature." With no hint of irony, he con-

cluded, "I wish an Indian could write this."[123] McCowan and Fletcher obviously believed in the innate value of "Indian music," but it is unclear whether they thought that the performance of such music by the band would better serve the needs of the students or those of the non-Indian public. Furthermore, whether or not an American Indian would write the music that McCowan hoped for the band to perform, it mattered little; for McCowan and Fletcher, the authenticity of the music ultimately lay in what they considered the proper execution of Indianness, and Indianness was composed of assumptions they had already agreed upon, assumptions that did not necessarily require the input of a Native person.

PAGEANTS:
THE APEX OF PERFORMANCE IN THE SCHOOLS

An evolutionary paradigm of musical programs assembled by school officials bound performances of Indianness with whiteness in a way that demonstrated the inevitability of white superiority while assuaging the demands of Indianness by non-Indian audiences. In 1926 the Haskell Institute orchestra performed in accordance with the competing desires for Indianness by the public and for assimilation by the OIA:

> The first half of the program . . . consists entirely of Indian music and during the time that that part of the program is being given the boys dress in Indian costume. The second half of the entertainment is made up of music similar to what any good orchestra would play and during the time that that part of the program is given the boys dress in evening dress. It can be readily understood that the contrast is striking and that the program is unique, no other organization being able to put on such a program.[124]

The program, however, was not unique in the slightest.

T. J. McCoy, of "Colonel T. J. McCoy's Last Great Council and Historical Spectacle Winning of the West" show, used a similar evolutionary structure in order to gain a government endorsement for his Wild West show at the Philadelphia Sesqui-Centennial Exposition in 1926. McCoy arranged with Wheelock, who had since retired from his

profession as a musician, to assemble an Indian band of thirty-two
school alumni, "not to have the Indian band arrayed in war paint and
feathers, but dressed in the most immaculate white uniform, in order
to show the contrast between the wild Indian and the finished product."[125] Indian schools and private entertainment groups seeking governmental approval reconciled their educational mandate with the
public longing to experience Indianness through an often vague evolutionary musical performance. During the performances students
would demonstrate an ability to perform both a contained Indianness
and a contrasting "civilized" whiteness with their horns, pianos, and
mandolins. The juxtaposition of "savagery" and "civilization" was
reminiscent of the "before and after" photographs that Pratt had used
in the late nineteenth century to advertise the "civilizing" effects of
the school. The difference here, however, was that following Leupp's
placement as the commissioner of Indian Affairs, school officials
began to deploy both whiteness and Indianness, whenever they
deemed it most useful to fit their particular needs. They might ask a
senior to dress in regalia and sing Indian-themed songs, for example,
not just students who had recently enrolled. Depending on the circumstances and the desires of the non-Indian public, OIA officials
asked their students to develop a repertoire from which they could
perform whiteness or Indianness, as if on command.

Despite the local struggles between the public and the schools over
how the young musicians and singers would represent themselves,
and the fact that many school officials requested students to conjure
up performances of Indianness and whiteness for different circumstances, the evolutionary narrative formed a common solution for the
school administrators when orchestrating public performances. This
type of display reached a pinnacle in school pageants, presented for
both the parents and the public during commencement exercises. In
these elaborate performances, administrators hoped to show a controlled form of Indianness within historical reenactments of American
history, thus forging a musical politics by joining a racial evolutionary
narrative with a nationalist one.

The pageants presented in Indian schools across the country
required the students to perform the roles of various European colonial "heroes" and Native American "foes" cast in the literary tradition

of Longfellow and other Puritan descendants. In the late nineteenth and early twentieth centuries, American historians and textbook publishers strove to rewrite American history in a manner that favored and exaggerated the role of the Puritans in creating a moral and civic compass for all Americans to follow. Just as Parson Weems created the story of George Washington and the cherry tree, these historians fashioned a narrative of good and evil in American history, with the Puritans acting clearly as the representative hallmark of the colonial conquest of North American tribes. This renewed patriotic fervor was due in large part to the massive influx of immigrants to the country in this period and was marked by increased nationalistic sentiment and the proliferation of patriotic pageantry.[126] According to David Glassberg, the pageant became "not only a new medium for patriotic, moral, and aesthetic education envisioned by genteel intellectuals, but also an instrument for the reconstruction of American society and culture using progressive ideals."[127] Although the pageants filled the auditoriums of public schools nationwide, in addition to federal Indian schools, it was the Native students who had to perform Indianness and whiteness in narratives that celebrated their own subjugation.

The pageants gained favor among the OIA officials in the years following Roosevelt's approval of Curtis's work and especially around the time that the OIA hired O'Hara to compose Indian music for the students. During the 1913 commencement exercises of the Seger School, fittingly in Colony, Oklahoma, the schoolchildren performed "A Colonial Pageant"—"a portrayal of the elements and influences operating in the growth of the Colonies into Nationality, 1650–1775."[128] The pageant included children dressing as students, Indians, Dutch settlers, Puritans, colonial ladies and gentlemen, plantation slaves, and a witch. Among the multiple scenes were "The Foundation of Manhattan" ("Indians are frightened at the approach of the white men. War Song follows. . . . Indians give presents to Dutch settlers who treat in return. Closes with the peace-pipe scene") and "The Rescue of Hadley," in which an Indian attack on the Puritans, while in church, was thwarted.[129] The evening closed with all of the students joining together onstage for a rendition of the song "America."[130]

The very next week at the Fort Sill closing exercises in Lawton, Oklahoma, the students pantomimed, to the music of the band, a

rendition of Longfellow's *Song of Hiawatha*. [131] The program began
with the school band performing the "Star-Spangled Banner" and
"Oklahoma," followed by piano solos by Alice Bear and Edith Poco,
"Merry June" by the Girl's Chorus, a duet, and then a recitation of
"Blackhawk's Farewell" by Samuel Mochodo and "Bob White" by
the primary pupils. [132] The largest segment of the performance, however, was the students' rendition of *Song of Hiawatha* in the following
pantomime:

Hiawatha's Childhood
The Killing of the Red Deer
Hiawatha Visits the Dakotas
Hiawatha's Friends
Hiawatha's Courtship
The Wedding Feast
The Ghosts
Death of Minnehaha
Hiawatha's Departure[133]

The performance concluded with all of the children singing a "Song
in the Indian Language." [134] The drills, songs, school choruses, and
individual numbers, according to a newspaper review, "brought out
with emphasis the good work being done by the teachers at the Ft. Sill
school." [135]

One review of the Fort Sill program fixated on the costumes that the
children wore during the pantomime. The children were clothed,
according to the review, in the "habiliments of the forest in a splendor
of array that only the Comanche tribe can present." Their dress was
"priceless" in value, in particular that of Hiawatha, who wore a "gorgeous war bonnet of eagle feathers, not a feather in which would cost
less than a dollar and a half." The girls, particularly the one who
played Minnehaha in this adaptation, wore shawls and "other gar-
ments of priceless value and great beauty." [136]

The program was attended by approximately one thousand people, about half of whom were Comanches, Kiowas, and Apaches who
lived on allotments within a radius of about forty miles, while the rest
of the audience consisted of "white guests" mostly from Lawton. [137]
Relatives of the children who aided them in the dining room as they

prepared for their scenes probably provided much of the dress for the pantomime.[138] The reporter, who paid close attention to the material value of the clothing and accoutrements, did not feel the need to exercise such interest in the names of the individuals, much less, ironically, in grammar: "the name of the Indian . . . [who wore the bonnet of eagle feathers] is to unspellable to try to reproduce."[139] Later in the review, the reporter added,

> It is difficult to individualize concerning the performers, but it would do positive injustice not to mention the dancing of the young man at the "wedding scene.["] His name likewise, tangles the alphabet too seriously for effort at reproduction by the uninitiated scribe. But [with] his grace of movement, ease of stage presence and perfect blending with the theme[,] he was exemplifying histrionic talent hardly to be expected in one of his race. In fact, the excellence of this entire presentation suggests the possibilities of the Indian as an actor not hitherto developed.[140]

The names were not important to the reporter because the children were evaluated not as individuals but in terms of whether or not their performances of Indianness satisfied the reporter's preconceptions. The parents, on the other hand, not only had a chance to visit their children and watch them perform, but they were also able to dress the children as they saw fit so that the children could at least perform Indianness in a physical expression that they could control.

Carlisle students began performing a pageant of an entirely different sort in 1908; it was so popular that they took it on the road to neighboring towns for a number of years thereafter. The pageant was an adaptation into a Pilgrim setting of Longfellow's "Courtship of Miles Standish," known throughout the schools (Carlisle was not the only Indian school to perform it) as "The Captain of Plymouth—A Comic Opera."[141] The 1909 performance at commencement resulted in three consecutive sold-out showings in a venue with a capacity of one thousand.[142] With Carlisle students dressed as both "Indians" and "whites," the pageant playfully engaged the founding myths, while ultimately emphasizing the superiority of the Pilgrims. When a Philadelphia reporter asked bandmaster Claude Stauffer why he selected "The Captain of Plymouth" for the students to perform, he replied that he chose the opera for its "civilizing influence." He continued:

I thought if Oscar Hammerstein can spend $1,000,000 to civilize Philadel-
phians, we could spen[d] a few weeks for the same civilizing influence on
the wards of the nation. And say, you know that I believe we got the better results. It is plain that the Indians are capable of taking up the white
man's burden, and before long these aborigines will realize how superior
to their peaceful tribal ways are the manners of church choirs and other
amateur musical organizations.[143]

The opera parallels the love triangle plot of Longfellow's story, but the
authors of the Carlisle adaptation included a twist in which Indian
Chief Wattawamat's people hold Standish captive. He is released after
promising to marry the chief's daughter, Katonka. Standish, completely disgusted by the princess, then refuses to marry her. In another
change from Longfellow's poem, Standish meets a group of Indians
in the forest with "friendship . . . in their looks, but in their hearts . . .
hatred." After receiving an insult from an Indian character named
Pecksuaot, Standish stabs Pecksuaot through the heart. The result is
an all-out war, culminating in the Pilgrims' victorious display of Chief
Wattawamat's decapitated head at the church. The Indians in the pageant serve only as instigators of the Pilgrim's travails, and in the end,
they face annihilation.[144] The odd twists inserted to include Indians in
the plot seem not only downright disturbing but also almost inexpli-
cable for a "comic opera."

Musical performances pervaded Indian schools across the country. Far
from considering music as an extracurricular activity, OIA officials
deemed the practice of music to be pivotal to their "civilization" campaign. This campaign, however, consisted in performances of both
whiteness and Indianness. For the majority of OIA officials who shaped
school curricula, one performance could simply not exist without the
other. Expectations of Indianness—considered at times as a demoralizing influence, at times as a romanticized critique of white society with
a real market value—played a profound role, one that should not be
understated, in the shaping of federal Indian policy, both on reservations and in the off-reservation boarding schools. To this end, ethnologists, composers, and the non-Indian public were greatly influential in
the design and execution of federal Indian policy in this period.

Philosophically speaking, the period was, as Tom Holm argues, one of great confusion.[145] To many, the deployment of Indianness in the schools seemed a direct challenge to the assimilationist rhetoric embodied in the ambitions of Richard Pratt. To officials such as Francis Leupp, lowered expectations of the abilities of Indian students contributed to OIA support of certain productions of Indian arts, crafts, and music, no matter how contrived they may have been. Competing philosophies left federal policy in the first quarter of the twentieth century mired in pragmatic orders and failed experiments that rarely signaled consistency on their face value.

Yet perhaps this "great confusion" exhibited by OIA officials rather resulted from the profound sets of assumptions buried deep within in their subconscious. As Lomawaima and McCarty assert, the officials defined for themselves what they deemed "safe" and "dangerous" cultural practices by Native peoples living on reservations or enrolled in schools. Those perceptions shaped the tolerance of, and at times the appetite for, the expressive cultural practices of Native peoples. This greatest confusion also resulted in the greatest tragedy, as the allotment campaign accelerated in this period. Those conceptions of "safe" and "dangerous" practices were perfectly consistent with the overarching civilization campaign—to liquidate Indian lands, detribalize Indian people, and produce a domesticated citizenry who could take pride in their ancestral past by exhibiting approved performances of Indianness but would never assert their difference in politically or culturally oppositional terms. In this sense federal Indian education policy in the 1880s through the mid-1930s was much more consistent than contrary or confused.

The character of federal Indian policy in this period, however, was also shaped profoundly by the resistance of Native peoples to allotment, assimilation, and to the assumptions of the OIA officials and non-Indian public. What did the students and their parents make of the school performances? On the one hand, the students, in many cases, had to enact narratives that supported the notion of their racial inferiority and celebrated violent rampages against their people. The bands and singers were made to perform evolutionary narratives that could simultaneously evoke what were considered their cultural deficiencies as well as their skills at "playing white." They were trained to become docile "Indians" as well as "proper" citizens, and their participation unwittingly justified for many the resultant failures of the assimilationist goals of federal Indian policy. The idyllic Indianness they learned in the schools shared little in common with the realities of their modern lives, yet that Indianness in many ways established a standard and an ideology by which they would be judged daily in the modern world. School administrators wielded unparalleled control over American Indians in the boarding schools, and with the noted exception of a handful of Native teachers such as Angel DeCora, through the 1920s most decisions relating to curriculum were made by non-Indians.

On the other hand, the perspective of the students is ultimately the most important to this story, and we can try to get a sense of how they felt "playing Indian" through a few extent accounts of it. Performances of Indianness in the schools must have felt in some ways liberating for many of the students. Ordinarily they were punished for speaking their Native languages at this time, but these opportunities at least allowed them to perform an ethnic construction of Indianness, if not alternatively a quite tribally specific construction of Indianness, in the midst of the assimilation campaign. Although within the confines of the school grounds they were charged to perform a narrative they could little control, they could certainly inflect their performances with dignity or devious humor.[146] From the early days of the "show Indians," Native people increasingly participated in the construction and consumption of Indianness that transfixed the imagination and opened the wallets of the American public. Education in off-reservation boarding schools, far away from their homes, did not seem to preclude the non-Indian public from investing in the authenticity of the pupils. The schools trained students to adopt this performative language of Indianness to engage non-Indians, but it also strengthened the tribal and pan-tribal bonds of students and provided another layer by which they would identify themselves as Native peoples.

One former boarding school student and later boarding school teacher, Esther Horne (Shoshone), recalled performing Indianness in school productions in 1928, her senior year at the Haskell Institute. She, like her peers and Native teachers, was quite cognizant of all of the contradictions facing students who performed Indianness, and she did not think twice about rejecting the message that the school officials hoped to impose upon the students and audience. For her, Indianness provided opportunity. She recalled:

> I accompanied Ruth Muskrat Bronson and other students to participate in programs that we presented to schools, to church groups and to service organizations. Instrumental and vocal music and talks relating to our Indian heritage were a part of the programs we presented. This was my first exposure to public speaking. . . . Both Ruth and Ella [Deloria] wanted us to learn to survive in a variety of environments. They wanted us to be proud of who we were as Indian people and as boarding school students but also to be comfortable in explaining our identity to the non-Indian world. I suppose one could say that this was a safe way of being Indian, that is, according to the expectations of white society. But for us it was not this way. With Ruth and Ella as our Indian mentors, these excursions became an expression of our Indianness that may not otherwise have been possible, given the poverty and discrimination so prevalent on most reservations.[147]

Ella Deloria (Dakota) and Ruth Muskrat Bronson (Cherokee), like Angel DeCora, became boarding school teachers, and like DeCora, they used their positions within the Indian Service to instill in the students pride in their tribal heritages. Horne considered Deloria and Bronson role models, and although the number of Native teachers in the schools remained low in this period, they clearly made a difference in teaching students another way to read the performance of Indianness—a way that did not contradict their own identities as tribal people but rather complemented their conception of tribal identity in a modern world. In fact, Horne was so taken by their work that she dedicated her own life to teaching Native students in the schools. From the beginning of her teaching career in the 1930s, Horne encouraged her students to take pride in tribalism: at times she even directed pageants, though they were conceived not by non-Indians but by the students themselves. The pageants included scenes of reservation dances as well as school life, and all were crafted out of pride, and not of narratives of racial inferiority.[148] One such pageant, named by an eighth-grade boy as "Buckskin to Broadcloth," did not evoke evolution or cultural obsolescence; rather, according to Horne, "it symbolized the changes that Indians had gone through without tolling the death bell for boarding school kids. For better or worse, a whole generation of Indian people were affected in one way or another by these institutions."[149]

Horne became quite savvy at challenging the directives of the Indian Service, taking its materials and reworking them to suit the needs of her homesick students at the Wahpeton Indian school in the 1930s, during the worst of the Great Depression, when fewer parents could travel to visit their children on a regular basis:

> I encouraged my students to draw scenes related to their home environments. . . . There were tribes from North Dakota, South Dakota, Minnesota, Nebraska, Iowa, Montana, and Wyoming, including Sioux, Chippewa, Cree, Blackfeet, Gros Ventre, Mandan, Hidatsa, Arikara, Mesquakie, Winnebago, Cheyenne, and Shoshone. When [OIA] supervisors came along, I was very adept at sweeping the Indian components under the table, so to speak. The philosophy of the boarding school was still to assimilate Indian children into mainstream culture. The creation of these reservation scenes evolved into a lot of after-school visiting in our room. We talked about differences in tribal regalia, dance, and language, and learned about each other's tribal cultures. We listened to a set of phonograph records of Indian music collected from all over the United States and Canada, and we got lonesome for home. We felt comfortable together because of our shared history and heritage, and we talked about pets and siblings and life. We visited about our homes and relatives, and frequently about folks we knew in common. I had gotten to know a lot of Indian families from across the United States through my friends at Haskell, and this created a bond between the students and myself. I tried to make Wahpeton a home away from home for these students.[150]

In addition, the songs recorded by ethnologists became useful; they captivated Horne and her students, and together with the students and nearby tribal community members she worked to teach the students how to dance along to them, even without live singers or a drum.[151] The Indianness that the OIA tolerated after Leupp's administration in fact often provided just enough performative space for Native teachers like Horne to foster students' pride in their tribal identities. For Horne, her classmates, and later her students, crafting Indianness in the classrooms or on the stage was a liberating and in some cases essential student, Indian experience. Horne observed:

> The traditions and memories that those records captured were so important to the students and to those of us who were teaching these kids the importance of remembering their past. When we heard the beat of the drum, we talked about it being the heartbeat of Mother Earth, who was the mother of us all. The kids, too, began to understand that getting along with one another was not so hard because they were all brothers and sisters. All of those values came together and made us strong. It is hard for me to convey the sense of pride and growth that those students and I felt in those days.[152]

The legacy of teaching musical Indianness in the schools established a far more complicated and oppositional set of meanings than commissioner Leupp could possibly have imagined.

Indeed, music instruction in the schools as well as sheet and recorded music served the students in multiple ways and affected their home communities as well, as an example provided by Willard Rhodes demonstrates. Beginning in the mid-1930s Rhodes recorded music on reservations at the encouragement of the OIA's Collier administration. His recordings were used by students in the "Indian clubs" they created following Collier's appointment. His work was also appreciated by many Native teachers. Praising Rhodes multiple times in her autobiography, Horne wrote, "All government school libraries received copies of these records, which were invaluable to us. They were so fine."[153] In fact the description of the Flagstaff powwow in the introduction of this book came from one of Rhodes's many recordings.

Rhodes was also a scholar of Indian music, however, and one article he wrote in 1958 is particularly revealing in terms of the years prior to Collier's tenure. Rhodes wrote a history of the diffusion of a song he called "Opening Peyote Song," and in the article he shared his correspondence with Elizabeth Willis DeHuff, an Indian schoolteacher and enthusiast of Native art who had recorded a performance of the song by two girls from Taos Pueblo on a wax cylinder in 1919.[154] DeHuff recalled:

According to their statement (the two girls), which was corroborated by several other Taos and Navajo pupils at the Santa Fe Indian School, where I collected it, the song originated among the Navajo and was adopted by the Taos Indians to use in their peyote ceremony. At that time, the Government was opposing the use of Peyote and I could not find out whether or not the Navajos used the song in a peyote ceremony.

She added, "I used it in an Indian play that year and it became popular with all of the Indian pupils and was disseminated when the pupils returned to their homes in Oklahoma, Arizona, New Mexico and among the Utes. It seemed to strike like a spark of dynamite."[155] DeHuff's recording was later harmonized for solo voice and piano by Homer Grunn and published as sheet music in 1924 under the title "Navajo Peyote Drinking Song." Soon after, the song, renamed "Peyote Drinking Song, Navaho Indiana [sic]," was commercially recorded on the His Master's Voice label by Mohawk baritone Chief Os-ke-non-ton. Os-ke-non-ton undoubtedly was not the only professional Indian singer to perform the song at fairs, rodeos, and powwows. War Bow (Harry Nieto) of Zuni recorded the song for Rhodes in 1941 and told him that "he had first heard it sung by an Indian 'Princess' at the Gallup Ceremonial." Rhodes concluded that since Nieto's version was so close to the published version, "one is led to believe that the Indian 'Princess' either learned the song from the printed score or by oral tradition as disseminated from the Santa Fe Indian School."[156] Regardless of the specific transmission of the song through Indian Country, it is clear that students engaged the instruction of Indianness in the schools to suit their own purposes. In this case, the knowledge of a song by one tribe spread quickly through the school, and through the children, to their home communities. Sheet music and a commercial recording by a Mohawk singer further distributed the song, demonstrating one process of selective dissemination of new songs and sounds across the continent.

Just as students found new opportunity in the safe space that the teaching of Indianness afforded, pageants also retained a life in Indian Country, well beyond the school grounds. Michael McNally describes the production by Ojibwas and Odawas (Anishinaabeg) of Longfellow's *Song of Hiawatha* at an amphitheater in Desbarats, Ontario. From

1901 through the 1960s, Anishinaabe actors performed the operatic adaptation for paying non-Indian audiences. McNally captures the sense of humor with which the actors staged their performances, and certainly their awareness reflects that of students performing the pageants as well. For this rendition, Ojibwe and Odawa songs filled the opera. McNally incorporated recollections of the 1950s production from performers, themselves former boarding school students, who saw the opera as an opportunity for financial gain and also experienced the work as an opportunity for fellow Anishinaabeg to gain solidarity through in-jokes made at the expense of the audience. This humor often originated through the necessity of the actors to grapple with a script that was borne out of a generic Indianness and not out of customs of the Anishinaabe people. For example, Longfellow's wedding scene challenged the performers, as McNally explains:

Anishinaabe people simply had no songs or dances specific to such affairs as weddings. When the cast was asked to introduce a festal song for the scene in 1902, [non-Indian composer for the pageant, Frederick Burton] remembered, "pains were taken to impress the Indians with the fact that what was wanted was such a song as they would sing on a jolly occasion. . . . After three days of thinking it over . . . they decided on a very ancient song." When Burton "heard it roared forth by forty powerful voices at a solemn adagio," he thought "there must have been some mistake, but when I understood the words I knew that, from the Indian point of view, nothing could have been more appropriate." Burton's later translation suggests something of the subterfuge going on:

Ambay ge way do che wah de wa bun gee gah gee kay ne me go minka hen ahkon e gayaung.
Let's go home before daybreak or people will find out what we have been doing.

McNally continues:

To those who knew Ojibwe, and this did not include the audience, the scene made room for some good old-fashioned Anishinaabe humor, for these introduced songs were bawdy songs of carousal. Picture, for example, an audience transported by Joe Chingwa's beautiful tenor as he sang the role of Chibiabos at the wedding of chaste Minnehaha and noble Hiawatha. Then consider the ribald song Chingwa had slipped in under cover of his own language:

kaninda-nibasi: nin :	*kidagogobanei*	*geinojinibasina*
I would not sleep	If there was anything	for which I could not sleep

"Apparently the inference," McNally adds, "was 'I wouldn't sleep if I had something to drink,' but Whitney Albert sang a version that was more direct, adding *waminikwaeya* ('that I could drink') in the first three repetitions, and then in the fourth, *gawiya nibane owisaena* ('if I had someone to sleep with')."[157]

In describing a similar entrepreneurial spectacle operated in the 1950s and 1960s by the Lac Du Flambeau band of Lake Superior Chippewa, Larry Nesper argues that the Wa-Swa-Gon Indian bowl provided them an opportunity to use the ignorance of the non-Indian audience as a means to forge their community ties. Songs were very specifically selected, and only those deemed appropriate for such venues—"the 'fun-type,' an indigenous category that had been evolving for a very long time on the intercultural middle ground"—were permitted, with close observation by tribal members to ensure that none of the sacred, Big Drum Songs were performed. The singers "knew that they knew something that the non-Indian spectators didn't," Nesper writes. "Solidarity in difference was realized by virtue of this gulf, even as culture was being objectified. Furthermore, Indian singers revealed what they knew of their traditions to each other by the ways in which they concealed it from the audience in innovative dissembling."[158] Without doubt, both the humorous liberties and vigilant care of musical performance taken by the Ojibwe, Odawa, and Lac Du Flambeau singers were also reflected in student performances in the early twentieth century, contributing to a sense of student solidarity at the expense of unknowing non-Indian teachers and audience members. In this way, students could certainly establish their own hidden transcripts of resistance within the scripted performances of Indianness that non-Indians increasingly demanded.

CHAPTER 5

Hitting the Road

Professional Native Musicians
in the Early Twentieth Century

The German torpedo struck the side of the British vessel *Carmania* around eleven o'clock on that cold night of 1918, and Tsianina Redfeather Blackstone, along with the rest of the passengers, was told that the ship would sink in fifteen minutes. Two water compartments had already filled with North Atlantic water, and the ship, only two days from reaching its destination of Liverpool, England, seemed doomed to a watery grave. Prior to the attack, Blackstone, a Creek-Cherokee mezzo-soprano widely known in the United States because of her extensive touring with acclaimed composer Charles Wakefield Cadman, had been entertaining the soldiers on board with her singing and accompaniment on the steel guitar. She had volunteered for the voyage in order to entertain the troops in England and France, but now she found herself rushing to her assigned lifeboat as the water's surface began to fill with the remains of the aquatic life that the torpedo had annihilated.[1]

Although Blackstone was the only American Indian entertainer on board the *Carmania*, she was a contemporary of hundreds of Native people who performed music derived originally from Euro-American or African American traditions for their local communities or on performance hall circuits that crisscrossed North America and Europe. All of their stories are unique. This chapter consists of five vignettes representative of the lives and ambitions of professional Native musicians who succeeded in adapting their musical training in creative ways, despite the arduous odds they often faced. In the difficult process of selecting a handful of professional musicians to feature in this chapter, many other prominent early twentieth-century professional performers were unfortunately relegated to the margins, including, to name but a few, Lucy Nicolar (aka Princess Watahwaso, Penobscot), Joe Shunatona (Pawnee-Otoe), Chief Os-ke-non-ton (Mohawk), Te Ata (Chickasaw), Dennison Wheelock (Oneida), and Robert Koon (Sioux). Three of the above—Lucy Nicolar, Te Ata, and Dennison Wheelock—have received recent scholarly attention.[2] With the exception of Blackstone, the subjects of this chapter have not received similar notice. However, their careers are compelling on their own terms, and when placed alongside each other, together they provide us with a window into the world that professional Native musicians inhabited in this period. They represent a wide range of financial and professional success as well as interest in using Indianness in their acts and in using their talents to engage federal Indian policy on a local or national level.

Each vignette provides a window into unique adaptations of training that derived principally from the boarding schools, and each illuminates different facets of the world of professional Native musicians in the early twentieth century. Musician and bandmaster Angus Lookaround (Menominee) dedicated his life to overcoming the lowered expectations of the school officials and to work with Native boys and girls. Fred Cardin (Quapaw) and Joe Morris (Blackfeet) logged thousands of miles on the road as they collectively played to a wide variety of audiences, from those in Seattle jazz clubs and reservation dance halls to U.S. presidents. Tsianina Redfeather Blackstone sang before boarding school children and before audiences of thousands at Santa Fe Fiestas and the Hollywood Bowl. Finally, Kiutus Tecumseh (Yakama-Cherokee) used the newly emergent technology of radio to broadcast his tenor vocals and strident concerns about federal Indian educational policies. Combined, they reflect an early twentieth-century cohort of professional musicians, well versed in the emergent modern music industry, who variously drew upon repertoires of both songs and Indianness to bring to widespread audiences their music and their experiences as modern Indian people.

Long before these performers had established their professional careers, Native peoples were familiar with music of non-Indian origin, particularly after the advent of recording and broadcast technologies. In 1904, for example, an American entrepreneur named W. M. Thompson hoped to leverage a trade deal with some Aleuts in the Bering Sea by introducing them to the phonograph. He recalled, "This was to be our magic, and with the god-box on our side, [the Aleut traders] could be induced to come down a few notches in their demands."[3] Upon docking at their village, Thompson planned to display for them the divine talking machine, whereupon he expected that they would fall to their knees, offering furs and ivory in an awestruck act of worship. Accordingly, Thompson cranked the phonograph, which pumped out the American favorite by Harry Williams and Egbert Van Alstyne, "In the Shade of the Old Apple Tree." Thompson was stunned to note, however, that rather than prostrating themselves as he had anticipated, after the first stanza "the crowd was still standing." He continued: "There were smiles on their faces as if they were waiting for something and when the chorus began we got the surprise of our lives. Every one of those unwashed denizens of the Arctic Circle chipped in with the chorus and sang it to perfection."[4] Thompson's chagrined surprise indicates that, even as far north as the Bering Sea, Native people were already fluent with an American musical dialect that would come to furnish many of them with an unexpected edge in many varieties of cultural barter.

Many American Indians had developed an early knowledge of recording technologies and the music industry in part because of the development of ethnology. Anthropologists and ethnologists such as Frederick Starr and Frances Densmore, along with composers hired by the OIA like Geoffrey O'Hara, had brought wax cylinder and phonograph recording devices to reservations as soon as they became portable, and by the 1920s these technologies were abundant in Indian Country. Non-Indians like Thompson consistently voiced surprise when they discovered that many Native people not only had listened through the devices since their advent but had recorded on them as well. In 1921, for example, a writer for the trade journal *Talking Machine World* was taken aback upon learning that a group of Blackfeet, hired to dance at the premiere of a movie in Newark, New Jersey, strolled over to a Victrola store after their exhibition in order to hear records they had recorded three years prior.[5] Some dancers even

adopted the new technology into their performance, such as a group
of Salish Indians from Arlee, Montana, who for a publicity stunt
danced at a 1926 Chicago rodeo to songs transmitted from a Thorola
radio receiver.[6]

Additionally, many American Indians developed an affinity for
American popular music early on, and local record dealers scrambled
to accommodate those who could afford their own phonographs and
records. The Pendleton Drug Company in 1920 reported that it had
sold not only many phonographs to local Indian community members but a "surprising . . . number of grand opera selections" to them
as well.[7] James Neece, Jr., manager of the Carney-Neece Music Shops
in both Okmulgee and Henryetta, Oklahoma, established a strong
clientele of local Native residents who bought records by the dozen.[8]
Perhaps because of the ubiquitous bands and drills on boarding
school campuses, a dealer for an Osage community noted that in 1917
"martial music was appreciated the most, as is the case with all the
Indians, band records selling like hot cakes."[9] In addition, many
Native communities had established their own brass bands by the
early twentieth century. The Oneidas of Wisconsin established their
Oneida National Band as early as the 1860s.[10] Thus, while many
American Indians in the early twentieth century were listening to
popular band and vocal selections, many performed them in their
own musical organizations as well.

Through access to modern technologies such as the phonograph
and radio, and through music education in the boarding schools,
American Indian musicians engaged not only the catalog of American
popular music but also, as Philip Deloria has shown, the expectations
of Indianness that permeated popular culture in the early twentieth
century.[11] While their Native audiences were well versed in the music
and the emergent technologies that supported them, their non-Indian
audiences were typically unwilling to recognize Native performances
of popular music as modern acts by modern people and in turn
sought to assign a different set of meanings to such performances—
in the symbolic universe of non-Indian Americans, as has been
shown, Native peoples often represented primitivism, the antithesis
of the modern world. It was up to Native musicians to determine how
they would handle those expectations in their own performances and

careers. Some exploited those expectations in order to further their opportunities, while others shunned all displays of Indianness in their acts. All struggled with those expectations in myriad ways as they sought to secure a living at a time when financial prospects on reservations were often extremely bleak. Some, however, also saw political opportunity in performing Indianness. During a period when Native values and cultural traditions were largely suppressed by OIA assimilation policies and the media largely ignored Native voices, a number of professional Indian musicians used musical performance to access influential non-Indian audiences, government officials, and the press—access that would have been denied them otherwise. In doing so, Native musicians used the pervasive tropes of Indianness in popular culture in order to further their own specific goals, ambitions, and political agendas. This chapter reveals the difficulties and limitations as well as the possibilities of working as a professional Native musician in the early twentieth century.

The politics of music by American Indians stretched well beyond the confines of reservations and boarding school grounds. Through the modern array of travel, recording and broadcast technologies, their voices and sounds infiltrated urban dance halls and theaters, filled the grooves of wax cylinders and 78 rpm records, and sailed hundreds of miles through radio transmissions. Through these media, the musicians could purvey the latest hits as well as launch public, political critique, and their access to these opportunities was unwittingly provided by the schools' music curricula. Not only did they learn a command of Euro-American styles in their lessons on the saxophone, the violin, or the singing of an operetta, but they also received training in the arts of Indianness, which taught them how to appeal to the imaginations of their non-Indian audiences. Their practiced familiarity with the role of "exotic" subject, especially in the technologies of the emerging entertainment industries, prepared them to subvert the ideologically fueled gaze of non-Indians by using for their own advantage the tools acquired in the schools.

Indian-themed music reached an apex in American popular culture within the first two decades of the twentieth century. Indianist composers brought music to the large theaters and opera houses frequented by the bourgeoisie, but the sounds of Indianness quickly

infiltrated all of the major musical arenas and genres, there meeting
with a more varied audience. Indian-themed songs resonated from
vaudeville, Tin Pan Alley, bandstands, jazz clubs, and dance halls. Of
the semiclassical variety, Lieurance's "By the Waters of the Min-
netonka" was one of Edison's six top sellers in October of 1920.[12]
"Indian Dawn" was a major hit in 1926, heard according to *Talking
Machine World* in "both concert and vaudeville."[13] Tin Pan Alley
meanwhile began cranking out hundreds of Indian-themed songs,
filling the air of theaters as well as family parlors and placing Indianness in an unceasing array of thematic and often bizarre contexts,
including that found in the following two-step, "Arrah Wanna: An
Irish Indian Matrimonial Venture":

> 'Mid the wild and woolly prairies lived an Indian maid,
> Arrah Wanna queen of fairies of her tribe afraid
> Each night came an Irish laddie buck
> With a wedding ring,
> He would sit outside her tent and with his bag pipes loudly sing.
> "Arrah Wanna, on my honor, I'll take care of you,
> I'll be kind and true we can love and bill and coo,
> In a wig-wam built of sham-rocks green, we'll make those red men
>   smile,
> When you're Misses Barney heap much Carney from Kilarney's Isle."[14]

These were the images of Indianness that Native musicians were
up against. Despite this debilitating and degrading economy of signifiers, however, the public interest generated by the work of ethnologists, Indianist composers, and the media coverage of the "dance
evil" debate created an economy of opportunity as well as a political
atmosphere that many Native musicians could manipulate.

Documentation exists about hundreds of Native musicians who
traveled the United States in the first three decades of the twentieth
century, and the evidence of their careers ranges from fleeting references in newspapers, names on phonograph records, and performance programs to personal correspondence, OIA records, oral
histories, and autobiographies. An examination of such materials
documenting the careers of the five musicians featured in this chap-

From the first decade of the twentieth century through the 1930s, Indian-themed music was very popular, and Tin Pan Alley published hundreds of compositions involving Native subjects that had little or nothing to do with the realities of Native peoples' lives but contributed to the imagery and sounds of Indianness prevalent in popular culture. Sheet music cover for the 1906 song "Arrah Wanna," words by Jack Drislane, music by Theodore Morse. From the author's collection.

In the 1900s through the 1930s, dozens of "all-Indian bands" like this unidenti-
fied one traversed the country, performing Indianness to access new audiences
and to express pride in their heritage in the midst of the government's campaign
of allotment and assimilation. Postcard from the author's collection.

ter illustrates that early twentieth-century Native musicians were an
extremely complex group of artists who daily navigated treacherous
expectations of Indianness along the bumpy and often harrowing
journey of potholed roads and missed trains that characterized the
typical life of a working musician. The OIA, as we have seen, used
musical training and the arts of Indianness with the intent to produce
contained, racialized, and docile citizens; those very "products" of the
schools, however, American Indians, often accepted the role of "the
authentic Indian" and in turn demonstrated their mastery of not only
their instruments but also the vocabulary of Indianness that typically
contradicted, yet shaped, their personal experience and occupation.
Each of their life stories contributes to a larger understanding of both
the diversity of the experiences realized by Native musicians in the
first decades of the twentieth century and the unique ways in which
expectations of Indianness influenced the possibilities afforded by
their careers as professional artists.

Many musical ensembles formed by American Indians traveled the world on extensive tours. The United States Indian Reservation Band, led by Joe Shunatona (Pawnee), is seen here at an appearance for the 1931 Exposition Coloniale Internationale in Paris. Photograph from the author's collection.

ANGUS LOOKAROUND: A VIEW FROM THE BANDSTAND

Federal Indian boarding schools had a profound influence on the students who attended them in the late nineteenth and early twentieth centuries. As we have seen, band music played heavily in the lives of some students who went on to establish themselves as professional singers and musicians. Angus Lookaround grew up in the boarding schools and eventually worked as a bandmaster in a number of Indian schools. Lookaround did not teach Native boys and girls how to assimilate or to develop shame for the expressive culture of their people; rather, he used his skills as a musician to serve as an example and to inspire his students to believe that they were entitled to lead as dignified an existence as any other people. He created opportunity out of his music education to infiltrate the schools as an OIA employee

The United States Indian Band poses with Vice President Charles Curtis in this 1929 photograph. Indian brass bands, both professional and school bands, performed at many inaugural parades and events that welcomed visiting dignitaries. This band is perhaps the organization that evolved into Joe Shunatona's United States Indian Reservation Band. National Photo Company Collection, Prints and Photographs Division, Library of Congress, LC-DIG-npcc-17380.

and to attack the educational philosophy of the early twentieth century that emphasized training merely in menial and domestic labor.

Lookaround dedicated his life and talents to the needs of Indian youth, perhaps partly motivated to do so because of the hardships that he and his own family had faced over the years. Lookaround was born on the Menominee Reservation in a log cabin on the banks of the Wolf River northeast of Keshena, Wisconsin.[15] His father, Henry Kaywah-tah-wah-poa of the Menominee Eagle clan, ran away at the age of fourteen to join the Union army.[16] Henry married Mary Murray of Menominee, Scotch, English, and French descent and later died of tuberculosis when Angus was fourteen. The Lookarounds faced significant trials during Angus's adolescence, as four of his siblings died of diphtheria. Despite these setbacks, he and his other four siblings continued to farm and to operate a lumber camp through the cold Wisconsin winters.[17]

Angus Lookaround spent his teens and early twenties in various Indian schools.[18] When he reached school age, the family relocated to Keshena so that he could enroll in the Keshena Indian School.[19] His time at Keshena was difficult; he later recalled defending his bread at mealtime by cracking the knuckles of older students with his knife, and being slapped when he spoke in his Native tongue.[20] Lookaround often had to leave the Keshena school in order to work on the farm, especially after his father died. By the age of sixteen he also patrolled the reservation, in snowshoes in the winters and by horseback in the summers.[21] He enrolled at the Tomah Indian School in 1908, where his brother Jerome was bandmaster. According to his wife, Phebe Jewell Nichols, "[Jerome was] determined that little brother should be a musician, too, and little brother was very willing. So began a long though frequently interrupted tutelage which resulted in his being able to play several instruments."[22]

Also adept in athletics, Lookaround graduated from the eighth grade in 1911, when he was twenty years old.[23] The next year, he enrolled himself at the Carlisle Indian School.[24] During the next three years at Carlisle, he spent the fall and spring playing football for Glenn "Pop" Warner's celebrated team and spent his summers on the Ford Model T assembly line in Highland Park, Michigan. Soon after his arrival at Carlisle, his brother Jerome died, which perhaps contributed to Angus's need to spend more and more time working and sending money home to his family.[25] Because of this strain, he often took leaves of absence during the school year to continue his work at the Ford plant.[26]

Lookaround built many lasting friendships while a student, but he also developed great disdain for the lowered expectations for Indian students that had developed in the OIA after Richard Pratt's departure. In his experience, the training in Indian "industrial" schools had become geared not toward gainful employment but instead toward the upkeep of the schools through labor in the barns, fields, laundries, and kitchens. Such menial training, he thought, denied the students

Angus Lookaround (Menominee) learned to play brass instruments at the Tomah Indian School under the tutelage of his brother Jerome, the school bandmaster. This photograph of Angus and Jerome Lookaround was taken at Tomah Indian School in 1911, the year that Angus completed the eighth grade. Jerome died shortly after Angus left Tomah for Carlisle. Wisconsin Historical Society, Madison, Wisconsin, WHi-57357.

ample opportunity to achieve their potential.[27] He was pained, he told his wife, by the philosophy that the schools "were designed to de-Indianize the Indians, strip them of their native pride, make them subservient and docile in an effort 'to make them good Americans.'"[28] After his death, Nichols recalled,

> He early began to resent the government's policy to strip the Indians of their native attitudes of mind and racial habits. He would have none of it. He prized his Indianhood. Very perspicacious, he resented the attempts at stultifying his initiative. He resented the implication that the whites were his betters and he was in the servant class. Always he came up against the government's policy to discourage leadership in its wards. The plodding and the docile were much less trouble, and as long as they could be kept plodding and docile there would be jobs for their guardians. He was sensitive to all this and could not be fooled, even when a young lad.[29]

Lookaround's negative perceptions of the school agendas affected him deeply for the rest of his life, so that in many ways he sought to live in a manner that would shatter the expectations of his former teachers.

Lookaround did not see his work at the Ford plant as the culmination of his education in the boarding schools. Instead, he attributed the experience to inspiring within him a renewed determination to challenge the shackles, as he saw it, of limited education for Native Americans. For the first time in his life he encountered groups of white people other than federal employees and noted that the immensely difficult economic situation of the Menominees was vastly more challenging than that of his white co-workers and friends. His wife recalled that at this point "he suddenly realized that as an Indian in his native land he was far from free." She continued: "He thought the Goddess of Liberty welcoming 'your poor, your downtrodden' was literally turning her back on him and his kind. Suddenly he knew what it was to be an *Indian*, one of an invaded, exploited people."[30]

By September 1916, Lookaround was ready to return to Wisconsin and asked Superintendent Lipps to close his bank account and send him the balance.[31] Lipps was clearly unhappy that Lookaround decided to go home, and with the requested check of eighty-one dollars and twelve cents, he wrote a note: "I have to say that all I can do is to give a man of your age and experience an opportunity. If you do not care to take advantage of this opportunity, I cannot force you to stay."[32] But Lookaround had loftier goals in mind, goals that the Ford plant fostered but could not actuate. After the United States became involved in World War I, he was one of the first Menominees to volunteer for service; he joined the navy in 1917.[33] Lookaround took his time in the navy very seriously and was proud to serve on the USS *New Hampshire*, a convoy escort, the next year.

It was onboard the *New Hampshire* that Angus Lookaround's musical abilities began to shape his experience in the post–boarding school world of adulthood. Owing to the skills he had developed under the influence of his late brother, Lookaround was able to join the ship's band as musician first class.[34] The band occasionally held evening concerts for the crew in order to lift their spirits. One such concert, performed during convoy duty on the Middle Atlantic on September 24, 1918, coincidentally included the popular fox-trot about a stuttering

Angus Lookaround (holding the tuba) with friends aboard the convoy escort USS *New Hampshire* during World War I. Lookaround's skills earned him the position of musician first class during the war, a time when an extraordinary number of American Indians volunteered for service. Wisconsin Historical Society, Madison Wisconsin, WHi-57360.

soldier, "K-K-K-Katy," written by Geoffrey O'Hara, the man appointed years earlier by the OIA to introduce Indian children to Indianist compositions.[35]

Lookaround returned home after the war with hopes that his opportunities would expand.[36] He was terribly disappointed when he was refused the job that had been promised him upon his return. In response to his disillusionment, Lookaround developed one of his strongest skills, his musicianship, to find work. At first he eked out a living in numerous small orchestras and bands, but over time his talent improved. As his wife put it, "he had learned his musicianship the hard way."[37] That talent in fact launched numerous touring seasons with the Royal Scotch Highlanders, the Forepaugh and Sells band,

and Barnum and Bailey's and Ringling's bands, as well as local Wisconsin performances (and a factory job) with the industrial Holton-Elkhorn Band.[38] He even performed and toured with the most famous band in the land, John Philip Sousa's. He largely enjoyed those experiences, but he bitterly recalled to his wife that while he "mingled with other musicians and athletes . . . [and] met with respect, . . . the whites always angled themselves into the positions of authority."[39] Nonetheless, between his seasonal stints with bands, he served as bandmaster and coached football for a number of white high schools. He was selected to perform with the American Legion Band in France in 1927, and he later received honorable mention for Indian achievement at Chicago's Century of Progress fair in 1934.[40]

Lookaround's main goal, however, was to teach and mentor Native children, and he used his skills as a musician to realize that goal. He accepted the job of bandmaster, boys' disciplinarian, and football coach at his alma mater, the Tomah Indian School. Because he was Native, he was paid only forty dollars a month—but low wages did not inhibit him from working with zeal. However, race-based harassment from fellow white employees eventually overcame him. When he arrived late to dinner one night and found nothing but bones on the table, he left and joined a circus band. Eventually he returned to the Menominee Reservation and led the Keshena Indian School band. According to his wife, "In three months['] time he taught Indian children from the non-Christian settlements who spoke no English . . . to play in his band. He insisted on taking their band to tournaments, housing it in the best hotels, having it served the best meals available, and it won outstanding honors."[41] Although he continued to work under white employees who he felt took credit for his results, he remained at the Keshena school until the Catholic Mission took it over in 1932.[42]

Lookaround worked a number of jobs after he left the school, but he maintained his dedication to his people, eventually serving as the director of the Menominee Reservation band, which was composed of many of his former pupils. He loved the work and remained dedicated to the band, which performed at social occasions for the tribe. As a perfectionist in his art, however, he occasionally voiced frustration to his wife when the band members would not practice as often as he preferred. He told his wife that he "could not understand how a man could be a member of a band year after year, never practice, turn up for concerts only and be satisfied to get no farther than the same first pieces learned."[43] He was so adept at music, in fact, that he could recall a tune from memory, or take a sample of a piece, and write all of the parts for his band in the key that he thought it should be played.[44] Despite his occasional frustration, however, he reveled in directing his people in the Menominee band.

During World War II, Angus Lookaround worked relentlessly at the Four Wheel Drive plant in Clintonville, Wisconsin, and was the featured player in its band. Lookaround believed that this was the best way he could help his stepson, who was incarcerated in a Japanese prison camp. Lookaround traveled forty miles a day to and from the plant; after working seven consecutive nights and performing three band concerts in a ten-day period, he suffered a cerebral thrombosis on September 3, 1944, and never fully recovered. A year and a half later he died and was buried by his Masonic Lodge brothers and a color guard from his Veterans of Foreign Wars post.

Angus Lookaround was seemingly as "all-American" as a person could be. He worked tirelessly, was a perfectionist, served in the navy during World War I and in a factory during World War II, played not only with John Philip Sousa but in circus bands as well, was a Mason, and was an active member of his local VFW post. But he was also embittered by racial discrimination. His experiences reflected those of many Native Americans at the time—he grew up on a reservation, was educated in boarding schools, and dealt with non-Indians who still relegated him to a second-class American citizenship despite all of the American ideals he embodied. Lookaround used his musical training not only to make a living on his own terms but also to challenge the limited expectations he faced from both Indian school officials and his various other non-Indian employers and co-workers. According to his wife, Lookaround was profoundly affected by his boarding school experience. Although he appreciated the friends he made there, and his musical and athletic training, he was dismayed by the OIA educational policy of the early twentieth century and he sought to rectify that policy on his own, by using music to inspire Native children to strive for higher ideals than many of their teachers expected of them. Unlike many other professional Native musicians of the time, Lookaround refused to perform Indianness to meet his goals. Rather, he incorporated hard work and seemingly "American" goals and ideals into an agenda that supported pride not only in tribalism but also in equal rights and opportunities for Menominees and indeed all American Indians.

FRED CARDIN:
A VIEW FROM THE CHAUTAUQUA CIRCUIT

In examining the life of Fred Cardin, we can gain a sense of the rigors of traveling and performing in lyceum and Chautauqua tours for one of the most recognized musicians to emerge from Carlisle Indian School. A Quapaw born in Kansas in 1895, Cardin graduated from Carlisle in 1912 and became particularly successful at an early age as a concert violinist.[45] During Cardin's enrollment at Carlisle he performed and was featured at practically every function that required music. Cardin enjoyed his life as a prominent musician at Carlisle and retained positive memories of his friendships there. After he graduated, he briefly took up postgraduate work in the business department of the school in order to continue his studies under Fred Stauffer, the Carlisle music director. Cardin craved further musical training, however, so that he could leave his mark on the world as a renowned violinist. He wished to continue his studies in a conservatory, but neither he nor his family was able to cover the cost of tuition or living expenses. They deeply suffered the effects of allotment. Too young to receive a two-hundred-acre parcel in the first division of the Quapaw reserve allotments, he instead received forty acres of "rough, untillable land" in the second division, land that could by no means provide him any revenue.[46] His father did no better, receiving an allotment of "undesirable" lands that brought him a scant income. To provide for his several children, Cardin's father labored in the railroad shops of the Missouri, Kansas and Texas Railway in Parsons, Kansas.[47] By the end of the summer of 1912, however, Cardin was awarded a scholarship to study the violin at Dana's Musical Institute in Warren, Ohio.[48] While at the conservatory, he became the protégé of musician Jake Gimbel.[49] Cardin studied at the conservatory on and off for at least the next three years. He periodically returned to Carlisle during those years and performed a violin duet with Caroline Hewitt at the 1913 Carlisle commencement concert.[50]

In his early career, Fred Cardin, like many other musicians, took various jobs wherever he found them, good and bad, in order to develop his skills and reputation and, moreover, simply to make ends meet. One of those jobs was a membership in the Chautauqua Institution's orchestra, but Cardin quickly contracted typhoid fever.[51] Unable to cover medical bills in New York, he returned to Carlisle and was admitted into the hospital there.[52] He recovered and briefly moved home to Parsons. From there he relocated numerous times, eventually even moving to Alabama for a short stint in a movie theater orchestra.[53]

What separated Cardin in his early career from most other musicians scrounging to make a living, however, was that he was sought-after both as a musician and as an Indian musician. The Indianist composer Thurlow Lieurance was early impressed by Cardin and wanted him to join his lyceum act in 1916.[54] Stretching back to the 1820s, lyceums in the United States were community institutions that organized weekly debates, entertainments, and lectures. Musicians lucky enough to join a lyceum circuit could expect a full calendar of performances that would take them throughout the region or even the country. Of his own volition, Cardin had begun to master popular Indianist compositions such as Charles Cadman's "From the Land of the Sky Blue Water" and Lieurance's "Pakoble (Cheyenne Melody)" and even wrote a piece of his own in 1915, entitled "Quapaw." He again returned to Carlisle on November 30, 1915, to perform these pieces in a violin recital.[55] Presented with numerous opportunities, in the spring of 1916 he accepted the position of first violin in the Indian String Quartet, based out of the Salem Indian School in Chemawa, Oregon.[56]

The Indian String Quartet, assembled by Indianist composer and Chemawa faculty member Ruthyn Turney, originally consisted of Turney and three young men who had received their musical training in various Indian schools. Administrative support of music at Salem was strong, because Superintendent H. W. Wadsworth saw Indian musicians as a prime generator of good public relations for his school. He lobbied for the Chemawa band to perform at the 1915 Panama-Pacific International Exposition in San Francisco, and he recruited Native musicians to attend Salem from other schools across the country and the U.S. territories.[57] Alex Melovidov, for example, from St. Paul of the Pribilof Islands, played second violin. Melovidov, an

The Indian String Quartet met with great success in the years before World War I, despite the hardships that they, like most musicians of the time, faced on the road. These photos from a promotional brochure show the quartet in the regalia they wore for half of their program, and in the tuxedos they wore for the other half. Papers of the Redpath Chautauqua Bureau, University of Iowa Libraries, Iowa City, Iowa.

Aleut, spent his early education in a local public school and a Russian school under the Greek Catholic Church. He arrived at the Chemawa school in the fall of 1911 principally to further his musical training.[58] Willie Reddie (a.k.a. Willie Reddy) from the Haida tribe of Wrangell, Alaska, played the cello.[59] Reddie had attended Chemawa since 1908 in order to study under Turney but later switched to the cello as his main instrument and began working with a master cellist in Portland.[60] Rounding out the quartet was William Palin, a Kootenai (Confederated Flathead), who, after attending Carlisle, joined the group at Chemawa as the viola player.

Palin and Cardin were peers and became fast friends at Carlisle, and it was Palin who proposed to the quartet that they locate and hire Cardin to take Turney's chair of first violin after the group's aspirations and potential extended beyond Oregon. Palin wrote Cardin, urging him to come on board. After some soul searching, Cardin agreed. He wrote,

> Now Bill, *confidentially*, I say this to you. I [have] become, (quite contrary to my make-up when you knew me) to a certain degree a thinking man. —I look at this job as an opportunity not as something to "get-by with" before the public—I am not yet a demonstrative artist but one at heart *also Indian* and in this work I hope to find that which is elevating and inspiring—*To*—Art for God's sake.[61]

Cardin's dedication reflected the motivation of all the young men in the quartet who were willing to chance the hardships of life on the road in order to celebrate both their art and their heritage as Indian people. By the time Cardin joined the band, the quartet was well on its way, having already met with much critical praise in its tours of the Northwest.[62]

A non-Indian named Richard Kennedy, the former chaplain at the Chemawa Indian School and a graduate of Harvard University, affixed himself to the group as road manager. Additionally, Kennedy provided lectures on Indian art and legends during the band's performances.[63] While Kennedy seemed to maintain a good rapport with the quartet during their many consecutive months of touring, he also understood the quartet as a vehicle to forward his own aspirations for a career in the entertainment business. In a brochure he ostensibly crafted for the quartet, he wrote, "In the role of narrative lecturer [Kennedy] is in a class by himself, and without any assistance whatever can provide an evening of intense interest and educational value."[64] Oddly enough, Kennedy often included lectures on seemingly unrelated topics such as Victor Hugo's Les Miserables while espousing on Native legends.[65] The quartet maintained a treacherous touring schedule throughout the year of 1917. After touring the Pacific Northwest in the spring, the group performed on seventy-two dates in Illinois and Indiana on the Meneley Chautauqua circuit without a single day off.[66] The quartet gathered much momentum, and in an effort to further its exposure, the band signed a contract for the 1917–18 season with the renowned Redpath Lyceum Bureau of Chicago.[67]

Life on the road for the Indian String Quartet during the Redpath season was filled with surprises and hazards. The fastest form of communication between the Redpath Bureau and the quartet was the telegram, but because the quartet sometimes performed six or seven days a week, in different cities, for six months straight, special care had to be taken to wire information and correspondence to the proper town, on the proper day.[68] Right before the quartet was to perform in Harlan, Kentucky, for example, the bureau wired the group in Benham, Kentucky, with the news that the show was canceled due to a smallpox outbreak. "Do not go in there," the bureau advised.[69] Cancellations and added shows, often at the last minute, caused the bureau to send the quartet changes in plan practically in midvoyage. After one cancellation for an April 10, 1918, appearance in Galesville, Wisconsin, the bureau wrote to the musicians, instructing them to "go there on the 11th and they will drive you from Galesville to Trempealeau to catch a 10:22 night train for St. Paul in order to catch the 800 Line over to Ladysmith."[70] Travel by train sometimes led to missed connections and canceled shows.[71] Extreme weather conditions in the winter of 1917–18 and curtailed public railroad traffic due to the war also created immense difficulties for the quartet as it bounded from one town to the next.[72] The Redpath Bureau desperately sought contact from the quartet after the tour had been paralyzed by a weeklong storm, writing that it was "anxiously waiting to hear from [Kennedy] as to when you are going to get out of the snow drift."[73] Even simple tasks such as laundry provided a challenge on the road, and at some points, when they sent their laundry out, it did not come back in time to catch the next train with the quartet and had to be mailed to the location of an upcoming show.[74] And then of course there were personal injuries or ailments that at times incapacitated the performers. On March 4, 1918, Kennedy wrote, "We missed Maple Rapids last week on account of a felon on the finger of the second violinist. I took a substitute to Lake Odessa Monday evening, but the only one I could get for Tuesday evening refused to make the trip when she learned that there would be an auto ride."[75] These conditions made road life particularly difficult and parsimonious at times for the quartet, who split a weekly salary of $150 from the bureau.[76]

The Indian String Quartet gained not only the favor of lyceum audiences but also that of fellow musicians. After the quartet was invited by the editor of the *Violinist* to perform before some of the "leading violinists" of Chicago, the American Guild of Violinists invited the group to perform at its Chicago meeting.[77] The quartet had already established a reputation in Illinois by the summer of 1917. The *Warren Tribune* considered the quartet "one of the best numbers that had been given" all season; the *St. Joseph Record* agreed, remarking that the quartet, "far above the average . . . gave the large audiences entertainments which were well worth listening to. . . . The Indians pleased with their rendition of the weird Indian music, and they also proved they could play the classics by giving some selections from the great masters."[78]

While the careers of professional American Indian musicians and their life on the road often reflected those of non-Indian musicians, their experiences also at times demonstrated the unique position of Native musicians who were called to perform not just music but also "weird Indian music," in order to fulfill the unique expectations of their non-Indian audiences and the desires of managers, booking agents, and other profiteers as well. This often led to the creation of programs that borrowed from the evolutionary paradigm that had been honed by boarding school officials and music instructors and with which these musicians were long familiar.

The Indian String Quartet attracted large audiences to its recitals of classical or classically influenced pieces juxtaposed with performances of Indianness, complete with "artistic Indian costumes."[79] Although prior to Cardin's inclusion in the quartet the boys had performed all of their pieces in suits, they decided to alter the program by performing their first, classical act, in suits, and then dressing in Native regalia for their more dramatic second act, which featured Turney's Indianist compositions.[80] In its early Chautauqua tours the quartet performed a Haydn, Beethoven, or Mozart quartet piece followed by several short "bright, varied, 'catching'" numbers in the first half, and then provided its renditions of Indianist pieces in the second.[81] To "give a better Indian effect," according to Kennedy, they played these songs from memory, with all of the musicians except for the cellist standing during the performance.[82] Performing pieces from memory while standing up was apparently meant to evoke a sense of "natural" racial talent exhibited by the young men, although whether it truly served any purpose other than creating discomfort and annoyances for the musicians is unclear. In between the sets, Kennedy would lecture about his displayed collection of baskets, beadwork, and Navajo rugs and would often introduce the Indianist songs with brief explanations.[83]

The program that the quartet performed for the Redpath tours typically ran an hour and a half. By the sixth week of the first tour, the group began to open all of the programs with "The Star-Spangled Banner."[84] Interestingly, after joining the Redpath organization, the quartet reversed the order of its program, performing the Indianist pieces in the first section, clad in full "Indian suits" that had, according to Kennedy, been "sent from the reservations."[85] After about a half hour of music, they retired from the stage while Kennedy delivered a lecture on Native crafts. At this point Kennedy also would typically inform the audience that "they have had a variety of Indian music, the only original American music that has not been Germanized," in an allusion to anti-German sentiment surrounding the war; then he would finish his talk with a "typical Indian legend."[86] After Kennedy's address, the quartet would return on stage in dress suits and continue with another round of music, consisting of two or three more Indianist compositions tossed in with a slew of classical pieces.[87]

Most of Turney's compositions were relatively melancholy in nature; when questioned by Redpath why the boys stuck to more somber material, Kennedy responded, "We could give some Indian songs and dances and a hip hip hooray entertainment that would raise the roof, but there would be nothing to it. We prefer to give one that leaves a good taste in the mouth and a pleasant memory that will last." The group planned to expand the program for the next year with a discussion of the "present conditions and the hopes of the race." Newspapers had already noted, however, that "it was easy to see that the speaker was in sympathy with the spirit of the tribes and felt that the Indian has suffered outrages at the hands of whites."[88] Clearly, Kennedy sought to maintain control over the aesthetics of the performance, much as boarding school officials sought to mold public performances of their students to suit their own vision and the justification of their means.

Cardin, however, was interested performing for Native audiences as well, and he repeatedly ensured that the quartet would perform at his alma mater. In the winter of 1917, for example, Cardin and Palin performed with the quartet on their old stomping grounds of Carlisle. The group performed the following program on the evening of December 10:

Allegro, from Quartet, 19 .... Mozart
Indian Suite .... Ruthyn Turney
    (a) Morning Song
    (b) Butterfly Dance
    (c) Prayer to the Rain God
    (d) Spirit Dance
Allegro, Modto, Quartet, 39 .... Haydn
Minuet .... Beethoven
Norwegian Dance .... Grieg
To a Wild Rose .... MacDowell
Cheyenne War Dance .... Skilton[89]

Cardin later wrote to the superintendent, "I have hoped for that opportunity because I wanted Carlisle to hear the organization of which I am proud, —because I am a part of it. We feel that we have been fortunate and regret that our visit was so brief."[90] Cardin also corresponded with the Carlisle staff in order to find and then invite his former classmates to his performances as the Indian String Quartet traversed the country.[91]

A number of boarding schools in fact endeavored to forward the success of the quartet. The Indian handiwork department of the Chilocco Indian School—a product of the OIA's efforts to continually exploit Indianness—sent Richard Kennedy two of the "choicest Navajo blankets in stock" to decorate the stage, with the understanding that after a few dates on the Redpath circuit, the department would receive due compensation.[92] However, Kennedy proved disinclined to reciprocate Chilocco for its support. Although the blankets received prominent attention in the quartet performances, he failed to respond to numerous attempts by the Chilocco school staff to secure payment.[93] The Redpath Bureau, still actively involved with the quartet, yet unwilling to help, simply denied knowledge of his whereabouts.[94] Kennedy in fact left a trail of unpaid debts in the wake of the quartet's travels across the country, leaving irate merchants to petition the bureau for redress.[95]

Despite the successes of the Indian String Quartet in its first Redpath Chautauqua tour, the group was very unsatisfied with the salary that Redpath provided. The war hampered the bureau from giving raises to any of its groups, however, and indicated that it would not be able to accommodate the needs as requested by the quartet.[96] Because the young men were not U.S. citizens, the conscription laws did not apply to them or threaten the existence of the quartet. In May 1917, Kennedy reported that he and the musicians "had considered the question of our duty carefully, and have decided not to enlist until our contracts are filled," and by November, Kennedy advised the bureau that the boys had decided to enlist in the war effort the next summer if the bureau would not agree to a salary increase.[97] Given the bureau's salary freeze, Fred Cardin enlisted in the army, serving in the 315th Cavalry and the 69th Field Artillery of the 95th Division.[98]

After the war, Cardin resumed his musical career, but this time he felt prepared to take greater control of it. By June 1920 he was leading a company of American Indian musicians on a circuit of New York State.[99] The group included Wanita Cardin (Quapaw) on piano, soprano Sensa Carey (Cherokee), and Te Ata, a Chickasaw singer.[100] Within the next month, Te Ata formed her own company, and

Cardin's old bandmate William Reddie joined Cardin on cello, as well as Paul Chilson (Pawnee), a tenor.[101] Billing themselves as Cardin's Indian Music and Art Company, the group worked with the management of Indianist composer Thurlow Lieurance, who by this point had assembled around a dozen musical groups to perform on the Chautauqua circuits.[102]

Cardin and his revolving cast of fellow Native musicians formed several musical groups in the 1920s and continued to tour throughout those years. In between tours, Reddie performed regularly with the Cincinnati Symphony Orchestra, and indeed Cardin and his peers often found pickup work beyond the purview of Indian-oriented acts.[103] Those acts remained successful draws, however, and in the fall of 1921 Reddie and Cardin formed the Cardin-Reddy American Indian Art and Ensemble Company, with soprano Gladys Gooding on vocals and piano. The group continued to wear "gorgeous costumes both Indian and full dress" and at times performed "Russian, Bohemian and other schools" of music for contrast to the Indianist melodies that Cardin and Lieurance developed.[104] Cardin continued his association with Lieurance over the next few years and by 1924 had assembled the Cardin Orchestral String Quintette.[105] By the end of the first decade of his professional career, Cardin had not only survived the difficulties of supporting oneself as a musician but in fact was thriving, creating numerous ensembles to advance his musical vision, which included using performances of Indianness when and where he saw fit.

Such performances of Indianness continued along with his career, but began to take a backseat as he focused his skills on composition and directing ensembles rather than merely performing within them. He continued his studies at the Curtis Institute in Philadelphia and the Conservatoire Institut in France and later pursued postgraduate work at Temple and Penn State universities.[106] In between his studies he directed theater orchestras for silent films.[107] He also served as a member of the Kansas City Orchestra and taught violin at the University of Nebraska School of Music.[108] In a further collaboration with Lieurance, he led the Cardin-Lieurance String Quintet through a number of successful seasons.[109] Perhaps influenced by the Carlisle pageants and his work with the Indian String Quartet, he composed

do you know that Indians are natural-born musicians?

The INDIAN Art and Musical Co. will be here at your community.... Chautauqua TO-MORROW.

In 1920 Fred Cardin (Quapaw), pictured on this brochure cover, formed the Indian Art and Musical Company with Wanita Cardin (Miami) on piano and singers Sensa Carey (Cherokee) and Te Ata (Chickasaw). Cardin created a number of all-Native ensembles after his prewar stint with the Indian String Quartet and was quite successful on Chautauqua circuits. Papers of the Redpath Chautauqua Bureau, University of Iowa Libraries, Iowa City, Iowa.

no less than ten pageants on American Indian history and his own Indian-themed songs. In 1930 one of his pageants, *Great Drum*, was performed in New York's Town Hall and was the only composition encored the next season due to popular demand.[110] The Carl Fischer publishing company released his "Cree War Dance" in 1924, and two of his collaborations with Lieurance, "Lament" and "Ghost Pipes (Indian Idyl)," were published by Theodore Presser Company in 1924 and 1932, respectively.[111] From 1936 to 1960 Cardin served as the director of the Ringgold Band and the Reading Civic Opera Society's productions and continued to perform as a member of the Reading Symphony Orchestra, all in Reading, Pennsylvania.[112] Cardin was enamored of music to the very end of his life. He died of a heart attack on August 29, 1960, at the end of a Ringgold Band rehearsal.[113]

Cardin's professional life was deeply rooted in his experiences as a Carlisle student. His collaborations reveal an extensive network of Native musicians and singers who often had met for the first time in boarding schools. Having performed with school ensembles, the students were all familiar with the desire of non-Indians to experience the long-encoded aural and visual signifiers of Indianness—the Plains war bonnets and associated regalia that had captured the non-Indian imagination since the early days of Wild West shows and the harmonized, pentatonic scales derived in part from ethnologists' interpretations of Native songs and in part from generic, musical interpretations of exoticness agreed upon by composers.[114] But many of them had also grown to love semiclassical and art music. The all-Indian quartets and quintets that Cardin and others formed gave them an opportunity to launch their musical careers in a way that benefited from the desire of audiences to experience authentic Indianness, but also allowed the musicians to work with each other, as colleagues who did not disparage Native people as Lookaround's non-Indian peers often had. Rather, they used the opportunity to take pride in their tribal heritages, and Cardin wrote several songs and pageants that allowed him to celebrate his Quapaw people and demonstrate his mastery of composition, the violin, and directorship of ensembles and orchestras.

JOE MORRIS: A VIEW FROM THE JAZZ CLUBS

While Cardin spent the majority of his touring career in bands that were contracted by lyceum organizations, other Native musicians were not as fortunate, finding themselves scrounging for jobs, particularly in the worsened economic conditions of the Depression era. It was in the 1930s that Joe Morris (Blackfeet) honed his skills not only on the trombone but in catching railway cars and stealing government automobiles to get to his shows as well. Morris self-published his autobiography in 2001, when he was eighty years old. A musician, a longshoreman, an occupier of Alcatraz from 1969 through 1971, Morris had had a long, eventful, hardscrabble life by that time, and his stories of his career as a musician are not nostalgic as much as they convey both his passion for jazz music and his hard times, including time spent in jail cells and fistfights in the bars he played night after night. Although he was most active as a professional musician in the mid-1930s and early 1940s, a few years beyond the most active years of the other musicians featured here, his stories are relevant in this context because they reveal with unmatched candor the life of an American Indian jazz musician in the Pacific Northwest.

Morris was born on the Blackfeet Reservation in East Glacier, Montana, and lived with his mother, who homesteaded a ranch just south of Glacier Park.[115] He enrolled at the Cut Bank Boarding School around 1929, right when the national economy began to fail. Like many Native people at the time, his primary motivation for attending the school was "not to get the education so much as to get something to eat." He adds, "No Indian can tell me he went to that school just to get an education; we went there to get some clothes and some food. We were all hungry and we came down there, all those families who couldn't support their kids."[116] His memories of Cut Bank are pained. In his autobiography, Morris describes a school where he was hit by teachers, where gang fights between Blackfeet students from Browning and Hard Butte were common, and where he even observed the school doctor self-injecting half of the morphine needed for a procedure to cut out gangrene-infected skin on Morris's toes.[117]

However, there were aspects of the school that he enjoyed as well. "The thing I liked best about the Cut Bank Boarding School," he writes, "was the little band at that school. It wasn't really a band, but we were learning to play instruments."[118] Music, all sorts of music, played a central role in his life, and he developed a positive relationship with Greely Billidoux, the music teacher. Morris continues,

> He and I used to play. I told him I wanted to play that upright horn, a mellophone. The government used to have old horns left over from the First World War, and it was kind of an old shin[y] instrument. I used to peck away on that, and I guess some of the people didn't like to hear me play it, but I liked to play that horn. I think music is part of the soul. Even singing, I used to like to sing. I would go to church. I was a Catholic, then I was a Protestant, then a Baptist; any kind of a church. I used to like to go in and sing even if I couldn't read the hymns. I went to the Methodist church and sang songs. That's where I learned to sing. And I liked to sing Indian, too. So whatever was around handy for me, I used to entertain myself or entertain other people.[119]

Morris, like many of his peers, absorbed every musical utterance he could find; for them, music was not categorized as savage or civilized, dangerous or safe. The only danger Morris encountered lay in not allowing his skills to develop. Despite his enjoyment of the music class and hymn singing, he left the school before completing the eighth grade and began honing his trombone skills on the road.

During those next few years, Morris alternated between hoboing across the Northwest, attending school in Fort Browning, Montana, and performing in the Blackfeet Tribal Band, consisting mainly of enrolled and returned students who had formed their own band to represent their tribe. He writes,

[The Blackfeet Tribal Band] would travel and play around in the summer months. I was always looking for a job, so I went on hoboing. I went and traveled up and down the country. I figure over a period of two or three years I must have gone twenty-five thousand miles on those freights, the rattlers. . . . I caught a freight out of Fort Browning to Spokane to buy my first trombone. I saved my money and had sixty bucks, so I went over there and bought a horn. When I came back home, my father was mad as hell at me for spending my money for a trombone. I was supposed to use the money to buy my clothes to go back to high school, to buy shoes and some jeans for the first day of school.[120]

Although Morris's father was upset at first, he eventually supported Morris's work as a professional musician when his son began making money.[121] Morris played with the Blackfeet Tribal Band between 1935 and 1940. His work with the band, like that of Lookaround's, demonstrates the vibrancy of band music on reservations at that time. As Morris recalled in his memoir, the Blackfeet band was hired for various tribal functions, including rodeos and Fourth of July celebrations. In addition, it provided the music for local fairs, such as that in Great Falls, Montana, and even played for President Franklin D. Roosevelt at East Glacier Park.[122] The band was very popular in the area, playing marching music as well as jazz, and was also well attuned to the added attraction that Indianness brought the group. According to Morris, "In the tribal band we all had to wear headdress war bonnets and look like Indians. It was important to wear the Indian outfits. I wore a headdress and a beaded vest."[123]

In those days, however, Morris was most fond of jamming to jazz tunes in dance halls, so besides playing with the tribal band, he took jobs with a number of jazz bands both to enjoy and support himself. As a Native jazz musician, Morris faced a unique set of circumstances in terms of racial segregation and local ordinances that prohibited American Indians from drinking in white establishments in the Pacific Northwest. On the one hand, even when playing in bands with white musicians, American Indians were not allowed to drink inside the bars they played: "I was not allowed to drink out in front with the white people. Some bartender would holler, 'OK, you go in the back room.' We had a trumpet man, I was playing the trombone, and we had a sax man, but we were all Indians. The drummer and the piano player were laughing like hell because we couldn't drink up front like the rest of the white people."[124] On the other hand, as an American Indian, Morris's rights were not as circumscribed as those of African Americans. He recalls a story, for example, when in 1943 jazz great Dexter Gordon, then a member of the Lionel Hampton band, asked Morris to sign for a room, because Gordon, an African American, was denied the right to rent a room with his girlfriend, a white woman.[125]

Some of the jazz clubs that Morris and his bandmates played were quite different from the halls in which Cardin and others on the lyceum circuit performed. A number of clubs Morris worked in Seattle, for example, were former bootlegging establishments and doubled as places to solicit prostitutes. At one predominantly African American club he worked in Seattle, the clientele had to check their knives, billy clubs, and other weapons at the door. Morris in fact played in African American clubs regularly; his fellow Native musicians seemed to feel more comfortable in such clubs, where they could drink in the club if they chose to and were not relegated to a storeroom.[126] Playing at African American clubs also afforded Morris and other Native musicians the opportunity to meet and play with some of the legendary jazz musicians of the time, such as saxophonist Lester Young, who sat in with Morris's band and socialized with Morris one night in Seattle while on tour with Count Basie.[127] Morris also regularly played dance halls on the north side of the Blackfeet Reservation. To get to the shows, Morris and his bandmates often stole a government car from the local agent, drove it along the back roads to avoid the police, and hid the automobile in the woods next to the dance hall during their performance.[128]

Regardless of whether the audience was predominantly white, American Indian, or African American, Morris experienced the typical incidents that would arise in an alcohol-fueled dance club environment. Occasional threats of violence, if not actual violence, were to be expected. He recalled a confrontation at one hall on the north side of the Blackfeet Reservation: "Some Cree Indian came in with a double-barrel shotgun, jealous over his girlfriend, and he shot the lights out. The bootlegger manager took the gun from the guy and put back the lights, and we started playing our music and the joint started jumping again."[129] In his memoirs Morris seemed to revel in his youthful exploits and adventures as a jazz musician in the 1930s.

Eventually Morris enrolled at Chemawa Indian School in Salem, Oregon, the birthplace of the Indian String Quartet. As a well-seasoned nineteen-year-old junior, he transferred his musical skills to that world, taking over the trombone duties in the school's jazz band, the Rhythm Chiefs. The band included Tony Shoulder Blade on drums, "Cash" Lobert on sax, Clifford Day on vocals, Robair Thomas on sax, and John Gerard on electric guitar.[130] Morris writes, "We had a pretty good deal. We played every Saturday night. We got no money but we got our food, and I liked it because we could get extra food."[131] He completed his high school education at Chemawa and later continued to play music at night while he worked during the day as a longshoreman in California. Morris retained close ties to the Blackfeet community as well as the San Francisco urban Indian community, and he coordinated the transportation of supplies from the San Francisco docks to Alcatraz during the 1969–71 occupation, even though he was much older by that time than most of the occupants.[132]

Morris's musical trajectory took him all over the West Coast, performing in all-Indian bands, in predominantly white bands, and in predominantly black bands. In some groups, such as the Blackfeet Tribal Band, he performed marching music and jazz in Plains war bonnets. In other instances he simply dressed in the latest fashions that any jazz musician would don. He saw no contradiction in wearing extensive regalia while performing jazz and band music, and in fact when I met him in 2003, he was signing copies of his book for sale at the Alcatraz Island bookstore, sporting a large and colorfully plumed headdress along with a longshoreman's union jacket. Music defined Morris's life in his youth, and he gained extraordinary experiences, playing for governors and the U.S. president, as well as patrons in white, black, and Indian dance halls across the Pacific Northwest. His musicianship on brass instruments originated from his boarding school education, but as was true of other jazz musicians of his time, his skills and his joy for playing grew out of his experiences on the road and the camaraderie he shared with his bandmates. Shunning the efforts of the OIA to categorize and compartmentalize his musical expressions, he devoured every note he could, using music to transgress the imposed racial barriers of the day.

TSIANINA REDFEATHER BLACKSTONE: A VIEW FROM THE HOLLYWOOD BOWL

Tsianina Blackstone, who survived the attack on the *Carmania*, was perhaps the most successful professional Native musician of the era. Distinguished by non-Indian audiences and critics through the combination of her beautiful voice, her engaging personality, and her performance of Indianness, she was also distinguished socially, as an entertainer, by her elegance, at least from the perspective of the elite cultural circles in which she mingled. Although she was probably better-traveled than the majority of her non-Indian audiences, having performed across the United States and Europe and studied for a year in Italy, they continually anticipated her as an embodiment of the primitive yet noble Indian princess. She seemed to delight in shattering those expectations at every social gathering she attended. For her musical proclivities, she had her own talents and her education to thank, but her high intercultural fluency derived in part from her role as one-half of a truly successful duo. The second half of this powerful partnership was Charles Wakefield Cadman, to whom she was introduced while studying under a piano instructor in Denver. Blackstone and Cadman embarked on a long professional relationship that took them on tours throughout the United States, in one season performing in forty-three states.[133] By 1916 the pair found themselves drawing crowds of more than seven thousand in towns as small as Kansas City.[134] Among her career highlights were her performances as a soloist with many orchestras, including the New York and Russian symphony orchestras. She served in the American Expeditionary Forces overseas during World War I and was the first American woman to cross the Rhine with the army of occupation.[135] Blackstone was an exceptional professional Native singer of semiclassical music who became adept at manipulating prevalent notions of Indianness in not only lucrative but also vital and creative ways.

Tsianina Blackstone perhaps found a worthy ally in Charles Wakefield Cadman. Like Fred Cardin, Blackstone built her career on her talents at performing both music and Indianness, yet Blackstone often played for more well-to-do audiences than did Cardin's various traveling lyceum acts. Cadman played a central role in her success by providing his own Indianist compositions and his legitimacy as an established composer in the eyes of the socialites, art music critics, and aficionados who filled the seats night after night. Cadman was at least as fortunate to have Blackstone's support, however, because, as a Creek singer of his works, she legitimated as authentically *Indian* his compositions for the same audience. She articulated publicly her strong belief in his mission to represent Indian melodies as "a classic, a living thing, that embodies all the beauty and dignity of the American Indian."[136] Like other Native musicians, Blackstone was quite conscious that she was "playing Indian" for the public. She viewed it as a great opportunity and at times a chance to challenge the public's views of American Indians by actually meeting her audience and, by revealing herself as a modern and cosmopolitan Creek woman, shattering their expectations. She forged a balance between asserting certain characteristics that the public desired, such as often invoking in her songs a tie to the natural world, while her non-Indian audience interpreted her travel experience throughout the country and Europe, her residence in urban centers, and her friendships with Cadman and members of the social elite as demonstrative of her modern sensibilities.

Blackstone and Cadman presented sold-out audiences with elaborate excursions into Indian song and dance. Throughout her career, Blackstone outfitted herself in a buckskin beaded dress of her own design that fairly typified the public's expectations of a "typical"

Tsianina Redfeather Blackstone (Creek-Cherokee) entertained people throughout the United States and Europe. She responded to her fans' requests for photographs and autographs whenever she could. Photograph from the author's
collection.

Indian "princess." She and Cadman performed on stages that they had together decorated with baskets, musical instruments, and Navajo rugs. Their songs were overwhelmingly of the Indianist tradition; in a single show an attendee might have heard them perform "I Found Him on the Mesa," "Invocation to the Sun God," "Ho!! Ye Warriors on the Warpath," and one of Cadman's most famous compositions, "From the Land of the Sky-Blue Water."[137] A review of one particular performance demonstrates the complex history and multicultural provenance of the pieces they performed, which were not embedded in specific tribal traditions as much as they reflected the essentializing evocation of Indianness: "A curious drum, decorated with the totem of the Alaskan Indians was used by Tsianina to illustrate the involved rhythm as used in the two Omaha ceremonial songs, which she sang. These songs were recorded by Miss [Alice] Fletcher, and the originals are in the Smithsonian collection at Washington."[138] What to make of an Omaha song, transcribed and harmonized by an ethnologist, adapted by a non-Indian composer, and then performed with the accompaniment of a drum decorated with an Inuit totem by a Creek singer in buckskin dress? The reporter certainly found nothing contradictory or inauthentic in the performance, and from what we can gather, neither did Blackstone.

Music in fact enabled many Native Americans like Tsianina Blackstone to interchange with ease such seemingly impermeable social and cultural categories. Recalling her travels years later in an autobiography, she felt a deep love for her Native heritage (Creek-Cherokee), her faith in the tenants of Christian Science, and her country (the United States), and, for her, none of these categories contradicted another. "The people's response to Indian music [when I was touring] gave me a love for my country and for being a Native American that I had not felt as strongly before," she said. "I was now a part of my song, a part of my heartbeat, and I knew where I was going, for I could feel the touch of the Holy One showing me the way."[139]

Although Blackstone seemed quite at ease in situating her identity along such multivalent lines, others were constantly bewildered and enthralled with what they interpreted as contradictions, in part because she simply broke the mold of the Indianness that they had anticipated. While touring and performing, Blackstone indeed met many people who did not quite know how to react to her. After one of her first performances, she and Cadman were invited to a party of Denver's high society. She wrote afterward that "many of them did not attempt to guard their talk in my presence because they did not think I could understand English—this, after a complete program in English."[140] Blackstone dealt with stereotypes among the Germans as well on an overseas tour. After staying in the home of a German family for a week, the daughter of the family confided to her that in the first few days of the visit, "because they were afraid of the Indian[,] she piled trunks and boxes against the door." Tsianina, however, then confessed that she had done the same thing.[141] Anthropologist Edgar Hewett at the 1916 Panama-California International Exposition took her to his American Indian exhibit and showed her his collection of Indian skulls. She wrote,

> I noticed him looking occasionally at my head. With no attempt at flattery, he said, "You have made so much out of your life in so short a time, and your head is so beautifully shaped, I would consider it a great contribution to the history of your people and archaeology if you would let us have your head when you depart for the Happy Hunting Ground." I made no reply, but inside I didn't feel so good. He frightened me, and I had a secret fear of having my skull on display for all to see. Imagine my relief when my beloved friend left for his Happy Hunting Ground before me.[142]

Despite her discomfort with his request, she befriended Hewitt, who invited her to perform for several years at the Santa Fe Fiesta program. After he died in 1955, Blackstone even took his widow, Donizetta Hewitt, into her home and cared for her until the latter's death five years later.[143]

Blackstone, like other Native musicians, was adept at using her public persona to attract attention to failed government policies in the allotment and assimilation era. When she and Cadman spoke at events such as the celebration of "Cadman and Tsianina Day" at the 1916 Panama-California fair, for example, Cadman would usually just turn the mic over to her. She wrote, "This was shocking to me at first, but the inner voice said, 'this is your opportunity to tell the truth about the Indian race.'"[144] She often swayed her audience and the press to sympathize with the problems that American Indians were facing. In one newspaper interview, for example, she said, "I want the American people to know the Indian as he is and has been, and not as he has been so grossly misrepresented to be. . . . Indian traditions and traits of character have been monstrously defamed. The popular conception seems to be drawn largely from motion picture characterization. I feel in justice to my people that I should do all in my power to dispel these illusions."[145] Her message appeared to have an effect, as she recalled in her autobiography: "Wherever I appeared people told me, almost with tears in their eyes, how they felt about the Indian question, how wrongly the Indian problem had been handled."[146] As one critic wrote, "Who, having heard Tsianina sing the tragic Indian lament, Into the Forest Near to God can ever forget this formidable arraignment of the pale-face civilization[?]"[147] Regarding one of her performances, Bugs Baer of the *San Francisco Examiner* remarked, "An American Indian is an alien born in this country. We cannot deny that this country belongs to him but we can refuse to admit it. Our Bureau of Indian Affairs considers it no affair of the Indians."[148]

Although Blackstone served overseas during World War I in the American Expeditionary Forces, her motives for doing so, like those of Native people who volunteered to serve in the military, were not bound in any particular desire to demonstrate her affinity for the U.S. government or the non-Indian population. She recognized the irony of the situation, noting, "Here I was—helping defend the homeland which in turn had robbed us of our heritage. Amazing! I wondered if I had all of my marbles!"[149] According to her autobiography, early on she "held a deep-rooted aversion for the white race in general . . . [and] resented . . . the false picture that was presented [of Indians] in school books."[150] She argued, "[The] white man claims that he brought civilization to America. By that he means *his* civilization."[151] Thus, she believed, "[the] white man is choosing his own way of life with its trail of tears—of deceit, intrigue, dishonesty, and inhumanity to man."[152] Because of the strong presence of American Indians who served in World War I, she felt that she "could look America squarely in the face . . . and tell the truth—the Indian had fought for his freedom, had won medals in the war along with every other soldier, and so had earned the right to be free."[153] Despite this anger early in her professional life, however, Blackstone would never have considered herself to be outspoken or antagonistic to white people as a race, nor did she see this as her main agenda on the stage. Later in life she began to direct her political grievances more particularly toward corrupt politicians whom she believed were not respecting Christian Science values or the Constitution: "The Indian question is not complicated, the complication is in America's leaders."[154] She added, "The core of the evil is politics, evasion of the Ten Commandments, evasion of the golden Rule, evasion of the Constitution of the United States."[155] Despite framing her later political grievances in such general terms, however, she remained dedicated to serving the specific needs of Indian people and cultivated relationships with Native communities after her retirement. In 1956 she established the Foundation for American Indian Education in Burbank, California, a group that provided financial assistance to American Indian children in need, including children in the Navajo Children's Home in Gallup, New Mexico.[156]

Blackstone considered as one of her crowning professional achievements her performance at the Hollywood Bowl of the opera *Shanewis (The Robin Woman)*, written in 1918 by Cadman and Nelle Eberhart and based on a story line by Blackstone. The plot centers around a love triangle between the characters Shanewis, an American Indian vocalist prodigy sponsored by a wealthy white woman to pursue her musical talents; Lionel, the future son-in-law of Shanewis's protégé; and Philip Harjo, Shanewis's foster brother, who has secretly loved her since childhood. In the first part of the one-act opera, Shanewis and Lionel meet in Southern California at a party thrown by her sponsor, Mrs. J. Asher Everton. Despite his engagement to Everton's daughter, Lionel pledges his love to Shanewis and promises to meet her family on the reservation. Once on the reservation, Lionel's fiancée confronts them both. Unaware that Lionel was engaged, Shanewis angrily chastises him and then pledges to redeem herself by leaving: "Into the forest, near to God I go." Lionel protests Shanewis's decision but is soon killed with a poisoned arrow by Harjo, and the opera draws to a close.

The plot of the opera is quite formulaic of any dramatic production of the era centered around a cross-race love triangle, the various conventions of which have been recently explored by Philip Deloria.[157]

What is interesting about the opera, however, is the second part, which takes place at a noticeably "modern" Oklahoma powwow. Instead of portraying a tribe, as many productions did, of backward, timeless Indians dancing in an assumed primitive fashion, the audience meets dancers in "mongrel" and "modern" dress, as well as "ceremonial" garb. The grounds include not only horses but "several Ford automobiles," and vendors sell crafts and food to the crowd, which includes "white spectators in holiday attire." In fact, with "booths decorated in red, white, and blue," it appears that the powwow is taking place on the Fourth of July. An eight-piece jazz band performs music in between the powwow dances.[158]

The powwow in *Shanewis* represents a significant digression from the typical depictions of Indian dances and songs as constructed by Indianist composers. The Fourth of July setting, modern dress, automobiles, and jazz band convey the incorporation and adaptation of various modern influences within the framework of an Oklahoma powwow. That Cadman, Blackstone, and Eberhart designed their opera as "modern" even though most performances of Indianness evoked Indian lives totally void of modernity, speaks volumes about their endeavors. Cadman was adamant in breaking with the tradition of representing Indian people as primitive, antimodern peoples, and his views were certainly influenced by his work with Blackstone and the story line that she provided him. Rather, he claimed, because the opera "deals with contemporary people in contemporary surroundings, and the principal woman character is Indian and the second scene passes in Oklahoma in an Indian reservation, the work does not in any way fill the ordinary definition of an Indian opera."[159] In the foreword to the score and text, he added, "There is no reason why this work should be labeled an Indian opera. Let it be an opera upon an American subject, or, if you will, an American opera."[160]

The opera debuted at the Metropolitan Opera House on March 23, 1918, and was performed eight times in two consecutive seasons.[161] *Shanewis* was one of several operas written by Americans that were performed during the war years at the Met, with patriotic fervor running unusually high . Cadman and the cast, along with Blackstone, received twenty curtain calls following their debut performance. Though Blackstone was slotted to perform the lead role, she was too nervous to accept it and instead coached the role of Shanewis to Sophie Breslau, a non-Indian.[162] Despite Cadman's claims that the opera should not be considered an Indian opera, per se, *Shanewis* was debuted on a night that featured two additional operas with race-based plotlines, one a "negro ballet" called *The Dance of the Place Congo*, and the other, "dealing with the Chinese in San Francisco," was an interpretation of *L'Oracolo*.[163] If Cadman and Blackstone needed a reminder that their cherished debut at the Metropolitan Opera House stage required a prodigious inflection of Indianness, despite their intentions to transcend the formulaic civilized/primitive dialectic that scored typical Indian operas, the racial overtones of the shared bill would have provided it.

Despite the circumstances of the debut, and the generally mixed reviews that *Shanewis* received, Blackstone eventually performed the title role for the two other renditions of the opera, first in Denver on December 5, 1924, and finally at the Hollywood Bowl on June 24, 1926. The Hollywood Bowl show attracted an audience of around twenty thousand, and "special interest," according to one paper, was directed at the reemergence of Blackstone on the American stage after a year of study in Rome.[164] She was joined on stage by Os-ke-non-ton (Mohawk), another prominent Native musician and a recording artist in his own right who performed the role of Philip Harjo.[165]

While Blackstone performed to significant audiences of non-Indians, she certainly had her share of Native fans, and she is perhaps remembered much more today by American Indians rather than non-Indian people. She and Cadman made it a priority to perform extensively at Indian schools, particularly between 1910 and 1917.[166] She also performed for the Native reform organization that Carlos Montezuma had cofounded, the Society of American Indians.[167] In addition, she was wildly popular in Santa Fe, as Pueblo Indians flocked to see her when she performed at the Santa Fe Fiesta on nine consecutive occasions. Recalling her 1917 performance in Santa Fe, she wrote,

> Many Indians from the different Pueblos came to the concert in their colorful costumes, making a bright splash in the auditorium. . . . It was revealing to observe how they received Mr. Cadman's music, based on melodies from their own people. They nodded their heads approvingly

Tsianina Redfeather Blackstone played the lead role of *Shanewis* in 1926 at the Hollywood Bowl. This photograph demonstrates the extraordinary attendance at the event. Reproduced with the permission of the Special Collections Library, The Pennsylvania State University Libraries.

after each number. . . . After we left Santa Fe, it was to the heart throb of the tom tom and the echo of the strongest cheers I have ever heard humanly expressed.[168]

Blackstone proudly remembered meeting artists Maria and Julian Martinez after the performance and in her autobiography seemed gratified that members of the Pueblos, who returned to see her sing for several years, extended an open invitation to her and accepted her music.[169] She received fan letters from Native soldiers in World War I and even satisfied the request of one such young man, wounded in action, who asked her to bring a package of Bull Durham tobacco to the London hospital during her visit.[170] She also attracted many Native fans to see her when she starred in *Shanewis* at the Hollywood Bowl.[171]

Tsianina moved about frequently in the years following her Hollywood Bowl success. For a time she resided in Chicago and founded the First Daughters of America, a federation of Native American women.[172] She retired from the stage in 1935 but remained active in Indian affairs and was often asked to speak at public events. Tsianina

In addition to singing, Blackstone played the piano and the Hawaiian steel guitar. Through her nineties, she continued to play Charles Wakefield Cadman's
prized grand piano in her living room, left to her in his will. George Grantham
Bain Collection, Prints and Photographs Division, Library of Congress, LC-DIG-
ggbain-30380.

lived to the age of 103 and led a remarkably full life that was formed around her work as an American Indian professional singer. Her musical career took her all over the world at a time when such travels were matched only by those of Native people who had worked in the earlier Wild West shows. Her travels brought her opportunity—to celebrate her heritage as a Creek woman with Native people all over the country, as well as to confront non-Indians that she encountered at performances and social gatherings who were unprepared to meet a quite modern American Indian woman.

KIUTUS TECUMSEH:
A VIEW FROM THE BROADCASTER'S BOOTH

Blackstone used her access to the non-Indian public and press to gain sympathy for the situation in which American Indians found themselves by the early twentieth century, but she did so by persuading her audience in terms that were more general than precise. Other musicians were much more direct in their calls for change in OIA policy and went so far as to engage in running correspondence over policy matters with the commissioners of Indian Affairs. Virtually denied any other means to engage U.S. politics on a public platform, music served these individuals much as writing served their literary peers such as Charles Eastman and Gertrude Simmons Bonnin.[173] Their efforts contributed to those of dancers on reservations who publicly refuted the assimilationist direction of the OIA and to those of professional, middle-class Indians such as Carlos Montezuma who contested the pessimistic philosophy that shaped the boarding school curriculum in the early twentieth century. These musicians formed a core component of the vanguard of urban Indians in this period who used their formal education and audience access to publicly challenge federal Indian policy, and their efforts would not go unheard, particularly when broadcast to potential audiences of millions through the advent of radio technology.

One of the first American Indians to take advantage of this innovation was tenor singer Herman W. Roberts (Yakama-Cherokee). A resident of White Swan, Washington, and a member of the Naval

Reserve during the First World War, he decided upon his discharge that he would like to pursue further education in both music and public speaking.[174] Although Senator Miles Poindexter wrote a letter on his behalf, Commissioner of Indian Affairs Charles Burke informed him that none of the Indian schools at present had the type of courses he desired.[175] This lack of advanced courses in the Indian schools spurred Roberts, who later renamed himself Kiutus Tecumseh, into a life of professional musical performance centered around a core message: the need to enhance the accessibility of higher education for all American Indians.

Although Tecumseh rigorously toured as other musicians did, he also grew adept, as musicians had to, at using the modern technology of the radio to further his own career ambitions. Despite limited opportunities for educational advancement, and the pessimism he encountered by the OIA in terms of brighter professional opportunities for American Indians, by 1924 Tecumseh had relocated to Chicago, managing to enroll in voice culture at the Chicago Musical College while also balancing a difficult schedule of touring the United States as a tenor soloist.[176] While in Chicago, he regularly performed on radio station WDAP, for which he received fan letters (that he sent home to his father) from as far as Montana and Massachusetts.[177] Radio consistently provided him with a widespread fan base. In 1929, for example, the *Spokane Chronicle* featured a photograph of Tecumseh standing next to an "Indian wigwam" constructed from eighteen thousand letters from his radio fans; an additional seventeen thousand fan letters filled the inside of it.[178] By 1925, Tecumseh had moved to New York City in order to advance his career and his vocal studies. There he accepted an offer to perform on station WEAF, where he also had the opportunity to sing with numerous prominent performers such as the famous Irish tenor John McCormack. In addition to numerous engagements on Chicago and New York stations that transmitted their signals across large swaths of the country, in 1927 he conducted a radio tour sponsored by the Calumet Baking Powder Company and stretching from Iowa to Washington State.[179] During the winter of 1929, he embarked upon a massive U.S. tour, singing at radio stations in thirty-three major cities from New Orleans (WSMB) to Boston (WNAC) and Salt Lake City (KSL). He was broadcast live

246
INDIAN BLUES

on all but 13 days of the 128-day tour.[180] Not only did Tecumseh find opportunities for himself through the radio, but he also sponsored radio appearances by other Native singers and performers, such as a group of Haskell students that traveled to Chicago to sing in 1926.[181] Although Tecumseh's career was not ultimately as financially successful as Blackstone's, he learned that he could use the public forums presented to performers, such as the radio, to serve a cause larger than his own.

Kiutus Tecumseh used his access to the public in political ways, particularly in his call to grant Native people greater access to higher education. Tecumseh often easily won over audiences in his criticisms of the OIA. The response of the leaders of a Virginia church where he performed in 1930 typified that of many. They applauded his presentation and wrote that Tecumseh, "proud to wear his native dress, with all the meaning attached thereto [brought a] real message of appeal for higher education for his race." They continued, "[Tecumseh] feels that if the American Indian is to make progress, he should be better understood—and not be the victims of exploitation of capital—not be driven from his own lands without recourse to lawful protection. He should be given advantage of college and university Education, thus enabling him to compete in the world of trade and industry and profession."[182]

Radio enabled Tecumseh to develop powerful political friendships. He frequently corresponded and met with Commissioner of Indian Affairs Charles Burke to discuss his own impressions of the work (or lack thereof) that the OIA was doing for American Indians.[183] Regarding his first visit with Commissioner Burke, Tecumseh wrote to the *Real American*, a newspaper run by Native Americans in the Northwest: "[Burke] explained to me why he did some of the things of which we criticize him for. I find that he is a very agreeable man to talk to and I sincerely believe if he is approached through [the] right channels that he would give the Real American cause every consideration."[184] Perhaps because Tecumseh was often very disappointed in the priority that the government was giving to furthering formal educational opportunities for American Indians, he continuously reached out to Commissioner Burke and often dedicated songs to him over the radio.[185] In 1926, for example, Superintendent James McGregor of the Rosebud Agency in South Dakota reported to Burke that people listening to radio station WJJD out of Chicago heard Tecumseh sing "Aloha Oe (Farewell to Thee)," a song written by deposed Hawaiian queen Liliuokalani with a dedication to the commissioner.[186] His intended message to Burke by singing that particular song is unclear, but a year earlier he wrote to Burke that it was an honor to sing his favorite songs over the air and that he was "sure that it will inspire other Indian boys with higher ideals."[187]

While attracting audiences initially through his "authenticity" and novelty as an Indian performer, Tecumseh attempted to influence the audience to reconsider current federal Indian policies and some Indian stereotypes, though he may have inadvertently reified others. When Tecumseh traveled and performed Indianist compositions in Plains Indian regalia, he frequently discussed his opinions of the OIA, the injustices against American Indians for which he felt non-Indians were responsible, and his "insider's perspective," both as a Yakama Cherokee and as a man who had established a relationship with Commissioner Burke. He wrote that he was often "called on by very prominent citizens to enlighten them on the American Indian question" and that he had been "asked to write several articles for newspapers through[out] the country."[188] Tecumseh virtually served as an ambassador and an educator, with no topic more important to him than that of Indian education.

Tecumseh and his piano accompanist, an Aleut named Simeon Oliver, kept an extremely busy road schedule, but they felt it was their duty always to visit Indian schools along the way in order to serve as role models for the students and to encourage the students to strive for higher education and go beyond limits of the training in manual and domestic labor that the schools offered.[189] In the middle of one radio tour, Tecumseh and Oliver made an unscheduled stop to entertain the children at the Chemawa Indian School, and in 1925 he asked for Burke's help in routing his tour for the year so that he could "stop at as many schools and reservations as possible, en route."[190] During an extensive tour of the West, Tecumseh visited several schools, including the Chemawa and Riverside schools, where both superintendents gave him a tour. The visits left him deeply concerned with the limited funding they received, and he wrote to Burke with the "hope that Congress in the near future will see fit to give our Indian

Kiutus Tecumseh (Yakama-Cherokee) enjoyed a professional career as a singer in the 1920s and 1930s. He often discussed his views of federal Indian policy on the radio during his extensive travels throughout the United States. In addition to singing, Tecumseh also composed music, such as "The Land of My Prairie Dreams," a song he published in 1926. Sheet music cover, from the author's collection.

Schools more money to carry on as I am sure that you are very anxious to see everyone of our boys and girls advance and the limited amount of funds that is being given towards that now does not give you a chance to do all that is necessary."[191]

After returning to Chicago to complete his courses necessary for graduation, he remained heartbroken that, during his tours and visits with schools, so many Native children were being "held back on account of no funds to carry on with along their chosen careers such as music, art, etc., which our Government does not seem to recognize."[192] "For many years," he wrote to Burke's successor, Commissioner Charles J. Rhoads, in 1931, "I have worked with one main object in view—it is recognition of the Redman and a suitable position for our young Indian boys and girls leaving college."[193] By 1930 Tecumseh had already been taking a more aggressive stance against the actions of the Office of Indian Affairs and the prejudices against American Indians. In an article in the *Washington Post* entitled, "Chief Holds Whites Responsible for Race," Tecumseh was quoted as saying, "I have been making these talks over the radio in connection with my singing . . . in an effort to better acquaint the public with Indian questions. It is my aim to place before the American people the honest facts concerning my race." He continued, "I am making every effort so that our boys and girls are given a fair chance to attend, not only grade and high schools, but colleges as well." He also stated that the government was prejudiced against hiring Indians even though there were many educated Indians who could perform the jobs just as well. He concluded, "Give the Indians a fair chance to obtain higher education . . . and they will make as good citizens as the white man."[194] According to the *Post*, Tecumseh had additionally informed Commissioner Rhoads that he believed that the Yakama tribe was owed compensation for land at the fork of the Wenatchee and Icicle rivers that had been unjustly taken by the U.S. government in 1894.[195]

Tecumseh was actively involved in the politics of Indian affairs well into the 1930s. Maintaining his tours of Indian boarding schools and concerned about the conditions children faced within them, in 1930 he sent crates of "Jim Hill" apples to many of the schools so that the children would have fresh fruit for Christmas.[196] Tecumseh continued lecturing his audiences on the state of Indian affairs for years into the

John Collier administration of the OIA, after Congress had passed the
"Indian New Deal" legislation spurred by the Wheeler-Howard Act of
1934, which ceased the allotment of land and largely quieted the efforts
of the federal government to restrict expressive culture on reservations
and in the schools. The new legislation was controversial in Indian
Country for its particular requirements related to tribal political organization and economic development, with some Native people seeing
those components of the bill as a positive sea change in policy, and others seeing them as an attempt by the federal government to gain even
greater oversight in tribal affairs. Tecumseh believed he had a role to
play in this concern as well.[197] He wrote to Collier in 1935,

> Personally, I think [the Wheeler-Howard bill] is a Godsend to the Ameri-
> can Indian. My radio and concert work takes me to all parts of the United
> States. I find that the American people are interested in the American
> Indian, but they have been so poorly informed as to the Indian's real need.
> My lectures and concerts have been well attended by citizens anxious to
> become more familiar with the Indian question. I have just recently fin-
> ished a tour of the Pacific Northwest, so have first hand information of
> what the Wheeler-Howard bill will really mean to my people. I would like
> all the printed material you have on this bill, as there may be some phases
> of it that I do not quite understand.[198]

Tecumseh actively engaged all of the commissioners of Indian Affairs
who were appointed during his professional career and made it a
point to inform them of his observations and positions on policies as
well as to provide his audiences with accurate information—audiences inside and outside Indian Country.

Music gave Tecumseh an opportunity he most likely would not
have had otherwise, to enter the public eye and voice his grievances,
"playing Indian" with a pointed, political message. He wrote to U.S.
senator Wesley Jones of Washington State,

> My personal visits to various radio stations throughout the United States,
> Canada, and Northern Mexico, have placed me in a wonderful position to
> bring our Indian question before the public in such a way as educating the
> public in the various real needs of the Redmen. My public appearances

before large audience[s] such as churches, clubs, schools, and various other institutions, have made it very eas[y] for me to deliver in person the real message concerning my people, which the majority of citizens know so little about. . . . [Although the government has hired people to discuss policy initiatives with the public,] none of them are in position to reach the vast audiences that I have access to, because they are only probably just lecturers, and therefore they do not get the time allotted them to speak and give radio programs that I have access to without any station charges whatever. . . . I have complete access to visit our various Indian schools throughout the nation, and in so doing, I am in a position to encourage thousands of students to become better educated and strive for higher ideals.[199]

His experience was multifaceted and modern, reflecting his generation and their experiences from Indian schools and home communities to the urban centers that they passed through or settled in. While he sought change for Native people as a whole, he also remained very concerned with the affairs of his Yakama community. Through his stage and radio performances, he articulated his pride as a World War I veteran and his disgust for the treatment of American Indians by the government. He invoked a nationalist rhetoric to argue that American Indians had already demonstrated patriotism and service to the country in World War I and, if given equal opportunities in education and employment, would become the "good citizens" to whom others would aspire.

The musicians profiled here were part of a generation of American Indians, educated in government schools, who combined their reservation and off-reservation experiences, boarding school education, modern technologies, and musical ambitions to adapt to the opportunities and difficulties that each encountered in a rapidly changing world. At a time when the vocational and domestic instruction taught in boarding schools was quite limited and prospects for work off the reservations not very promising, these performers were able to make a decent living doing what they loved to do. Beyond that, opportunities to actually confront and address the public were very limited for Native people at this time, and the performance of music became one of the most accessible media for American Indians to do just that.

Music gave these performers an inroad for inspiring boarding school students and influencing the public perception of American Indians, while also alerting the public as to the difficulties that Native people were facing. The musical performances of those who manipulated Indianness in their act were often infused with complex and simultaneous affirmations of aural and visual stereotypes as well as tribal and pan-Indian pride, patriotism and service to the U.S. government as well as critique and disdain. As Philip Deloria argues in *Playing Indian*, the messages that public Native figures tried to deliver may have easily been outweighed by the stereotypical notions of Indianness that drew most of the members of their audiences to them.[200] The ability to control the message their audience was receiving was extremely uncertain. Yet they often did what they could to serve as "authentic" spokespeople for American Indians, using the cultural authority vested in their performance of Indianness to demonstrate to the non-Indian public that Native people were not disappearing but instead were active, capable and deserving of asserting a voice and leadership in their own affairs.[201]

At the same time, it is also clear that these five individuals, at least, loved the music that they performed. Lookaround sought perfection in his fellow Menominee bandmates and pushed his students to reach for those difficult to find notes. Cardin created several ensembles of his fellow Native musicians and spent years on the road, spreading their art before the country. Morris reveled in jazz music and, through his music, traversed the racially segregated dance halls that he played. Blackstone delighted in her songs and her collaborative work with Cadman, and Tecumseh pushed himself to access as many American Indian and non-Indian audiences as he could. Their music did not merely shape their lives; it *was* their lives. And even when playing the music that boarding school educators hoped would help sever their ties with their people, they made it their own, creating new traditions of decidedly Indian music.

EPILOGUE

"It's all about identity," says Rex Smallboy of the Cree hip-hop group War Party.[1] War Party has been together for twelve years, with five albums; several Canadian Aboriginal Music Awards; a guest appearance by Public Enemy's Chuck D on its 2005 album, ""*The Resistance*; and a touring history with the likes of Wu-Tang Clan, Mack 10, and Ice-T. "We made the hip hop music, hip hop music doesn't make us," he continued.[2] The members of War Party feel that they have much to say, and hip-hop seems the best vehicle to get their message of self-empowerment and pride in Native identity across to young indigenous peoples throughout the continent. According to their MySpace page, their mission is as follows: "To lead, inspire and empower all youth to believe in themselves and in their dreams to promote successful and positive attitudes. To educate through Rap music to create a better awareness and understanding towards First Nation's issues in Canada."[3] Their music is as politically charged as Native music ever has been. Smallboy notes that the band has received death threats from "people who didn't like Indians." He adds, "They called us Mongoloids, told us to go back to the reserve and drink Lysol. Shit like that."[4] And just as returned Carlisle students on the Lakota reservations caused concern among their elders for performing the Rabbit Dance and other new practices of music, War Party's hip-hop musicality has caused controversy among the group's own people as well.[5] Despite the difficulties, however, Smallboy talks with elders to find out what they should be writing about in order to "represent the Indian experience in a responsible way."[6]

Along with the Aleuts who gleefully sang the chorus of "In the Shade of the Old Apple Tree" in 1904, War Party's devotion to hip-hop illuminates the degree to which Native people spanning the North American continent have, for a very long time, creatively appropriated and made their own a multitude of musical styles. War Party's musical influences traverse many strains of contemporary music, and in fundamental ways its use of music as a form of Native politics is also linked to the histories of the singers, dancers, and musicians described in this book. Today some reservation-based marching bands such as that at Zuni Pueblo persist, powwow culture has grown exponentially since Native peoples successfully resisted the government attempts to restrict it in the 1920s, the Native American Music Awards cover more than thirty categories, and thousands of Native singers, musicians, and dancers of all varieties continue to access every available musical arena, including of course that of cyberspace.[7] By doing so, Native people have maintained their use of music as, among many other things, a potent political instrument.

In important ways, the OIA changed course in policy with the advent of the "Indian New Deal" in the 1930s, inaugurated by the Indian Reorganization Act (IRA) of 1934, which seemed to turn the tide against the suppression of Indian arts and traditions by the government. Certainly many forces contributed to the shift, including reports of corruption and mismanagement by the OIA, as well as the publication of the Meriam Report in 1928, which revealed in shocking detail the deteriorating health, educational, and economic conditions that resulted from the allotment and assimilation policies.[8] Another factor was the reform organizations led by John Collier and others in the 1920s that were philosophically invested in the value of Indianness for non-Indian citizens as well as the protection of the religious rights of Native peoples.[9] Native expressive culture meanwhile continued to gain currency for non-Indian Americans as they sought to forge new identities in the modern world.[10]

But reformers and American identity crises were only partially responsible for causing the reevaluation of the role and rights of American Indians in the country. American Indians played a crucial role in the shift in federal Indian policy away from cultural suppression and toward greater autonomy and self-determination. It was not Collier who caused the shift; it was decades of efforts made by American Indians that led to the transformation of official policy in 1934. According to Tom Holm, "The underlying ideas of assimilation collapsed because Natives simply refused to vanish as peoples or as individuals into the American mainstream. The resiliency of peoplehood militated against assimilation and caused whites to rethink the policy."[11] The defense of dance on the reservations and the opportunities for public speaking and engagements that music provided loosened the grip that government officials attempted to hold over the lives of American Indians. Native music became politically charged, not necessarily because of its content but because of how it was used. Grass Dancers confronted the assimilation policy and manipulated ideas of Americanness and citizenship such that their demands for control over reservation-based expressive culture were heeded by local OIA agents. Students made their musical experience on campus their own, disregarding the efforts of the administrators to control its meaning. In the semiclassical and art genres, singers and musicians like Cardin, Blackstone, and Tecumseh—whether onstage, through the radio, or in conversation with the public that music brought before them—were now able to present their politics and their own sense of cultural entitlement for a broad audience. Far from representing the federal government's success in detribalizing Indian peoples, these dancers, singers, and musicians demonstrated the willingness, the ability, and even the economic viability to assert their difference as tribal peoples in a polyphonic, modern American society.

After the appointment of John Collier as the commissioner of Indian Affairs and the passage of the IRA and other "Indian New Deal" legislation, the politics of music in the schools seemed to change dramatically. As a first step, on January 4, 1934, Collier issued circular 2970, "Indian Religious Freedom and Indian Culture," which stated, "No interference with Indian religious life or ceremonial expression will hereafter be tolerated. The cultural liberty of Indians is in all respects to be considered equal to that of any non-Indian group."[12] Then the monumental IRA, also known as the Wheeler-Howard Act, effectively reversed the Dawes Act, ceasing the further allotment of reservation land and condemning the assimilation policy.[13] The legislation additionally provided for economic development on reservations and attempted to provide a framework by which tribes could organize new forms of self-government. Finally, the tide of official governmental policy seemed to be turning. With an initiative dedicated to celebrating Native expressive culture rather than suppressing it, Collier, in his second year as commissioner, suggested that the Indian bureau "try the experiment of throwing overboard all of our conventional teaching of European music . . . and of superseding it with work designed to bring into the consciousness of the young people all of the values of their native music and an increased skill in rendering it."[14] The idea in some ways reflected the plan initiated by Commissioner Francis Leupp in 1907 to teach the students how to become "proper" Indians, yet Collier's plan called for a direct education in Native music by Native teachers, with no intermediaries.[15] Individual music teachers in the schools took their own initiatives as well. Virginia Bailey and Helen Kinnick worked with the people of the Santa Maria, Paraje, Encinal, Isleta, and Chicale Pueblo communities in an effort to plan music education for the children with their parents' approval. Kinnick reported to Collier in 1935, "We are not using Indian songs unless the community approves, and in any case only those which they deem suitable."[16] Educator Alida Bowler of the Carson Indian School in Stewart, Nevada, told Collier that she felt that "Indian music, as taught, should be a living thing, not a mere preservation of a dead or dying art."[17] In this regard the Carson school hired George La Mere (Ho-Chunk) to teach music, dancing, and "dramatic expression" to the students.[18] Collier was determined to support a full-fledged educational initiative in Native cultural traditions.

La Mere's role in the new movement with the Indian bureau, however, also reflected the changing ways in which "Indian music" was being defined. After attending the Haskell Indian school, he was trained at the University of Miami on a scholarship won by a vocal audition. Trained in voice and cello, he contributed the "Indian melodies" used in composer Charles Skilton's "Suite Primeval." He performed Indianist compositions, including his own, at the Wisconsin Dells.[19] But he also spent weeks working with the Paiute and Washoe communities to "acquaint himself more fully with local songs" before his appointment at Carson.[20] La Mere was therefore familiar with a variety of Native performative traditions as they existed in the 1930s. And he also knew, as did Bowler, that the students were as interested in "conventional (or jazz!)" music as they were in the other sounds of music that surrounded them.[21] The ethnic or racial distinctions that the OIA had attributed to music in that era were as blurred as those represented by the hip-hop of War Party today.

By the late 1930s students and Native teachers had created "Indian clubs" in nearly all of the schools, and students found greater and greater opportunity to use the schools as a means to treasure and expand tribal traditions to a degree that would have seemed impossible twenty or even ten years before. As Esther Horne recounted,

> It was about this time (1936–37) that I began to think about creating an Indian club at the Wahpeton Indian School. As I thought about how I would begin, I envisioned that the purpose of this club would be to create some carry-over from the reservation to the school and to instill in the children a sense of their worth as individuals as well as members of particular tribal groups. . . . [T]he Indian Club would be a teaching tool for the students, staff, and anyone else with whom we might share our music, dance, philosophy, and way of life. Even in the boarding school, our culture was being maintained and nourished. . . . Those days were so exciting! Finally, we no longer had to hide the fact that we were incorporating our cultural values into the curriculum and student life.[22]

Indeed, thanks to the efforts of Native dancers, singers, and musicians on reservations, on school grounds, and in public performance sites, it seemed as if a new day had dawned, with Native expressive culture no longer actively combated by the federal government.

In other ways, however, little changed in the aftermath of the IRA, and Native peoples had to remain vigilant to protect what victories they had won. Collier's vision for Indian reform was jeopardized by the bureaucratic challenges of revamping Native educational policies that had been entrenched for decades. In addition, although previously the federal government had worked to maintain its paternalistic prerogative to detribalize Native peoples, Collier's

administration could not quite escape a "paternalism that romanticized them."[23] Lomawaima and McCarty argue that while the Collier
administration encouraged instruction in tribal art, histories, and
music, students were not exposed, for example, to studying treaty
rights or the workings of Native governments.[24] In that sense, the
authors contend, education in the Native schools (though by then
principally reservation and public day schools) remained squarely
within a "safety zone" that the federal government continued to
define.[25] Furthermore, and for good reason, many Native people
remained highly skeptical that any good would come from simply
the latest regime change in OIA administration.[26] Just as the skeptics
foresaw, the federal government actually extended its power over
tribes in certain ways through the IRA tribal governments, and after
Collier left office, a new congressional campaign in the 1940s called
once again for the termination of tribes.[27] It was clear that Native peoples could not depend on the federal government, regardless of who
was in charge or what policies were previously reversed.

In that sense the era of tribal self-government promised by the IRA
represented but a small step toward Native peoples' longstanding
goals of self-determination, control over education, and protection of
their lands, treaty rights, languages, and cultural and religious practices—indeed, struggles to meet these goals persist today as never
before. The seeds of their efforts to wrest the control over tribes from
the federal government, however, were planted by the toil of thousands of American Indians during the late nineteenth and early twentieth centuries, and their victories along the way were guarded with
vigilance. Performers like Cardin, Blackstone, and Tecumseh made
Indianness their own, rendering Indianness "in play" and thus pene-
trating the tapestry of ideologically driven symbols that had obfus-
cated the real damage to Native communities wrought by federal
Indian policy during the allotment and assimilation era. Just as
Omaha dancers at times metaphorically wrapped their dances in the
American flag to ensure not just their survival but their innovation
and proliferation, these musicians cloaked their challenges to the limited expectations of OIA officials, and indeed the non-Indian public,
within their play of Indianness. Performers and audience members
negotiated the meaning of those performances, and the meanings

they derived were often complex and contradictory. However, it is clear that all of these performers, just as Angus Lookaround rallied his students and Joe Morris rattled the rooftops of white, Indian, and African American jazz clubs, embraced the political possibilities and the power of music, and their efforts certainly contributed to the beginnings of the modern struggle for self-determination in Indian Country. For them, the practice of music was as potent a weapon as any they could muster.

ARCHIVES AND ABBREVIATIONS

BLUCB Bancroft Library, University of California, Berkeley
  PPIER Panama Pacific International Exposition Records
CCHS Cumberland County Historical Society, Carlisle, Pa.
  CISOHP Carlisle Indian School Oral History Project
FACHL Beatrice Chauvenet Collection, Fray Angélico Chávez
    History Library, Santa Fe, N.Mex.
LOC Library of Congress, American Folklife Center, Washington,
    D.C.
NAA National Anthropological Archives, Washington, D.C.
  AFP Alice Fletcher Papers
  BAE File: Densmore, Frances, Bureau of American Ethnology
    Correspondence (1909–50)
  FDP Frances Densmore Papers
NARA National Archives and Records Administration, Records of
    the Bureau of Indian Affairs (Record Group 75), Washington,
    D.C.
    CCF Central Classified Files
    BIS Bismarck Indian School
    CA Carlisle Indian School
    CHS Chilocco Indian School
    FIS Flandreau Indian School
    GSF General Service File
    HIS Haskell Indian School
    HA Hopi Agency

PIS Phoenix Indian School
RA Rosebud Agency
RLA Red Lake Agency
SI Sherman Institute
SIS Salem Indian School
SRA Standing Rock Agency
TRS Theodore Roosevelt Indian School
YA Yakima Agency
CSSR Entry 1327, Carlisle Indian School Student Records, 1879–1918
OCCL Entry 133, Orders, Circulars, and Circular letters: Replies to Circulars 1907–1935, Answers to Circulars 1646–1666, no. 1665, Box 102
RLS Entry 996, Records of the Library Section
NYPL New York Public Library, Music Division, Performing Arts Library, New York
UISC University of Iowa Libraries, Special Collections Department, Iowa City
RCC Redpath Chautauqua Collection
WHS Wisconsin Historical Society, Madison
ALPJNP Angus Lookaround and Phebe Jewell Nichols Papers (Oshkosh MSS BG)

NOTES

PREFACE

1. I borrow from Aaron Fox in his meta-reading of country music discourse. Fox, "Jukebox of History."

2. Loretta Lynn, *Your Squaw Is on the Warpath* (Decca Records, 1969). Lynn sings this song in concerts to this day.

3. Cam Smith, "Squaws along the Yukon," lyrics. Performed by Hank Thompson on *The Best of Hank Thompson* (Capitol Records, 1963).

4. Tommy Barnes, Gene Simmons, and John D. Loudermilk, "Indian Outlaw," lyrics. Performed by Tim McGraw on *Not a Moment Too Soon* (Curb Records, 1994).

5. Johnny Cash, *Bitter Tears: Ballads of the American Indian* (Columbia/Legacy Records, 1964).

INTRODUCTION

1. Willard Rhodes, Sound recordings 9519A, 9519B, 9520A, 9520B, 9521A, LOC. The recordings were commissioned by the Education Division, Office of Indian Affairs, and these particular performances took place on July 5, 1941.

2. Ibid. Clarence Taptuka was born in 1891 in the Hopi village of Moencopi. He attended the Sherman Institute beginning around 1909, and by 1912 he was playing in the Martinez Indian band, an Indian boarding school band based in Thermal, California. Author's correspondence with Matthew Sakiestewa Gilbert, July 23, 2008.

3. Logan, *Pale Moon*; Cadman, *From the Land of the Sky-Blue Water*.

4. Whenever possible, I refer to the many individual Native people in this book by their specific tribal affiliation(s). I also at times refer to tribes and nations when describing the overarching political/familial entities that Native peoples affiliate with, especially when dealing with the federal government. Throughout the book, I also use interchangeably the terms "Native American," "American Indian," "Indian,"

"Native," and "indigenous," particularly when referring to large or comprehensive multitribal groups of people, or when discussing the impact of broad policy initiatives by the government. All of the terms are flawed, but none seems particularly better suited, or accepted, than another.

5. Overviews on federal Indian policy in this era include Prucha, *Great Father*; Hoxie, *Final Promise*; V. Deloria and Lytle, *American Indians, American Justice*; McDonnell, *Dispossession of the American Indian*; and Holm, *Great Confusion in Indian Affairs*.

6. McCool, Olson, and Robinson discuss the relationship between American Indians and U.S. citizenship in their *Native Vote*. In the first chapter, they provide an excellent introduction to the complicated history of U.S. citizenship in Indian Country, partially summarized here. The U.S. Constitution originally exempted American Indians from citizenship status. The Fourteenth Amendment was passed with the express understanding that it did not offer citizenship protections to American Indians. The 1868 Treaty of Fort Laramie provided that the Lakotas and Arapahoes could gain citizenship "by receiving a patent for land under the foregoing provisions . . . and be entitled to all the privileges and immunities of such citizens, and shall, at the same time retain all [their] rights to benefits accruing to Indians under this treaty." Quoted in ibid., 5. This treaty provision would have in effect allowed select Lakotas to become citizens "and still maintain their status and rights as Indians" Ibid. The provision was not effectively utilized, however, and the federal government and court system continued to largely deny citizenship status to American Indians (see *Elk v. Wilkins*, 112 U.S. 94 [1884]). The General Allotment Act (or Dawes Act), however, laid the cornerstone for the government's vision of granting U.S. citizenship to those American Indians "who availed themselves of the act's provisions and accepted allotment or completely abandoned their tribe and adopted Anglo culture." Ibid., 6. Citizenship legislation continued to unfurl haphazardly for American Indians. The Burke Act of 1906 provided the secretary of the interior with the ability to judge individuals as "competent" or "incompetent" in an effort to facilitate the bestowal of citizenship and ostensibly to protect American Indians from being defrauded of their allotments. The Oklahoma Enabling Act bestowed U.S. citizenship on Indians living in that territory (formerly Indian Territory), and all World War I veterans received citizenship status in 1919. By the early 1920s, two-thirds of the American Indians were U.S. citizens, and the rest became U.S. citizens through the Indian Citizenship Act of 1924, an act that did not expressly require them to give up their tribal affiliations in doing so. This act, however, did not ensure the enfranchisement of American Indians, and indeed, many remained disenfranchised in their states for decades following the passage of the Indian Citizenship Act. McCool, Olson, and Robinson, *Native Vote*, 6–10. For additional discussions of U.S. citizenship and American Indians, see Wilkins, *American Indian Sovereignty*, 118–36. See also Bodayla, "'Can an Indian Vote?'"; and Stein, "Indian Citizenship Act of 1924." Alan Trachtenberg, in *Shades of Hiawatha*, juxtaposed American Indians and European immigrants in the national citizenship debates and rhetoric of the early twentieth century.

7. Each head of a family was to receive one-quarter of a section (160 acres); each single person over the age of eighteen, one-eighth of a section (80 acres); and each person under the age of eighteen when the act was passed, one-sixteenth of a section (40 acres).

8. V. Deloria and Lytle, *American Indians, American Justice*, 9.

9. Quoted in Harmon, "American Indians,"106. Harmon juxtaposes this rhetoric with condemnations of American Indians who amassed land among the so-called Five Civilized Tribes.

10. These school-oriented Americanization programs reflect in many ways the experiences of African Americans in Reconstruction through Jim Crow–era schools as well as the Americanization programs of Mexican American and European immigrant children in the early twentieth century. For the education of African Americans in this period, see Anderson, *Education of Blacks*; and Fairclough, *Teaching Equality*. For the education of Mexican Americans, see García, *Desert Immigrants*; and Sánchez, *Becoming Mexican American*. For the education of European Immigrants, see Weiss, *American Education*; Carlson, *Americanization Syndrome*; and Pozzetta, *Education and the Immigrant*.

11. Adams, *Education for Extinction*, 52. This text provides an excellent overview of the assimilation policy enacted in the boarding schools. Over the past fifteen years, scholars of American Indian education have focused not simply on the imposition of the assimilation campaign in the schools but also on how students and their parents experienced that campaign or resisted it. These works include Trafzer, Keller, and Sisquoc, *Boarding School Blues*; Katanski, *Learning to Write "Indian"*; Child, *Boarding School Seasons*; Lomawaima, *They Called It Prairie Light*; Mihesuah, *Cultivating the Rosebuds*; Archuleta, Child, and Lomawaima, *Away from Home*; Riney, *Rapid City Indian School*; and Ellis, *To Change Them Forever*.

12. V. Deloria and Lytle, *American Indians, American Justice*, 10.

13. For evidence of this and the rest of the guesses, see www.pacifier.com/~ascott/they/tamildaa.htm.

14. Radano, *Lying Up a Nation*; Radano and Bohlman, *Music and the Racial Imagination*; Sotiropoulos, *Staging Race*.

15. *Powwow*, edited by Ellis, Lassiter, and Dunham, offers an exceptional collection of essays on both the historical and social components of the powwow in many fascinating contexts. Recent and informative scholarship that addresses lyrical and notational analysis along with some historical context includes Heth, *Native American Dance*; Black Bear and Theisz, *Songs and Dances of the Lakota*; Jackson and Levine, "Singing for Garfish"; Jackson, *Yuchi Ceremonial Life*; and Powers, *War Dance*. More significant contextual studies of Native music include Vander, *Songprints*; Lassiter, *Power of Kiowa Song*; Lassiter and Ellis, "Commentary"; Lassiter, "Charlie Brown"; Lassiter, Ellis, and Kotay, *Jesus Road*; Ellis, "'Truly Dancing Their Own Way'"; Ellis, "'We Don't Want Your Rations'"; Ellis, "'There Is No Doubt'"; and Ellis, *Dancing People*. Ellis and Lassiter provide insightful analyses of the community meanings of powwow and religious dances for Kiowa and other tribes of the southern plains. See also McNally, *Ojibwe Singers*. Murphy, in *The People*, examines the Indian dance debate

and modern dance troupes. Tara Browner published an excellent book, *Heartbeat of the People*, on the complexities and empowerment of contemporary northern powwows. She points out that the cultural significance, attributes, and meanings of many songs and dances lie within the intellectual property of individuals or clans. While the music and performances transcribed and recorded by ethnologists and observers since the late nineteenth century retain value for tribal members seeking historical information, they also, in the eyes of many, represent a further act of thievery by non-Indians. I focus less on such particulars of these performances primarily because such analysis does not serve my present purposes and because I wish to avoid an inadvertent replication of this thievery through the publication of sensitive knowledge. For Browner's discussion of the "political minefield" that scholars walk when discussing the cultural knowledge of individuals and tribes in regard to their songs and dances, see ibid., 11–17.

16. Pisani, *Imagining Native America in Music*.

17. Browner, "'Breathing the Indian Spirit.'"

18. Young Bear and Theisz, *Standing in the Light*, 38.

19. McClary, *Feminine Endings*, 21.

20. De Certeau, *Practice of Everyday Life*, 170.

21. Morgan (1818–81) was an American "anthropologist" before the profession really got off the ground. He was a materialist and is best known for his work *Ancient Society* (1877), in which he argued that all groups of the human family exist in a state of savagery, a state of barbarism, or a state of civilization.

22. Lomawaima and McCarty, "To Remain an Indian," 2–3; emphasis in original. See also Lomawaima, "American Indian Education."

23. Scott argues that hidden transcripts of resistance occur "behind the scenes . . . [when the oppressed] create and defend a social space in which offstage dissent to the official transcript of power relations may be voiced." These hidden transcripts represent "a critique of power spoken behind the back of the dominant." He goes on to suggest that such transcripts are "typically expressed openly—albeit in disguised form." Following this theory, the request of the Lakotas to hold a Grass Dance in order to celebrate the Fourth of July seems a clear example of such a public, hidden transcript of resistance. Such a dance created a social space in which the dancers could seemingly appease OIA officials through a celebration of a patriotic American holiday while simultaneously affirming their own difference as Lakota people, therefore resisting the policy of assimilation. Scott, *Domination and the Arts of Resistance*, xi–xiii.

24. P. J. Deloria, *Playing Indian*. The classic study concerning representations of American Indians is Berkhofer, *White Man's Indian*. See also R. D. Green, "Tribe Called Wannabee"; R. D. Green, "Indian in Popular American Culture"; Bird, *Dressing in Feathers*; Dilworth, *Imagining Indians in the Southwest*; Moses, *Wild West Shows*; Meyer and Royer, *Selling the Indian*; Whitt, "Cultural Imperialism"; and S. L. Smith, *Reimagining Indians*.

25. Leah Dilworth, in *Imagining Indians in the Southwest* (pp. 4–5), argues: "For its practitioners, primitivism is a source of authority, a gesture that demonstrates the essential nature or the primacy of their notions, because the primitive is imagined at

a state somehow previous to modernity and therefore more real, more authentic. Primitivism seems to offer a cure for what ails modernity, because it imagines that differentiation is a later, inauthentic development, that things were more whole, more harmonious at some time 'before.'"

26. Philip Deloria's reading of the relationship between authenticity, modernity, and Indianness in the late nineteenth and early twentieth centuries, as well as his discussion of the scouting movement, is particularly insightful. See his *Playing Indian*, 95–127.

27. P. J. Deloria, *Indians in Unexpected Places*.

28. Ibid, 236–89. See also Browner, "'Breathing the Indian Spirit,'" 265; and Pisani, *Imagining Native America in Music*.

29. Alternately, images of the "ignoble savage" persisted as well, with women and men alike depicted in an extremely derogatory manner. But most of the non-Indian public interested in consuming Indianness constructed images of "noble savages," equally derogatory through their denial of humanity.

30. Pfister, who has exceptionally investigated the role of the Carlisle Indian School in facilitating the "individualization" of the students, refers to those American Indians who use stereotypes of Indianness to their advantage as "faking Indian." Pfister, *Individuality Incorporated*, 122. Katanski utilizes anthropologist Paul Kroskrity's notion of "repertoires of identity" to explain how students did not "lose" their tribal identities in the schools but rather gained ways in which they self-identified. Katanski, *Learning to Write "Indian,"* 7–8.

31. Leah Dilworth details the relationship of the Fred Harvey Company with the local Native populations and the rise in southwestern tourism in *Imagining Indians in the Southwest*, 77–124. For Buffalo Bill's and other shows, see Moses, *Wild West Shows*.

32. For example, Melissa Parkhurst is writing a study of music at the Chemawa Indian School, and Matthew Sakiestewa Gilbert and William Oscar Medina both examine the experiences, musical and otherwise, of Sherman Institute students in their current manuscripts.

33. Samuels, *Putting a Song on Top of It*.

CHAPTER 1

Epigraphs: Young Bear and Theisz, *Standing in the Light*, 43; Transcript of Proceedings, "Investigation into the Practices of the Sioux Indians on the Dakota Reservations with Particular Reference to the Indian Dance," File 10429–1922-063, GSF, CCF, NARA (hereafter "Practices of the Sioux Indians"), 52.

1. This chapter focuses on events that took place primarily on the Rosebud, Pine Ridge, Cheyenne River, and Standing Rock Sioux reservations. These reservations are inhabited primarily by the Lakota people, although the Standing Rock reservation is also inhabited by their close relatives, the Dakotas and Yanktonais (the Yanktonais are often grouped as the Nakotas), who all speak different dialects of the same language. These three peoples were called the "Nadoweisiweg by their Ojibwe neighbors, meaning 'little or lesser snakes/enemies.'" The French later corrupted the word and

shortened it to "Sioux." The seven groups of people who affiliate as Lakotas are the Hunkpapas, Sihasapas, Itazipcos, Miniconjous, Oohenumpas, Sicangus, and Oglalas. The Sihasapas and Hunkpapas were grouped onto the Standing Rock reservation, with the Sihasapas to the south of the South Dakota–North Dakota border, which traverses the reservation. The Sihasapas also reside on the Cheyenne River Indian reservation, which is also the reservation of the Miniconjous, the Sihasapas, the Oohenumpas, and the Itazipcos. The Sicangus reside on the Rosebud Lower Brule reservation, while the Oglalas reside at the Pine Ridge reservation. The Yanktonais, Hunkpatinas, and Cut-head bands of Dakota and Nakota peoples reside in parts of the northern section of the Standing Rock reservation. Unfortunately, most of the archival materials that I use in this chapter are unspecific when it comes to describing individuals on the reservations as Lakota, Dakota, or Nakota, much less their subgroup affiliations or even, often, their names. I struggled to come up with a way in which to refer to those dancers and singers whom I could not properly identify. I could have lumped them under the name "Sioux," as did the OIA officials, but because most of the reservations that I discuss in this chapter were composed of Lakotas, with one reservation (Standing Rock) also including Dakotas and the Yanktonai peoples, I decided to refer to the dancers as Lakotas, making exception when specifically referencing the Standing Rock reservation or individuals whom I could readily identify. Although this solution was not perfect, it seemed to reflect the subjects of this chapter with the greatest accuracy. My thanks to Mark Thiel, Robert Galler, Brian Hosmer, and Clyde Ellis for helping me sort this issue out. The above information on the Lakota, Dakota, and Nakota bands and their affiliations and reservations is taken from Sprague, *Images of America*, 7.

2. There are, of course, important exceptions, the most prominent being the output of Native writers such as Charles Eastman or Carlos Montezuma and the development of Native-organized reform groups such as the Society of American Indians. Certainly such opportunities were fewer and farther between for reservation-based, non-urban Indians.

3. Scott, *Domination and the Arts of Resistance*, xi.

4. For an excellent introduction to the complexities, vitality, and nuances of the tribal and intertribal powwow world, see Ellis, Lassiter, and Dunham, *Powwow*.

5. Horne and McBeth, *Essie's Story*, 85.

6. Powers, *Lakota Warrior Tradition*, 18.

7. Biolsi, *Organizing the Lakota*, 5.

8. Powers, *Lakota Warrior Tradition*, 18.

9. Maddra, *Hostiles?* 18; Biolsi, *Organizing the Lakota*, 11.

10. Biolsi, *Organizing the Lakota*, 11.

11. Ibid., 7.

12. Ibid., 17–19.

13. Ibid., 18–19.

14. Admittedly, characterizing allotment as a grand failure for tribes disregards those Native peoples, in every tribe, who believed that allotment was not a bad idea, at least due to the promise that the government would no longer control their

resources. However, it is clear that, for the majority of the Lakotas, the allotment policy did not help them but ultimately led to a tremendous liquidation of remaining tribal lands.

15. Gibbon, *Sioux*, 136.

16. Biolsi, *Organizing the Lakota*, 24.

17. Lazarus, *Black Hills, White Justice*, 150–51.

18. Biolsi, *Organizing the Lakota*, 24.

19. Lazarus details the remarkable attempts of Lakotas to recover the Black Hills during this period through diplomatic efforts and the courts, but they have yet to recover the territory from the U.S. government. See Lazarus, *Black Hills, White Justice*.

20. Young Bear and Theisz, *Standing in the Light*, 55.

21. Holm, *Great Confusion in Indian Affairs*, 34.

22. Ibid.

23. Quoted in James, *Pages from Hopi History*, 186.

24. Greci Green, "Performances and Celebrations," 27, 29.

25. Focused mainly on the 1880s and 1890s, Holler gives an account of the Sun Dance ban and suppression on the Sioux reservations in his *Black Elk's Religion*, 110–38.

26. Greci Green, "Performances and Celebrations," 11.

27. Kavanagh, "Southern Plains Dance," 109–11.

28. Greci Green, "Performances and Celebrations," 50–51.

29. Thiel, "Omaha Dance," 5.

30. Young Bear and Theisz, *Standing in the Light*, 55–56.

31. Quoted in Browner, *Heartbeat of the People*, 21.

32. Thiel, "Omaha Dance," 5.

33. Young Bear and Theisz, *Standing in the Light*, 56–57.

34. Greci Green, "Performances and Celebrations," 125.

35. Thiel, "Omaha Dance," 6.

36. Browner, *Heartbeat of the People*, 23, 26.

37. See, e.g., Powell, *Sweet Medicine*, 338–41; Greenwald, "'Hurrah! 4th July!'"

38. Greci Green, "Performances and Celebrations," 55, 81, 84.

39. Thiel, "Omaha Dance," 5.

40. Ibid.; Greci Green, "Performances and Celebrations," 54–97.

41. Greci Green finds the first documentary evidence of a Lakota Fourth of July dance in 1889, but certainly the tradition took root before then. Greenwald recounts a tale by Crow leader Plenty Coups in which he stumbled across some sort of Lakota Fourth of July celebration in the prereservation days. Greci Green, "Performances and Celebrations," 58; Greenwald, "Hurrah! 4th July!" 5.

42. Young Bear and Theisz, *Standing in the Light*, 55.

43. Thiel, "Omaha Dance," 9.

44. Moses, *Wild West Shows*, 22.

45. This definition of Indianness owes an intellectual debt to Philip Deloria's work on the expectations of American Indians in his *Indians in Unexpected Places*.

46. Quoted in Murphy, *The People Have Never Stopped Dancing*, 70.

47. Moses, *Wild West Shows*, 33; Murphy, *The People Have Never Stopped Dancing*, 70–73.

48. Murphy, *The People Have Never Stopped Dancing*, 72–73.

49. Moses, *Wild West Shows*.

50. Greci Green, "Performances and Celebrations," 117.

51. Young Bear and Theisz, *Standing in the Light*, 97.

52. Holm, *Great Confusion in Indian Affairs*, 40.

53. "Practices of the Sioux Indians," 18. Father Bernard was referring to the murders, committed by Lieutenant Bull Head and Second Sergeant Red Tomahawk, of Sitting Bull and eight others from his camp in front of his house. Six policemen were also killed, including Bull Head. Sitting Bull was heavily involved with the Ghost Dance movement that had taken form within many of the Sioux communities. The Wounded Knee massacre occurred shortly thereafter. See Mooney, *Ghost Dance*, 218–20; and Demallie, "Lakota Ghost Dance." Maddra explores the revelation that a number of the Indian policemen hired to suppress the Lakota Ghost Dance had previously taken up work with Buffalo Bill's Wild West Show. See Maddra, *Hostiles?* 86–111.

54. Greenwald, "Hurrah! 4th July!" 10.

55. Ibid.

56. Ibid., 10–11.

57. Thiel, "Omaha Dance," 7. The noted exception was Rev. Francis M. Craft, himself of Mohawk or Seneca ancestry, who recognized the virtues celebrated in Omaha dances. He worked on the Pine Ridge and Rosebud reservations in the mid-1880s and was inducted into the Omaha society.

58. Ibid.

59. Harmon P. Marble, Superintendent of the Crow Creek Indian Agency, to Charles Burke, March 2, 1922, File 10429–1922-063, GSF, CCF, NARA.

60. Ibid. McLaughlin, the Standing Rock agent during the manifestation of the Ghost Dance movement in the Dakotas, was responsible for arranging the arrest of Sitting Bull, which resulted in the latter's murder. Mooney, *Ghost Dance*, 216.

61. Arthur Pratt to E. D. Mossman, October 16, 1922, File 75420–19-063, SRA, CCF, NARA.

62. Ibid.

63. "Practices of the Sioux Indians," 15.

64. Ibid., 46.

65. Ibid.

66. Ibid, 50.

67. Ibid, 51.

68. Ibid, 50.

69. P. J. Deloria, *Playing Indian*.

70. "Practices of the Sioux Indians," 29–30.

71. Katanski, *Learning to Write "Indian*," 42–48.

72. McDonnell, *Dispossession of the American Indian*, 123.

73. File 71473–08-751, SRA, CCF, 75, NARA.

74. Ibid. Stealing, destroying, or otherwise mishandling a drum is practically unthinkable among Native singers and would almost certainly devastate them, which was probably what the agent intended.

75. "Practices of the Sioux Indians," 15–16.

76. Ibid.

77. Ibid., 47.

78. E. D. Mossman, Superintendent of the Standing Rock Agency to Charles H. Burke, February 10, 1922, File 10429–1922-063, GSF, CCF, NARA.

79. Young Bear and Theisz, *Standing in the Light*, 86–87. The Office of Indian Affairs was renamed the Bureau of Indian Affairs in 1947.

80. Quoted in Murphy, *The People Have Never Stopped Dancing*, 91.

81. For information on Hollow Horn Bear's life, see www.dlncoalition.org/dln_nation/chief_hollow_horn_bear.htm.

82. "Conversation in the Commissioner's Office between Hollow Horn Bear and Acting Commissioner Abbott, Mr. Estes—Interpreting," March 6, 1913, File 29466-13-063, RA, CCF, NARA, 7–10.

83. F. H. Abbott, Acting Commissioner, to Hollow Horn Bear, March 7, 1913, File 29466-13-063, RA, CCF, NARA.

84. *An Act to Provide for the Allotment of Lands in Severalty to Indians on the Various Reservations*, U.S. Statutes at Large 24 (1887): 388–91, 390.

85. *An Act to Amend Section Six of an Act Approved February Eighth, Eighteen Hundred and Eighty-Seven*, U.S. Statutes at Large 34 (1910): 182–83.

86. Prucha, *Great Father*, 793. The granting of U.S. citizenship, however, did not entitle American Indians to the right to vote.

87. Superintendent of the Tongue River Agency to Charles H. Burke, April 6, 1923, File 10429–1922-063, GSF, CCF, NARA. Presumably, "National Indian Day" refers to Indian Citizenship Day, a holiday created for students of Indian boarding schools to celebrate the passage of the Dawes Act of 1887. Adams, *Education for Extinction*, 196.

88. James H. McGregor to the Commissioner of Indian Affairs, January 20, 1923, File 7141–23-063, RA, CCF, NARA.

89. Superintendent C. W. Rastall to Charles H. Burke, April 13, 1923, File 10429-1922-063, GSF, CCF, NARA.

90. Superintendent of the Pine Ridge Agency to Charles H. Burke, April 5, 1923, File 10429-1922-063, GSF, CCF, NARA.; James B. Kitch to the Commissioner of Indian Affairs, March 6, 1919, File 109123-17-063, SRA, CCF, NARA.

91. Young Bear and Theisz, *Standing in the Light*, 55.

92. "Practices of the Sioux Indians," 11.

93. Ibid., 52.

94. Mary Patterson Lord to John Barton Payne, Secretary of the Interior, October 5, 1920, File 109123–17-063, SRA, CCF, NARA.

95. Holm, *Strong Hearts, Wounded Souls*, 99. See also Britten, *American Indians in World War I*.

96. Holm, *Strong Hearts, Wounded Souls*, 101.

97. Powers, *Lakota Warrior Tradition*, 32.

98. Holm, *Strong Hearts, Wounded Souls*, 101.

99. Quoted in ibid., 99, 101.

100. Ibid., 101.

101. Powers, *Lakota Warrior Tradition*, 33.

102. Ibid., 39. Powers does not attribute this particular song to any one singer, but he recorded these songs from the following individuals: Henry White Calf and his son Isidor, LeRoy White Whirlwind, Edgar Red Cloud, Oliver Red Cloud, Clarence Janis, Harry Jumping Bull, Frank Afraid of Horse, William Horn Cloud, and Matt and Nellie Two Bulls. Ibid., 35.

103. Theisz, *Sending Their Voices*, 22.

104. Ibid., 23.

105. Powers, *Lakota Warrior Tradition*, 40.

106. Superintendent of the Pine Ridge Indian Agency to Burke, April 5, 1923, File 10429–1922-063, GSF, CCF, NARA.

107. Holler, *Black Elk's Religion*, 136.

108. "Memorandum on Reports of Superintendents of Sioux Reservations in North Dakota and South Dakota Relative to Dancing Among the Indians of their Respective Reservations," James McLaughlin, Inspector, Office of Indian Affairs to Burke, February 27, 1922, File 10429-1922-063, GSF, CCF, NARA. Standing Rock Indian School superintendent James Kitch stated that about 130 boys from this school alone served in the army during World War I. Britten, *American Indians in World War I*, 65.

109. Mossman to Burke, February 10, 1922, File 10429-1922-063, GSF, CCF.

110. Ibid. According to Bishop Burleson, Red Cross officials encouraged many Lakotas to raise money through such dances. "Practices of the Sioux Indians," 17.

111. No Heart et al. to Cato Sells, June 7, 1919, File 109123-17-063, SRA, CCF, NARA.

112. Ibid.

113. Apparently, a few months earlier Thomas Frosted had traveled to Washington, D.C., to complain personally to the commissioner about the dance prohibition that Kitch had established. James B. Kitch to the Commissioner of Indian Affairs, September 8, 1919, File 75420-19-063, SRA, CCF, NARA. Brown, also known as Mato-ska, or White Bear, was a Yanktonai born in 1859. At one time the chief of the Indian police at Standing Rock, he also worked to secure redress for the theft of the Black hills, His two adopted sons, August and John Brought Plenty, both fought in the war. See Lazarus, *Black Hills, White Justice*, 149, and www.rootsweb.ancestry.com/~nalakota/sc/oldchiefpassesaway_scpa122332.html.

114. Thomas Frosted and John Brown to the Commissioner of Indian Affairs, October 7, 1918, File 109123-17-063, SRA, CCF, NARA. The Sioux communities and Red Cross officials did not always get along in their wartime efforts. In one instance, the Sioux of the Wakpala District of Standing Rock raised $125 for the Red Cross through a basket social and supper, yet they refused to turn the money over to the Red Cross

after "the white people of Wakpala failed to include them in any of their local offices." James B. Kitch to Cato Sells, September 10, 1918, File 109123-17-063, SRA, CCF, NARA.

115. Ibid.

116. Young Bear and Theisz, *Standing in the Light*, 58.

117. Smith Pain on Hip to Burke, March 11, 1923, File 10429-1922-063, GSF, CCF, NARA. A group of Washington State Indians, appointed by the Colville general council, responded to Burke's 1923 order to cease giveaways by arguing that "no poor person is solicited to make any gift, and no one gives his friends more than he can afford." Charley Wilpocken, John Hayes, and Joe Moses to Burke, March 23, 1923, File 10429-1922-063, GSF, CCF, NARA.

118. Young Bear and Theisz, *Standing in the Light*, 57.

119. Ibid.

120. C. H. Gensler, Superintendent of the Lower Brule Indian Agency to Burke, February 10, 1922, File 10429-1922-063, GSF, CCF, NARA.

121. Ibid.

122. "Practices of the Sioux Indians," 44.

123. Ibid.

124. James B. Kitch to the Commissioner of Indian Affairs, January 9, 1920, File 109123-17-063, SRA, CCF, NARA.

125. Ibid.

126. Ibid. Fee-patent Indians were those who had received full title to their allotments clear of any conditions or restrictions set forth by the government.

127. Arthur Pratt to E. D. Mossman, October 16, 1922, File 75420-19-063, SRA, CCF, NARA.

128. "Practices of the Sioux Indians," 50, 55.

129. Ibid.

130. Ibid., 56–57.

131. James B. Kitch to Commissioner of Indian Affairs, January 9, 1920, File 109123-17-063, SRA, CCF, NARA.

132. E. B. Meritt to David M. Means, February 8, 1921, File 75420-19-063, SRA, CCF, NARA.

133. Ibid.

134. "Memorandum on Reports of Superintendents." See also Holler, *Black Elk's Religion*, 126.

135. Biolsi, *Organizing the Lakota*, 24.

136. Mossman to the Commissioner of Indian Affairs, August 12, 1924, and Mossman to Farmers, July 1, 1924, File 60373-24-062, SRA, CCF, NARA.

CHAPTER 2

1. "A Message to All Indians," Charles H. Burke, Commissioner of Indian Affairs, February 24, 1923; Charles H. Burke to C. M. Blair, Superintendent of Chilocco School, March 14, 1923; and Blair, C. M., Superintendent of Chilocco School, February 6, 1923, all in File 10429-1922-063, GSF, CCF, NARA.

2. Kelly, "Charles Henry Burke," 259.

3. "Indian Dancing," circular no. 1665, Office of Indian Affairs, File 10429-1922-063, GSF, CCF, NARA.

4. Ibid.

5. Ibid.

6. Ibid.

7. "Practices of the Sioux Indians," 3.

8. Hoxie, *Final Promise.*

9. Government farmers (also called OIA farmers, farm agents, or boss farmers) were "subagency official[s] stationed at the local farm station in the reservation district." Biolsi, *Organizing the Lakota,* 16–18.

10. Which Native community or mission Shaw was a member of is unclear. "Practices of the Sioux Indians," 28.

11. Ibid., 53. Mossman had reported the existence of the star club earlier in the year to Charles H. Burke. E. S. Mossman, superintendent of SRA to Charles H. Burke, February 10, 1922, File 10429-1922-063, GSF, CCF, NARA. It is likely that such "underground" dances were not a recent phenomenon on the reservation but had only recently come to the attention of the superintendents.

12. Holm, *Great Confusion in Indian Affairs,* 189–90.

13. Kelly, *Assault on Assimilation,* 213–54. See also Holm, *Great Confusion in Indian Affairs,* 183–84.

14. Lomawaima and McCarty, *"To Remain an Indian,"* 64–65.

15. For Collier's role in this debate, see Kelly, *Assault on Assimilation,* esp. 295–348. Collier (1884–1968) served as commissioner of Indian Affairs from 1933 to 1945. He was an outspoken critic of Charles Burke's dance order, and after President Franklin Roosevelt appointed him commissioner, he turned to anthropologists for guidance instead of to missionaries. Philp, "John Collier, 1933–45."

16. For an introduction to the involvement of Native people in world fairs, see Moses, *Wild West Shows,* and Rydell, *All the World's a Fair.*

17. It is unclear which Dr. Riggs appeared at this meeting. "Practices of the Sioux Indians," 20–21.

18. Ibid., 48. Presumably this individual was superintendent C. D. Munro.

19. Ibid.

20. Ibid., 61.

21. "Indian Dancing."

22. "A Message to All Indians."

23. Ibid.

24. Ibid.

25. "A Message to All Indians." This copy of the circular (in File 10429-1922-063, GSF, CCF, NARA) was not printed at Chilocco but is typewritten, with the recommendations at the end, presumably for superintendents, missionaries, and other interested organizations or parties.

26. Kelly, *Assault on Assimilation*, 306.

27. William E. Johnson, "Civilizing Indian Dances," *Western Christian Advocate* (Cincinnati), June 27, 1923, in Hopi: Dance Ban Reports in Favor Of, Newspaper Clippings, ca. 1923–24, Ceremonial Dances Box 1, RLS, NARA (hereafter "Hopi: Dance Ban Reports in Favor Of").

28. "Mr. Welsh on Indian Dances," Open Letters from the Editor's Mail Bag, *Philadelphia Record*, May 5, 1923, in Hopi: Dance Ban Reports in Favor Of. Interestingly, Welsh's first impression of Native dances took place in 1882 when he arrived a few days after the annual Sun Dance at Rosebud, South Dakota. Although he recognized the potential benefit of social gatherings, he thought the "barbarous tortures" kept alive "old and savage customs." He immediately chastised the practice of the giveaways, in which the Lakotas provided gifts to those "less fortunate or more lazy than themselves." Welsh even suggested that they "turn this heathen festival into a Fourth of July picnic, offer some servic[e]able reward to those who had proved themselves industrious during the year past, discourage a baneful generosity on the part of those whose labors had won success, and entirely prohibit the degrading spectacle of self-torture." Hagan, *Indian Rights Association*, 6–7.

29. "Association Is Seeking Franchise Rights for Indians," *Washington Times*, April 26, 1924, in Hopi: Dance Ban Reports in Favor Of. Franklin asserted the main goals of the IRA: "the uplift of the Indian of America in every way and the eventual granting to them the right of franchise." The IRA claimed no political allegiance and swore that its advocacy remained aligned not with the government but with American Indians. Yet its philosophy of assimilation, as well as that of Burke's, on a majority of issues was one and the same.

30. Ibid.

31. "Indians Urged to Give Up Their Snake Dances," *Pomona (Calif.) Bulletin*, October 9, 1923, in Hopi: Dance Ban Reports in Favor Of.

32. Ibid.

33. Jacobs, *Engendered Encounters*, 106.

34. Ibid, 110.

35. "Secret Dances of the Pueblos," To the Editor of the New York Times, *New York Times*, written November 1, 1924, in Hopi: Dance Ban Reports in Favor Of. Similarly, the *Western Christian Advocate* of Cincinnati reported. "Orgies [resulting from some Indian dances] are of such a nature that they cannot be publicly described. But the Indian Rights Association has a large number of affidavits made by Indians themselves who recognize the horrible character of these affairs and are co-operating to eliminate them." See Johnson, "Civilizing Indian Dances."

36. "Secret Dances of the Pueblos."

37. Ibid.

38. "Banned Indian Dances Immoral, Is Charge of Mission Worker," *Chicago American*, April 27, 1923, in Hopi: Dance Ban Reports in Favor Of.

39. Ibid.

40. "What Readers Say," *New York Tribune*, March 29, 1923, in Hopi: Dance Ban Reports in Favor Of.

41. Ibid.

42. "Thirty-two Dances of Indians Beat Jazz, Says 'Y,'" *New Orleans Times Picayune*, July 15, 1923, in Miscellaneous Information, Newspaper Clippings, ca. 1923–24, Ceremonial Dances Box 1, RLS, NARA (hereafter "Miscellaneous Information, Newspaper Clippings"). Samuel Eliot of the Board of Indian Commissioners agreed as to the detrimental nature of the giveaways: "In some tribes, the dances are occasions for what we would call robbery. The lazy good-for-nothings of the village assemble before the house of a hard-working Indian and compel him to share his goods with them. This proceeding may be religious tradition, but when traditions hurt the welfare of the Indians, it is time for them to be abandoned." See "Indian Dances to Be Banned: Commissioners Believe That Rites Have Lost all Their Religious Meaning," *New Bedford (Mass.) Mercury*, November 17, 1923, in Miscellaneous Information, Newspaper Clippings.

43. Jacobs, *Engendered Encounters*; Jacobs, "Making Savages of Us All."

44. "Indian 'Give Away' Dance Very Often Has Serious Consequences," *Rochester (N.Y.) Post-Express*, May 24, 1923, in Hopi: Dance Ban Reports in Favor Of.

45. "Indian Dances to Be Banned." The Board of Indian Commissioners was established in 1869 to provide input on federal Indian policy initiatives and to thwart corruption by overseeing contracts and annuity disbursements. The board wielded influence on the shape of federal Indian policy until it was terminated during Collier's reign as commissioner of Indian Affairs. For more information on the Board of Indian Commissioners, see Hagan, *Indian Rights Association*.

46. "Indian Dances to Be Banned."

47. Kelly, *Assault on Assimilation*, 305–306.

48. Ibid.

49. "Commissioner Burke Put Ban on Indians' Snake Dance," *Danville (Va.) Bee*, May 30, 1923, in Hopi: Dance Ban, Reports Against, Newspaper Clippings, ca. 1923–24, Ceremonial Dances Box 1, RLS, NARA (hereafter "Hopi: Dance Ban, Reports Against").

50. "Taking the Indianism Out of the Indian," *Literary Digest* (New York City), in Hopi: Dance Ban, Reports Against.

51. "The Indian Dances," *Utica (N.Y.) Observer Dispatch*, April 23, 1923, in Hopi: Dance Ban, Reports Against.

52. "The Indian's Dances: Every True American Will Want to See Them Preserved," *New York Herald*, April 25, 1923, in Hopi: Dance Ban, Reports Against.

53. "Indian Customs," *Helena (Mont.) Record Herald*, June 26, 1923, in Hopi: Dance Ban, Reports Against.

54. "An Amazing Order," *Santa Fe New Mexican*, March 26, 1923, in Hopi: Dance Ban, Reports Against.

55. "Museum Takes Indian Order at Its Face Value, Stated: Meanwhile, Subordinates Say Decree Sent to Pueblos Doesn't Mean Anything," *Santa Fe New Mexican*, March 27, 1923, in Hopi: Dance Ban Reports in Favor Of.

56. Gere, "Art of Survivance," 673.

57. For a cogent discussion of the antimodern primitivism movement, see P. J. Deloria, *Playing Indian*, 95–127. Likewise Sherry Smith argues that, in the face of increasing industrialization, urbanization, and immigration, middle-class white Americans took refuge within their interpretation of primitivism found in Indianness. Smith, *Reimagining Indians*.

58. "A Plea for the Primitive," *Chicago News*, July 20, 1917, newspaper clipping in File 95989–16-063, RLA, CCF, NARA.

59. Dilworth, *Imagining Indians in the Southwest*, 21–22. Dilworth details the rising interest in the snake dance and the issues of representation that surrounded that interest in ibid., 21–76. For the origins of the dance, see James, *Pages from Hopi History*, 18–22.

60. James, *Pages from Hopi History*, 170–73.

61. "Stirring Up Trouble," *Bisbee (Ariz.) Review*, June 22, 1923, in Miscellaneous Information, Newspaper Clippings.

62. "Club Aid on Indian Dance Issue Asked," *Los Angeles Illustrated Daily News*, June 7, 1924, in Hopi: Dance Ban, Reports Against.

63. Philp, *John Collier's Crusade*, 61.

64. "The Last Snake Dance," *Oakland (Calif.) Post-Enquirer*, August 30, 1923, in Hopi: Dance Ban, Reports Against.

65. "The Indians' Dances," *Louisville (Ky.) Post*, August 22, 1923, in Hopi: Dance Ban, Reports Against.

66. "Prohibition—of Dancing," *Chicago Evening Post*, March 30, 1923, in Hopi: Dance Ban, Reports Against.

67. "The Indian Commissioner's Blue Laws," *Detroit Free Press*, April 11, 1923, in Hopi: Dance Ban, Reports Against.

68. For a cogent discussion of the appropriation of African American music and dance by whites in the 1910s, see Sotiropoulos, *Staging Race*, 219–26.

69. H. I. Phillips, "The Once Over: Banning the Indians' Dances," *Houston Post*, April 3, 1923, in Hopi: Dance Ban, Reports Against. Phillips's column appeared in newspapers across the country, including the *St. Louis Post-Dispatch* on March 30, 1923.

70. "Jazz for the Indians," *Meridian (Miss.) Star*, May 2, 1923, in Hopi: Dance Ban, Reports Against.

71. "Saving the Indians' Culture," *El Paso Times*, June 2, 1923, in Hopi: Dance Ban, Reports Against.

72. "Religious Freedom and the Pueblo Tribal Dances," *Fresno (Calif.) Bee*, April 11, 1923, in Hopi: Dance Ban, Reports Against.

73. "The Indian Dances," *Utica (N.Y.) Observer Dispatch*, April 23, 1923, in Hopi: Dance Ban, Reports Against.

74. "Indian Dances," *Outlook* (New York City), May 2, 1923, in Hopi: Dance Ban, Reports in Favor Of.

75. "Indians Will Dance Despite U.S. Ruling," *Everett (Wash.) News*, July 8, 1923, in Hopi: Dance Ban, Reports Against.

76. "Indian 'Blue Laws?' Ugh!: 'Bootleg Dances Be Worse,' Says Ponca Chief, Who Defends Tribal Dance as Most Artistic in America," *Kansas City (Mo.) Times*, March 12, 1923, in Hopi: Dance Ban, Reports Against.

77. Ibid.

78. "Ponca and Otoe Indians Defend Tribal Customs in Reply Made to Charles H. Burke," *Daily Oklahoman* (Oklahoma City), April 1, 1923, in Other Tribes Pro and Con, Newspaper Clippings, ca 1923–24, Ceremonial Dances Box 1, RLS, NARA.

79. "Navajo Asks U.S. to Spare Tribal Dance: Government Order against Medicine Men Astounds Indian," *Joliet (Ill.) Herald News*, November 21, 1923, in Hopi: Dance Ban, Reports Against.

80. Ibid.

81. Ibid.

82. For a discussion of the Puebloans' use of the religious freedom argument in the dance debate, see Wenger, "'We Are Guaranteed Freedom': Pueblo Indians and the Category of Religion in the 1920s," 89–113.

83. Philp, *John Collier's Crusade*, 60–61. The boys were not returned until their religious training was completed.

84. "Don't Dance for the Fun of It, Indians Tell Commissioner," *Santa Fe New Mexican*, April 11, 1923, in Hopi: Dance Ban, Reports Against. See also "The Pueblos on Their Dances," *New York Tribune*, April 20, 1923, in Hopi: Dance Ban, Reports Against.

85. "Don't Dance for the Fun of It." Eventually Burke was compelled to assure the Pueblo leaders that he would not allow the OIA to interfere with their ceremonials.

86. Kelly, "Charles Henry Burke," 259.

87. Kelly, *Assault on Assimilation*, 306.

88. Charles H. Burke to R. E. L. Daniel, Superintendent, Holbrook, Ariz., August 21, 1923, File 63710-23-063, HA, CCF, NARA.

89. Otto Lomavitu, "Dances Should Stop," *Coconino Sun*, July 28, 1923, newspaper clipping in File 10429-1922-063, GSF, CCF, NARA.

90. Whiteley, *Deliberate Acts*, 272, 283.

91. Lomavitu's political aspirations are noted in ibid., 327 n. 13.

92. Lomavitu, "Dances Should Stop," *Coconino Sun*, July 28, 1923, newspaper clipping in File 10429-1922-063, GSF, CCF, NARA.

93. Ibid.

94. Ibid.

95. Ibid.

96. Ibid.

97. Ibid.

98. J. Preston Myers, Principal, Oraibi Day School, "The Orabi Christmas Entertainment," Copy to E. K. Miller, Superintendent, Keams Canyon, Ariz., January 1924, File 000-24-063, Hopi Agency, CCF, NARA.

99. Peo-peo-tah-likt, Nez Perce Agency to Charles H. Burke, March 12, 1923, File 10429-1922-063, GSF, CCF, NARA.

100. Bird Above to Charles H. Burke, March 17, 1923, File 10429-1922-063, GSF, CCF, NARA.

101. C. H. Asbury, superintendent of the Crow Agency to Charles H. Burke, April 4, 1923, File 10429-1922-063, GSF, CCF, NARA.

102. Nina Big Day and Annie Pryor, Montana, to C. H. Asbury, Superintendent, Crow Agency, February 28, 1923, OCCL, NARA.

103. Ibid.

104. Horses Mane, Paul Kills, Ben Gardner, Joseph Hill, Barney Old Coyote, F. H. Does It, Alfonso Childs, William Moore, Fine or Five, Mike B. Chief, Thomas Long Tail, Jacob Big Hair, Eagle Turn Around, Mrs. Old Coyote, Mrs. Mary Takes a Gun, Takes A Gun, Rides A Pretty Horse, Mrs. Does Everything, Shot in the Nose, Woman That Sits Down, Susan Gardner, May Old Coyote, and Susie B. Chief to Charles H. Burke, April 10, 1923, File 10429-1922-063, GSF, CCF, NARA. Emphasis in original.

105. Ibid.

106. Juan Pablo Garcia, Governor of Acoma Pueblo; Felicano Tenorio, Governor of Santo Domingo; Thamasitu[?] Tenorio, Lt. Governor; Andreas Velasque, Lt. Governor of San Felipe Pueblo; Daniel Otero, Governor of Santa Ana Pueblo; Martin Shandoh, Governor of Jemez Pueblo; Lorenzo Lucero, Governor of San Dia (Sandia) Pueblo; Juan Bautista Aneno [?], Governor of San Juan Pueblo; Olojio Naranjo, Governor of Santa Clara Pueblo; Juan Vigil, Gubernado Sanchez[?] puebulo [sic]; Jose Padilla, Governor of Isleta Pueblo; and Jose Alcario Montoya, Governor of Chochiti Pueblo, New Mexico, to Charles H. Burke, April 9, 1923, File 10429-1922-063, GSF, CCF, NARA. John Collier and other Indian policy reformers met with the Pueblo leaders and discussed the implications of the circular as well as strategies for defending themselves. A few weeks after their initial letter to Burke, Collier worked with them to draw up a statement regarding their right to dance as a matter of religious liberty. Philp, *John Collier's Crusade*, 295–348.

107. Frank Anwash to Charles H. Burke, March 27, 1923, File 10429-1922-063, GSF, CCF, NARA.

108. Ibid.

109. H. M. Tidwell, Superintendent of Pine Ridge Indian Agency to Charles H. Burke, April 5, 1923, File 10429-1922-063, GSF, CCF, NARA.

110. Smith Pain on Hip to Charles H. Burke, March 11, 1923, File 10429-1922-063, GSF, CCF, NARA.

111. Ibid.

112. Ibid.

113. Charley Wilpocken, John Hayes, and Joe Moses to Charles H. Burke, March 23, 1923, File 10429-1922-063, GSF, CCF, NARA.

114. No Heart et al. to Cato Sells, June 7, 1919, File 109123-17-063, SRA, CCF, NARA.

115. Joseph No Hearts to the Commissioner of Indian Affairs, February 18,1921, File 75420-19-063, SRA, CCF, NARA.

116. John Joseph to Charles H. Burke, March 25, 1923, File 10429-1922-063, GSF, CCF, NARA. Presumably John Andrew was a local who traveled around the country, and possibly overseas, as Joseph seems to indicate, entertaining audiences with dances and demonstrations of Native culture.

117. Ibid.

118. The Wichita Nation Association to Charles L. Ellis, Supervisor of Indian Affairs, File 10429–1922-063, GSF, CCF, NARA.

119. They wrote, "All are farmers and have been for many hundreds of years before the United States came into existence. What sort of people would be so considerate of each other's welfare and happiness[?] . . . Certainly not the evil-minded. What a very fine thing it would be if all the races were as fine in character!" Ibid., 4.

120. "Perhaps some few have taken on some of the evil ways of the white folks. But most of them do not." Ibid.

121. Ibid., 5–6.

122. Ibid., 6.

123. Ibid.

124. Arthur Pratt to E. D. Mossman, Superintendent, Fort Yates, North Dakota, March 22, 1924, file 1 of 5, OCCL, NARA.

125. Ibid.

126. Ibid.

127. H. W. Sipe to R. E. L. Daniel, Superintendent, Yankton Agency, March 19, 1924, file 1 of 5, OCCL, NARA.

128. Ibid.

129. Dr. Jacob Breid, Superintendent and Physician, Sac and Fox Sanatorium, to the Commissioner of Indian Affairs, April 2, 1924, file 2 of 5, OCCL, NARA.

130. Ibid.

131. F. C. Causpleece, Superintendent, Blackfeet Agency, Browning, Mont., to the Commissioner of Indian Affairs, March 29, 1924, file 2 of 5, OCCL, NARA.

132. Edward G. Martin, Agency Farmer, to R. E. L. Daniel, Superintendent, Yankton Agency, Wagner, S.Dak., March 28, 1924, file 2 of 5, OCCL, NARA.

133. Ibid.

134. J. B. Brown, Superintendent, Phoenix Indian School, to the Commissioner of Indian Affairs, March 20, 1924, file 2 of 5, OCCL, NARA.

135. N. C. Nillshare, Sisseton Indian Agency, to the Commissioner of Indian Affairs, March 26, 1924, file 2 of 5, OCCL, NARA.

136. W. E. Dunn, Superintendent, Grand Rapids Agency, Wisconsin Rapids, to the Commissioner of Indian Affairs, March 14, 1924, file 3 of 5, OCCL, NARA.

137. Ibid.

138. Ibid.

139. H. P. Marble, Superintendent, Southern Pueblos, to the Commissioner of Indian Affairs, March 17, 1924, file 2 of 5, OCCL, NARA. Presumably this is the same Marble who, as superintendent of the Crow Creek agency in 1922, had condemned the role of young people in dances in correspondence with Charles Burke.

140. H. D. Lawshe, Superintendent, Coeur d'Alene Indian Agency, April 3, 1924, file 1 of 5, OCCL, NARA.

141. R. J. Bauman, Superintendent, Zuni Indian Agency, Blackrock, N.Mex., to the Commissioner of Indian Affairs, April 28, 1924, file 1 of 5, OCCL, NARA.

142. See Institute for Government Research, *Problem of Indian Administration.*

143. "Civilizing the Indians," *Great Falls (Mont.) Daily Tribune*, April 10, 1923, newspaper clipping in File 10429-1922-063, GSF, CCF, NARA.

144. C. E. Kell to James H. McGregor, July 23, 1923, File 64023-23-063, RA, CCF, NARA.

145. James H. McGregor to Charles H. Burke, July 31, 1924, and Charles H. Burke to James H. McGregor, August 8, 1924, both in File 59136-24-062, RA, CCF, NARA.

146. For Shaw's views, see "Practices of the Sioux Indians," 30.

147. Joseph Otter Robe et al. to Charles H. Burke, January 17, 1927, File 8058-27-063, SRA, CCF, NARA. The Naslohan Wacipi, probably the dance referred to here as the Slide Naslohan Dance, is a Round Dance. All of the dances in the complaint are couples dances, and presumably this caused the greatest concern for Otter Robe and the rest.

148. Ibid.

149. Ibid.

150. E. D. Mossman to the Commissioner of Indian Affairs, March 10, 1927, File 8058-27-063, SRA, CCF, NARA.

151. Ibid.

152. Ibid.

153. Joseph Otter Robe et al. to Charles H. Burke, January 17, 1927.

154. Ibid.

CHAPTER 3

1. Katanski, *Learning to Write "Indian,"* 54.

2. Ibid., 45–94.

3. *Indian Helper*, December 5, 1890, 2.

4. Katanski, *Learning to Write "Indian."*

5. *Indian Helper*, December 12, 1890, 2.

6. Ibid.

7. *Indian Helper*, December 26, 1890, 2.

8. Moses Culbertson clarified to Pratt that they had not been killed. *Indian Helper*, January 30, 1891, 1.

9. *Indian Helper*, February 27, 1891, 1.

10. Ibid.

11. Katanski, *Learning How to Write "Indian,"* 68.

12. Burgess appropriated the first name of a real Carlisle student and the photograph of another in order to create her fictional character.

13. Burgess, *Stiya*, 59. For an extensive treatment of *Stiya*, see Katanski, *Learning How to Write "Indian,"* 64–82.

14. Adams, *Education for Extinction*, 52. Exceptions in practice to Pratt's binary absolutism existed in all of the schools. Gilbert, for example, notes that some elements of Hopi cultural practices and knowledge were acknowledged by teachers in the classroom, but that such cultural references were typically used only to further educational goals of assimilation, not to validate those references or to support tribalism. Gilbert, "Education beyond the Mesas," 122–23.

15. Adams, *Education for Extinction*, 57–58.

16. Maddox, *Citizen Indians*, 19.

17. Quoted in Adams, *Education for Extinction*, 276.

18. Medina, "Selling Indians at Sherman Institute," 116–18.

19. Lomawaima and McCarty, *"To Remain an Indian,"* 2–3, 5.

20. Interview with James Garvie by Helen Norton, December 3, 1980, CISOHP, CCHS, 8.

21. "Indians Display Musicalability [*sic*]: Cases of Exceptional Talent Pound at Carlisle Indian School," *Pittsburgh Gazette-Times*, October 9, 1914, CIIS drop files, CCHS.

22. Ibid.

23. Ibid.

24. Hauptman and McLester, *Oneida Indians*, 122.

25. Stauffer, "Hail to Thee, Carlisle."

26. "Chilocco," in Lomawaima, *They Called It Prairie Light*, v.

27. H. B. Peairs to A. F. Corbin, President, Indian Normal School, Pembroke, North Carolina, July 9, 1923, File 53984-23-814, GSF, CCF, NARA.

28. Ibid.

29. Ibid.

30. Section 10, "Report of Harwood Hall, Supervisor of Indian Schools, Subject—General Inspection Sherman Institute, Riverside, Cal.," November 6, 1909, File 91083-10-751, SI, CCF, NARA.

31. Flandreau Indian School, *Bow and Arrow*, 20–21. The Indian String Quartet is featured in chapter 5.

32. Lomawaima and McCarty, *"To Remain an Indian,"* 57.

33. In *They Called It Prairie Light*, Lomawaima demonstrated the school officials' fixation on the bodies of the Chilocco Indian students.

34. Quoted in Adams, *Education for Extinction*, 118.

35. Annual School Calendar, U.S. Indian School, Carlisle, Pa., "15–16," Carlisle: Carlisle Indian Press, September, 1915, in Box 1, Records of Carlisle Indian School, Miscellaneous Publications and Records, ca. 1908–18, Entry 1349 C, Records of Non-Reservation Schools, NARA.

36. Luther Standing Bear, *My People the Sioux*, 149.

37. Interview with James Garvie by Helen Norton, 1–2.

38. Quoted in Ellis, "'We Had a Lot of Fun,'" 74.

39. Quoted in McBeth, *Ethnic Identity*, 102–103.

40. Adams, *Education for Extinction*, 117.

41. Medina discusses the marketing of the Sherman Institute through its musical groups in "Selling Indians at Sherman institute," 108–28.

42. Pratt, *Indian Industrial School*, 37.

43. Student attendance increased from 754 in 1891 to 878 in 1899. Hauptman and McLester, *Oneida Indians*, 135 n. 22.

44. Moses Friedman, Superintendent of the Carlisle Indian School, to the Commissioner of Indian Affairs, January 8, 1913, File 2819-1913-047, CA, CCF, NARA; "Is Oneida's Counselor," *Red Man*, April 1912, 354.

45. "Is Oneida's Counselor," 352–54; Pratt, *Battlefield and Classroom*, 299–300.

46. Pratt, *Battlefield and Classroom*, 295. Laurence Hauptman wrote an in-depth essay on the musical life of Dennison Wheelock. See Hauptman and McLester, *Oneida Indians in the Age of Allotment*, 112–38.

47. Quoted in Katanski, *Learning to Write "Indian,"* 90.

48. For a study of Native experiences at the fair, see Parezo and Fowler, *Anthropology Goes to the Fair*.

49. *Government Official Indian Band*.

50. Ibid.

51. Ibid.

52. Harwood Hall, Superintendent Sherman Institute to the Commissioner of Indian Affairs, February 17, 1909, File 9588-09-929, SI, CCF, NARA. See also File 54448–09-929, SI, CCF, NARA.

53. Medina, "Selling Indians at Sherman Institute."

54. Ralph P. Stanion to the Commissioner of Indian Affairs, May 21, 1928, File 00-28-814, TRS, CCF, NARA.

55. *Annual Report*, 1931, Narrative Section, BIS, CCF, NARA.

56. "Campus News," *Phoenix Native American*, December 6, 1930, 244.

57. Medina, "Selling Indians at Sherman Institute," 115.

58. Harry Welch to C. W. Goodman, February 18, 1914, File 22198-14-929, PIS, CCF, NARA.

59. "Indians Capture Bishop," *Owens Valley Herald*, March 20, 1914, clipping in File 48264–14-047, BIS, CCF, NARA.

60. Ibid.

61. Ibid.

62. Ibid.

63. "Indian Show," *Inyo County Register*, March 26, 1914, clipping in File 48264-14-047, BIS, CCF, NARA.

64. Ibid.

65. Ibid.

66. Edgar H. Miller to E. B. Merritt, Commissioner of Indian Affairs, September 20, 1917, File 22954-17-047, GSF, CCF, NARA.

67. "Second Department, Indian Exhibit, Director, Edgar K. Miller," File 22954-17-047, GSF, CCF, NARA.

68. Edward K. Miller, Superintendent Indian School, Greenville, California to the Commissioner of Indian Affairs, May 22, 1917, File 22954-17-047, GSF, CCF, NARA.

69. Edgar H. Miller to E. B. Merritt, Commissioner of Indian Affairs, September 20, 1917, File 22954-17-047, GSF, CCF, NARA. The prize money ($300) had to be returned to the state agricultural society after it was determined that even though the boys had not yet graduated, some of them were too old to participate in the competition. Despite the age infraction, however, the boys did surprisingly well, given that Sherman Institute had not had a permanent band leader at the school in the months leading up to the fair—the band had not practiced in months. Only two weeks before the fair, Superintendent Conser hired a temporary employee to get the band into shape for the event. F. M. Conser to the Commissioner of Indian Affairs, October 13, 1917, File 95282-17-047, SI, CCF, NARA.

70. *Morning Star*, March 1886, 11.

71. Joseph Weber, President, American Federation of Musicians to Hubert Work, Secretary of the Interior, February 12, 1926, File 6088-26-929, HIS, CCF, NARA.

72. Owen Miller to T. E. Leupp, Commissioner of Indian Affairs, August 26, 1908, File 44146-08-929, SIS, CCF, NARA.

73. Joseph Weber to Hubert Work, February 3, 1926, NA File 6088-26-929, HIS, CCF, NARA.

74. NA CCF Salem, File 44146-08-929; Owen Miller, Secretary of the American Federation of Musicians to Walter G. Fischer, Secretary of the Interior, February 27, 1913, File 105850-13-929, SI, CCF, NARA.

75. The American Federation of Musicians protested on numerous occasions to the OIA with regard to Indian bands, even when they were private bands and not at all connected to the schools or the OIA. See their protest in 1909 against an Indian band of Onondaga, New York, in File 42783-09-929, GSF, CCF, NARA.

76. J. M. Shott to Carl Hayden, M. A. Smith, H. F. Ashurst, and the Commissioner of Indian Affairs, May 20, 1913, File 66058-13-929, PIS, CCF, NARA.

77. Cato Sells to John M. Shott, September 15, 1913, File 66058-13-929, PIS, CCF, NARA.

78. Dr. Francis H. Redewill to Supt. Goodman, October 3, 1913, and E. B. Meritt, Assistant Commissioner of Indian Affairs to the Honorable Carl Hayden, House of Representatives, March 2, 1914, both in File 66058-13-929 PIS, CCF, NARA.

79. Charles W. Harris to Franklin K. Lane, Secretary of the Interior, May 7, 1915, File 53142-15-929, PIS, CCF, NARA.

80. Throughout the correspondence from which this material is drawn, Redewill's band is referred to interchangeably as the First Infantry Band, the First Regiment Band, and the First Regimental Band.

81. Edgar Grinstead to J. B. Brown, superintendent of the Phoenix Indian School, May 26, 1915, File 53142-15-929, PIS, CCF, NARA.

82. Ibid.

83. The dances generally lasted from 7:15 P.M. until 9:30 P.M. Section 22, "Report of Harwood Hall, Supervisor of Indian Schools, Subject—General Inspection Sherman Institute, Riverside, Cal," November 6, 1909, File 91083-22-750, SI, CCF, NARA.

84. "Indian Life and Culture Reflected by the Carlisle Indian School," transcript 10, tape 1, interview with Luana Mangold by Helen Norton, January 19, 1981, Norristown, Pa., CISOHP, CCHS.

85. Quoted in Adams, "Beyond Bleakness," 52.

86. Quoted in ibid., 52.

87. Quoted in ibid.

88. Ellis, "'We Had a Lot of Fun,'" 83–84.

89. Riney, "Loosening the Bonds," 132.

90. Charles L. Davis, Inspection Report, January 15, 1910, File 5805-10-752, GSF, CCF, NARA, 2.

91. Ibid., 2–3.

92. Ibid., 3. In 1916, Assistant Secretary of Indian Affairs Bo Sweeney indicated that the OIA "do[es] not require dancing in the Indian schools and do[es] not prohibit it." Bo Sweeney to J. W. Brink, August 2, 1916, File 82353-16-752, GSF, CCF, NARA.

93. Charles L. Davis, Inspection Report, January 15, 1910, File 5805-10-752, GSF CCF, NARA, 3. Emphasis in original. Davis recognized the argument that dance "gives the Indian youths ease and grace of bodily movement and in company of the other sex, all of which is admitted." He added, "But there are other forms of amusement which will accomplish the same end, against which the objections raised above can not be urged. The grand march, to the accompaniment of the orchestra, the piano, or even the phonograph, does much to bring out the backward pupils, and I can see no objection to such figure movements as the Virginia reel, and similar forms of amusement, if engaged in as mere amusement and not made a part of a dance." Ibid, 4.

94. Ibid., 4.

95. Jacobs, "Working on the Domestic Frontier."

96. Lomawaima and McCarty, "To Remain an Indian," 12.

97. "When Garvie Blew His Horn, Indian School 'Fell Out,'" June 19, 1983, Harrisburg (Pa.) Sunday Patriot News, CIIS drop files, CCHS. Interview with James Garvie by Helen Norton, 12.

98. Interview with James Garvie by Helen Norton, 2.

99. Ibid.

100. Trennert, Phoenix Indian School, 127.

101. Ibid., 128.

102. Ibid.

103. Interview with James Garvie by Helen Norton, 23.

104. Ibid., 19.

105. Ibid., 23.

106. Ibid., 26.

107. Ibid.

108. Standing Bear, *My People the Sioux*, 148.

109. Ibid., 171. Emphasis in original.

110. Trennert, *Phoenix Indian School*, 127–28.

111. Gilbert, "Education beyond the Mesas," 134.

112. Child, *Boarding School Seasons*, 23.

113. Horne and McBeth, *Essie's Story*, 44.

114. *Red Man*, February 1896.

115. "Indian School Is Strongly Endorsed," clipping of unknown newspaper article, July 15, 1909, CIIS drop files, CCHS.

116. "Why Band Did Not Play Flag Salute," *Carlisle (Pa.) American Volunteer*, July 1, 1909, CIIS drop files, CCHS.

117. "Attacks Head of Indian School," *Carlisle (Pa.) American Volunteer*, July 8, 1909, CIIS drop files, CCHS.

118. Ibid.

119. "Ex-Students Who Took Training, but Did Not Graduate," *Chilocco Graduates, 1894 to 1932*, ed. Ms. Claude Hogg Hayman, ed., n.d., File 64151-34-820, CHS, CCF, NARA.

120. Ibid.

121. "Class of 1927," in *Chilocco Graduates, 1894 to 1932*, 99.

122. "Class of 1929," in *Chilocco Graduates, 1894 to 1932*, 123.

123. Lomawaima, *They Called It Prairie Light*, 82–83.

124. Ibid., 65, 86.

125. Gilbert, "Education beyond the Mesas," 133.

126. Moses Friedman to the Commissioner of Indian Affairs, May 1, 1908, File 29456-08-814, CA, CCF, NARA.

127. Annual Narrative Report, 1933, BIS, CCF, NARA.

128. J. F. House, Superintendent Flandreau Indian School to the Commissioner of Indian Affairs, October 16, 1923, File 80994-23-814, FIS, CCF, NARA. See also Child, *Boarding School Seasons*, 70.

129. "Ex-Students Who Took Training, but Did Not Graduate."

130. "Class of 1928," in *Chilocco Graduates, 1894 to 1932*, 102.

131. "Class of 1930," in *Chilocco Graduates, 1894 to 1932*, 127–8.

132. "Class of 1920," in *Chilocco Graduates, 1894 to 1932*, 56.

133. When, by 1934, Armstrong had not been heard from in some time, interviewer Claude Hogg wrote that "whether or not she is still there, no one [in her home of Eldorado, Kansas] seems to know." "Class of 1930," 126.

134. Ellis, "'We Had a Lot of Fun,'" 79.

135. "Class of 1917," in *Chilocco Graduates, 1894 to 1932*, 35; "Class of 1919," in *Chilocco Graduates, 1894 to 1932*, 48.

136. "Class of 1921," in *Chilocco Graduates, 1894 to 1932*, 59.

137. "Class of 1928," 106.

138. "Class of 1908," in *Chilocco Graduates, 1894 to 1932*, 26.

139. "Class of 1917," 35.

140. "Class of 1922," in *Chilocco Graduates, 1894 to 1932*, 68.

141. Ibid., 69.

142. "Class of 1929," 118.

143. "Class of 1924," in *Chilocco Graduates, 1894 to 1932*, 77.

144. La Flesche, *Middle Five*, 100.

145. Gilbert, "Education beyond the Mesas," 109.

146. Ibid., 119.

147. Ibid., 122.

148. Ibid., 124.

149. Ibid.

150. Ibid., 126.

151. Ibid., 127.

152. Ibid., 129.

153. Ibid.

154. Silko, *Yellow Woman*, 161.

155. Ibid., 163.

156. Ibid., 164.

157. "Class of 1929," 121.

CHAPTER 4

1. "Indians Entertain," *Inyo County Register*, March 5, 1913, clipping in File 48264-14-047, BIS, CCF, NARA.

2. "Entertainment Planned for Band Benefit Big Success," *Owens Valley Herald*, March 6, 1913, clipping in File 48264-14-047, BIS, CCF, NARA.

3. George Simeral to F. H. Abbott, March 29, 1913, File 43895-1913-814, BIS, CCF, NARA.

4. "Entertainment Planned for Band Benefit."

5. "Indian Show" program for February 28, 1913, File 43895-1913-814, BIS, CCF, NARA.

6. "Entertainment Planned for Band Benefit."

7. Ibid. See also "Indians Entertain."

8. "Entertainment Planned for Band Benefit."

9. Earlier, Superintendent of Indian Schools William Hailmann (1894–98) argued for the economic benefit of the instruction of Indian art in the schools. Gere, "Art of Survivance," 653–54.

10. Moses, *Wild West Shows*, 8.

11. Ibid., 4.

12. Ibid., xiii.

13. Ibid., 3, 63, 199.

14. P. J. Deloria, *Playing Indian*, 105.

15. P. J. Deloria, *Indians in Unexpected Places*, 191.

16. Maddox, *Citizen Indians*, 5.

17. Pisani, *Imagining Native America in Music*, 12–13.

18. Ibid., 252, 266–67.

19. Browner, "'Breathing the Indian Spirit,'" 265. See also *Imagining Native America in Music*, Michael Pisani's excellent and exhaustive history of American Indian-themed classical, semiclassical, Broadway musical, and film score compositions.

20. Because not all composers who wrote Indian-themed pieces were considered Indianists, Browner's use of the term is fitting for the present work: "'Indianist' is used here to refer to any American who used Native American music as source material for art music on a consistent basis (as opposed to just once or twice) between 1890 and 1920." Browner, "'Breathing the Indian Spirit,'" 266. For more information on these composers, in addition to Browner and Pisani, see Block, "Amy Beach's Music"; and P. J. Deloria, *Indians in Unexpected Places*, 236–89.

21. For the development of Asian stereotypes in early twentieth-century American music, see Lancefield, "Hearing Orientality."

22. P. J. Deloria, *Indians in Unexpected Places*, 184.

23. Ibid., 222.

24. McHugh and Perillo, *Indian Blues*.

25. Abrahams, *Big Chief Killahun*. Some 10,000 Native troops had joined the armed forces by 1918, and 85 percent of them had volunteered. Cato Sells reported in 1920 that American Indians had bought more than $60 million in Liberty Bonds, with an immediate outpouring of $25 million in cash. Holm, *Great Confusion in Indian Affairs*, 178.

26. McNutt, "John Comfort Fillmore," 61.

27. For examples of their work, see Curtis, *Indians' Book*; Hofmann, *Frances Densmore and American Indian Music*; Fletcher, *Study of Omaha Indian Music*.

28. In an interview with Minnesota Public Radio, Larry Aitken, former president of Leech Lake Tribal College, emphasized the value of her works for Ojibwe people today and added that "her books and her writings are timeless." Stephen Smith, "Song Catcher." Tom Holm recognizes that Alice Fletcher's work at least assured the "partial survival" of the songs. Holm, *Great Confusion in Indian Affairs*, 106.

29. It is important to note, however, that by the 1930s Densmore took a greater interest in the process of song creation in the modern era. See, for example, Densmore, "Songs of Indian Soldiers" and "Influence of Hymns."

30. Densmore, Extract from Diaries, "Chronology of the Study and Presentation of Indian Music from 1893 to 1944 by Frances Densmore," Box 1, FDP, NAA.

31. "I Heard an Indian Drum," Manuscript for Autobiography, File 16, Box 2, FDP, NAA, 7.

32. Densmore, Extract from Diaries, 1904.

33. Ibid., 1906.

34. Ibid.

35. "Record of the Field Work by Densmore for the BIA, 1907–1941, on the Music and Customs of the American Indians," Personal Memoranda, 1943, File 25, Box 2, FDP, NAA, 28; Frances Densmore to F. W. Hodge, July 17, 1914, Box 27, BAE, NAA, 1–2.

36. F. H. Abbott to Frances Densmore, June 7, 1913, GSF 751, CCF, NARA.

37. Mark, *Stranger in Her Native Land*, 73.

38. Ibid., 75, 92–93, 118–19, 200.

39. Frances Densmore to F. W. Hodge, July 11, 1911, Box 26, BAE, NAA.

40. See chapter 1 for a discussion on returned students.

41. Hofmann, *Frances Densmore and American Indian Music*, 20.

42. Ibid.

43. Frances Densmore to F. W. Hodge, August 10, 1914, Box 27, BAE, NAA, 1.

44. Ibid.; Densmore, "Incidents in the Study of Ute Music," File 20, Box 2, FDP, NAA, 2.

45. Ibid., 4.

46. Ibid. Emphasis in original.

47. Brady, *Spiral Way*, 93.

48. Quoted in ibid.

49. Kvasnicka and Viola, *Commissioners of Indian Affairs*, 221–31.

50. Hoxie, *Final Promise*, xiii.

51. Lomawaima, "Estelle Reel."

52. For the example of the Sherman Institute, see Medina, "Selling Indians at Sherman Institute," 116–17.

53. Pfister, *Individuality Incorporated*, 87. Pfister's work on Leupp and especially Leupp's ideas regarding race is particularly instructive.

54. Quoted in ibid., 89. William Hailmann, superintendent of Indian schools from 1894 to 1898, briefly expressed interest in facilitating the commodification and production of Native art in the schools. He believed that such work might inculcate among the students the value of thrift and provide an introduction to wage labor. Gere, "Art of Survivance," 653.

55. Holm, *Great Confusion in Indian Affairs*, 162.

56. Quoted in Pfister, *Individuality Incorporated*, 89.

57. Quoted in Holm, *Great Confusion in Indian Affairs*, 162.

58. Pfister, *Individuality Incorporated*, 85. Friedman served as the superintendent of Carlisle from 1908 to 1913.

59. Quoted in Holm, *Great Confusion in Indian Affairs*, 175.

60. Littlefield, "B.I.A. Boarding School"; Littlefield, "Learning to Labor," 43.

61. Quoted in Kvasnicka and Viola, *Commissioners of Indian Affairs*, 227.

62. Ibid., 249.

63. Ibid., 227–28, 230.

64. F. E. Leupp, Education Circular 175, December 3, 1907, File 56074-1934-814, GSF, CCF, NARA. Emphasis added.

65. Kvasnicka and Viola, *Commissioners of Indian Affairs*, 231.

66. In Curtis, *Indians' Book*, xxv.

67. Curtis, "Mr. Roosevelt and Indian Music," 399.

68. Pfister, *Individuality Incorporated*, 88.

69. Michael Castro argues that Curtis's work, even with Roosevelt's endorsement, "did little to soften the overall governmental oppressions." This is true, as can be seen by the acceleration of allotment and the continuity of the assimilation philosophy. Yet the valuation (severely flawed as it was) of Native culture as exemplified by Curtis and supported by Roosevelt, along with consistent resistance to assimilation by American Indians, did cause Leupp and his successors to attempt new strategies to forward their agendas. Castro, *Interpreting the Indian*, 9.

70. Lomawaima and McCarty, *"To Remain an Indian,"* 2, 5.

71. "Graduation Exercises," program, April 4, 1907, Carlisle Indian School, CIIS drop files, CCHS.

72. R. G. Valentine to Cromwell Childs, September 13, 1911, File 76581-11-751, GSF, CCF, NARA. This first effort by the OIA did not produce results, however, as the appointee "failed to appreciate the work in which he was engaged and practically nothing was accomplished."

73. "Pima Indian Children Sing Tribal Chants for Composer," *Musical America*, April 11, 1914, in Clippings—Names, Cadman, Charles W., NYPL. Tsianina Redfeather accompanied Cadman and performed for the children.

74. Thurlow Lieurance to the Indian Office, May 6, 1912, File 47389-13-751, GSF, CCF, NARA.

75. Thurlow Lieurance to P. P. Campbel, April 2, 1913, File 44814-13-751, GSF, CCF, NARA.

76. T. B. LeSieur, "The Shoshoni Sun-Dance," *Red Man*, November 1911.

77. Ibid.

78. *Red Man*, November 1911.

79. Katanski, *Learning to Write "Indian,"* 47–48.

80. *Indian Helper*, June 17, 1887, 1.

81. Ibid.

82. There were occasional exceptions. Gilbert documents the performance of the Eagle Dance by Hopi students in 1907. Gilbert, "Education beyond the Mesas," 126–27.

83. Albert Beedon to Franklin K. Lane, Secretary of the Interior, March 20, 1913, File 39494-13-751, GSF, CCF, NARA.

84. Lewis G. Laylin to Frank Parker Stockbridge, April 29, 1913, File 46377-13-751 GSF, CCF, NARA.

85. F. H. Abbott to A. S. Ely, May 16, 1913, File 64029-13-751, GSF, CCF, NARA.

86. "Big Chiefs Hesitate before Singing into Phonograph Horn," *Carlisle Evening Herald*, April 7, 1913, CIIS drop files, CCHS, 1.

87. O'Hara, *Navajo Indian Songs*.

88. Senator William S. Kenyon to Cato Sells, November 24, 1914, and Cato Sells to Senator William S. Kenyon, November 30, 1914, both in File 75297-13-751, GSF, CCF, NARA. O'Hara recorded at least eight cylinders' worth of music by American Indians in 1913. Chief Clerk to J. W. Fewkes, January 29, 1926, File 4976-26-751, GSF, CCF, NARA.

89. Stauffer, "Tammany."

90. Stauffer, "Cheyenne"; Stauffer, "My Wife's Gone to the Country."

91. In 1914, the year that Friedman was suspended from the service for various improprieties, some involving corporal punishment, Stauffer was fired for beating an eighteen-year-old Potawatomi student named Julia Hardin. Because Hardin had not had time to pack her trunk to prepare for an outing assignment, she refused to leave for the 5 P.M. train. Stauffer was called to the room by two matrons; he slapped Hardin across the face and then, after the matrons held her down, he grabbed a board from a windowsill and struck her several times in the head. Episode recounted in Adams, *Education for Extinction*, 325.

92. R. G. Valentine, Acting Commissioner of Indian Affairs, to Henry T. Finck, May 10, 1909, File 36178-09-751, GSF, CCF, NARA, and letters of introduction in same file to each school superintendent.

93. Ibid.

94. See, e.g., C. F. Hauke, Acting Commissioner of Indian Affairs to Mrs. L. C. Short, Silver Beach, Wash., June 27, 1913, File 75667-13-751, GSF, CCF, NARA.

95. Mr. and Mrs. Mazzini Slusser to Lane Franklin, March 20, 1913, File 39495-13-751, GSF, CCF, NARA.

96. Lucy J. Barlow to the Supervisor of Indian Music, December 11, 1908, File 83086-08-751, GSF, CCF, NARA.

97. J. M. Conser to Lucy J. Barlow, December 15, 1908, File 83086-08-751, GSF, CCF, NARA.

98. J. H. Bratley to the Commissioner of Indian Affairs, April 2, 1909, and John Francis, Jr., to J. H. Bratley, April 14, 1909, both in File 26376-09-751, GSF, CCF, NARA.

99. Between 1890 and 1899 a growing number of teachers were Native, constituting a high of 19 percent of Indian Service teachers by 1897. The teachers were typically former boarding school students who discovered upon graduation that the only employer near their reservations who would hire them was the Indian Service. The number of Native employees had begun a steady decline by 1899, however. In 1905, only 50 of 450 teachers in the Indian Service, or 11 percent, were Native. Of this number, only a handful taught courses in Native arts like DeCora. See Ahern, "Experiment Aborted."

100. Pfister, *Individuality Incorporated*, 88. For a recent study of DeCora, see Gere, "Art of Survivance."

101. Quoted in ibid.

102. J. W. Gibson to the Honorable Secretary of the Interior, March 30, 1913, File 43092-13-751, GSF, CCF, NARA.

103. F. H. Abbott to J. W. Gibson, April 22, 1913, File 43092-13-751, GSF, CCF, NARA.

104. The Yavapai are sometimes referred to as the Mohave-Apaches. Montezuma was often referred to by the public as simply an Apache. Iverson, *Carlos Montezuma*, 3–4.

105. Hertzberg, *Search for an American Indian Identity*, 43–44.

106. "Stirs Chicago Indian," newspaper clipping, File 64029-13-751, GSF, CCF, NARA.

107. John M. Oskison, a Cherokee Indian to Franklin K. Lane, Secretary of Interior, April 1, 1913, File 87252-13-751, GSF, CCF, NARA.

108. F. H. Abbott to A. S. Ely, May 16, 1913, File 64029-13-751, GSF, CCF, NARA.

109. Ibid. Emphasis added.

110. Quoted in Maddox, *Citizen Indians*, 25.

111. Moses Friedman to Rev. William B. Humphrey, May 8, 1911, File, 40586-11-047, CA, CCF, NARA.

112. Frances Densmore to F. W. Hodge, July 17, 1914, Box 27, BAE, NAA.

113. Ibid.; Frances Densmore to F. W. Hodge, June 28, 1911, Box 27, BAE, NAA.

114. Moses Friedman to James Mumblehead, May 8, 1911, File 40586-11-047, CA, CCF, NARA.

115. Moses Friedman to Rev. William B. Humphrey, May 8, 1911. Friedman subsequently reprimanded the missionaries.

116. Pratt, *Battlefield and Classroom*, 283.

117. Holm, *Te Great Confusion in Indian Affairs*, 155.

118. *Oklahoma Oil and Gas News* 1, no. 42 (February 18, 1915), clipping in File 26966-15-047, CHS, CCF, NARA, 1, 4.

119. Edgar Allen to the Editor, *Oklahoma Oil and Gas News*, March 1, 1915, clipping in File 26966-15-047, CHS, CCF, NARA. For Sells's inquiry into and rebuttal of this charge, see Cato Sells to Edgar A. Allen, Superintendent of Chilocco School, February 25, 1915, clipping in File 26966-15-047, CHS, CCF, NARA.

120. *American Volunteer* (Carlisle, Pa.), October 1896, CIIS drop files, CCHS.

121. Hauptman and McLester, *Oneida Indians*, 119.

122. Ibid., 112–38. Dennison Wheelock is a fascinating and controversial figure in Oneida history. Hauptman has written an in-depth account of Wheelock's musical career, so I felt compelled to focus more attention, in chapter 5, on other, lesser-known Native musicians.

123. S. M. McCowan to Alice Fletcher, May 27, 1904, File: Incoming Correspondence, 1903–1904, Box 2, AFP, NAA.

124. H. B. Peairs to the Commissioner of Indian Affairs, February 11, 1926, File 6088-26-929, HIS, CCF, NARA.

125. T. J. McCoy to Charles H. Burke, Commissioner of Indian Affairs, November 27, 1925, File 65346-1925-047, GSF, CCF, NARA; "Is Oneida's Counselor," 352-54; "Echoes from Flandreau, S.D.," *Red Man and Helper* 18 (June 27, 1902), CIIS drop files, CCHS.

126. For a discussion of the relationship between immigration and Indian citizenship in this era, see Trachtenberg, *Shades of Hiawatha*.

127. Quoted in Maddox, *Citizen Indians*, 20.

128. Seger School, program, June 19–20, 1913, File 120567-13-047, GSF, CCF, NARA.

129. Ibid.

130. "A Colonial Pageant," Seger School, June 19–20, 1913, File 120567-13-047, GSF, CCF, NARA.

131. "Closing Exercises, Fort Sill U.S. Indian School," program, June 20, 1913, File 120567-13-047, GSF, CCF, NARA. Michael D. McNally's "Contesting the Real Indian" is an interesting essay on the *Song of Hiawatha* pageant history among the Anishinaabe.

132. "Program, Academic Department, 8:00 P.M.," *Program, Closing Exercises, Fort Sill U.S. Indian School, Lawton, Oklahoma, June 20, 1913*, File 120567-13-047, GSF, CCF, NARA; "'Draped in the Habiliments of the Forest' Indians Act," newspaper clipping, unknown newspaper, n.d., File 120567-13-047, GSF, CCF, NARA.

133. "Program, Academic Department, 8:00 P.M.."

134. Ibid.

135. "'Draped in the Habiliments of the Forest' Indians Act."

136. Ibid.

137. Ibid.

138. Ibid.

139. Ibid.

140. Ibid.

141. H. C. Eldridge to Robert G. Valentine, Commissioner of Indian Affairs, April 28, 1910, File 37199-10-814, CA, CCF, NARA; "Indian Opera Company Off on Special," *Carlisle (Pa.) Evening Sentinel*, April 1 1910, CIIS drop files, CCHS, 2; E. B. Meritt to W. I. Endicott, August 17, 1927, File 38143-27-751, GSF, CCF, NARA.

142. Pfister, *Individuality Incorporated*, 72.

143. "The Captain of Plymouth—A Comic Opera," *Indian Craftsman*, May 1909, 47.

144. This set of quotes and summary of the pageant is derived from Barbara Lee's excellent discussion of "Captain of Plymouth" in Lee, "Romanticizing of a Puritan Romance."

145. Holm, *Great Confusion in Indian Affairs*.

146. For examples of students invoking humor through appropriating Indianness, see Neuman, "Students, Wordplay, and Ideologies of Indianness."

147. Horne and McBeth, *Essie's Story*, 49.

148. Ibid., 99.

149. Ibid.

150. Ibid., 66–67.

151. Ibid., 84–86.

152. Ibid., 86.

153. Ibid.

154. Rhodes, "A Study of Musical Diffusion," 45. DeHuff was married to Santa Fe Indian School superintendent John David DeHuff. She was a patron of Native music and maintained a close friendship with Hopi artist Fred Kabotie. Her husband had to leave the Indian Service after his and his wife's the couple's enthusiasm for Indian art and crafts led to charges that under his watch the students would "revert to paganism." http://rmoa.unm.edu/docviewer.php?docId=nmu1mss99bc.xml.

155. Rhodes, "Study of Musical Diffusion," 45–46.

156. Ibid., 46. In 1953 David McAllester recorded Walter Taylor's rendition of the song; Taylor had heard it sung in 1935 by two Hopis in 1935, Robert Lomodofkie and Edward Nequatewa. Taylor recalled that that he had also heard the song sung the previous year by a Zuni workman "on a dig being directed by Frank H.H. Roberts Jr." Ibid., 47.

157. McNally, *Ojibwe Singers*, 125–26.

158. Nesper, "Simulating Culture," 457.

CHAPTER 5

1. Blackstone, *Where Trails Have Led Me*, 3rd rev. ed., 142–45.

2. See McBride, "Lucy Nicolar"; Richard Green, *Te Ata*; and Hauptman and McLester, *Oneida Indians*.

3. "Talking Machine Fails to Win Fortune in Arctic," *Talking Machine World*, September 15, 1919, 3.

4. Ibid.

5. "Blackfeet Indians Return Call," *Talking Machine World*, June 15, 1921, 10.

6. "Thorola Set Used by Indians," *Talking Machine World*, September 15, 1926, 110.

7. "Oregon Indians Buy Opera," *Talking Machine World*, August 15, 1920, 163.

8. "Record Trade with the Indians," *Talking Machine World*, July 15, 1922, 19.

9. "Selling Talkers to Indians Requires Special Gifts," *Talking Machine World*, October 15, 1917, 105. Many Osages who received large mineral rights payments at this time were known by record salesmen to spend extravagantly on records.

10. Hauptman and McLester, *Oneida Indians*, 139.

11. P. J. Deloria, *Indians in Unexpected Places*.

12. "From Our Chicago Headquarters," *Talking Machine World*, October 15, 1920, 144.

13. "'Indian Dawn' a Hit," *Talking Machine World*, July 1926, 126. The song had longevity as well, circulating as early as April 1925, and was performed by numerous non-Indian and Indian singers such as Rose Raisa, Frances Alda, Tsianina Blackstone, Anna Case, Barbara Maurel, and Marjory Moody. Ibid.; "Indian Concert Artist Praises 'Indian Dawn,'" *Talking Machine World*, April 15, 1925, 160. See also the advertisement for "Indian Dawn," *Talking Machine World*, August 15, 1925, 162–63.

14. Morse, *Arrah Wanna*.

15. Phebe Jewell Nichols, "Brief Biography of Angus F. Lookaround," in ALPJNP, WHS.

16. Lookaround's parents were Mary Weso Murray Lookaround, who died at age seventy-four in 1928, and Henry Kay-wah-tah-wah-poa, who died in 1908. His name, which meant "sharp looking around (lightning) of the Thunderbird (eagle)," influenced his given English name, "Look-around," when the first Menominee tribal rolls were recorded." Ibid.

17. Ibid.; Medical Record, Gus Lookaround (Augustus Looks), April 12, 1912, File August (Angus) Lookaround (4624), Menominee, Wisc., Box 111, CSSR, NARA (hereafter "File August Lookaround"). Mary and Henry Lookaround were married around 1868. Angus Lookaround's living siblings included Angeline Lookaround Adams, Elizabeth Lookaround Tourtillott, Jerome, and Peter. Family History Tracing the Collateral Relatives of the Late Angeline Smith Camdem, enclosure from B. O. Angell, Examiner of Inheritance, to Melvin L. Robertson, Superintendent, Menominee Indian Agency, Biography and Miscellany, ALPJNP, WHS. This family history puts Henry Lookaround's death three years later than his wife indicates in his biography.

18. Lookaround went by several other names as well, according to the Carlisle records, including Gus Lookaround, August Lookaround, and Augustus Looks. To avoid confusion, I will refer to him as Angus Lookaround.

19. Nichols, "Brief Biography," in ALPJNP, WHS.

20. Ibid.

21. Ibid.

22. Ibid.

23. Application for Enrollment in a Nonreservation School, August Lookaround, File August Lookaround.

24. Medical Record, Gus Lookaround (Augustus Looks), April 12, 1912, File August Lookaround.

25. Family History Tracing the Collateral Relatives of the Late Angeline Smith Camdem, enclosure from B. O. Angell, Examiner of Inheritance, to Melvin L. Robertson, Superintendent, Menominee Indian Agency, Biography and Miscellany, ALPJNP, WHS; Superintendent to Gus Lookaround, July 7, 1915, File August Lookaround.

26. Carlisle Indian School, Descriptive and Historical Record of Student, August Lookaround, File August Lookaround.

27. Nichols, "Brief Biography," in ALPJNP, WHS.

28. Ibid.

29. Ibid.

30. Ibid. Emphasis added.

31. Gus Lookaround to O. H. Lipps, September 12, 1916, File August Lookaround.

32. Superintendent to August Lookaround, September 15, 1916, File August Lookaround.

33. Nichols, "Brief Biography."

34. Ibid.

35. "Evening Concert," USS *New Hampshire*, September 24, 1918, Iconographic Collection, ALPJNP, WHS. In addition to entertaining the men, he played quarter-

back and coached the ship's football team. The team excelled and won the Atlantic Fleet championship in 1917. Nichols, "Brief Biography."

36. Nichols, "Brief Biography."

37. Ibid.

38. Ibid.

39. Ibid.

40. Ibid.

41. Ibid.

42. Ibid.

43. Ibid.

44. Ibid.

45. Elmer, *Musical Remembrances*, 61.

46. Ira C. Deaver, Superintendent, Seneca School, Wyandotte, Okla., to O. H. Lipps, Supervisor in Charge, United States Indian School, Carlisle, Pa., July 23, 1914, File Cardin, Fred (5529), Box 140, CSSR, NARA.

47. Ibid.

48. "Fred Cardin Honored," undated clipping in File Cardin, Fred (5529), Box 140, CSSR, NARA.

49. "Talented Indian Boy on Visit Here," *Vincennes Sun*, undated clipping in File Cardin, Fred (5529), Box 140, CSSR, NARA.

50. Program, "The Carlisle United States Indian Band," Commencement Concert, April 1, 1913. CIIS drop files, CCHS.

51. The Chautauqua Institution was founded in 1874 in New York State as a summer retreat for Sunday school teachers on Lake Chautauqua. With a base of white middle-class participants, it was imbued with the principles of the Social Gospel movement, and the teachers were exposed to a series of lectures and entertainments during their residency. Such "constructive entertainments" quickly gained popularity throughout the United States. Rieser, "Canopy of Culture," 3–6.

52. Arthur Bestor, President, Chautauqua Institution, to David DeHuff, Superintendent and Principle, Carlisle Indian School, August 31, 1915, File Cardin, Fred (5529), Box 140, CSSR, NARA.

53. Fred Cardin to William Palin, March 7, 1916, File 33873-16-929, SIS, CCF, NARA.

54. Thurlow Lieurance to William Colledge, October 24, 1916, Thurlow Lieurance, Talent Correspondence and Brochures, Box 139, RCC, UISC.

55. "The Cardin Violin Recital," *Carlisle Arrow*, December 3, 1915, 3. The newspaper reported, "To those who appreciate good music, the concert was indeed a treat. Mr. Cardin plays with a depth of feeling surprising in one so young, and each number was beautifully executed."

56. Fred Cardin to O. H. Lipps, March 13, 1916, File Cardin, Fred (5529), Box 140, CSSR, NARA.

57. He wrote to the director of the exposition, stating, "We consider it one of the best bands in this part of the north-west and aside from their being Indian boys you

will be pleased with them, I am sure." Despite Wadsworth's stirring sales pitch, the offer was declined. H. E. Wadsworth to the Director, Panama Pacific Exposition, February 4, 1914, Box 81, Folder 17, PPIER, BLUCB.

58. *The Indian String Quartet: From the Indian Training School, Chemawa, OR.*, brochure in File 33873-16-929, SIS, CCF, NARA.

59. *The Indian String Quartet: And Richard H. Kennedy*, James, Kerns and Abbot, Portland[, Ore.], n.d., brochure in RCC, UISC, 3.

60. *Indian String Quartet: From the Indian Training School.*

61. Fred Cardin to William Palin, March 7, 1916, File 33873-16-929, SIS, CCF, NARA. Emphasis in original.

62. A brochure of press notices and personal letters for the Indian String Quartet, printed in 1915 or early 1916, included over a dozen glowing newspaper reviews written on their behalf. *Indian String Quartet: From the Indian Training School.*

63. *Indian String Quartet: And Richard H. Kennedy*, 3. Kennedy wrote Commissioner Cato Sells that the addition of Cardin "will give us a full Indian quartet, all clean, manly young men, of high ambition, earnest purpose and industrious habits." R. H. Kennedy to Cato Sells, March 22, 1916, File 33873-16-929, SIS, CCF, NARA.

64. *Indian String Quartet: From the Indian Training School.*

65. Ibid.

66. "Indian String Quartet and Richard Kennedy, Itinerary, Summer of 1917," in letter from Fred Cardin to Redpath Lyceum Bureau, September 17, 1917, and R. H. Kennedy to L. B. Crotty, January 16, 1917, both in Talent Correspondence and Brochures, Indian String Quartet, RCC, UISC.

67. Manager Concert Contract between Richard H. Kennedy and the Redpath Lyceum Bureau, December 19, 1916, Talent Correspondence and Brochures, Indian String Quartet, RCC, UISC. The Redpath Lyceum Bureau first made the offer on October 30, 1916, which originally consisted of twenty consecutives weeks in the 1917–18 lyceum season at $150 per week plus transportation. William A. Colledge to Richard H. Kennedy, October 30, 1916, Talent Correspondence and Brochures, Indian String Quartet, RCC, UISC. The Redpath Lyceum Bureau was the flagship bureau of many such institutions that combined the spirit of the Chautauqua Institution's dedication toward social uplift and education with the traveling entertainment-oriented programs offered by lyceum circuits. The Redpath bureau stretched throughout the midwestern states. The "Circuit Chautauquas" were typically commercial ventures organized by talent agents and entrepreneurs and were at times scorned by cultural elites. Tapia, *Circuit Chautauqua*, 19–24.

68. Talent Schedule, 1918–19, Indian String Quartet, RCC, UISC.

69. Redpath Bureau to Mr. R. Kennedy, Western Union Telegram, April 22, 1918, Talent Correspondence and Brochures, Indian String Quartet, RCC, UISC.

70. Redpath Bureau to Richard Kennedy, Galesville, Wisc., April 8, 1918, Talent Correspondence and Brochures, Indian String Quartet, RCC, UISC.

71. R. H. Kennedy to L. B. Crotty, March 14, 1918, Talent Correspondence and Brochures, Indian String Quartet, RCC, UISC.

72. Redpath Bureau to Hicks Chatten Engraving Company, March 18, 1918, Talent Correspondence and Brochures, Indian String Quartet, RCC, UISC.

73. Redpath Bureau to R. H. Kennedy, January 17, 1918, Talent Correspondence and Brochures, Indian String Quartet, RCC, UISC.

74. R. H. Kennedy to the Redpath Bureau, April 12, 1918, Talent Correspondence and Brochures, Indian String Quartet, RCC, UISC.

75. R. H. Kennedy to L. B. Crotty, March 4, 1918, Indian String Quartet, Box 115, RCC, UISC.

76. Manager Concert Contract between Richard H. Kennedy and the Redpath Lyceum Bureau. In contrast, singer Lucy Nicolar (Penobscot), a.k.a. Princess Watahwaso, made $75 per week during her 1917 Redpath lyceum tour. McBride, "Lucy Nicolar," 147.

77. R. H. Kennedy to L. B. Crotty, February 2, 1918, Talent Correspondence and Brochures, Indian String Quartet, RCC, UISC.

78. "Warren Chautauqua Ends Monday Evening with One of Strongest Numbers," clipping from *Warren Tribune*, August 10, 1917, and "Chautauqua Closes," clipping from *St. Joseph Record*, June 29, 1917, both in Talent Correspondence and Brochures, Indian String Quartet, RCC, UISC.

79. R. H. Kennedy to Cato Sells, March 22, 1916, File 33873-16-929, SIS, CCF, NARA.

80. Ibid.

81. R. H. Kennedy to William A. Colledge, October 24, 1916, Talent Correspondence and Brochures, Indian String Quartet, RCC, UISC.

82. Ibid.

83. Ibid.

84. R. H. Kennedy to William A. Colledge, November 8, 1917, Talent Correspondence and Brochures, Indian String Quartet, RCC, UISC.

85. R. H. Kennedy to the Redpath Bureau, December 8, 1916, Talent Correspondence and Brochures, Indian String Quartet, RCC, UISC.

86. Kennedy to Colledge, November 8, 1917, and Redpath Lyceum Bureau to William A. Colledge, October 25, 1917, both in Talent Correspondence and Brochures, Indian String Quartet, RCC, UISC.

87. "Warren Chautauqua Ends Monday Evening"; Kennedy to Colledge, November 8, 1917.

88. R. H. Kennedy to L. B. Crotty, November 10, 1917, Talent Correspondence and Brochures, Indian String Quartet, RCC, UISC.

89. "The Indian String Quartet," *Carlisle Arrow and Red Man*, January 4, 1918, 19.

90. Fred Cardin to Superintendent John Frances, Jr., December 14, 1917, File Cardin, Fred (5529), Box 140, CSSR, NARA.

91. Fred Cardin to Chief Clerk, U.S. Indian School, Carlisle, Pa., Received January 26, 1918, Talent Correspondence and Brochures, Indian String Quartet, RCC, UISC.

92. Homer H. Hill to the Redpath Bureau, May 7, 1918, Talent Correspondence and Brochures, Indian String Quartet, RCC, UISC.

93. Ibid.

94. Redpath Bureau to Homer H. Hill, May 11, 1918, Talent Correspondence and Brochures, Indian String Quartet, RCC, UISC.

95. See, e.g., F. E. Andrews, Hicks-Chatten Engraving Co., to Redpath Bureau, February 27, 1918, Talent Correspondence and Brochures, Indian String Quartet, RCC, UISC.

96. Redpath Bureau to R. H. Kennedy, November 12, 1917, Talent Correspondence and Brochures, Indian String Quartet, RCC, UISC.

97. R. H. Kennedy to William A. Colledge, May 6, 1917, May 6, 1917; Kennedy to Crotty, November 10, 1917.

98. Gridley, *Indians of Today*, 57.

99. Thurlow Lieurance to H. P. Harrison, June 21, 1920, Thurlow Lieurance, Box 139, Redpath Chautauqua Correspondence, RCC, UISC.

100. Ibid. Te Ata led a long, professional life as a Chickasaw entertainer, primarily as a storyteller. Richard Green wrote a very detailed biography of her life in his *Te Ata*. It is unclear how or if Wanita was related to Fred Cardin.

101. Thurlow Lieurance to H. P. Harrison, July 30, 1920, Talent Correspondence and Brochures, Thurlow Lieurance, RCC, UISC.

102. Cardin not only led the group but also sang "the primitive songs of his people and [explained] their meanings." List of Lieurance's Companies and Descriptions for the 1920 Lyceum season, Talent Correspondence and Brochures, Thurlow Lieurance, RCC, UISC.

103. Thurlow Lieurance to H. P. Harrison, October 1, 1920, Talent Correspondence and Brochures, Thurlow Lieurance, RCC, UISC.

104. Thurlow Lieurance to L. B. Crotty, October 5, 1921, Talent Correspondence and Brochures, Thurlow Lieurance, RCC, UISC.

105. Thurlow Lieurance to H. P. Harrison, n.d., Talent Correspondence and Brochures, Thurlow Lieurance, RCC, UISC.

106. Elmer, *Musical Remembrances*, 61.

107. Ibid.

108. Gridley, *Indians of Today*, 57.

109. Ibid.

110. Elmer, *Musical Remembrances*, 62; Gridley, *Indians of Today*, 58. I have been unable to locate any of Cardin's pageants.

111. Elmer, *Musical Remembrances*, 62. "Cree War Dance" was reprinted in the March 1925 issue of the *Violinist*.

112. "Ringgold Band: Band History," www.ringgoldband.com/history.htm; Elmer, *Musical Remembrances*, 61.

113. Elmer, *Musical Remembrances*, 62. Reading citizen Bill Seidel made tremendous efforts to assist my search for further information on Fred Cardin's life in Reading. Cardin and his wife had no children, and we were unable to determine the existence of his personal papers or music-related materials in the Reading area.

114. Pisani, "'I'm an Indian Too,'" 233. See also P. J. Deloria, *Indians in Unexpected Places*, 183–203.

115. Morris, *Alcatraz Indian Occupation Diary*, ix.

116. Ibid., 3–4.

117. Ibid., 9–11.

118. Ibid., 12.

119. Ibid.

120. Ibid., 16.

121. Ibid., 60–61.

122. Ibid., 51.

123. Ibid.

124. Ibid., 17.

125. Ibid., 52.

126. Ibid., 30.

127. Ibid.

128. Ibid., 27.

129. Ibid.

130. Ibid., 26.

131. Ibid., 18.

132. Ibid., 169.

133. Blackstone, *Where Trails Have Led Me*, 2nd ed., 27, 104.

134. "7,000 Hear Cadman and Tsianina," *Musical Courier*, December 14, 1916, Clippings—Names, Cadman, Charles W., NYPL.

135. Blackstone, *Where Trails Have Led Me*, 2nd ed., 104.

136. Ibid., 34.

137. Ibid., 31–32.

138. "An Eveni[n]g with Cadman and Tsianina," n.d., Clippings—Names, Cadman, Charles W., NYPL.

139. Blackstone, *Where Trails Have Led Me*, 2nd ed., 110.

140. Ibid, 27.

141. Ibid., 103.

142. Ibid., 37–38.

143. Tsianina Blackstone to Jennie Avery, April 16, 1955, Tsianina Evans-Jennie Avery Correspondence, FACHL. Carter Jones Meyer explores more closely the relationship between Blackstone and Hewett in Meyer, "Edgar Hewett, Tsianina Redfeather."

144. Blackstone, *Where Trails Have Led Me*, 2nd ed., 36.

145. Blackstone, *Where Trails Have Led Me*, 3rd rev. ed., 229.

146. Blackstone, *Where Trails Have Led Me*, 2nd ed., 116.

147. Ibid., 111.

148. Ibid., 107.

149. Ibid., 93.

150. Ibid., 28.

151. Ibid., 115. Emphasis added.

152. Ibid., 114.

153. Ibid., 104.

154. Ibid., 82.

155. Ibid., 113.

156. Ibid., 136–37; Blackstone, *Where Trails Have Led Me*, 3rd rev. ed., 264–65.

157. P. J. Deloria, *Indians in Unexpected Places*, 84.

158. The full text of the work is available at Stanford University's opera information server, *Opera Glass*, http://opera.stanford.edu/Cadman/Shanewis/libretto .html, which is also the source of the synopsis and quotations in the text.

159. "A Little of Ragtime to Cadman's New Opera," n.d., Clippings—Names, Cadman, Charles W., NYPL.

160. "Shanewis," *Pittsburgh Post*, n.d., Clippings—Names, Cadman, Charles W., NYPL.

161. "Indian Opera and Negro Ballet Make New American Bill at the Metropolitan," *New York Herald*, March 24, 1918, clipping in Charles Cadman and Nelle Eberhart Scrapbook, 1893, 1907–25, 1935, Clippings, NYPL.

162. Blackstone, *Where Trails Have Led Me*, 2nd ed., 118. Alice Gentle was to play the lead role but within four days of the performance she developed laryngitis and bowed out.

163. "Indian Opera and Negro Ballet."

164. "Shanewis Applauded by 20,000," June 25, 1926, Clippings—Names, Cadman, Charles W., NYPL.

165. Ibid.

166. "Pima Indian Children Sing Tribal Chants for Composer," *Musical America*, April 11, 1914, Clippings—Names, Cadman, Charles W., NYPL.

167. Patterson, "'Real' Indian Songs," 53.

168. Blackstone, *Where Trails Have Led Me*, 2nd ed., 39–40.

169. Ibid., 40.

170. Ibid., 93.

171. Ibid., 38. P. J. Deloria, *Indians in Unexpected Places*, 276.

172. Blackstone, *Where Trails Have Led Me*, 3rd rev. ed, 233.

173. Bonnin was also known for her skills as a concert violinist.

174. Charles H. Burke to the Honorable Miles Poindexter, U.S. Senate, January 5, 1922, File 328-22-814, YA, CCF, NARA. Roberts's grandfather on his mother's side was Yakama, but he had left the reservation many years prior to 1924 and moved east. He eventually married a white woman in Indiana and there raised a girl named Julia, Tecumseh's mother. Tecumseh's grandmother on his father's side was a North Carolina Cherokee, "said to be full blood," who moved to Indiana as well, married a white man, and had a son named J. W. Roberts. J. W. Roberts and Julia married in Indiana and unsuccessfully attempted to enroll in the Oklahoma Cherokee tribe after moving to the Cherokee Strip of Oklahoma. Denied an allotment, they moved to the

Yakima Reservation around 1909. Evan W. Estep to Charles H. Burke, September 24, 1924, File 10185-36-033, YA, CCF, NARA.

175. Burke to Poindexter, January 5, 1922.

176. Evan Estep, Superintendent, Yakima Indian Agency, to Charles H. Burke, Commissioner of Indian Affairs, March 29, 1924, File 27541-240-814, YA, CCF, NARA; Nutchuk and Hatch, *Back to the Smoky Sea*, 38.

177. Estep to Burke, March 29, 1924.

178. "Western Indian Tenor Wins Fame," *Spokane Chronicle*, August 22, 1929, State History Box 141, Resource Identifier sh141-429, Wallis and Marilyn Kimble Northwest History Database, http://content.wsulibs.wsu.edu/pncc/NW_history/index.php.

179. Kiutus Tecumseh to Charles H. Burke, January 30, 1927, File 10506-25-751, GSF, CCF, NARA.

180. "1929 Radio Broadcasting Itinerary, Chief Tecumseh," author's collection.

181. Clipping, n.d., enclosed in letter from Kiutus Tecumseh to Charles H. Burke, Commissioner of Indian Affairs, July 9, 1926, File 10506-25-751, GSF, CCF, NARA.

182. Mathew F. Woodar, "To Whom This May Come," December 22, 1930, File 10506-25-751, GSF, CCF, NARA.

183. Kiutus Tecumseh to Charles H. Burke, Commissioner of Indian Affairs, February 8, 1925, File 10506-25-751, GSF, CCF, NARA.

184. "Real American Popular with Eastern Indians," *Real American*, Hoquiam, Wash., November 7, 1924, clipping in File 10506-25-751, GSF, CCF, NARA, 1.

185. Tecumseh to Burke, February 8, 1925.

186. James H. McGregor to Charles H. Burke, January 8, 1926, File 10506-25-751, GSF, CCF, NARA.

187. Kiutus Tecumseh to Charles Burke, February 18, 1925, File 10506-25-751, GSF, CCF, NARA.

188. Tecumseh to Burke, February 8, 1925.

189. Kiutus Tecumseh to Charles H. Burke, Commissioner of Indian Affairs, March 3, 1925; Kiutus Tecumseh to Charles Burke, March 27, 1925; Kiutus Tecumseh to Charles H. Burke, August 5, 1926, all in File 10506-25-751, GSF, CCF, NARA. Burke sent the superintendent of the Cherokee Indian Agency a letter of introduction on behalf of Tecumseh. Charles H. Burke to James E. Henderson, January 28, 1928, January 28, 1928. Simeon Oliver became a writer under the name of Nutchuk. His published memoirs include Nutchuk and Hatch, *Son of the Smoky Sea*, and Nutchuk and Hatch, *Back to the Smoky Sea*.

190. Kiutus Tecumseh to Charles Burke, April 13, 1925, File 10506-25-751, GSF, CCF, NARA.

191. Kiutus Tecumseh to Charles Burke, October 7, 1925, File 10506-25-751, GSF, CCF, NARA.

192. Ibid.; Kiutus Tecumseh to Charles H. Burke, December 17, 1925, File 10506-25-751, GSF, CCF, NARA.

193. Kiutus Tecumseh to Charles Rhoads, February 14, 1931, File 10506-25-751, GSF, CCF, NARA.

194. "Chief Holds Whites Responsible for Race," *Washington Post*, November 24, 1930, clipping in File 10506-25-751, GSF, CCF, NARA.

195. Ibid.

196. Sam B. Davis to Kiutus Tecumseh, January 6, 1931, File 10506-25-751, GSF, CCF, NARA; H .B. Peairs to Kiutus Tecumseh, December 31, 1930, File 10506-25-751, GSF, CCF, NARA.

197. Kiutus Tecumseh to John Collier, Commissioner of Indian Affairs, March 11, 1935, File 10506-25-751, GSF, CCF, NARA.

198. Ibid.

199. Kiutus Tecumseh to Senator Wesley L. Jones, U.S. Senate, 1931, File 10506-25-751, GSF, CCF, NARA.

200. P. J. Deloria, *Playing Indian*, 126.

201. Ibid., 125.

EPILOGUE

1. Skelton, "Native Rappers."

2. Ibid.

3. www.myspace.com/officialwarparty.

4. Gragg, "Hobbema Hip-Hoppers."

5. Ibid.

6. Elaschuk, "Shooting Straight from the Hip."

7. http://nativeamericanmusicawards.com.

8. Lomawaima and McCarty, *"To Remain an Indian,"* 64–65.

9. Holm, *Great Confusion in Indian Affairs*, 186–90.

10. P. J. Deloria, *Playing Indian*.

11. Holm, *Great Confusion in Indian Affairs*, xiv.

12. Prucha, *Great Father*, 951.

13. On the congressional floor, coauthor Edgar Howard said, "[Our] formula for civilizing the Indians has always been the policy of intolerance and suppression combined with a forcible religious and educational proselytism designed to compel the Indian to give up his own beliefs and views of life, his languages and arts and customs, and accept those of the white man. In permitting and encouraging the destruction of everything that was uniquely Indian, whether art or language or social custom, mythology or religion, or tribal and clan organization, the Government has not only destroyed a heritage that would make a colorful and priceless contribution to our own civilization, but it has hampered and delayed the adaptation of the Indian to white civilization." Many Native community leaders felt, understandably so, that the Indian Reorganization Act should not be trusted, and 78 of the 252 tribes and bands that were eligible to accept the access to revolving funds and other resources included in the legislation refused to do so, an act of defiant self-determination in

itself. Nevertheless, the cessation of allotment and invasive assimilation policies was an overwhelming victory for all tribes and bands of the United States. Quoted in Dippie, *Vanishing American*, 315, 318.

14. John Collier to Signor Guilio Silva, September 7, 1934, File 56074-1934-814, GSF, CCF, NARA. Collier also said he believed that the "present policy of practice [of music education] can only be hurtful to the Indians," and he added, "We teach them European music through tenth-rate teachers." John Collier to Albust Elkus, September 7, 1934, File 56074-1934-814, GSF, CCF, NARA.

15. Silva, Giulio to John Collier, September 14, 1934, File 56074-34-814, GSF, CCF, NARA.

16. Helen L. Kinnick, Demonstration Teacher, Elem., to Rose K. Brandt, Supervisor Elementary Education, Office of Indian Affairs, May 12, 1935, File 56074-34-814, GSF, CCF, NARA.

17. Alida C. Bowler to the Commissioner of Indian Affairs, April 25, 1935, File 56074-1934-814, GSF, CCF, NARA.

18. Ibid.

19. Ibid.

20. Ibid.

21. Ibid.

22. Horne and McBeth, *Essie's Story*, 84–86.

23. Lomawaima and McCarty, *"To Remain an Indian,"* 68.

24. Ibid., 75.

25. Ibid.

26. Ibid., 74.

27. Holm, *Great Confusion in Indian Affairs*, 194.

BIBLIOGRAPHY

NEWSPAPERS

Arrow. Weekly. Carlisle Indian School Press, Carlisle, Pa. 1904–1908. Continued under the name *Carlisle Arrow,* 1908–1917.

Indian Helper. Weekly. Carlisle Indian School Press, Carlisle, Pa. 1885–1900.

Morning Star. Monthly. Carlisle Indian School Press, Carlisle, Pa. 1882–87.

Native American. Weekly. Phoenix Indian School Press, Phoenix. 1900–1931.

Red Man. Variable frequency. Carlisle Indian School Press, Carlisle, Pa. 1888–1900 and 1909–17.

Red Man and Helper. Weekly. Carlisle Indian School Press, Carlisle, Pa. 1900–1904.

BOOKS, ARTICLES, DISSERTATIONS, AND SHEET MUSIC

Abrahams, Maurice. *Big Chief Killahun.* Lyrics by Alfred Bryan and Edgar Leslie. New York: Waterson, Berlin, and Snider Co., 1918.

Adams, David Wallace. "Beyond Bleakness: The Brighter Side of Indian Boarding Schools, 1870–1940." In Trafzer, Keller, and Sisquoc, *Boarding School Blues.*

———. *Education for Extinction: American Indians and the Boarding School Experience, 1875–1928.* Lawrence: University Press of Kansas, 1995.

Ahern, Wilbert H. "An Experiment Aborted: Returned Indian Students in the Indian School Service, 1881–1908." *Ethnohistory* 44, no. 2 (1997): 263–304.

Anderson, James D. *The Education of Blacks in the South, 1860–1935.* Chapel Hill: University of North Carolina Press, 1988.

Archuleta, Margaret L., Brenda J. Child, and K. Tsianina Lomawaima, eds. *Away from Home: American Indian Boarding School Experiences, 1879–2000.* Phoenix: Heard Museum, 2000.

Baraka, Amiri [aka Leroi Jones]. *Blues People: Negro Music in White America.* 1963. Reprint, New York: Harper Perennial, 1999.

Berkhofer, Robert F. *The White Man's Indian: Images of the American Indian from Columbus to the Present.* New York: Vintage Books, 1978.

Biolsi, Thomas. *Organizing the Lakota: The Political Economy of the New Deal on the Pine Ridge and Rosebud Reservations.* Tucson: University of Arizona Press, 1992.

Bird, S. Elizabeth, ed. *Dressing in Feathers.* Boulder, Colo.: Westview, 1996.

Black Bear, Ben, Sr., and R. D. Theisz. *Songs and Dances of the Lakota.* Aberdeen, S.Dak.: North Plains Press, 1976.

"Blackfeet Indians Return Call." *Talking Machine World* 17, no. 6 (1921): 10.

Blackstone, Tsianina. *Where Trails Have Led Me.* 2nd ed. Burbank, Calif.: Tsianina Blackstone, 1968.

Blackstone, Tsianina Redfeather, Princess. *Where Trails Have Led Me.* 3rd rev. ed., in collaboration with Dora Jean. N.p.: private printing, Princess Enterprises, 1982.

Block, Adrienne Fried. "Amy Beach's Music on Native American Themes." *American Music* (Summer 1990): 141–166.

Bodayla, Stephen D. "'Can an Indian Vote?' *Elk v. Wilkins,* a Setback for Indian Citizenship." *Nebraska History* 67, no. 4 (1986): 372–80.

Brady, Erika. *A Spiral Way: How the Phonograph Changed Ethnography.* Jackson: University Press of Mississippi, 1999.

Bredenberg, Alfred R. "Natalie Curtis Burlin (1875–1921): A Pioneer in the Study of American Minority Cultures," *Connecticut Review* 16, no. 1 (1994): 1–15.

Britten, Thomas A. *American Indians in World War I: At Home and at War.* Albuquerque: University of New Mexico Press, 1997.

Browner, Tara. "'Breathing the Indian Spirit': Thoughts on Musical Borrowing and the 'Indianist' Movement in American Music." *American Music* (Fall 1997): 265–84.

———. *Heartbeat of the People: Music and Dance of the Northern Pow-wow.* Urbana: University of Illinois Press, 2002.

Burgess, Marianna [as Embe]. *Stiya: A Carlisle Indian Girl at Home.* Cambridge: Riverside, 1891.

Cadman, Charles Wakefield. *From the Land of the Sky-Blue Water.* Lyrics by Nelle R. Eberhart. Boston: White-Smith Music Publishing Co., 1909.

Carlson, Robert A. *The Americanization Syndrome: A Quest for Conformity.* London: Croom Helm, 1987.

Castro, Michael. *Interpreting the Indian: Twentieth-Century Poets and the Native American.* Norman: University of Oklahoma Press, 1983.

Certeau, Michel de. *The Practice of Everyday Life.* Translated by Steven Rendall. Berkeley: University of California Press, 1984.

Child, Brenda J. *Boarding School Seasons.* Lincoln: University of Nebraska Press, 1998.

Curtis, Natalie. *The Indians' Book: An Offering by the American Indians of Indian Lore, Musical and Narrative, to Form a Record of the Songs and Legends of Their Race.* Reprint, New York: Bonanza Books, 1987. Orig. published in 1907.

———. "Mr. Roosevelt and Indian Music," March 5, 1919, *Outlook* 121:399–400.

Deloria, Philip J. *Indians in Unexpected Places.* Lawrence: University Press of Kansas, 2004.

————. *Playing Indian*. New Haven, Conn.: Yale University Press, 1998.

Deloria, Vine, Jr., and Clifford M. Lytle. *American Indians, American Justice*. Austin: University of Texas Press, 1983.

Demallie, Raymond J. "The Lakota Ghost Dance: An Ethnohistorical Account." *Pacific Historical Review* 51, no. 4 (1982): 385–405.

Densmore, Frances. "The Influence of Hymns on the Form of Indian Songs." *American Anthropologist* 40, no. 1 (1938): 175–77.

————. "The Songs of Indian Soldiers during the World War." *Musical Quarterly* 20, no. 4 (1934): 419–25.

Dilworth, Leah. *Imagining Indians in the Southwest: Persistent Visions of a Primitive Past*. Washington, D.C.: Smithsonian Institution Press, 1996.

Dippie, Brian W. *The Vanishing American: White Attitudes and U.S. Indian Policy*. Lawrence: University Press of Kansas, 1982.

Eastman, Charles A. [Ohiyesa]. *Indian Boyhood*. Boston: Little, Brown, and Co., 1902.

Elaschuk, Gary. "Shooting Straight from the Hip." *Alberta Sweetgrass News*. August 2002.

Ellis, Clyde. *A Dancing People: Powwow Culture on the Southern Plains*. Lawrence: University Press of Kansas, 2003.

————. "'There Is No Doubt the Dances Should Be Curtailed': Indian Dances and Federal Policy on the Southern Plains, 1880–1930." *Pacific Historical Review* 70, no. 4 (2001): 543–69.

————. *To Change Them Forever: Indian Education at the Rainy Mountain Boarding School, 1893–1920*. Norman: University of Oklahoma Press, 1996.

————. "'Truly Dancing Their Own Way': Modern Revival and Diffusion of the Gourd Dance." *American Indian Quarterly* 14, no. 1 (1990): 19–33.

————. "'We Don't Want Your Rations, We Want This Dance': The Changing Use of Song and Dance on the Southern Plains." *Western Historical Quarterly* 30, vol. 2 (1999): 133–54.

————. "'We Had a Lot of Fun, but of Course, That Wasn't the School Part'": Life at the Rainy Mountain Boarding School, 1893–1920." In Trafzer, Keller, and Sisquoc, *Boarding School Blues*.

Ellis, Clyde, Luke Lassiter, and Gary Dunham, eds. *Powwow*. Lincoln: University of Nebraska Press, 2005.

Elmer, Cedric N. *Musical Remembrances*. Reading, Pa.: Berksiana Foundation, 1976.

Fairclough, Adam. *Teaching Equality: Black Schools in the Age of Jim Crow*. Athens: University of Georgia Press, 2001.

Flandreau Indian School. *The Bow and Arrow, 1930*. Flandreau, S.Dak. Flandreau Indian School, 1930.

Fletcher, Alice C. *A Study of Omaha Indian Music*. 1893. Reprint, Lincoln: University of Nebraska Press, 1994.

Fox, Aaron A. "The Jukebox of History: Narratives of Loss and Desire in the Discourse of Country Music." *Popular Music* 11, no. 1 (1992): 53–72.

"From Our Chicago Headquarters." *Talking Machine World* 16, no. 10 (1920): 144.

García, Mario T. *Desert Immigrants: The Mexicans of El Paso, 1880–1920.* New Haven, Conn.: Yale University Press, 1981.

Gere, Anne Ruggles. "An Art of Survivance: Angel DeCora at Carlisle." *American Indian Quarterly* 28, nos. 3–4 (2004): 649–84.

Gibbon, Guy. *The Sioux: The Dakota and Lakota Nations.* Malden, Mass.: Blackwell, 2003.

Gilbert, Matthew Thomas. "Education beyond the Mesas: Hopi Student Involvement at Sherman Institute, 1902–1929." Ph.D. diss., University of California, Riverside, 2006.

The Government Official Indian Band, Organized by the U.S. Government Expressly for the Louisiana Purchase Exposition, St. Louis, 1904. Chicago: Hollister Brothers, Engravers and Printers, 1904.

Gragg, Russell. "Hobbema Hip-Hoppers." *See Magazine,* December 5, 2002.

Greci Green, Adriana. "Performances and Celebrations: Displaying Lakota Identity, 1880–1915." Ph.D. diss., Rutgers University, 2001.

Green, Rayna D. "The Indian in Popular American Culture." In Wilcomb E. Washburn, ed., *History of Indian-White Relations.* Washington, D.C.: Smithsonian Institution, 1988.

———. "The Tribe Called Wannabee: Playing Indian in America and Europe." *Folklore* 99, no. 1 (1988): 30–55.

Green, Richard. *Te Ata: Chickasaw Storyteller, American Treasure.* Norman: University of Oklahoma Press, 2002.

Greenwald, Emily. "'Hurrah! 4th July!': The Ironies of Independence Day on Western Reservations." Draft manuscript in the possession of the author.

Gridley, Marion E. *Indians of Today.* 3rd ed. Chicago: Towertown Press, 1960.

Hagan, William T. *The Indian Rights Association: The Herbert Welsh Years, 1882–1904.* Tucson: University of Arizona Press, 1985.

Harmon, Alexandra. "American Indians and Land Monopolies in the Gilded Age." *Journal of American History* 90, no. 1 (2003): 106–33.

Hauptman, Laurence M., and L. Gordon McLester, eds. *The Oneida Indians in the Age of Allotment, 1860–1920.* Norman: University of Oklahoma Press, 2006.

Hertzberg, Hazel W. *The Search for an American Indian Identity: Modern Pan-Indian Movements.* Syracuse, N.Y.: Syracuse University Press, 1971.

Heth, Charlotte, ed. *Native American Dance: Ceremonies and Social Traditions.* Washington, D.C.: National Museum of the American Indian, Smithsonian Institution, with Starwood Publishing, 1992.

Hofmann, Charles, ed. *Frances Densmore and American Indian Music: A Memorial Volume.* New York: Museum of the American Indian, Heye Foundation, 1968.

Holler, Clyde. *Black Elk's Religion: The Sun Dance and Lakota Catholicism.* Syracuse, N.Y.: Syracuse University Press, 1995.

Holm, Tom. *The Great Confusion in Indian Affairs: Native Americans and Whites in the Progressive Era.* Austin: University of Texas Press, 2005.

———. *Strong Hearts, Wounded Souls: Native American Veterans of the Vietnam War.* Austin: University of Texas Press, 1996.

Horne, Esther Burnett, and Sally McBeth. *Essie's Story: The Life and Legacy of a Shoshone Teacher.* Lincoln: University of Nebraska Press, 1999.

Hoxie, Frederick E. *A Final Promise: The Campaign to Assimilate the Indians, 1880–1920.* Cambridge: Cambridge University Press, 1984.

Huhndorf, Shari M. *Going Native: Indians in the American Cultural Imagination.* Ithaca, N.Y.: Cornell University Press, 2001.

"Indian Concert Artist Praises 'Indian Dawn.'" *Talking Machine World* 21, no. 4 (1925): 160.

"Indian Dawn." *Talking Machine World* 21, no. 8 (1925): 162–63.

"'Indian Dawn' a Hit." *Talking Machine World* 22, no. 7 (1926): 126.

Institute for Government Research. *The Problem of Indian Administration.* Studies in Administration. Baltimore: Johns Hopkins Press, 1928.

Iverson, Peter. *Carlos Montezuma and the Changing World of American Indians.* Albuquerque: University of New Mexico Press, 1982.

Jackson, Jason Baird. *Yuchi Ceremonial Life: Performance, Meaning and Tradition in a Contemporary Native American Community.* Lincoln: University of Nebraska Press, 2003.

Jackson, Jason Baird, and Victoria Levine. "Singing for Garfish: Music and Community Life in Eastern Oklahoma." *Ethnomusicology* 46, no. 2 (2001): 284–306.

Jacobs, Margaret D. *Engendered Encounters: Feminism and Pueblo Cultures, 1879–1934.* Lincoln: University of Nebraska Press, 1999.

———. "Making Savages of Us All: White Women, Pueblo Indians, and the Controversy over Indian Dances in the 1920s." *Frontiers: A Journal of Women Studies* 17, no. 3 (1996): 178–209.

———. "Working on the Domestic Frontier: American Indian Domestic Servants in White Women's Households in the San Francisco Bay Area, 1820–1840." *Frontiers: A Journal of Women Studies* 28, nos. 1–2 (2007): 165–99.

James, Harry C. *Pages from Hopi History.* Tucson: University of Arizona Press, 1974.

Katanski, Amelia V. *Learning to Write "Indian": The Boarding School Experience and American Indian Literature.* Norman: University of Oklahoma Press, 2005.

Kavanagh, Thomas W. "Southern Plains Dance: Tradition and Dynamism." In Heth, *Native American Dance.*

Kelly, Lawrence C. *The Assault on Assimilation: John Collier and the Origins of Indian Policy Reform.* Albuquerque: University of New Mexico Press, 1983.

———. "Charles Henry Burke, 1921–29." In Robert M. Kvasnicka and Herman J. Viola, eds., *The Commissioners of Indian Affairs, 1824–1977.* Lincoln: University of Lincoln Press, 1979.

Kvasnicka, Robert M., and Herman J. Viola, eds. *The Commissioners of Indian Affairs, 1824–1977.* Lincoln: University of Nebraska Press, 1979.

La Flesche, Francis. *The Middle Five: Indian Schoolboys of the Omaha Tribe.* 1900. Reprint, Lincoln: University of Nebraska Press, 1978.

Lancefield, Robert Charles. "Hearing Orientality in (White) America, 1900–1930." Ph.D. diss., Wesleyan University, 2005.

Lassiter, Luke E. "Charlie Brown: Not Just Another Essay on the Gourd Dance. *American Indian Culture and Research Journal* 25, no. 4 (1997): 75–103.

———. *The Power of Kiowa Song.* Tucson: University of Arizona Press, 1998.

Lassiter, Luke E., and Clyde Ellis. "Commentary: Applying Communitas to Kiowa Powwows: Some Theoretical and Methodological Problems." *American Indian Quarterly* 22, no. 4 (1998): 485–91.

Lassiter, Luke E., Clyde Ellis, and Ralph Kotay. *The Jesus Road: Kiowas, Christianity, and Indian Hymns.* Lincoln: University of Nebraska Press, 2002.

Lee, Barbara S. "Romanticizing of a Puritan Romance: Commencement at the Carlisle Indian Industrial School." Attached in personal email correspondence from Barbara Landis to the author, September 26, 2001.

Lee, R. Alton. "Indian Citizenship and the Fourteenth Amendment." *South Dakota History* 4, no. 2 (1974): 198–221.

Littlefield, A. "The B.I.A. Boarding School: Theories of Resistance and Social Reproduction." *Humanity and Society* 13 (1989): 428–441.

———. "Learning to Labor: Native American Education in the United States, 1880–1930." In J. Moore, ed. *The Political Economy of North American Indians.* Norman: University of Oklahoma Press, 1993.

Logan, Frederick Knight. *Pale Moon.* Lyrics by Jesse G. M. Glick. Chicago: Forster Music Publishers, 1920.

Lomawaima, K. Tsianina. "American Indian Education: By Indians versus For Indians." In Philip Deloria and Neil Salisbury, eds., *Blackwell Companion to American Indian History.* Malden, Mass.: Blackwell Press, 2002.

———. "Estelle Reel, Superintendent of Indian Schools, 1898–1910: Politics, Curriculum, and Land." *Journal of American Indian Education* 35, no. 3 (1996): 5–32.

———. *They Called It Prairie Light: The Story of Chilocco Indian School.* Lincoln: University of Nebraska Press, 1994.

Lomawaima, K. Tsianina, and Teresa L. McCarty. *"To Remain an Indian": Lessons in Democracy from a Century of Native American Education.* New York: Teachers College Press, 2006.

Maddox, Lucy. *Citizen Indians: Native American Intellectuals, Race, and Reform.* Ithaca, N.Y.: Cornell University Press, 2005.

Maddra, Sam A. *Hostiles? The Lakota Ghost Dance and Buffalo Bill's Wild West.* Norman: University of Oklahoma Press, 2006.

Mark, Joan T. *A Stranger in Her Native Land: Alice Fletcher and the American Indians.* Lincoln: University of Nebraska Press, 1988.

Martin, Jill E. "'Neither Fish, Flesh, Fowl, nor Good Red Herring': The Citizenship Status of American Indians, 1830–1924." *Journal of the West* 29, no. 3 (1990): 75–87.

McBeth, Sally J. *Ethnic Identity and the Boarding School Experience of West-Central Oklahoma American Indians.* Washington, D.C.: University Press of America, 1983.

McBride, Bunny. "Lucy Nicolar: The Artful Activism of a Penobscot Performer." In Theda Perdue, ed., *Sifters: Native American Women's Lives*. Oxford: Oxford University Press, 2001.

McClary, Susan. *Feminine Endings: Music, Gender, and Sexuality*. Minneapolis: University of Minnesota Press, 1991.

McCool, Daniel, Susan M. Olson, and Jennifer L. Robinson. *Native Vote: American Indians, the Voting Rights Act, and the Right to Vote*. Cambridge: Cambridge University Press, 2007.

McDonnell, Janet A. *The Dispossession of the American Indian, 1887–1934*. Bloomington: Indiana University Press, 1991.

McHugh, Edwin, and C. Perillo, Jr. *Indian Blues*. Arranged by Charles M. Smith. New York: Joe Morris Music Co., 1919.

McNally, Michael D. "Contesting the Real Indian in *Song of Hiawatha* Pageants, 1901–1965." *American Quarterly* 58, no. 1 (2006): 105–36.

———. *Ojibwe Singers: Hymns, Grief, and a Native Culture in Motion*. New York: Oxford University Press, 2000.

McNutt, James C. "John Comfort Fillmore: A Student of Indian Music Reconsidered." *American Music* (Spring 1984): 61–70.

Medina, William Oscar. "Selling Indians at Sherman Institute, 1902–1922." Ph.D. diss., University of California, Riverside, 2007.

Meyer, Carter Jones. "Edgar Hewett, Tsianina Redfeather, and Early-Twentieth-Century Indian Reform." *New Mexico Historical Review* 75 (April 2000): 195–220.

Meyer, Carter Jones, and Diana Royer, eds. *Selling the Indian: Commercializing and Appropriating American Indian Cultures*. Tucson: University of Arizona Press, 2001.

Mihesuah, Devon. *Cultivating the Rosebuds: The Education of Women at the Cherokee Female Seminary, 1851–1909*. Urbana: University of Illinois Press, 1993.

Mooney, James. *The Ghost Dance*. North Dighton, Mass.: JG Press, 1996.

Morgan, Lewis Henry. *Ancient Society; or, Researches in the Lines of Human Progress from Savagery through Barbarism to Civilization*. London: MacMillan and Co., 1877.

Morris, "Indian Joe." *Alcatraz Indian Occupation Diary: Nov. 20, 1969–June 11, 1971, Also Early Life on Blackfeet Reservation and Linda C. Morris' Tragic Love Story*. N.p.: private printing, 2001.

Morse, Theodore F. *Arrah Wanna*. Lyrics by Jack Drislane. New York: F. B. Haviland Publishing Co., 1906.

Moses, L. G. *Wild West Shows and the Images of American Indians*. Albuquerque: University of New Mexico Press, 1999.

Murphy, Jacqueline Shea. *The People Have Never Stopped Dancing: Native American Modern Dance Histories*. Minneapolis: University of Minnesota Press, 2007.

Nesper, Larry. "Simulating Culture: Being Indian for Tourists in Lac du Flambeau's Wa-Swa-Gon Indian Bowl." *Ethnohistory* 50, no. 3 (2003): 447–472.

Neuman, Lisa K. "Students, Wordplay, and Ideologies of Indianness at a School for Native Americans." *American Indian Quarterly* 32, no. 2 (2008): 178–203.

Nutchuk [Simeon Oliver], and Alden Hatch. *Back to the Smoky Sea*. New York: Julian
    Messner, 1946.
————. *Son of the Smoky Sea*. New York: Julian Messner, 1941.
O'Hara, Geoffrey. *Navajo Indian Songs/Blackfoot Indian Tribe, Gambler's Song*. Victor
    Records 17635.
"Oregon Indians Buy Opera." *Talking Machine World* 16, no. 8 (1920): 163.
Parezo, Nancy J., and Don D. Fowler. *Anthropology Goes to the Fair: The 1904 Louisiana
    Purchase Exposition*. Lincoln: University of Nebraska Press, 2007.
Patterson, Michelle Wick. "'Real' Indian Songs: The Society of American Indians and
    the Use of Native American Culture as a Means of Reform." *American Indian Quar-
    terly* 26, no. 1 (2002): 44–66.
Pfister, Joel. *Individuality Incorporated: Indians and the Multicultural Modern*. Durham,
    N.C.: Duke University Press, 2004.
Philp, Kenneth R. "John Collier, 1933–45." In Robert M. Kvasnicka and Herman J.
    Viola, eds. *The Commissioners of Indian Affairs, 1824–1977*. Lincoln: University of
    Nebraska Press, 1979.
————. *John Collier's Crusade for Indian Reform, 1920–1954*. Tucson: University of Ari-
    zona Press, 1977.
Pisani, Michael V. *Imagining Native America in Music*. New Haven, Conn.: Yale Uni-
    versity Press, 2005.
————. "'I'm an Indian Too': Creating Native American Identities in Nineteenth- and
    Early Twentieth-Century Music." In Jonathan Bellman, ed. *The Exotic in Western
    Music*. Boston: Northeastern University Press, 1998.
Powell, Peter J. *Sweet Medicine: The Continuing Role of the Sacred Arrows, the Sun Dance,
    and the Sacred Buffalo Hat in Northern Cheyenne History*. Norman: University of
    Oklahoma Press, 1998.
Powers, William K. *The Lakota Warrior Tradition: Three Essays on Lakotas at War*. Kendall
    Park, N.J.: Lakota Press, 2001.
————. *War Dance: Plains Indian Musical Performance*. Tucson: University of Arizona
    Press, 1990.
Pozzetta, George E., ed. *Education and the Immigrant*. New York: Garland, 1991.
Pratt, R. H., General. *The Indian Industrial School, Carlisle, Pennsylvania*. 1908. Reprint,
    Carlisle, Pa.: Cumberland County Historical Society Publications, 1979.
Pratt, Richard Henry. *Battlefield and Classroom: Four Decades with the American Indian,
    1867–1904*. New Haven, Conn.: Yale University Press, 1964.
Prucha, Francis Paul. *The Great Father: The United States Government and the American
    Indians*. Vol. 2. Lincoln: University of Nebraska Press, 1984.
Radano, Ronald. *Lying Up a Nation: Race and Black Music*. Chicago: University of
    Chicago Press, 2003.
Radano, Ronald, and Phillip V. Bohlman, eds. *Music and the Racial Imagination*.
    Chicago: University of Chicago Press, 2000.
"Record Trade with the Indians." *Talking Machine World* 18, no. 7 (1922): 19.

Rhodes, Willard. "A Study of Musical Diffusion Based on the Wandering of the Opening Peyote Song." *Journal of the International Folk Music Council* 10 (1958): 42–49.

Rieser, Andrew C. "Canopy of Culture: Chautauqua and the Renegotiation of Middle Class Authority, 1874–1919." Ph.D. diss., University of Wisconsin–Madison, 1999.

Riney, Scott. "Loosening the Bonds: The Rapid City Indian School in the 1920s." In Trafzer, Keller, and Sisquoc, *Boarding School Blues.*

———. *The Rapid City Indian School, 1898–1933.* Norman: University of Oklahoma Press, 1999.

Rydell, Robert W. *All the World's a Fair: Visions of Empire at American International Expositions, 1876–1916.* Chicago: University of Chicago Press, 1984.

Samuels, David W. *Putting a Song on Top of It: Expression and identity on the San Carlos Apache Reservation.* Tucson: University of Arizona Press, 2004.

Sánchez, George J. *Becoming Mexican American: Ethnicity, Culture, and Identity in Chicano Los Angeles, 1900–1945.* New York: Oxford University Press, 1993.

Scott, James C. *Domination and the Arts of Resistance: Hidden Transcripts.* New Haven, Conn.: Yale University Press, 1990.

"Selling Talkers to Indians Requires Special Gifts." *Talking Machine World* 13, no. 10 (1917): 105.

Silko, Leslie Marmon. *Yellow Woman and a Beauty of the Spirit: Essays on Native American Life Today.* New York: Simon and Schuster, 1997.

Skelton, Caroline. "Native Rappers Aim to Deliver Hip Hop Hope." *Times Colonist* (Victoria, B.C.), June 27, 2004.

Smith, Sherry L. *Reimagining Indians: Native Americans through Anglo Eyes, 1880–1940.* Oxford: Oxford University Press, 2000.

Smith, Stephen. "Song Catcher: Radio Biography Script." MPR regional broadcast, November 22, 1994. http://news.minnesota.publicradio.org/features/199702/01_smiths_densmore/docs/radiodoc1.shtml.

Sotiropoulos, Karen. *Staging Race: Black Performers in Turn of the Century America.* Cambridge: Harvard University Press, 2006.

Sprague, Donovin Arleigh. *Images of America: Standing Rock Sioux.* Charleston, S.C.: Arcadia Publishing, 2004.

Standing Bear, Luther. *My People the Sioux.* Lincoln: University of Nebraska Press, 1975.

Stauffer, Claude Maxwell. "Cheyenne." In Stauffer, comp., *Songs and Yells.*

———. "Hail to Thee, Carlisle." In Stauffer, *Songs and Yells.*

———. "My Wife's Gone to the Country." In Stauffer, *Songs and Yells.*

———, comp. *Songs and Yells: U.S. Indian School, Carlisle, Penna.* Carlisle, Pa.: Carlisle Indian Press, a department of the U.S. Indian School, n.d.

———. "Tammany." In Stauffer, *Songs and Yells.*

Stein, Gary C. "The Indian Citizenship Act of 1924." *New Mexico Historical Review* 47, no. 3 (1972): 257–74.

"Talking Machine Fails to Win Fortune in Arctic." *Talking Machine World* 15, no. 9 (1919): 3.

Tapia, John E. *Circuit Chautauqua: From Rural Education to Popular Entertainment in Early Twentieth Century America.* Jefferson, N.C.: McFarland and Co., 1997.

Theisz, R. D. *Sending Their Voices: Essays on Lakota Musicology.* Kendall Park, N.J.: Lakota Books, 1996.

Thiel, Mark. "The Omaha Dance in Oglala and Sicangu Sioux History, 1883–1923." *Whispering Wind* 23, no. 5 (1990): 5–17.

"Thorola Set Used by Indians." *Talking Machine World* 22, no. 9 (1926): 110.

Trachtenberg, Alan. *Shades of Hiawatha: Staging Indians, Making Americans, 1880–1930.* New York: Hill and Wang, 2004.

Trafzer, Clifford E., Jean A. Keller, and Lorene Sisquoc, eds. *Boarding School Blues: Revisiting American Indian Educational Experiences.* Lincoln: University of Nebraska Press, 2006.

Trennert, Robert A., Jr. *The Phoenix Indian School: Forced Assimilation in Arizona, 1891–1935.* Norman: University of Oklahoma Press, 1988.

Vander, Judith. *Songprints: The Musical Experience of Five Shoshone Women.* Urbana: University of Illinois Press, 1988.

Weiss, Bernard J., ed. *American Education and the European Immigrant: 1840–1940.* Urbana: University of Illinois Press, 1982.

Wenger, Tisa. "We Are Guaranteed Freedom": Pueblo Indians and the Category of Religion in the 1920s." *History of Religions* 45, no. 2 (2005): 89–113.

Whiteley, Peter M. *Deliberate Acts: Changing Hopi Culture through the Oraibi Split.* Tucson: University of Arizona Press, 1988.

Whitt, Laurie Anne. "Cultural Imperialism and the Marketing of Native America." *American Indian Culture and Research Journal* 19, no. 3 (1995): 1–31.

Wilkins, David E. *American Indian Sovereignty and the U.S. Supreme Court: The Masking of Justice.* Austin: University of Texas Press, 1997: 118–36.

Young Bear, Severt, and R. D. Theisz. *Standing in the Light: A Lakota Way of Seeing.* Lincoln: University of Nebraska Press, 1994.

Zitkala-Ša [Gertrude Bonnin]. *American Indian Stories.* Washington, D.C.: Hayworth Publishing House, 1921.

INDEX

CPSIA information can be obtained at www.ICGtesting.com
Printed in the USA
LVOW081414300613

340850LV00002B/2/P